P9-DWP-558

REST IN PEACE RURAL AMERICA

BY
CHARLES L. CIANCIO

Publisher: VicToria Freudiger
Entry Way Marketing and Publishing
www.entrywaypublishing.com
www.entrywaymarketing.com
entrywaypublish@aol.com

© Copyright 2007, Charles L. Ciancio

All Rights Reserved.

No part of this book may be reproduced, stored in a
retrieval system, or transmitted by any means,
electronic, mechanical, photocopying, recording,
or otherwise, without written permission
from the author, Charles L. Ciancio.

Printer: Bookmasters, Inc. Services
www.bookmasters.com
ISBN: 978-0-9793944-0-9

CREDITS

Thanks to:

Kelly Stalker
Dave Vogel

Practical professionals who helped show the way

Aunt Dorothy

Who provided information

Friends and Family that helped

FOREWORD
FROM THE AUTHOR

I have reached a point in life where I can freely state some things that need to be said, and maybe passing on what I have learned in the real world can be useful in making things better.

The material in the book involves application of logic and common sense; so, some folks may need to proceed with caution.

This book is an interesting read, because many ideas and information provided in this book are not routinely promoted or distributed by the standard media, academic community, and other professionals. Some readers will find the saying "truth can be stranger than fiction" applicable to segments of the book.

I am not a biologist, hydrologist, watershed specialist, or professional writer. I am just a working stiff that qualifies to be called a forester as additionally verified by being California Registered Professional Forester Number 317.

Working as a professional **FIELD** forester since 1966 and being born and raised in the rural areas of California, gave me the opportunity to experience many good things associated with the rural way of life and to learn about the problems facing Rural America. The good things have included watching my kids experience the thrill of catching a trout as I did. The bad things have involved watching an unaccountable regulatory community take this simple thrill away from my grandkids.

I intimately lived through the creation of the current California Forest Practice mess and many other regulatory processes affecting rural landowners in the western United States. This experience and real world field experiences have provided me with and extensive background and knowledge that allows me to provide a practical and factual presentation of problematic situations occurring in the wildlands of this country.

Information provided in this book is believed to be factually and truthfully correct to the best of my belief and knowledge, and I attempt to provide an understanding of the ever-changing and elusive regulatory processes in this country. Different opinions and conclusions do exist regarding the issues and information I provide, and many will take exception to things I say.

By using actual real world examples involving species protection, regulatory problems, public relation efforts, management and no management options, rural community economic situation, water issues, wildlife, diversity, spotted owls, old-growth trees, and so on, I factually and truthfully point out how and where things have gone wrong and are continuing to go wrong.

To show I am not alone in my thoughts about Rural America's problems and the Fourth Branch of Government, I have utilized information, quotes, and examples from others that support and emphasize my points of view. I have tried to not change the intent of chosen information, and changes in presentation have only been made to provide a better understanding of what I believe is intended to be said.

I see the rural way of life as I have experienced it slipping away to the detriment of everyone in this country, and while change is inevitable and it may be time for the rural way of life to go, I provide ways to slow the unnecessary demise of the rural way of life.

The production of natural resource products (lumber, cattle, minerals, food) provides the key to keeping Rural America alive, and I show how shutting down natural resource use is causing Rural America to disappear.

It will be obvious I give few pats on the back to those involved with rural community issues, and many will not take kindly to what I have to say. I have found an unwillingness to invest personal time and resources to do what is needed to stop negative things that are happening, and a review of what has happened to rural communities does not find many that deserve a pat on the back.

One purpose for writing this book is to bring attention to a lack of accountability demonstrated by a Fourth Branch of Government (all public agencies, appointed commissions and boards, and the lower court system) that now runs our lives. Discussing how this regulatory group is bringing down Rural America provides an intimately familiar way to expose how authorized regulatory procedures are being ignored, and how environmental and regulatory thinking is routinely not based on site specific facts, time tested proven science, logic, and common sense.

This book is a collection of environmental and regulatory issues affecting our everyday lives and the use of natural resources. There is a push for regulatory control of everything such as seat belts for dogs in cars, restricted use of horses in wilderness areas, trimming trees in your backyard, what color you paint your fence and on and on. In the hurry to create many regulations, clarity and justification are being sacrificed, and a lack of clarity is giving the Fourth Branch of Government the power to misinterpret and misapply many laws and regulations without having to be accountable.

This book shows how resilient Mother Nature can be in providing diversity and in healing areas of concern, and the book describes how proper management, not preservation, is mandatory in order to provide wildland values everyone says they want.

It may appear the many provided examples and stories used to illustrate the issues and problems discussed in the book are localized and limited in scope; however, a close review will find the provided information and stories do span the nation and parts of the world. Many references have been utilized, and provided information spans more than fifty years.

To those who take issue with utilized information, quotes, and examples, I say relax, do not get sidetracked with minor issues, and move-on. The provided information, quotes, and examples are used to highlight main points of discussion, and main points of discussion will not change based on the right or wrong of any single piece of supporting information.

Some may say I am against all governmental authority. This is not true. I acknowledge policemen, firemen, and the armed services need flexibility and leeway to do their job, and I only advocate governmental actions be supported by authorized regulations and smart use of time tested and peer reviewed science, site specific facts, logic, and common sense. To do otherwise, opens the door to letting inappropriate actions by the Fourth Branches of Government go unchecked.

Losing Rural America means losing a lot of good things.

I do not know if I have the quote exactly right, but when asked, "where will we find the men that gave their all at Normandy on D-Day in World War II", I heard Ronald Reagan answered:

"Where we have always found them. In the farms, villages, towns."

While the cities and some towns will be around, I wonder if the farms and villages of Rural America will be around the next time we call for help?

Rest in peace Rural America. You have done well. You have provided natural resource products needed to keep this country independent and strong. You have provided direction and purpose of life to many and a perspective on life that will be lost when you are gone. You have provided sons and daughters with a strong moral base and appreciation for honesty and a hard day's work and a patriotic desire to defend and protect this country.

Job well done Rural America.

INDEX

CREDITS..iii
FOREWARD FROM THE AUTHOR v
INDEX ix

Chapter One: OUR FOREFATHERS WHERE VERY VERY
SMART AND ALMOST GOT THE JOB DONE 1

Chapter Two: CRY OF WOLF THAT IS FOR REAL 10

Chapter Three: REGULATIONS AND REGULATORS
RUNNING AMUCK-ENDANGERED SPECIES ACT (ESA)......... 62

Chapter Four: PROTECTING THEM TO DEATH - ROADS
GONE/NO ACCESS/NO MANAGEMENT/NO
DISTURBANCE/NO DIVERSITY/NO CONIFERS/NO
LWD/NO FOOD/NO FISH/NO WILDLIFE 88

Chapter Five: THE FOLLY OF THE BROKEN HEARING
AND PETITION PROCESSES.. 133

Chapter Six: FAULTY LEGALESE... 144

Chapter Seven: BYE BYE DOLLARS 160

Chapter Eight: A CASTLE FOR A SMALL TOWN 184

Chapter Nine: A SHORT STORY - THE LAST BALE 189

Chapter Ten: HI HO! HI HO! IMPORTATION IS ACOMING.... 194

Chapter Eleven: A NEEDED KICK IN THE SHINS (A FOCUS
ON THE RURAL FOLKS - DARN THEM ALL)........................... 209

Chapter Twelve: POOR POOR MISINFORMED PUBLIC 225

Chapter Thirteen: WE GET WHAT WE PREACH 250

Chapter Fourteen: DOST THO PROTEST TO MUCH 264

Chapter Fifteen: THE CIRCLE 279

Chapter Sixteen: NEW FORESTRY - A LITTLE NEW AND
A LOT OF OLD 283

Chapter Seventeen: BURN BABY BURN 288

Chapter Eighteen: WHERE OH WHERE HAVE OUR
NATURAL RESOURCES GONE? - RESTORATION!
RESTORATION! SET-ASIDE! SET-ASIDE! CONSERVATION
EASEMENT! CONSERVATION EASEMENT! PARKS AND
WILDERNESS! PARKS AND WILDERNESS! - READY OR
NOT TAXPAYERS HERE WE COME 306

Chapter Nineteen: IT'S ACCOUNTABILITY STUPID 329

Chapter Twenty: A LONG ROAD TO ACCOUNTABILITY
(THE GODDARD GULCH STORY) 347

Chapter Twenty-One: FACE-OFF - HOW DO WE STOP THE
SKY FROM FALLING? PUTTING ACCOUNTABILITY BACK
INTO THE REGULATORY PROCESS 352

Reference Information 393

OUR FOREFATHERS WERE VERY VERY SMART AND ALMOST GOT THE JOB DONE

Chapter One

After 38 plus years since I graduated from college, I am far from being a constitutional scholar, and I can only speak from what I have learned and understand as an average citizen about our government and the constitution. Recently I have found it easier to understand the thinking of our forefathers and the constitutional terms that my teachers made so complicated in school. Maybe the exposure to these things over the years or my ability to better interpret and understand things is the cause for my recent enlightenment. In any case, I see and understand many things I did not see and understand before.

The writing of this book has caused me to delve into many aspects of our system of government. I have found where some governmental processes can work to help Rural America. Mostly I have found where excesses by a layman populous and a Fourth Branch of Government consisting of public agencies, governmental entities, appointed commissions and boards, and the judicial system beneath the United States Supreme Court are working to hurt Rural America.

I was taught our forefathers recognized the potential for populated states to control less populated states. While living and working with the regulatory situation faced by Rural America, I have seen how straight majority rule gives control to the populated areas, and I am very aware of the concerns regarding populated areas dominating less populated areas. Many current majority rule processes are allowing a layman and disconnected populous to inappropriately control the lives of rural minorities, and as illustrated in the 2000 presidential election, it is very possible for the most populated areas in a minority of the country to inappropriately control the larger part of the country.

In the past-maybe not now-it was taught that our forefathers did a lot of negotiating among themselves, and the less populous state representatives held out until they felt their interests were protected. My overall interpretation of the government intended by our forefathers is of a Senate in which each state had an equal say, a Congress possibly controlled by the populated areas, a Presidency possibly slanted by geographical thinking, and an impartial Judicial system. The negotiations covered a lot of other complicated procedural limitations and restrictions which are covered in the constitution and beyond my ability to discuss; however, these negotiations did create two items which involve Rural America that are worth discussing.

1. As set up by our forefathers, our system of government per the constitution is a representative Republic and not a Democracy. My teachers did not do a good job of making this fact clear to me, and I know many other people have trouble accepting the concept of our country being a government run by representatives versus populous majority rule. Having a Senate where big and small, heavily populated and lightly populated states have an equal say helps to hold back legislation that would hurt Rural America. To me, this provides additional support for thinking our forefathers understood how straight majority rule when not evenly distributed over a knowledgeable and educated public could lead to mob rule and all kinds of other problems. The complexities of this issue are out of my league and I leave this discussion to the historians and others more qualified. But, I now get it.

2. Another result of the negotiations was to put an electoral college process in place to be used in electing the President. To me, the electoral college process was another way to provide rural, less populated areas a more equitable say in one of the three branches of government-the Presidency-which exercises a lot of control over rural areas. The power of a more sympathetic Presidency could also be utilized to rebut anti-rural actions by a Congress that was controlled by population centers.

It looks like areas with low populations such as Rural America were given two ways, the Electoral College and the U.S. Senate, to slow potential adverse impacts from majority rule. Unwittingly, I believe, these two ways additionally give some, but not a lot, of protection from abusive actions by a Fourth Branch of Government.

Although there has been a lot of stumbling along the way, I can see how our government is able to flex and change without breaking and how the constitution serves this country well.

While our current regulatory system of representative government seems to have developed in a practical and reasonable manner, I believe our forefathers never foresaw all the control and influence that the presidency and a layman populous have gained over rural areas.

Through appointments to head of federal agency positions, control of federal employees, and land and natural resource set-aside powers, the President has more control over rural areas than the other two branches of government. Federal governmental agencies controlled by the President control the economies and lives of Rural America, and presidential powers allow the President to set aside use of natural resources without full consideration of the impacts to rural communities. The amount of federal ownership in the western part of this country which is mostly rural, gives the President a lot of control over what happens in the rural communities in the western United States. Last I heard Idaho is around 90 percent in public, mostly federal, ownership, California is close to or exceeds 50% public ownership, and the western states in general are all heavily owned by the Federal government. President Clinton's designation of the 327,769 acre Sequoia monument(1) showed how the power of the Presidency can be used to adversely affect rural communities without much if any consideration for local impacts.

The populated areas mostly consisting of a layman populous heavily control what happens in rural areas through majority rule. The rules and regulations being applied by a Fourth Branch of Government are developed and put in place by a simple majority vote by those that are put in place by a simple majority vote, and by boards, committees, and commissions appointed by those put in place by a simple majority vote. With the regulations and laws being made by a simple majority vote that is controlled by the populated areas, the folks in the rural areas are being knocked around and controlled by the thinking and political pressures developed in this country's population centers. By restricting use of natural resources through use of unclear and unsupported by the truth laws and regulations that are created through simple majority rule by federal and state elected representatives and legislatures and the many appointed boards, commissions, and committees, rural communities are being slowly rubbed out.

California, where both state legislative houses are based on population, provides a prime example where the process of providing equitable representation to Rural America's communities has been corrupted. By basing northern California's representation on population, northern California's legislative representatives are overwhelmed by the sheer numbers of representatives from other parts of the state, and this situation is slowing hurting and eliminating California's rural communities. This abuse of majority control really shows itself in the "taking" and control of northern California's water and restricting the use of natural resources in California.

News article(2) states "Rural California..." "...comprises 60 percent of the state,..." "...whose residents make up only 6 percent of its population.", and "...rural counties have little power in the legislature." In California, the populations of southern California and the Sacramento to San Francisco region control what happens in the rest of the state. The referenced news article states "...Del Norte, Siskyou, Trinity, Shasta, Tehama, Glenn, Yuba, Sutter, Colusa, and parts of Nevada, Placer, and Butte counties are represented by one senator. Lassen, Plumas, Sierra, Nevada, and Yuba counties and part of Butte County are represented by one Assembly member." It is hard to keep up with the continually changing and expanding legislative boundaries of my corner of northwestern California, however, I believe two senators and a couple Assembly members represent an even larger area than that described for the two representatives listed in the news article. This news article goes on to say "By contrast, 25 Assembly members and 13 senators represent Los Angeles County." alone!!!! Rural legislators "...just don't have the horsepower in the (state) legislature."

The U.S. Congress is routinely setting aside protected areas and restricting or stopping use of natural resources to the detriment of rural communities. The Endangered Species Act is being applied in ways supported by population centers that are causing detrimental problems for Rural America. Details on how this is happening are provided throughout this book and specifically in Chapters 3 and 7.

A Fourth Branch of Government, which is heavily influenced by Presidential appointments and majority opinion, gives Rural America little say in the economic and social decisions that affect and support its existence. The list of public and governmental agencies that control Rural America is without end: Forest Service, Bureau of Land Management, Agricultural Department, Bureau of Interior, Federal Fish and Wildlife Service, Federal Marine Agency, Corp. of Engineers, many federal agencies handling endangered species issues, Environmental Protection Agency, agencies handling safety, commerce, employment, the thousands of appointed boards, commissions, committees, and their staffs, the layman legal system of unelected layman officials and judges, all the involved state agencies (Water Quality, Fish and Game, Forestry, Parks, Archaeological, etc.), all the involved city and county agencies, and on and on and on.

A bottom line is Rural America has been left underrepresented with no way to effectively protect the rural way of life.

The 2000 and 2004 Presidential elections will go down in history as a clear demonstration of the battle between a popular majority vote and an Electoral College vote.

As we all watched the Electoral College votes be counted, the country turned red for Bush. Except for minor exceptions, the blue for Gore and Kerry areas were heavily confined to the populated, nonrural areas. When this was put on a county basis, the emphasis between rural and populated areas was even more graphic.

But for gyrations of the legal system and the Electoral College, a very small portion of the country (Los Angeles and New York for example) almost elected a president that had much different beliefs and thinking than the majority of the territorial United States. If Gore or Kerry had been elected President, a small territorial portion of the country and its ideas could have been inappropriately forced on a majority area of the country. Different areas and different people create different philosophies, and our forefathers went to great pains to assure one area or mindset did not have an unjustifiable ability to adversely impact other territorial ways of life and thinking.

There was another unpublicized recognized battle going on in the 2000 and 2004 presidential elections which involves a rear guard action by Rural America to maintain use of this country's natural resources and to maintain a certain rural way of life. As illustrated by the vote, Rural America understands how a Gore or Kerry Presidency would have hurt Rural America and how important the presidency and Electoral College are to Rural America.

Granted Rural America's influence over actions by the President is very limited and often looks nonexistent, but there is no question things would have been much much worse under a Gore or Kerry Presidency.

Under a Gore presidency, many of the distorted environmental ideas and layman policies espoused by Gore as illustrated in his book "Earth in the Balance" and by Gore's supporters in the heavily populated areas would have devastated Rural America.

Kerry's position on the environment did not seem to be clearly presented. The loud, hateful rhetoric towards Bush by the Kerry campaign did a lot to confuse and drown out Kerry's position on other issues such as the environment. While Kerry's position on environmental issues may have not been clear, the locations of the country that voted for Kerry were very similar to Gore's areas of support, and this showed a clear indication Kerry's supporters were of the same mindset as Gore and his supporters. There is no

5

logical reason to think a Kerry Presidency would have been any better than a Gore Presidency for rural communities.

During the Kerry/Bush election, there was a lot of questioning and agonizing over why the country was so divided. While conservative thinking and different family values are major factors in causing this division, my experiences tell me another factor is helping to fuel the division, and this factor is the growing mistrust of regulators and current enviro thinking. The very graphic division represented by the red versus blue, rural versus populous areas, map highlights how Rural America and populated centers think differently and are being treated differently.

The 2000 and 2004 Presidential elections also brought additional attention to the pitfalls of straight majority rule.

While there is a logical basis and argument for the president being determined by the majority of the populous, our forefathers found this argument to be flawed and not in the best interest of all the states and all the multiple groups to be found in this country. We are a country where the majority is used to establish many laws and to make many decisions; however, our forefathers saw the wisdom and need to not let all decisions be made by straight majority rule.

A simple to understand example of how a majority can use its power to force a minority to do their bidding through the ballot box is provided by a news article(3). The article states "Supporters…effort to tax millionaires to fund mental health care system…have collected 640,000 signatures- about 70 percent more than the required number-to put the issue before voters." Without getting involved in the plight of the poor millionaires, can you imagine all the ways a majority can use the majority vote process to get their way with all kinds of minorities?

Another example of a populous questionably controlling a rural majority is provided by a radio report(4) involving folks in the state of Maine. Some governmental jurisdictions overlap population centers and island communities, and some island folks think they may be getting the short end of the stick. Apparently at least one island community has succeeded from a governmental body that controlled them, and they formed their own controlling governmental body. Other island communities are thinking about doing the same thing.

The island community being discussed said they expected their own governmental body would result in things like reduced taxes, better use of their tax money on local projects, and better handling of local concerns.

One example of potential tax reduction involved reducing shoreline parcel taxes from $14,000 to $2,000 annually.

The island community did not think a cost consolidation measure being considered by the mainland was a good idea. This idea involved having young third and fourth graders on their own getting to and taking a ferry, riding the ferry, being around open water, and finding their way to school on the mainland. Such a reduction in their school size might also be an invitation to completely eliminate schooling on the island.

Where one community has succeeded from a larger city governmental body, there is a story told how the community had tried for years to get a rock removed in the middle of a street. The controlling governmental agency kept saying it could not be done. As soon as the new road manager was put in place under the newly formed island government, he took a pick and shovel and removed the rock.

It was interesting in the radio report how the defenders of big government were the members of the Fourth Branch of Government. Succession would mean smaller government and less authority for the Fourth Branches of Government, and it sounded like a little self-interest was in play regarding this secessionist issue. It was also interesting to hear one of the defenders of large government say succession was not democracy because decisions would not be made to benefit the whole group.

A news article (5) tells of another secessionist movement involving a rural area and a population center. "...Central Coast City..." and "...Santa Barbara County..." "...have struggled to exist under one (county) government roof..." "The liberal positions didn't sit well in the solidly middle-class North." Again "...succession opponents argue that a breakup would create financial problems and lead to cutbacks in services, higher taxes (for who???) and limited political clout in Sacramento. Supporters counter that government now favors the south, and a new county would be better for development and bring more efficient government closer to home." I find it interesting how the one mentioned as against the breakup is again a member of the Fourth Branch of Government. These Fourth Branches of Government sure do not want to lose their power.

Have democratic principles become so warped that minorities are required to do the biding of the majority to the benefit of the majority even when the minority is abused? Wasn't the Civil War partly caused by some miss-used majority thinking? The south may have lost and was forced to do the bidding of the majority, but that didn't make the majority lily white in what happened to the south. Would the slaves still be slaves if the majority of white thinking had been allowed to stand? Just like the poor millionaires, I wonder who is next to openly be forced to do the bidding of some majority. The path being laid by those saying democracy requires unchallenged allegiance to the majority is not leading to a good place.

If smaller government provides for proper and fair distribution and control of a community's assets and affairs and the majority is unfairly taking from a community, then succession is justified. Is this not what happened in the revolutionary war? The rights of a group versus the rights of a portion of a group will always be in some kind of conflict, and a workable democracy seems to require all parties to have equal treatment and protection of their interests while at the same time protecting the interests of the group. Extreme positions should not be allowed to cause unjustified harm or damage to the whole or the parts. When minority interests are unjustifiably being hurt by being forced to be part of a group, the minority needs the ability to change things. When minority interests will unjustifiably hurt the welfare of the group, then minority interests have to give way to the group's interest. When majority interests are unjustifiably being hurt by a minority interest as illustrated by the issues involving Christmas, the majority interests should not be ignored. If we allow unjustified harm to a minority or majority to go unchecked, then we no longer have fair and balanced regulatory rule, and such a situation leads to all kinds of bad things as historically experienced by slaves, indentured servants, and Native Americans.

While it seems many folks seem to meddle where they shouldn't be meddling, I am not saying the people in populated areas and nonrural folks are not good people that can not make good decisions. I believe some of the reason for folks in nonrural areas to think differently than rural folks regarding rural area issues is due to a lack of adequate exposure to the truth and what it takes to support and hold rural communities together. Nonrural folks are exposed to a lot of inaccurate and slanted information in a manner that leaves them in the dark about how Rural America is being hurt. Thanks to a kind of "perception is reality" thinking and a broken hearing and information distribution process where the loudest and most politically correct are in control (media, governmental staffs, Fourth Branch of Government, and politicians), the folks in the populated areas and a lot of the general population are not provided complete and truthful information based on peer reviewed and time tested science, site specific facts, logic, and common sense. The result is Rural America's interests and the truth are not given fair and adequate exposure, and incomplete and inaccurate information that is readily available and easy to absorb is routinely used by nonrural folks in deciding how to vote on rural issues.

In summary, this chapter has included a discussion of how majority control influences and controls the actions of many different levels of government. This book provides additional discussion and examples of how this influence and control is routinely allowing some unjustified and inappropriate detrimental impacts regarding proper use of natural resources, the environment, and maintenance of viable rural communities to occur.

As it could lead to all kinds of problems, it would be wrong to eliminate existing safeguards which include use of the Electoral College to elect the President and other built-in safeguards regarding majority rule that were conscientiously and carefully put in place by our forefathers.

Allowing a popular vote to determine the presidency could inappropriately allow a small portion of the country to influence what happens in the larger remainder portion of the country. The folks in the nonrural, populated areas routinely have different ideas and values than rural area folks, and they do not understand or know what it takes to maintain and keep the rural way of life alive. Populated areas have shown a desire to control what happens in rural areas, and when it is not appropriate, this desire to meddle and control needs to be checked and controlled.

Currently without any changes, inadequate use of site specific facts and proper time tested, peer reviewed science, is allowing the majority decision process which routinely involves inexperienced and unknowledgeable decision makers to hasten the end of Rural America as we now know it. As Rural America goes, so goes this country's independence from others for natural resources and so goes the values and benefits that rural life has provided this country.

The title of this chapter says our forefathers were very smart as illustrated by what they accomplished, and except for the damage being caused by a Fourth Branch of Government and a layman populous excesses, they almost got the job done. Hopefully ways to control these excesses will be found and applied; so, they do not continue to contribute to the downfall of Rural America and a beautifully created system of government.

I would like to think some of Rural America can survive all this and be more than a footnote in the history books.

CRY OF WOLF THAT IS FOR REAL

Chapter Two

A Fourth Branch of Government without an effective means of accountability now controls our lives.

An obvious reaction is to ask "Where do I get such an idea?"

I can assure you I am not a radical, card carrying kook. I am nothing more than a working family man who has lived what I consider to be a typical and average middle class life. As I write this book, I have raised four kids during 34 years of marriage, and I am a grandfather six times over with one grandchild in the oven. Other than maybe being overly opinionated on some matters, I think I am a pretty ordinary and average guy.

As I have become seasoned by my professional life as a forester and my family life as a member of the of the rural communities in California, I have become aware of something that has, like a wolf in the night, slowly and methodically taken control of our lives. I call this thing a Fourth Branch of Government, and I see it consisting of all the public agencies, governmental entities, appointed commissions and boards, and the judicial lower court system beneath the United States Supreme Court. This group contains many unelected officials that are not accountable to an electorate, and all the members of this branch of government pretty well do as they want without fear of being held accountable for inappropriate actions. This group includes many people that are commonly called "Public Servants".

The creation of a Fourth Branch of Government with the ability to control things without being held accountable for inappropriate actions did not occur overnight. It evolved while a lot of folks looked the other way, and when accountability problems started to appear, little to nothing was done to force the members of the Fourth Branch of Government to be accountable.

This lack of accountability evolved into allowing this Fourth Branch of Government to do more than interpret and apply our laws and regulations. Through repeated and unquestioned use of internally developed guidelines and incorrect interpretations of existing regulations, this group is allowed to apply and enforce laws itself develops. This group is allowed to make "new law" outside authorized regulatory review procedures.

The influence of this Fourth Branch of Government permeates all places of employment and all walks of life. The system of checks and balances needed to assure accountability based on responsible application of authorized regulations, proven and time tested science, site specific facts, logic, and common sense is skewed in the favor of the members of this group.

While discussing the creation of a County General Plan, some developers in news article(6) provide a logical perspective on how and why some members of this Fourth Branch of Government think and act as they do. They say in the article "...the planners are all basically environmental people who are going to school to get out of college to become planners. So, you have basically no-growth minded people that are in essence running the cities.", and "The city councils are getting weaker because - who the hell wants to be a city councilmember?" One spokesperson said he made "...a legal trip to Cuba..." and went "...holy smokes!... The people aren't rewarded for doing good deeds..." and he saw "...a lot of the same things..." that are happening in this country. "...there's a disconnect between the people in charge making the decisions - their qualifications as to how to tell us what to do - and they have the ultimate authority."

At this point, you may just say you have already heard others cry about governmental abuses, and there is little I can add to what you have already heard. Like the boy who cried wolf too often, the messengers of the problem have been many. The message has become old hat and easy to ignore.

I believe I have taken an approach in presenting the involved subject material that is different from what others have done. In developing the description of what I call a Fourth Branch of Government, I had to look for similarities in the actions of regulatory groups and in the reasons behind their actions. This knowledge of similarities and my experiences with the various involved groups has allowed me to develop information and ideas that are not routinely discussed.

My professional background as a forester for over thirty eight years and a member of rural communities all my life has provided me with perspectives and information not available to a lot people. During my involvement with all phases of forest management matters (appraisal work, contractual supervision, harvesting activities, application of regulations), you name it, and it seems I have at least an acquaintance with it. Maybe a light acquaintance, but at least an acquaintance. In practicing forestry and all the other disciplines that go with the practice of forestry, you can not avoid coming in contact with many, many environmental issues and regulations. The number of Fourth Branch of Government members that deal with forestry and environmental issues are legion and include the following: United States Forest Service, Department of the Interior, Bureau of Land

Management, Department of Agriculture, California Department of Forestry, Department of Mines and Geology, Federal Occupational Safety Administration, California Occupational Safety Administration, California Department of Fish and Game, US Fish and Wildlife Service, National Marine Fishery, Federal Environmental Protection Agency, Public and Native American Archeological groups, California Water Quality Agencies, Federal Clean Water Folks, Air Quality Agencies, and various city, county, local, and district agencies. My experiences have taught me how all these departments and agencies do not have a review and accountability process in place that assures their personnel, collectively or individually, can not abuse their authority.

TYING THINGS TOGETHER

PROVIDING SOME FOCUS

First, let's discuss some nonproblem things.

I think we can all agree most of the actions by this Fourth Branch of Government involve some pretty benign and not worth mentioning situations, and there is no need to get hung up on the trivial problem situations. In writing this book, I concentrate on significant inappropriate actions and the lack of accountability involving these actions. I accept the fact there will always be a need for some regulators in order to have a safe, sane, and productive society.

Because they put their lives on the line for us, we need to have a soft spot for the policemen, firemen, and armed forces. These groups need some leeway in order to properly protect us and to provide for the general public's safety. While some peer review of what and how things are done by this group is needed, improperly applied rigid controls over these folks can give bad results.

Even though their silence on the matters discussed is very noticeable and shows a lack of professionalism, the dedicated, knowledgeable, and experienced members of the involved Fourth Branches of Government who can and will do a proper and correct job if given proper direction and supervisorial support are not the focus of this book. I do not see these folks as the ones directly promoting the misinterpretation and inappropriate application of regulations; however, I do see their silence on needed changes regarding existing regulatory problems as a problem.

JUST WHO IS THE PROBLEM CHILD?

The following provides a listing of similarities that shows why the members of the Fourth Branch of Government fit together. This listing of similarities also helps to show how this group is collectively being abusive.

I see the birth of many problems involving a Fourth Branch of Government starting with the creation of unclear regulations that are open to multiple and changing interpretations. This allows the Fourth Branches of Government to interpret regulations to fit their needs and to alleviate any pressures that may be applied to them. This group is allowed a lot of leeway when interpreting how to apply laws and regulations that helps protect their power base. Self-preservation is a powerful thing.

Part of the clarity problem is due to a lovefest over the use of words by those developing rules and regulations. Excessive use of verbiage is causing a loss of clarity in many laws and regulations.

I see decisions and approved regulation routinely not being based on good science and the truth. Instead I see more and more regulations being developed based on political correctness, compromise, and who wins the point and counter point battle. The fact the layman court system is putting technical legal requirements into place, which were never intended to be applied and often make little or no sense, illustrates the lack of clarity in many regulations.

Those being regulated constantly run into road blocks when trying to make the Fourth Branches of government accountable for inappropriate actions. The Fourth Branches of government are full of smart people. They have learned they have the ability and power to routinely sidestep attempts at making them accountable.

Permit appeal processes involving inappropriate actions by the Fourth Branch of Government are routinely not available, or are ineffective, costly, and purposely made cumbersome and unworkable by the members of the Fourth branch of Government.

The Fourth Branch of Government demonstrates its knowledge of its freedom and power by routinely not requiring everyone involved in permit and approval processes to be accountable for their input and actions. Sister governmental agencies and the general public are routinely not required to provide full and adequate explanation and justification for requested permit requirements. In violation of authorized regulatory time line requirements, sister governmental agencies and the general public are routinely allowed to be late with reports and to unjustifiably delay permit review and approval.

Many members of this Fourth branch of Government, especially laymen Boards and Commissions, do not control and often can not control their staffs. Their heavily reliance on staff input and staff directed agendas routinely allows staff to inappropriately control the handling of issues. Legitimate and factual input provided during hearing processes is routinely allowed to be buried and ignored.

I see a lack of leadership and supervisorial backbone in providing needed direction, instruction, and support regarding regulatory limitations and responsibilities by the members of the Fourth Branch of Government. Without proper training and instruction, inexperienced personnel are routinely put into the field and told to apply and interpret thousands of unclear laws.

Watchdog processes overseeing actions by members of the Fourth Branch of Government are lacking or nonexistent. There is not enough being done to assure our laws, rules, and regulations are properly interpreted and applied as intended. Peer review by experienced and qualified professionals and by those who make our laws routinely does not occur. Without proper guidance and oversight, upper levels of the Fourth Branches of the Government and lower level supervisors unintentionally and sometimes purposely incorrectly interpret and apply many unclear laws and regulations.

Use of their regulatory authority routinely allows for use of oppressive, erroneous, and incorrect rule interpretations. Routinely operational and permit requirements are not justified and supported by peer reviewed science, site specific facts, logic, and common sense.

The government has grown so large, the other three branches of government do not and can not oversee the Fourth Branch of Government; so, the members of the Fourth Branch of Government pretty well operate as they see fit.

IT IS NOT MY PROBLEM

It is not my problem. When we examine this statement, we need to do a little honest sole searching.

If anyone takes an honest look back, I bet they will find some member of this Fourth Branch of Government that has affected their life or the life of someone they know. I believe most people can think of at least one situation where they didn't like how a member of this Fourth Branch of Government has acted.

What have you done when you thought a regulator has acted improperly? What could you do? Have you found there is little you can do to check if a regulator has done the right thing? Do you feel pretty hopeless when dealing with a regulator? If you have had these thoughts and questions, you are not alone.

In my life, especially my professional life, I have run across numerous situations, especially involving governmental permits and enforcement of regulations, where an unjustifiable and unauthorized action by a member of this Fourth Branch of Government has occurred. I have seen such inappropriate actions result in financial damage to someone, in damage to the environment, and in damage to the support base for rural communities. I have seen where the never ending stream of new, unclear, and hard to interpret environmental law is giving a Fourth Branch of Government a lot of unaccountable power and is causing damage.

Like most people, for multiple reasons, I did nothing when I first came into contact with regulatory abuse and inappropriate governmental actions. As I became more experienced in what was happening and looked around for ways to counter and appeal inappropriate regulatory actions, I found-like many other people-that there was little that could be done. As I became even more experienced and was able to better understand what was happening, I began to see how our lives in numerous ways were being controlled by a group of unelected people that could not effectively be held accountable for inappropriate, unjustified, and unauthorized regulatory actions. My experiences, professionally and personally, with this unaccountable group provided me the ability to develop a description of this group and to discuss how this group is allowed to operate.

RECAPPING THE SEEMINGLY HOPELESS?

In many ways, we now have a Government lacking accountability and feared by the people.

The problem of governmental accountability is rarely if ever approached as being more than a single agency problem. The larger problem of multiple agencies having the same problem is being missed.

Governmental accountability problems are being presented in fragmented segments and are routinely shuffled off as a nonproblem being created by some malcontents. The "why can't we all just get along" attitude is routinely allowed to drown out legitimate accountability issues.

Over time, our system of government in a broad way does work and bends to accommodate and resolve problems such as the current out of control Fourth Branch of Government; however, a lot of damage can occur before an extreme position is reached that forces correction to occur, and corrections are usually full of compromise and imprecise solutions.

Those who have to deal on a professional level with the Fourth Branches of Government know there is a need for more experienced peer review of the building inspectors, the county employees, the state employees, the federal employees, and all other members of the Fourth Branch of Government.

To demonstrate the problem of holding those accountable for inappropriate application of our many laws and regulations, try to think of when a public employee has ever been let go for abusing his authority. Try to think of an agency that has ever voluntary allowed nongovernmental peer review of their activities. Try to think of when internal disciplinary action within a public agency has ever been taken. At best, such actions are very few and hard to find. I know of a couple cases where disciplinary action was taken, but the action taken was initiated by those outside the government.

More commitment and pressure is needed. While citizen involvement and participation in lawsuits, legislative action, and use of the hearing processes must continue to try and not let things get worse, there is an obvious lack of commitment to apply enough pressure through these corrective avenues to cause meaningful change. Politicians continue to make laws subject to multiple interpretations, and the Forth Branches of Government continue to routinely not base their actions on authorized regulations, time tested proven peer reviewed science, site specific facts, logic, and common sense.

While this book capsulizes the problems surrounding the Fourth Branch of Government, it also provides a collection of useful information and suggestions, ammunition if you will, for making government more accountable.

The kettle is building a head of steam. Hopefully, when the kettle blows, the right things will be done.

AN OUNCE OF PREVENTION IS WORTH A POUND OF YOUR HIDE

There is a trend to develop requirements for permits and regulations based on speculation which some call professional judgment. The intent is to second guess what might happen and to load up permits and regulations with so many things you are suppose to do and not suppose to do that nothing wrong can happen.

These requirements are routinely called prescriptive requirements.

Many end-result, performance based standards are being replaced with requirements based on second guessing about what may or may not happen.

While some upfront proven preventive actions are appropriate and do some good, there is a flood of subjective, unnecessary, unproven, and inappropriate prescriptive regulations being put in place. The subjectivity of many requirements is routinely twisted by the regulators to the point permitees are guilty until proven innocent. This flood of unnecessary and inappropriate regulations is causing many unjustified and unnecessary costs, unintended damage to humans and the environment, and giving the unaccountable Fourth Branch of Government even more power.

To illustrate what I see happening, I chose two major but totally different issues, the practice of medicine and the handling of environmental activities, to discuss.

I am not qualified to get technical regarding the medical situation, but as with the rest of you, I know medical costs are going up, and there are problems with having enough medical professionals. I understand part of the reason for this problem is the fear of losing lawsuits. There seems to be a lot of lawsuits decided against medical providers without proof of actual damage or deciding the right or wrong of the involved issues. Time tested and peer reviewed knowledge is being ignored as everyone covers themselves with more costly insurance coverage and by doing more and more routinely unnecessary medical tests and laboratory work. Collectively this thinking is leading to higher medical cost problems, a shortage of medical professionals, and changes in medical practices that may not be the best for the patient.

On a radio program, I heard where the "C" section process used to be a choice of last resort, but due to lawsuit awards for unproven claims of misconduct, "C" sections, while generally considered more dangerous than natural child birth, are now routinely applied. This increased use of the "C" section process is happening, because, the potential for a lawsuit is lower than waiting for natural child birth to occur.

By applying all kinds of costly, unnecessary, and unjustified prevention and prescriptive measures, the handling of environmental activities parallels the medical situation.

The practice of environmental regulators requiring a whole bunch of preventive measures is becoming routine. The motto seems to be "pile on the prevention measures" no matter the cost.

17

Under a subjective prescription requirement process, a lot of unnecessary and unjustified violations are likely even when there is no real or potential environmental damage. The regulators do not have to prove environmental damage has occurred to give a violation. Many prescriptive requirements are not physically doable, do not work, are open-ended, and subject to multiple interpretations. A regulator can subjectively determine that a prescriptive requirement has not been fulfilled and give a violation. An unpredictable Mother Nature can come along and destroy whatever work has been done, and a violation may still be given.

Some folks are being asked to spend time and money doing the impossible which includes second-guessing an unpredictable Mother Nature. Some of this unjustified and unnecessary cost can be passed onto the consumer and some can't.

An illustration of "penalty without damage" thinking is provided by the handling of water Quality issues by California's Water Quality (WQ) North Coast Regional Water Board and staff. This board has made changes to their regulations which allows violations and citations to be applied based on hard to challenge determinations of violations by staff personnel without proving actual detrimental damage.

The following information demonstrates how the new and current WQ regulations are inappropriately different from older WQ regulations and how regulatory abuses may occur under the new regulations.

Original Basin Plan regulations applicable to determination of a violation of the California Porter Cologne Water Quality Act were as follows:

- The discharge of soil, silt, bark, slash. or organic and earthen material from any logging, construction, gravel mining, agricultural grazing, or other activity of whatever nature into any stream or watercourse in the basin in **quantities deleterious** to fish, wildlife, or other beneficial uses is prohibited.

- The placing or disposal of soil, silt, bark, slash. or organic and earthen material from any logging, construction, gravel mining, agricultural grazing, or other activity of whatever nature at locations where such material could pass into any stream or watercourse in the basin in **quantities deleterious** to fish, wildlife, or other beneficial uses is prohibited.

As I interpret it, the new, provided standard for giving a WQ violation is as follows:

The occurrence of any controllable discharge resulting from human activities (which is implied to include human handling of animals and natural movement of landscapes where human activities have occurred) **that can influence the quality of the water** (along with associated species habitats and beneficial uses) **of the State that can be reasonably controlled through prevention, mitigation, or restoration** (as judged applicable by Water Quality staff) **is a violation and has to be mitigated.**

A simple review of problems with the new WQ regulations provides the following:

1. Actual detrimental damage does not have to occur and be proven to have occurred for a citation to be given. I repeat,

ACTUAL PROVEN DELETERIOUS DAMAGE DOES NOT HAVE TO OCCUR TO GIVE A CITATION

If you have not done what WQ thinks needs to be done to prevent the "possibility" of a discharge before a discharge or any damage has occurred, you may be cited and fined.

By doing provable, defendable, and professional work, provides some protection against misapplication of WQ regulations. Doing everything WQ instructs may or may not provide the same protection. WQ has shown a propensity to routinely require use of internally developed unworkable ideas that have not been time tested and scientifically peer reviewed, and WQ has been known to force permitees to do things that have resulted in environmental damage and violations.

2. A citable action is a legal action that needs to be based on clear and easily understood legal definitions, and there is a lack of clear and easily understood legal definitions that accompany the new WQ regulations. This lack of clarity will be used by WQ to freely interpret the regulatory wording as they see fit. WQ staff will be able to play God.

While many assume WQ will not abuse their authority, my experiences say otherwise. WQ personnel routinely lack experience and training in making many of the decisions they make, and I have seen many unjustified

19

and unsupported decisions made by WQ staff. Once cited, landowners routinely lack resources and means of recourse to rebut and correct inappropriate actions by WQ.

How comfortable would you be having use of your property being subject to the following WQ standard?

- A citation can be given for any discharge of any substance which influences any waters (and associated species habitats and beneficial uses) when humans have done something in the discharge area prior to the discharge if WQ staff determines the discharge to have been controllable by past actions.

This is quite a mouth full, isn't it.

The current WQ regulations require California landowners to be asking themselves the following kind of questions:

- Will the ground cover reduction from grazing and wet weather tracking by horses, goats, and livestock in soft soils, now and in the future, cause soil movement or other effects that may influence the waters in California?

- Am I required to do something with the natural sliding and unstable condition located on my property because not doing something may influence the waters in California?

- Will the plowing of a field or garden area, now and in the future, cause soil movement or other effects that may influence the waters in California?

- Will development of a water source for me or my animals, now and in the future, cause something to happen that may influence the waters in California?

- Will cutting some trees which exposes the ground to increased weather related impacts, now and in the future, cause soil movement or other effects that may influence the waters in California?

- Will burning of woody debris, now and in the future, cause soil movement or other effects that may influence the waters in California?

- Will grading, culvert work, and road placement involving access road(s), now and in the future, cause soil movement or other effects that may influence the waters in California?

- Will placement of property developments (swimming pool, patio, septic system, or house) and associated movement of soils, now and in the future, cause soil movement or other effects that may influence the waters in California?

Keep in mind wet, moist areas, rain created running water, and rain created pools of water need to be considered as waters of California.

Don't forget protection of California waters also includes protection of associated species' habitats and all beneficial uses of California waters.

If you feel you need to be a good conscientious law-a-biding citizen, you may want to go to WQ and see if you need a permit. If WQ does not give you a pass for now, a permit for a new project can require a filing fee maybe up to or over $800 per year during the life of the permit. Amount of fee depends on what you are doing and what WQ decides they want you to pay. An application must be prepared which contains letter(s), maybe a Form 200 or equivalent document, a project document which may include or be other state approved permit(s) if they are required, and multiple technical documents which may not be part of a project document. At their discretion, Water Quality staff will be allowed a long time, possibly around 90 days, to review and approve the application.

A lot of this sounds kind of silly doesn't it. Californians won't think silly when the word finally gets out how WQ Action Plans and Implementation plans are slowing being required of everyone in California for activities like those mentioned in the above questions. A little selective enforcement of the WQ rules and regulations has kept the lid on where and how WQ permit requirements are suppose to now be applied. The army of WQ regulators needed to enforce all the WQ regulations now in place does not exist, and the state of California is too broke to hire the needed army.

Currently, Californians are in a grace period as far as what is coming under WQ regulations.

A WATER QUALITY CITATION IN CALIFORNIA CAN MEAN WHAT?

To complete the Water Quality situation in California, I provide a short review of what can be involved regarding citations in California.

Civil penalties under CWC Section 13350 of the California Porter Cologne Water Quality Act applicable to violations of the new regulations are as follows:

When there is a discharge as determined by staff and a clean-up and abatement order as prepared by staff and approved by board is put in place, board can give a fine for a violation which can not be less than $500 nor more than $5,000 for each day staff determines discharge occurs. In this situation, superior court can give fine for violation that does not exceed $15,000 for each day staff determines discharge occurs.

When there is a discharge as determined by staff and no clean-up and abatement order has been put in place, board can give fine for violation that does not exceed $10 per gallon of discharge (sediment, muddy water, whatever type of material staff chooses to use) as calculated by staff. In this situation, superior court can give fine for violation that does not exceed $20 per gallon of discharge (sediment, muddy water, whatever type of material staff chooses to use) as calculated by staff.

When there is no discharge but an order such as the new regulations are violated as determined by staff, board can give fine for violation not less than $100 nor more than $1,000 for each day staff determines violation is occurring. In this situation, superior court can give fine for violation that does not exceed $10,000 for each day staff determines discharge occurs.

While I do not feel a lot of sympathy for the generally well-to-do folks that own vineyards or public agencies that do not do a proper job, it is still worth noting what WQ is doing to these folks. There are examples of where Water Quality has given violations and assessed $40,000, $90,000, $225,000, $450,000, and $500,000 fines to grape vineyard owners, dairy farmers, building developers, and municipalities. These fines indicate to me, WQ wouldn't break a sweat assessing a $5,000 or even $10,000 fine to a small individual landowner.

Water Quality folks will say I am exaggerating which I agree is correct for now. But just you wait. I come from the position, rules and regulations should not be put in place that are not going to be clearly and equally applied and are eligible to be applied in a frivolous and abusive manner. If a rule is on the books and available for use, some regulator somewhere, sometime is going to take the opportunity to give it a try.

While the focus of Water Quality regulations in California has mostly been on timber harvesting, the ranchers and farmers are getting more and more attention. Dairies have especially been targeted. More attention is being given to the activities on county and city roads. Rural subdivisions are in WQ's cross-hairs. I have heard where a municipality has been required to get a WQ permit to mow the vegetation in a river flood by-pass channel when it was not flowing water. When all human activities that create supposedly controllable sediment discharge sources are brought into the mix which is currently being done by California Water Quality Agencies through the Environmental Protection Agency's Total Maximum Daily Load process, all human activities will technically require WQ permits in the state of California.

Big Brother in the name of Water Quality has really arrived in California, and these folks may have finally regulated the small timberland owner out of wanting to keep his trees standing. The annual $873 permit fee and costs associated with conforming to an unclear and abusive permit process controlled by WQ staff and an unsure regulatory future may just do the trick. The old folks will say "Se la vee" as privately owned trees in California are fell to pay extra WQ permit fees and to avoid the need for future WQ permits. Those who can leave, will sell out and leave California for the few remaining areas that do not punish people for trying to manage and grow trees.

THE WORLD OF FINES AND PENALTIES IS VERY REAL

The small landowners or producers of natural resource products do not want to get crossways with the regulators or to get violations. The consequences of getting violations are routinely not good. The regulators' control over the penalty processes allows them to set fines and penalties at levels that can break landowners and producers of natural resource products. Handling citations and assessed probation and jail time can interrupt operations which is costly and simply not good for business. Future relations with regulators are not enhanced by fighting with them.

It is obvious environmental laws are here to stay and in some cases fines and corrective work are justified; however, I have a hard time believing a person should serve jail time unless significant harm to humans or human society has occurred.

Rather than locking up the bad guys, I believe the better good is served providing punishment that makes the bad guys correct or contribute towards correcting whatever bad thing has happened to the environment.

A news article(5) provides an example of apparent regulatory overkill. While this news article lacks details on the true extent of involved environmental damage, it can be assumed some oak trees were killed, and some regulatory agency was involved. When a "Man who cleared 300 trees goes to jail…" for "…210 days…", he had better have done something pretty bad. This fella is to additionally pay "…$500,000 to the Ojai Land Conservancy for an oak restoration program. He was also placed on probation for 60 months." Without putting the guy in jail, $1,666.67 per oak tree and five years of probation is a pretty hefty punishment by itself. Have we reached the point where human freedom takes second place to the concerns about oak trees and other nonhuman species? When real criminals are not receiving similar punishment, something just doesn't feel right about what happened to this guy.

My research into fine and citation situations has raised some questions about how readily and cavalierly criminal actions and big fines and are being applied by the regulators. The following information and examples describe violatable offenses and resulting penalties which provides some insight to how the penalty processes are being applied.

Another news article(8) describes how "...two felony and 11 misdemeanor charges relating to water pollution..." were applied to a developer and a corporation. The article mentions how "County Community Planning Department Director...said he was not aware of the complaints...and...developer has complied with all pertinent planning regulations..." "...a failure in the old road...to access the property..." occurred "...but...repairs to the hillside were made." "...County Engineer...said...we checked it this winter and there was no problem at all,...It was clean as a whistle." "...a geological study, as well a several engineering reports..." had been "...done on the project..." "It happens...he had a blow out...which caused sediment to enter the creek..." Felony and misdemeanor violations can lead to jail time and are nothing to be considered lightly, yet the California Department of Fish and Game feels someone who apparently has done about all he can needs to be treated this harshly. A follow-up news article(317) shows this matter ended up with developer getting "...fined $20,000 and sentenced to five years probation for roiling the salmon bearing waters of Gilbert Creek..." If there was a legitimate wrong done, then the fine is kind of okay, excessive, but okay. The whole story bothers me and still looks like an excessive use of regulatory authority for just "roiling" a creek when natural processes routinely cause slides that roil creeks all year long. All this makes you realize how vulnerable you are and how easily a regulatory agency can put anyone in a position to go to jail.

Several water quality violation situations are provided in another news article(9). "A Sonoma County vineyard owner agreed to pay $1 million to settle criminal charges that work on his lands damaged streams that feed the Russian River." Another vineyard owner "...agreed to pay $225,000 in damages for harming..." streams feeding "...the Russian River." A large wine producing company "...paid about $500,000 in fines and repair costs after development at a vineyard triggered a mudslide into another stream." "District Attorney said...at least four other cases are pending... and a settlement with at least one vineyard owner... could come in the next six weeks."

In a news article(10), a "...homebuilder is facing a $40,000 fine for leaking large amounts of dirt into the Russian River...from a 445 home development…" which could "…smother insect larvae that fish…depend on for food…" and "The runoff that carried the silt was worse than it had to be."

As illustrated in a news article(11), there is no mercy for accidents as "…failure of a pump near…" a "…dairy's waste water lagoon sent an estimated 1.3 million gallons of manure tainted (tainted mind you) water into irrigation canals (note irrigation canals)…", and "…dairy operators…face a $90,000…fine…from the California Regional Water Quality Control Board…" Now, 1.3 million gallons of wastewater is a lot of wastewater, but I have to wonder if putting a kind of fertilizer into irrigation water is really a bad thing and justifies a $90,000 fine.

As mentioned in news article(12), the dirt police are not stopping at going after their brethren public officials. "The city of Redding (California) will pay a $450,000 fine for allowing…7.1 million gallons of silty water…to escape a sports park last winter…into a nearby creek and wetlands." "The silt possibly hurt salmon spawning in the creek and potentially stunted several vernal pool plants by muddying the water and blocking the sunlight." While it sounds like a pretty big deal, $450,000 of taxpayer dollars could go to better uses than to pay another public body for a few salmon and vernal pool plants.

It sounds like there are an awful lot of bad people out there; or, the regulators are flexing their muscles because they can.

Right or wrong, hear come the dirt and manure police.

DUE PROCESS? WHAT'S THAT?

The following information, helps to outline my concern in how regulators are handling accused violators of environmental laws, and shows why I see a lack of due process for accused violators.

News article(13) mentions how "GMO ban draws constitutional concern…" by "…District Attorney…" who "…pointed to a clause in the proposed ordinance, which voters will decide on Nov. 2, that allows the county agricultural commissioner to impose jail sentences on anyone caught growing or producing genetically modified crops…", and "…also calls on the agricultural commissioner to impose fines on would-be violators." "Such punishment measures could be in conflict with the U.S. and state constitutions, which leave the power to jail people exclusively with the court system." "There is no due process rights connected with the ordinance's means of imprisonment, and that …is unconstitutional,…"

After reading this article, I got to thinking about how other public agencies are handling violatable offenses, and I see many situations where governmental agencies routinely act in a manner the District Attorney finds objectionable.

The simple version of what I have seen happen when a public official cites someone for an environmental violation is as follows:

A process starts where there is little due process and the accused violator has little ability to control what is happening. The regulatory powers put the accused through a battery of internal public agency processes which are controlled by the regulators. Even though these processes may eventually end in front of a layman judge, the accused rarely has the resources and ability to last out the process long enough to get in front of a real judge. If the accused makes it in front of a real judge, there is still no assurance that a usually layman judge, faced with a more powerful presentation provided by the regulators will be able to sort out the truth, understand the issues, and make a fair, impartial, and knowledgeable decision.

My review of the California situation has found violations involving the California Forest Practice Act (FPA) may be handled through a fine and infraction process, through a criminal misdemeanor process which allows for judge and jury peer review; or, through a civil process involving monetary fines.

Even though I have intimate knowledge of the FPA processes and I have followed the FPA infraction process for years, this process remains a mystery to me. There have been continual changes over the years in how, when, and where the process is applied. While I know of no recent use, I understand this infraction process, which handles an infraction like a traffic ticket with a ticket, is still in play.

Under the FPA criminal misdemeanor process, fines and jail time determinations are controlled and limited by written law. Under this process within a short time period, the accused has the option to present what has happened before a jury of their peers or before a supposedly impartial judge. I have been closely involved with various FPA misdemeanor situations, and with a couple of exceptions, the results have been justified and fair.

I understand the FPA civil citation process starts with a California Department of Forestry (CDF) field inspector's report which is passed up the line for review by supervisors and eventually Sacramento. The amount of civil penalty or fine is developed as the report moves up the line. The accused is then given notice of a hearing before the full California Board of Forestry, and at this time, the accused decides to appeal the citation at a hearing or to just give-in and pay the fine. If an appeal is requested, the chairman of the board decides if the appeal will be before the full board, a board committee, or before an administrative judge. If the appeal goes to an administrative judge, the board chairman can have the judge give a final decision or only give a proposed decision. Administrative judge can change fine amount or the board can change the fine amount; however, I understand the board does not have to accept the administrative judge's decision. The board has full control over the process, and over the outcome. If the board does not like the judge's or anyone else's input, the board has the ability to override any thinking contrary to the board's thinking.

Adabba dabba dabba do. Are you lost yet?

Please note the amount of control exercised by the regulators over the citation process and the lack of access by the accused to the court system and to review by their peers. Does this process provide for required due process?

If the accused loses the appeal of the citation, the fine must be paid in 20 days. If wanted after all the board actions are exhausted which must be done first, the accused can then appeal final board decisions to a local superior judge and eventually to the State Supreme court if wanted.

While being allowed back to the courts at the end of the California Forest Practice civil citation process, it is hard to see how any average accused operator, landowner, or person has the resources and ability to hang-on through the one-sided FPA review and hearing process. Most accused violators, guilty or not, do not attempt to fight the regulators. They generally give up, and pay whatever fine is established by the Board of Forestry. The FPA civil citation process is being handled very quietly and receives little attention; so, the extent of its use is not well advertised. I do know from contacts with Sacramento that the process is in full swing and the number of FPA civil citations is growing.

Although the FPA misdemeanor process provides fair and justified results by providing timely results in a local court with review by your peers at a reasonable cost to everyone involved, the CDF avoids using this process. I was told the FPA misdemeanor process was considered to be too much work for the regulatory community and was not getting the number of wanted convictions.

THE FOURTH IS COMING TO CONTROL ALL OF US

The following is a listing of numerous real life examples illustrating how a Fourth Branch of Government is working towards control of all facets of our lives.

PERMITS GALORE

Even the activists and protesters face the inability to offset actions by the Fourth Branches of Government as illustrated by two news stories (14 and 15).

In Mill Valley, California a formal process for processing parade permits was put in place by the city council which allows the council to chose who participates in the Memorial Day Parade. This does not make the Marin Peace and Justice Coalition group happy.

In Santa Rosa, California the city council modified a trespass ordinance to allow the banning of anyone from a shopping center for up to a year, and this change in the ordinance was done to keep rowdies away. The news article quoted a local activists as saying "It may seem like a safety issue or good business to other people, but what I find troublesome is there is no way to ensure it will be applied fairly".

So, what's new? The producers of natural resources have been facing the fact there is no way to ensure environmental laws will be applied fairly for years.

These two stories illustrate how the media gives attention to rather small incidences of possible governmental abuse involving activists and protesters, but the many daily stories of regulatory abuse involving the producers of natural resources basically go unnoticed.

A simple news story(16) illustrates how the physical field situation is not fully understood before creating and applying some rules and regulations. The simple use of a highway into a rural area by livestock trucks requires repeated legislated exemption action every so many years. While other highway areas may require application of the regulation, why is the involved highway not permanently exempted from the regulation, and the continual effort and waste of time to re-do the exemption every so many years stopped? Either the road can handle the livestock trucks or it can not. Obviously the granting of the exemption indicates the involved highway can physically handle use by livestock trucks, and the politics of the situation seem to favor the livestock trucks; so, the problem of livestock truck use must be coming from a different direction. Could it be the involved regulatory authority is interpreting the base law as being applicable to the involved highway when in reality there is no need to apply the involved regulation to the involved highway?

In a following news story(17), it appears the livestock trucking and highway problem is back again. The story is titled "Cattlemen suffer under highway restrictions". The article indicates there is some kind of change to what has been happening up to this point in time, and "…an emergency waiver of trucking rules…" is being requested. While extra safety precautions may be needed, why is there a change in what has been physically done in the past? Is the change due to some inappropriate regulatory determination? The article has the cattle people saying "The regulations right now are almost unworkable…" for the "…number of cattle loads per year out of Humboldt County…" which is "…between 400 and 600…"

Sounds like this highway use problem will go on until the cows come home.

DO IT OUR WAY OR ELSE

Another newspaper story(18) involving the Environmental Protection Agency (EPA), illustrates how a governmental agency interprets and applies laws as interpreted by itself which appears to favor the environmental community. This article tells how the EPA has reached a settlement with some environmental groups over how to apply some farm emission standards.

The first problem illustrated by this article is the many laws and regulations being foisted upon us that are unclear which allows public agencies such as the EPA a free hand in how to interpret and apply them. As in this case, internally developed guidelines were called into question by some environmental groups, and this action apparently required court action to resolve the issue. Resolution of interpretation disagreements over unclear laws and regulations is not a bad thing; and is something that has to be done; however, this example illustrates how time, effort and cost are needed to make corrections. The use of the courts is often the only recourse in many similar situations, and court action does not always provide proper and best solutions.

In this EPA case, the article indicates the permitting processes will be applied as wanted by the environmental groups, and who knows if what is wanted by the environmental groups is what was intended by the legislature. Additionally since the EPA has the ability to apply whatever guidelines they want, who knows if the settlement is based on properly peer reviewed science, site specific facts, logic, and common sense; or, if the resolution was just a way for the EPA to side step the pressures from the environmental groups at the expense of the farmers.

This type of thing happens everyday in the resolution of the many unclear laws and regulations where the governmental agencies or layman courts get to decide what is right or wrong in the application of unclear laws. As illustrated by the environmental group's legal action, it can take political connections, time, and financial resources to take on a governmental agency's internally developed guidelines. For basically all producers of natural resource products and especially small landowners, political connections, time, and financial resources are in short supply and usually not available.

POLLUTION
NOISE, AIR, AND SMELL

In news article(19), snowmobile police were held at bay as "The House voted…to let snowmobiles continue using Yellowstone and Grand Teton national parks…" "…the machines cause pollution and noise, and pose a danger to the park's wildlife." From my perspective and experience, winter fun on top of the snow in already limited snowmobile access areas does little to no environmental damage, and I doubt much wildlife sticks around to be hurt. It is hard to believe the pollution problem is not resolved as it is dissipated into the vast amount of atmosphere over the park lands and surrounding mostly lightly populated rural area. "…a ban would devastate the local economy around the parks…" which means a lot of tourists must be coming to the parks which the enviros continually say are needed to replace the reducing use of natural resources. It seems to me this is really about the desire of a few to limit use of a massive park and wilderness area to those wanting quiet and no human interference with Mother nature.

A couple of news articles(20 and 21) mention how literally the bullsh…t (BS) police are on their way. Air Quality regulators are "…to regulate smog-forming emissions from cow manure…" from "…cows in Southern California dairies…" "Farms and dairies that annually produce more than 12.5 tons (how this will be determined is anyone's guess) of the gases that contribute to smog must apply…for local air quality permits, pay hundreds of dollars in annual fees and begin accounting for the air pollution produced by their farms and dairies." Another news article(22) says these new air quality regulations will affect "…dairies with at least 50 cows…" in "…300 dairies in the Chino area,…" and "It is expected to cost…" about "…$15,000 per dairy…" I thought open space agricultural uses were being promoted and wanted due to their ability to provide for clean air and open space lands, but one news article(23) contradicts this thinking by saying "…government agencies…" have "…older state analysis…" supporting "…a claim…" that "…ammonia and other gases from the…San Joaquine …valley's massive dairy industry and other animal waste create more pollution than cars,…" By putting these new regulations and high added air quality permit and regulatory operational costs in place, it sounds like someone has changed their mind about wanting to provide incentives for maintaining dairy open space lands.

I will grant you being downwind of a collection point of dairy cows will bring you the sweet smell of meadow muffins, and you have to be a rancher, farmer, or dairy person to appreciate what the smell represents; however, it is hard to logically believe gases from cow manure piles mean much in the overall scheme of things as they rise and dissipate into the large expanse of air over dairy farms. Will attempts to control such gases really do much to alleviate larger smog problems? It looks like those with cows and bulls will have another row to hoe. For sure, more regulation is not going to help now struggling dairies and to promote preservation and maintenance of lands in an open space condition. More development here we come.

LOVE THOSE ANIMALS

For obvious and some not so obvious reasons, dog lovers, which I am one, have a lot of regulations and problems heading our way. The time of being able to walk your dog without needing to abide by some form of regulatory restriction has come to an end for many folks, and will soon end for those wanting to walk dogs around other people, other dogs, and for many other reasons. We have all heard about the many conflicts that come from this practice, and it has only been a matter of time before something had to be done to reduce and eliminate such conflicts. Dog fights, harassment of wildlife, harm to humans, and even a case of a dog killing a person have occurred.

News article(24) provides how restriction on beaches are being applied. "Under California law, dogs are not allowed on state beaches unless specifically allowed in the jurisdiction...per State Park superintendent..." State Parks "...is looking out for the threatened snowy plover." A letter to the editor(25), shows some folks are really upset about what is happening, and the letter shows confining dog use to certain areas has its own problems by saying "...ever since State Parks and Recreation closed all their beaches to dogs, Dry Lagoon has been overrun. It seems like every dog in Humboldt County is now at Dry Lagoon, which I guess must be the only place people have to take their dogs anymore."

A news article(26) shows the animal protection police are on their way in Europe. "...Spain's first animal cruelty law...banned killing of abandoned cats and dogs in animal shelters..." which indicates Spain's law will help the cat and dog food industries while raising the question how they themselves intend to properly care for these animals and avoid the listed penalty of $24,200. "...Germany plans to phase out caged farming of caged chickens..." which means free-range chickens running around town could be the in-thing. "Austria's new Law...outlaws use of lions and other wild animals in circuses and makes it illegal to restrain dogs with chains, choke collars or...electric shock...invisible fences..." which all indicates a circus in Austria will apparently be limited to only human acts and Austrian kids will never see an animal circus, and leather will be the in thing for those who wish to walk the dog. In Austria "Violators will be subject to fines of $2,420...up to $18,160..."

In this country an example of silly and not well thought out regulation is described in news article(27) where "Santa Fe, N.M...is rethinking a proposed rewrite of its animal control ordinance that would have required dogs to wear seat belts in cars." While there is a need to control dogs, the idea of restraining a dog in a seat belt would really lead to major stress problems for the dog, and the idea is most likely not physically doable for every type of dog. It is laughable to anyone who knows dogs to imagine them being forcibly held in any kind of firm restraint apparatus. Talk about stress and cruelty to animals.

While dog protection police are busy in Europe and other places, another news article(28) shows Oakland, California "City officials are considering an ordinance that would limit the number of dogs in most households to four." "Puppies less than 4 months old..." will be "...exempt from the proposed ordinance." While nuisance and poor care situations involving animals needs to sometimes be handled by legal means, this kind of policing opens the door to all kinds of problems such as unavoidable selective enforcement and conflict with private home rights. "Knock! Knock! This is the doggie police! We understand you have not been able to get ride of all your puppies quick enough, and you have more than four dogs over four months of age in your home. The doggie ordinance is just another example of ways vague, unclear, and questionable regulations are being developed that allow the Fourth Branch of Government to selectively chose who to bother and who not to bother without having to be accountable.

Regulatory controls involving animals has been taken to new heights as illustrated in internet report(29) "...in which the San Francisco Chronicle reported...A California law requires a trapping license in order to kill mice." "...anyone who takes furbearing mammals or non-game animals must purchase a trapping license by passing a complex test and paying a fee of $78.50,..." "The (California) Fish and Game Code 4005 defines non-game animals as including mice, rats, gophers and moles,..." Selective enforcement is planned as "...chief of law enforcement for the (California) Department of Fish and Game, said the law would not be enforced for personal use (which can mean what???).", but "...the statute is enforced for commercial use..." meaning "...gardener or pest control service..." Setting traps could result in someone facing "...arrest without a permit." The next time you hire a pest control person to handle a rodent problem, ask them if they have the needed trapping license.

I understand no matter how large or isolated your property you can not legally dispose of any dead animal on your property. It appears all the dead gold fish and tweety birds buried in folks backyards are potential violatable offenses, and I assume dog and cat burials are major offenses. I am not sure of all the legal requirements involved in dead pet situations, but I imagine regulators or some health official need to get involved. Can you imagine the overload at disposal facilities if all dead animals were properly delivered and processed. As mentioned in letter to the editor(30), one rural area has been affected by "...closure of the Tallow Works..." and officially dead animals have to be transported out of the affected area for long distances to properly dispose of the animals. I agree dead animal disposal can be a real health problem in populated areas, but in the rural areas, these things have been and can continue to be handled as in the past without all the fuss that is being created. If the regulators want to really do something worthwhile, they could provide a legitimately needed service and help out the public, farmers and ranchers, but instead they seem to concentrate on legal enforcement activities and leave the public, farmers, and ranchers hanging. I wonder what police label we should apply to the regulators who have to handle enforcing dead animal disposal requirements. How about DAD (dead animal disposal) police?

EATING AND BREATHING HAZARDS

Those making regulations love to require all kinds of warning labels be posted whether they are justified or do any good. Everywhere you look you see warning labels. Hot drinks are labeled "Warning drinks are hot". Liquor stores list "Warning alcoholic beverages may be hazardous to you and your baby's health".

Cigarette containers state how "Smoking is hazardous to your health". Gas stations list "Gasoline can cause cancer". A recent news article(31) really caught my eye when I read there is an attempt to "...require signs in restaurants and stores warning that French fries may cause cancer." as part of a "...right-to-know law..." passed by California voters. Another news article(32) mentions "...Proposition 65 – a 1986 ballot measure...requires businesses to warn consumers about known carcinogens or reproductive toxins.", and "...tuna companies...are failing to warn consumers their products contain mercury."

While all this may have created new industries and jobs to supply, service, and police all this labeling, consumers often out of necessity and simply because they like a product are still buying the products with warning labels which raises the question about how much good all the labeling is doing. Especially in cases where dangerous quantities of intake and contact involving a deadly substance are not realistically possible to achieve, some of this labeling has gotten pretty silly and is wasting a lot of time, resources, and money that could be better utilized on more worthwhile endeavors.

Two radio shows(270) carry personal responsibility to a new low by mentioning there is a movement in England to only allow knives to have rounded points. The goal is to not allow any knives to have sharp points

News article(33) discusses a proposal to require "Boats...to post a sticker warning of the dangers of carbon monoxide poisoning,..." The intent is to make "...boaters aware they are breathing dangerous levels of carbon monoxide from the boat's engine..." Now, I am not a boating person and do not know how true it is that boaters intake dangerous levels of carbon monoxide from the boat engines, but it seems a lot to do about nothing by some regulators who do not have enough to do. Most lakes have a lot of open, smog free type air to help dissipate carbon monoxide fumes, and while it may provide a little educational value, I believe the expense and time spent will basically be a waste; because, water skiers and boaters will pay zilch attention to such labeling. This just sounds like another nuisance regulation that will be selectively enforced and cost someone a lot of wasted time and money to avoid being hassled, fined, and ticketed by a regulator.

The next logical step is to apply a similar labeling requirement to all types of machinery that gives off carbon monoxide. Here come the car carbon monoxide label police.

Regulatory issues involving smoke and smog are always a major concern in populated nonrural areas. Especially during cold weather in areas where a lot of wood burning smoke just hangs in the air, smoke can be a legitimate problem for some folks, and in some areas, fireplaces, burn barrels, and basic burning of any kind is being banned.

News article(34) describes the burn ban situation in the San Francisco Bay. "Thirty-five San Francisco Bay Area cities and counties have passed woodburning laws, but only four have…banned burning on smoky nights." "The city…Fairfield…is considering a ban on fireplaces and woodburning stoves (which use a renewable resource, wood and not petroleum products) to help fight winter air pollution." "…on cold nights… smoke hangs close to the ground,…" "Fairfield could …make it a misdemeanor (you can go to jail) to burn on so-called "spare the air" nights." The misdemeanor idea opens the door to the knock on a cold night by the smoke police who can ticket you and send you to jail for trying to keep warm. If really justified, an infractionable fine regulation may be something to utilize, but to give the unaccountable Fourth Branch of Government the discretion to make wood smoke a jailable offense is wrong.

While the reasons for such bans may appear obvious and such bans may even do some good in smoggy metropolitan areas, trying to eliminate a little discomfort from smoke in rural communities is causing a lot of problems. Many burn regulations do not make a lot of sense, and what is good for the metropolitan, populated areas of California is not necessary good for rural California. In rural areas, hanging smoke problems generally dissipate throughout the day, and legitimate health problems are not occurring in many areas being targeted as potential health problem areas.

Without using some common sense and factual information, a lot of the burning bans are being justified and controlled by conditions in nonrural areas. Without providing an advertised site specific and scientifically proven factual basis, burn barrel restrictions have been placed in rural areas which do not have smog problems, and burn controls are being applied based on nonapplicable measurements and information provided from outside the rural areas being restricted. A Letter to the Editor(35) provides an example of how nonsite specific information from distant and different conditions is inappropriately being used to determine burn days. The letter says "Our burn days (in Eureka on the coast) are determined by what the weather is like in Ukiah (over 100 miles away and over 20 miles inland) at 5,000 feet in an airplane."

Without having to be accountable for what they say, air quality regulators say the small amount of smoke coming from burn barrels is polluting the air as it climbs into the large expanse of airspace over my rural area, Eureka. Eureka is surrounded by miles and miles of undeveloped areas to the north, east, and south and the Pacific Ocean immediately to the west; so, to any logically thinking person, the air quality regulators are full of it.

Under the burn barrel ban, even paper can not be burned, and this has increased the amount of garbage going to landfills. It was interesting to watch how this ban caused a run on paper shredders needed to destroy papers containing personal information, and in today's world, personal papers amount to a lot of paper. I do not know exactly how others were affected, but even with some recycling, our family's contributions to the landfill have at least tripled. Those making paper shredders and the garbage companies are having a hay day raking in the increased revenues, and it is easy to think they help lobby for burner barrel bans.

The burn barrel and garbage situation shows how members of the Fourth Branches of Government do not co-ordinate their activities to avoid problems. One result of the burn ban will be an increase in illegal dumping by those trying to avoid extra garbage disposal fees. In my work overseeing various properties for clients, I find illegal dumping to be a big problem for rural landowners. Various public agencies require landowners to clean up illegally dumped materials and to stand the costs for doing this clean-up. News article(36) has a law enforcement person saying "Illegal dumping of garbage and other waste has become a serious problem inside Eureka,..." "Instead of taking the time and spending the money to get rid of garbage responsibility, we find people dumping it wherever they can." Note the two key words, time and money. While fines and penalties are applied such as "...between $250 and $1,000...", a simple check will find these fines are little deterrent in rural areas where law enforcement coverage is light and catching illegal dumping is rare.

At the same time the burner barrel ban was put in place in my area, permit and fee requirements for all burning were put in place. The process of getting a burn permit to burn some leaves now involves a public agency that does not have the time and resources to do the job right. The already referenced Letter to the Editor(35) demonstrates the frustration felt by rural folks and illustrates how the regulators are not held accountable for their actions. The letter mentions how "The vast majority of the people that attended (hearings)…was adamantly against the banning of burn barrels. We were told that we really did not have a say…" "At no time…were we told that there would be a…$12…tax for burn permit…" "Then on the news I hear the Eureka fire chief state that 'We decided to ban all burn barrels,' not the people…but the fire chief." Several letters to the editor were sent regarding the burn barrel ban and another Letter to the Editor(37) says "Enough is enough. We may have air pollution, but it isn't from burn barrels. It's from the mouths of the people controlling the office (Air Quality Management District). I believe it is called power."

As the situation in my area demonstrates, those in control, the regulators, have decided it is better to put more garbage into the landfills, have more illegal dumping, and to ship the garbage problem off to someone else (like we do to Oregon); rather than, have a little benign burning. The elimination of burn barrels in rural areas with fireplaces soon to follow, is forcing a lot of time, money, and resources to be needlessly wasted.

If there wasn't so much money in handling garbage, maybe someone would have the incentive to find a better and more efficient way to burn garbage and produce much needed power. Whoops, I said the "burn" word.

Agricultural burning is also coming under more and more regulatory control, and the ability to eliminate agricultural wastes and reduce the potential for fire is becoming more and more limited. The burning of agricultural wastes and the use of fire to reduce fire fuels is a very useful and effective tool if correctly utilized; however, those in control, the regulators and uninformed public, do not realize and understand the benefits and requirements involved in using this tool. Regulations and restrictions on burning are resulting in less burning, and when agricultural waste and wildland fuel loads are allowed to sit around, unburned, the potential for fire and more damaging fire increases.

A surprising source of particulate pollution that is bothering the regulators is discussed in news article(38) that says "…the smoggiest in the nation…regions…are also the worst in…particulates so small they can easily enter the lungs and bloodstream." "…13 counties around Los Angeles and the San Joaquin Valley failed …new limits for tiny particles in the air." "…paved road dust (**paved road dust I say**) was among the biggest…" pollution sources in San Joaquin Valley, Los Angeles, and San Diego regions. "In San Diego and the San Joaquin Valley...residential fuel combustion, including wood-burning stoves and fireplaces..." were among "...the biggest sources..." of pollution. It is going to be interesting to see how the dust and particulate police go after the paved road dust problem in the land of automobiles, Southern California.

Smokers, you are running out of places to smoke, and the Fourth branch of government can't seem to find enough ways to get at you. While I am not a smoker, my folks were heavy smokers, and I think I understand both sides of the issue. I do not support smokers, but I am starting to feel sorry for them, because I do not like the way the regulators are going after some folks that just can't hep it. News article(39) mentions how a California Senate bill bans "...smoking...on the sand..." of "...the 64 state-owned beaches..."; or, face a fine of "...$100..." I am among the many who do not like seeing cigarette butts on a beach, but I do not like the idea of the regulators having more authority and unclear regulations to selectively enforce in chasing a pretty petty problem.

A news article(40) discusses "...a (California state) bill that would prohibit the production and sale of foie gras, a delicacy derived from the livers of force-fed geese and ducks." I do not know why livers from other geese and ducks are not as good as foie gras, and since I do not eat the stuff, I guess I do not really care that much about what happens to the foie gras industry. I do care enforcement of such a very, very low priority concern will take up time and resources that could be better used elsewhere. I also care that food restrictions could be inappropriately expanded to cover other foods produced in rural communities.

The food police are on their way. I wonder how far they will be allowed to go?

GARDENERS BEWARE

Due to all the fires in Southern California and elsewhere, there is talk of having brush trimming and plant approval police. While there is a need to do fire prevention work, using the regulatory process to force such work to be done has some pitfalls if the regulations are not clearly spelled out and if the regulators are not held accountable for their actions. As I say throughout this book, I have a soft spot for the firemen and enforcement people, but there is a need to be sure the ones who would be enforcing brush trimming and approving plant species are not given too much unaccountable authority. As mentioned regarding Fairfield's idea to make smoke misdemeanor regulations, it would not be right to send someone to jail for not trimming their bushes or planting the wrong plant based on some regulator's chosen specifications.

You may say this thinking is far fetched, but there is no assurance that this type of thinking won't end up in regulation as mentioned in a news article(41) where "...Sierra Club lobbyist who's been working with insurance companies in crafting fire legislation, said there is an effort afoot to give the California Department of Forestry more authority to require work around homes be done." "...bills that could strengthen or expand existing demands that brush and trees be cleared around houses..." are being promoted. "...defensible space is...also socially responsible,...", "...at a minimum - is a 30-foot area cleared of flammable plants...", and "minimum clearing could be set at 100 feet."

Same news article(41) provides an alternative to regulatory approaches to fire prevention that makes a lot of sense. "In Colorado, State Farm is giving residents in fire-prone areas two years to clear brush around homes or risk having their policies canceled..." While some may say allowing the big insurance companies and the market place handle things will be too harsh and will result in a lot of folks not having insurance, I say this is only true for those who do not act responsibly. This approach at least gives landowners more say about what happens on their property versus letting unaccountable politicians and regulators determine what happens to them and their property.

BETTER LEAVE THE CRITTERS ALONE

Remember when kids could be kids, and with and without their folks, they could have fun playing and messing around with tadpoles and frogs in an innocent quest to learn about nature? It was fun to catch tadpoles, raise them, and watch them turn into frogs. Well, no more can this be done in California without getting in trouble with the frog police. Species protection laws prevent messing with such species as red-legged frogs, tailed frogs, and many other amphibian species that are being found all over the place. In fact, in California anyone 16 years of age or older (I assume including teachers) needs a fishing license or some kind of special permit to mess around with tadpoles and frogs and needs to be sure they are following listed regulations; otherwise, they can be cited for violation of Fish and Game laws.

Those who think I exaggerate the potential for "Tadpole" penalties might keep in mind what happened to an experienced "...former federal wildlife manager who says he moved about 400 protected tadpoles from a backyard pond to a refuge for their own safety..." The news article(277) says the wildlife manager "...agreed to pay a $3,500 fine to avoid a criminal charge." If an experienced professional who voluntarily tries to do the right thing has the potential to be "criminally charged", you can believe there is nothing to stop regulators from socking it to the uniformed. Playing with the wrong tadpoles can be a very costly adventure and can make you a criminal potentially subject to jail time. Additionally, in getting ride of any standing water to eliminate breeding mosquitoes that can spread the West Nile virus, you better make sure there are no tadpoles living with the mosquitoes; or, you might commit a criminal action.

Are you getting confused about what you can and can't do? If you are, welcome to the current real world of overlapping, gotcha regulations being applied by the Fourth Branch of Government. Read on. There is more.

A mixed bag of regulations has been put in place regarding the red-legged frog, ferry shrimp, and tiger salamander. News article(43) mentions how "...U.S. Fish and Wildlife Service is proposing to designate 4.1 million acres as critical habitat for the threatened California red-legged frog..." which involves by my count 28 counties that make up the southern end of California and a lot of the Sacramento Valley. Keep in mind the rest of the state has red-legged frogs, and there are a whole lot of red legged frogs out there; but, don't let a large population of frogs get in the way of a good chance to regulate some folks.

This designation will cause landowners, farmers, and ranchers to be "...bound by...provisions of the Endangered Species Act (ESA).", and restrictions already in place are affecting how they can utilize their lands.

While I have not been directly involved with what is happening in the southern end of California, I had a wildlife biologists explain to me what Environmental Protection Agency (EPA) and California Department of Fish and Game (DFG) are doing to ranchers and landowners. Very expensive surveys (around $75,000 has been mentioned) for the red-legged frog, ferry shrimp, and tiger salamander are required in 50 year potential flood plain areas. Rain and flood levels are very unpredictable, and many lakes and pool type areas are created during any rain which quickly dry up. This results in **a lot of area being called potential habitat,** and a lot of area (a whole bunch) has to be surveyed over long periods of time. I understand cattle grazing operations that have been in place for 100 years or more are exempt from the survey and ESA requirements, but put a plow to the ground or disturb the ground and you better know if a ferry shrimp once lived there or if a tiger salamander has passed by. I suspect the ones mainly affected by these survey and ESA requirements are the larger rural landowners and anyone trying to build houses and develop an area. The smaller landowners are probably being given a pass for now. It probably is only a matter of time before the Red Legged Frog, Ferry Shrimp, and Tiger Salamander police come knocking on all Southern California and Sacramento Valley doors.

HERE COME THE FISH AND GAME PEOPLE

Another California Fish and Game law that can bring the punch card police and jail time down on you involves a salmon and steelhead punch card. One day while reading the paper I read in news article(44) "Violation of the mandatory return..." of "...Steelhead Report Cards...requirement is a misdemeanor". Since I understand a misdemeanor carried jail time with it, I went to the California Department of Fish and Game to verify just what could be done to a person who didn't return their punch card. Sure enough, you could go to jail for not returning your punch card. I refer you to Title 14 Section 1.74, Section 12000, and other Freshwater Sport Fishing requirements found in California's 2003 Fish and Game Code Regulations for exact regulatory wording.

To summarize the punch card situation, if you might catch or hook a steelhead trout that is 16 inches or longer in any anadromous waters (in any waters that allow unimpeded access to the Pacific Ocean), you better get a punch card. You are to voluntarily go get this card, pay your money, and for trying to be an up straight responsible citizen, you can pay a $1,000 fine and possibly go to jail for six months if you forget to mail your punch card back on time. While I would be the first to agree having any judge apply the maximum penalty would be an extreme rarity, I have a problem with anyone being given the authority to apply such an extreme penalty in such an abusive manner for such a benign problem.

Oh, by the way, for those who think I exaggerate the potential for abuse of punch card regulations, abuse is happening right now. If you know of anyone that likes to pick the rocks or skin-dive for abalone in California, tell them I have heard someone forgetting to mail in his punch card was fined $410 by DFG. No jail time in this case, but wow!

In my book, punch card penalties are good examples of where the punishment does not fit the crime.

In California, trout fishing has become so complicated and so costly it is not worth the risk and cost to do it. As a kid, I and other friends spent hours fishing streams which allowed us to learn a lot. Now, there is no chance for other kids to do the same without violating some questionable or benign law or regulation. This type of activity used to be the way a lot of young people could spend their time learning to be independent versus not having anything to do and getting into trouble. Fishing has been relegated by the regulators to the older folks who are the only ones who have a chance at understanding all the complicated rules and regulations. A lot of kids who get to fish probably believe fish come from a truck that comes and dumps them into the artificial lake, pond, or concrete box where they have been allowed to fish.

How much harm would it do to just let the kids under 16 years of age go fish anywhere and catch whatever they can catch? Huh, California department of Fish and game? Think the benefits to the kids would outweigh the loss of a few fish?

People with bird feeders better watch out, because the DFG is coming after you. News article(45) says "...bird feeders "might" be spreading a deadly disease." and "...it is best to stop feeding altogether,..." and "...recommends ditching feeders altogether." Those feeding the birds "...poo-pooed...idea..." and said "If you keep feeders clean it shouldn't be a problem." Is DFG again chasing a windmill and applying a blanket restrictive policy to the whole state of California when the involved disease problem may only exist in areas with certain site specific conditions? Will the DFG make a stand and become bird feeder and bird feeder cleaning police? Don't be surprised if DFG goes after folks feeding birds, because without having to justify and support their actions, you never know how far regulators will go.

Another example of an out of control regulatory permit process is the California Department of Fish and Game's (DFG) 1600 stream alteration permit process. This regulatory process has been mostly developed internally by the DFG without much public input, and can apply to such low order waterways as wet and moist areas, indentations in the ground which only flow water during rainfall, and underground piping of water.

DFG arbitrarily makes-up rules and regulations without public input for the 1600 permit processes. The following outline shows changes effective 1/1/2004. Sixteen hundred stream alternation permits obtained under the older 10/12/2001 requirements are routinely hard to get and take a long time. Under the new requirements, permits routinely taking 90 days to get will take even longer, because DFG has given themselves even more review time.

Changes to the 1600 process for 2004

10/21/2001	1/1/2004
DFG has 30 days to notify the person notification is complete.	DFG has 30 days to determine notification is complete. (notification to permitee deleted)

DFG has 30 days to respond.
  -If DFG fails to respond, activity may commence.
	DFG has 60 days to provide draft agreement.
	  -If DFG fails to provide draft agreement, activity may commence.
	(30 more review days added)

If DFG's proposals are unacceptable, DFG shall meet with permitee within seven days.	If DFG's proposals are not acceptable, DFG shall met with permitee within fourteen days. (Review delayed another seven days)
If mutual agreement is not reached, a panel of arbitrators will resolve disagreements.	If mutual agreement is not reached, a panel of arbitrators will resolve disagreements. (No pressure is really put on DFG to resolve disagreements until the end of the process, and resolution is by an unspecified panel and unclear arbitration process.)

As in most permit review processes, the permitee is required to provide information and act according to firm guidelines, but the DFG has the ability to play around with requirements all through the long review process. The permitee does not know what the permit will say until the end of permit review, and permitee is routinely forced to grant extensions of review periods to work out disagreements or to utilize an unknown and questionably fair arbitration process.

It seems there is no end to the creation of more and more environmental laws for the Fourth Branches of Government to apply.

Two internet reports(64)(65) outline how a new Invasive Species law is being put in place. This law is being elevated "...to that of wetlands and Endangered Species within the NEPA (Environmental Policy Act of 1969) process." "Briefly...Invasive Species...is defined as any organism that is non-native and could cause harm to the environment." How's this for a broad definition? The new law will "...hand the Interior Dept., authority to decide which plants, animals, fish, birds and insects are invasive, or of foreign origin to a particular land area, and are therefore threatening to those species regarded as native."

While this new regulation seems to focus on invasive weed plant species, the internet reports say "It will not stop with the plant kingdom, either. Rainbow trout, brown trout, pheasants, goldfish, and honeybees are invasive according to the definition (foreign origin, harmful to the environment by way of replacing/ threatening native species). The entire biological realm is open to DOI's interpretation." "Once it's discovered (as determined by the regulators) your property is home to an invasive species, Interior folks have all the justification they need to oversee, manage, analyze, prevent and control the damage (as perceived by the regulators) from these invaders".

Because I have seen how regulatory authorities can twist and control things through their unaccountable interpretations of existing unclear laws, I can see how this new invasive species law has the potential to be applied as described in this internet report. As mentioned in another story in this book, rainbow trout are considered an invader species in the Grand Canyon which makes killing rainbow trout a candidate project under this new regulation. The potential for the Department of the Interior showing up to do things on your property without your say is very real.

SOME ODDS AND ENDS

Public bodies use questionable environmental reasons and their regulatory authority in some pretty questionable ways. Nonresident parking police here we come. I am not talking about routine parking tickets and parking meter police. I am talking about what news article(46) says happened to "Out-of-towners who attended a benefit concert at a nature preserve..." They "...were required to park their vehicles farthest from the stage and then wait to be escorted into the show by someone who could show proof of residency."; because, "Palo Alto...City Council invoked a little known law that says the 1,400 acre preserve is only open to Palo Alto residents and their guests." This all came about, because an environmental member "complained...the preserve, populated by quail, deer, and mountain lions, shouldn't be used for a concert at all." I wonder if all the funds to purchase, maintain, and support the preserve only come from Palo Alto residents? This shows how public agencies have the authority to control some pretty mundane and questionable things.

As illustrated in a news article(47), the Fourth Branch of Government's ability to set policy and create regulations does not stop with natural resource issues. In this article, how our kids and schools operate is involved. "…the anti-discrimination policy for all California Schools…" uses "…a state law that defines gender as a person's actual or perceived sex…" and "…a Christian legal rights group…" finds this "…immoral…" and conflicting "…with the state penal code - which defines gender as a person's biological sex - therefore schools should not be required to comply with it." This may sound like splitting hairs, and maybe this time the Fourth Branch of Government will be held accountable for inappropriate actions; however, how often are similar actions by the Fourth Branch of Government actions held up to the spotlight and scrutinized as in the case of this situation? This situation illustrates how easy it is for the Fourth Branches of Government to slip in and change things to their way of thinking without going through required legislative and other regulatory formation processes.

While the idea of separation of church and state is being pushed by the American Civil Liberty Union and others, the public's right to revere symbols and have traditions of any kind are being taken away by using the Fourth Branch of Government's powers. A news article(48) presents a situation where some folks created "…a war memorial and a place of worship at a Southern California desert site known as Sunrise Rock …in the Mojave National Reserve…" that can be used and observed by anyone. "…the 9th Circuit Court of Appeals…ruled against…an 8-foot cross…on behalf of a retired National Park Service employee who objected to the religious symbol…" The involved site "…has… attracted Christian worshippers." While the attack on the showing of the cross in anyway connected to a public activity or body is nothing new, this situation further illustrates how the Fourth Branch of Government can interfere with even the simplest of activities, and there is little to no recourse for anyone including a majority to do anything about it. Onward the cross police.

In another public lands issue involving the Forest Service, internet report(49) tells how "The Forest Service…" through a "…recreation forester…has told California vacationers…flagpoles are not authorized for recreation residences…" and "…to remove poles flying the U.S. flag from property the service has leased to them." One vacationer said "My flagpole has been up for more than 23 years, and like many in our cabin tract I am a patriotic American who has a flagpole." So sorry Charlie, but it looks like the Forest Service feels flying the American Flag is not politically correct on public lands.

Other Forest Service requests provided in the internet report(49) have included Taking "...down a clothesline tied to a tree...", painting "...aluminum door a dark color to better match the cabin.", and "Saunas, spas and hot tubs may be approved if incorporated into the main structure or deck, are not visible by neighbors or from public vantage points, and do not cause negative environmental impacts,..."

It sounds like the Forest Service is tightening their interpretation of leases, and you lessees, especially patriotic lessees, better be ready for some harassment by a member of the Fourth Branch of Government.

LOCAL GOVERNMENTS JOIN THE FRAY

The following example demonstrates how county regulators are some of the most pushy and unaccountable regulators around. In this example a landowner was wanting to simply remove some old logs for aesthetic and fire protection reasons, and the county sent him a 2/1/99 listing of required fees and forms to be completed. A short outline of what the county sent is as follows.

A cover letter from County Planning Division said: A special county permit may be required, and failure to get permit constitutes a violation of Humboldt County Code which may subject the landowner to enforcement action by the county.

The letter was accompanied by a whole bunch of listed requirements which required the use of a professional contractor such as a professional forester. A short sample of information requested by the county included things like estimated timber volumes, names of all involved parties including contractors, contract fees to be paid, acreage to be harvested, building and service facility locations, survey monument information, watercourse location, and on. Why all the requested information was needed or relevant was a big question mark.

Types of operations needing a county permit were listed as Christmas tree collection, removal of dead, dying, or diseased tree, production of fuelwood or split wood products, fire hazard reduction work, work on substantially damaged land, less than three acre operations, public agency or utility right-of-way work, emergency operations, work under a modified timber harvest plan, and any conversions. Despite extensive state review of all these operations, the county still wanted to do additional review and get paid fees.

A fee schedule was provided as follows:

Preliminary, just to talk to county fee was $55.00.
Inspection fee was $50 per inspection.
Environmental Health review fee was $42 per thirty minute review.
Final map inspection fee of $125.

Over fifty other potentially applicable fees were listed, and full cost recovery fees were mentioned as a possibility. A $750 dollar fee which was far more than the value of the few logs to be removed was requested by the county, and it seems something like a $1,600 review fee was mentioned at one point.

The correspondence was enough to boggle the mind of average homeowners, and the landowner was understandably confused and baffled. Right off the bat, the county says their review of the situation is required and a fee of $55 needs to be paid. The county described how they would review the project and make determinations about sensitive habitats, wetlands, environmental concerns, and other regulations whether they are qualified or not to do the review. To do what the county wanted done would result in an expenditure in the thousands of dollars.

The involved landowner came to me for help, and by directly confronting the county with how they were out of line, the matter was resolved by giving the county $55 of the landowner's hide to avoid more conflict.

County governments are full of up-and-coming regulators who get to apply a lot of questionable regulations, and examples of questionable county regulatory actions routinely occur.

Another landowner with an approved state permit to remove some windfall trees on a homesite parcel was told a county permit was additionally required even for noncommercial use of the trees such as firewood. Landowner saw what was required to get a permit and decided to just leave the trees to go to rot.

County employees without adequate biological training routinely make decisions about wet area restrictions, and such an employee used their regulatory authority to inappropriately designate an area as a wet area and to tell a contractor the area could not be used to load a few logs.

A person applied for a fire safe exemption permit from the state and contacted the county about what was being done. County said a swale holding some water overflow from a tank was a wet area, and county would not give a permit costing $1,000 until other professionals such as a biologist reviewed the wet area for species of concern.

County regulators routinely get involved in irrigation work on irrigation ditches that have been maintained and used for years.

How would you feel in the situations faced by landowners involved in the listed examples and specifically by the landowner involved in the described "remove some old logs" example? Would you feel a little intimated and helpless? Do you think you could have effectively handled these situations without professional outside help? As illustrated by these examples, governmental regulations can be overwhelming and very confusing, and this puts most landowners pretty well at the mercy of how the county and other governmental agencies interpret and apply our many laws and regulations. These examples are only a small sample of what is happening all over this country regarding the many governmental entities and how they are routinely able to operate without being held accountable for inappropriate and unnecessary regulatory actions.

Another example of how local governmental inspectors have the upper hand is provided in a news article(50) that describes how new store owners who bought an ongoing business thought they "…were taking over a turn-key business." Why would they think otherwise when the business was actively doing business prior to their purchasing it which indicated everything was up to snuff. They had obtained all the permit licenses they understood were needed. Whoops, along came the "…County Department of Health and Human Services, Division of Environmental Health (must have pretty big badge to say all this)… inspector…" who "…came up with…three pages of items…" including "…upgrading the store's two-basin sink to one with three basins, relining a wall in the walk-in and installing shatter-proof covers over the light fixtures." and various work "…primarily in the deli and walk-in refrigerator." They "…reopened the store…" after the inspection to sell "…dry groceries, candy, snacks, and sodas…" while "…not operating the deli or selling beer…" which seemed logical and legal until the inspection list items could be handled. Sounds logical, but obviously not good enough in the mind of the regulator. "…inspector returned…" and they "…were told they had to close their doors until the walk-in repairs and certain upgrades in the deli were completed."

The inspector said "It's our policy to work with the new owners…" This story makes it sound like the county's interpretation of "working with new owners" is a one-sided arrangement where the county's showing up to tell you what you can do is their contribution to working with you. Where were the regulators when the previous owners were operating the store? Are the involved regulations really written so strictly as to specify a three basin sink is required versus a two basin sink?

As this case illustrates, many business owners have little option but to do what the regulators tell them to do. Who would they go to; or, what could they do to rebut inappropriate actions by the regulator. While I strongly support health regulations, these kinds of situations indicate how regulators are in a position to do whatever they want, and there is little to no way to hold them accountable for inappropriate actions.

There are many hidden regulations that landowners have no clue exist. An example of such a law is described in a news article(51) where "The California Senate approved (proposed) legislation…that means a certain number of trees would have to be kept in a 200-foot buffer along recreational rivers…used for recreation (which unless defined somewhere means all rivers)…, as well as (designated) wild and scenic rivers." I wonder how many landowners adjacent to unclearly defined recreational rivers know this regulatory requirement is coming? Spare that tree or face the consequences you landowners.

A news article(6) tells us there is a regulatory group that focuses on controlling dust. Per the article "…badge-wearing airborne guys…" say dust "…can't leave your property line…" in residential neighborhoods. While the article refers to a residential development project and simple watering probably handles the problem, it makes you wonder how far this type of regulatory authority goes or will eventually go.

CAMPERS BEWARE

Even the homeless are subject to the power of the Fourth Branch of Government. A news article(53) shows regulators are using wetland protection and environmental protection laws as a basis for going after the homeless. "Key West, Florida…officials say the squatters…" at a mangrove tree site "…must go because they're damaging the protected and environmentally sensitive mangrove wetlands." "…assistant city manager…said…It looks like its not too Bad…But it's in endangered wetlands. They're violating the law.

49

In my professional life, I have had to deal with illegal camps and the filth and garbage created by the homeless on private lands; so, I agree there needs to be control over homeless camping. However, I see a little hypocrisy regarding wetland protection advocates running the homeless off. Many in the eviro community live like the homeless and promote the homeless way of living. Yet, many of these same people are promoting more and more wetland protections and support what is being done to the homeless in the Florida article. Talk about your contradictions and strange bedfellows.

Speaking of camping, a news article(54) is letting wilderness campers know the human pooper police are coming. "The Forest Service..." has put regulations in Place "...in Smith River National Recreation Area (and assumably other similar wilderness type areas)..." that require "...human waste...to be buried 6 to 8 inches deep and at least 100 feet from a stream." While the regulations have some value and validity, it is interesting that the bears and other wild species can poop anywhere in anyway they want without getting a ticket. It must take a really dedicated regulator to do the field checking required by these regulations.

Good luck campers.

DON'T TOUCH THAT OLD THING; OR, FOR THAT MATTER THAT NEW THING

Controls over signs, types, sizes, shapes, colors, you name it, are becoming a big deal, and this area of governmental control looks like it is run by the opinion of those in power and not by logic, practicality, aesthetics, and common sense. Take a walk through any big city where you would suspect signing controls exist. Then, tell me the placement and use of signs has been controlled by logic, practicality, aesthetics, and common sense. I assume the mess found in the cities is what those wanting to control signing want to avoid, but to me, signing controls have not done much to correct the big city problems. Signing controls have mainly provided another way for regulators to hassle some folks.

Governmental authorities of all kinds are getting intensively involved in the details of all kinds of work being done in and on specially designated historical areas and buildings. The hysterical historical police are on the way.

A news article(55) describes how a "...city's Design Review Commission..." is reviewing projects "...to restore and paint...historic structure...facade..." and "...window design change...at coffeehouse and general store..."

California Coastal Commission routinely gets involved in color of paint and fencing work on properties in the Coastal zone and really gets with it when a historical coastal town is involved.

A couple new articles(56)(57) explain how the Mills Historical Preservation Act in California is being applied by one city which started with sending a letter giving "...owners the opportunity to "opt out" of the (historical) ordinance by mailing a notice to the city."; however, many landowners never saw the letter or never sent back the notice. "The statewide act allows cities to grant a 50 percent tax reduction...in return..." property owner agrees to "...a 10-year renewable contract to maintain the property's original character." Alterations require application to "...Historic Preservation Commission..." "...cost of that application is $370." While many home owners may not remember getting the notice and the tax break, the historical preservation police are available to make sure they are reminded through stop work orders and instructions to pay a $370 application fee if they ever try to remodel their houses. Another article(58) states during an ongoing altercation between the city and one property owner "...commission...voted...thin shingle with more of a flat appearance like stucco..." out, and "...voted to limit (property owner's) option to stucco and another horizontal type siding...that resembles stucco." In referenced articles property owner states "...he did not know the house was on the list when he bought it at an auction last year (which raises a disclosure issue for the seller)...", and the commission decision "...is condemning the house to a life of mediocrity. I wouldn't be proud of it. I would be embarrassed by it."

Through the judicial process and questionable application of environmental and historical protection laws, unsuspecting rural landowners and rural folks can lose control over their property, be forced to pay significant sums of money, and be forced to abide by the wishes of various advocacy groups. A news article(59) illustrates how this can happen by describing how a "Sutter County Heritage group, sued...Yuba City ...over the destruction...of a historic Sutter County home...built in the 1880s...on property that was slated for development...saying...city...violated the California Environmental Act CEQA." While the home may have warranted saving which is sometimes not justified due to poor conditions and questionable historic value, the "...Ranch owner..." was forced to "...give $50,000..." and lost control over something he owned. Why the rancher was the one who had to lose something of value, and how the city got off scott free when the city was obviously a party to what happened needs an explanation. The use of CEQA as the basis for the lawsuit also points out how environmental laws can be used to take private property from landowners.

Historical preservation ideas are causing all kinds of disruptions for local communities. News article(60) has a developer ready to kill a $23 million dollar redevelopment project which is tied up due to problems involving retention of an old theater and some other old buildings. News article(61) wakes some local folks up to how establishment of an historical protection act could create a "...hit of more than $41,115 to the county's general fund, $3,866 to the financially strapped library system, $1,496 to the...Municipal Water District, $1,190 to the...Recreation and Conservation District." In news article(62), a private landowner wants to move an old mansion to avoid destroying it, but the move is being stopped. There are many other examples where historical protectionists are denying private property owners full use of their property, and potentially beneficial redevelopment projects are being delayed and stopped. Senior citizens and private property owners are being forced to do some costly things many can not afford for some pretty questionable reasons.

As illustrated in one situation, speculated historical value can open the door to get folks coming and going and possibly land folks in jail. This situation is described in a news article(325) which tells how a "...mayor...has been charged with two misdemeanors...", because the mayor "...did not get a demolition permit or a historical building review." "The mayor said he became concerned for the structure's safety when floors started buckling, and walls began leaning." The "...Planning Department... twice...told..." the mayor a permit was not needed"...if portion of the building was left standing." "Neighbors protested the demolition, saying it was an architectural loss to the city.", and "...the mayor could face $500 fine or time in the county jail,..."

Since it appears historical review had not yet occurred, just neighbors raising a ruckus about speculated historical value can be used to put folks in jail. It also looks like trying to avoid unsafe building violations and accompanying liability and following instructions from a member of the Fourth Branch of Government is not good enough for other members of the Fourth Branch of Government. Maybe some demolition permit requirements were overlooked, and maybe a fine which could be put to some good use was appropriate; but, yee gads, having laws which allow sending someone to jail under the described circumstances for a low human impact situation are not right.

ARE YOU SURE YOU QUALIFY?

Governmental bodies control development of salaries and requirements for Civil Service and public agency positions with little involvement by those outside the government. While there is some review and participation by elected officials and a few other groups, development of salaries and requirements is heavily influenced and controlled by the Fourth Branches of Government without a lot of scrutiny. A lot of ways are found to allow placement of chosen individuals into chosen positions. Political appointments especially involving top positions routinely place unqualified, inexperienced, and biased thinking folks into positions of authority.

As illustrated in a news article(63) the control over who can work for what public agency can be based on some questionable internally developed requirements. This article in its entirety says, "The San Mateo County Board of Supervisors has adopted a strict policy that bars smokers from being hired as sheriff's deputies, sergeants (which I guess can be assumed to mean no promotion to sergeant and beyond if you are a smoker), jail officers, and district attorney inspectors. The change, which will not apply to existing public safety employees, is designed to reduce workers comp claims in light of a law that classifies cancer and heart disease as job-related illnesses for all public safety officers."

Since smoking is suppose to affect cancer and heart problems in everyone who works, it would seem this action by the San Mateo Board of Supervisors involves some kind of selective discrimination against those wanting to be a public safety officer. There are a lot of unhealthy habits that can lead to health problems; so, what is to stop this idea from prohibiting the hiring of folks with other declared unhealthy habits that can lead to later health problems such as use of alcohol? If left unchecked, hiring prohibitions involving all kinds of physical and physiological reasons could be developed and applied by the Fourth Branches of Government.

Additionally, it is understood there is a shortage of available qualified public safety people, and the ban on using smokers is going to exacerbate this shortage problem.

While there is a need for some physical job standards to be in place for some physically demanding jobs such as firemen and policemen, the idea a person's bad habits, that may or may not interfere with their ability to do the job, can prevent their being hired leads us down a very questionable road. Because of a lot of unknowns and subjectivity in application, members of the Fourth Branches of Government have a lot of leeway in how these types of restrictions are applied. Because they can, members of the Fourth Branch of Government will come down hard or find ways around these type of regulations as it suits their needs. These regulations will also provide someone, somewhere the basis for a lawsuit to fight not being employed based on their unproven potential to have future health and workers comp claims problems. Until all the legal issues get sorted out, here come the bad habit, background check, and unemployable determination police.

SOME OFF-THE-WALL THINGS

To me things are really getting weird when news article(66) describes how the "Los Angeles... council..." has tied "...shootings..." to "...cyber café..." businesses. The council has "...proposed..." an "...ordinance..." requiring "...cafes with at least five computers (appears video games count as computers) to obtain police permits, install cameras, and ban minors during school hours..." and was stimulated by an incident where "...a man was followed home from...a melee at a...cafe...and killed." How restrictions on a cyber (which I understand to be something involved with computers and video games) business owner will somehow stop illegal and criminal activities that occur away from a business location is a mystery to me. If the problem is a gathering of kids that leads to bad behavior, then more than one kind of gathering place is eligible to become a target for this type of ordinance. I guess I do not understand how the cyber cafe situation warrants special added restrictions by the regulators and how these restrictions are going to solve the involved problem. Oh well, I do not live in L.A.; so, I guess what the cyber cafe police do with this Don Quixote windmill won't be affecting me for quite awhile.

Another proposal to regulate a product in trying to control bad human behavior is described in two news articles(67)(68). "Los Angeles...City council says silly string is a serious threat to public safety. One article says "...the committee voted...to ban the use or possession of silly string on city property, including streets and parks.", and the other article says "City Council members have decided to craft an ordinance that would ban the use of silly string in Hollywood on Halloween." "Several other communities including Santa Clarita and New Orleans, have restrictions against the use of silly string." "...residents and business groups complained that their streets get jammed on Halloween…" "…spraying among rival string slingers can endanger officers, particularly those on horses." and "…more and more it becomes a flashpoint where disorder occurs." It will be interesting to see how this ordinance is enforced and interpreted regarding some unknowing kid spraying some silly string, how start and stop times for Halloween are determined, and what kind of fines or penalties are applied.

The silly string deal mixed with the cyber cafe deal sounds like the involved city council is trying to stop bad behavior by restricting targeted locations and products instead of targeting the perpetrators of the bad behavior. I guess the idea is if the targeted location or product does not exist, the bad behavior will go away. The possibility that other locations and products can be utilized to cause the same bad behavior seems to elude the thinking of the regulators, and I guess their solution is to eliminate all locations and products involved in bad behavior until there is no more bad behavior. I guess you better not go to L.A. with any business that serves the general public or with any product like silly string, because the city counsel may decide your product leads to bad behavior or bad behavior is possible at your place of business.

Just when you wonder what other simple product or business location will be considered bad and restricted next, along comes the happy, friendly ice cream truck. A news article(302) headline says "Napa (California) wants Ice cream trucks to turn volume down". "Napa City Council…asked city manager to set a decibel limit for ice cream trucks." One resident said those "…who complain must have no life. If they don't, they should go out and get one,…" In Napa, the kids will need to grow bigger ears to avoid missing their ice cream.

STUPID IS AS STUPID DOES

There are some just outright pretty "stupid is as stupid does" type regulatory actions that I guess I am too logical and stubborn to ever accept.

The regulators who regulate fisheries are on the top of my list of those doing stupid things. I have provided various examples of illogical and abusive actions by these folks throughout this book and to add to this information I provide the following:

In restricting the catch of certain fish sizes and species, the regulators often apply a requirement that accidentally caught illegal fish have to be release and thrown overboard. Now, anyone that knows anything about fishing knows once a fish is caught especially from deep depths it is going to be traumatized and probably physically hurt as it is horsed up and onto a boat. While not all caught fish will die when thrown back, a lot of them will die. Fishermen up and down the west coast talk about accidentally catching a lot of coho and having to throw them back even when they are hurt. In the past this same practice of throwing fish back was also required when a regulated undersize, shaker fish was caught with the same results.

As a logically thinking person, does it make sense to throw back to their death a lot of hurt fish? If any fish of any size and species were required to be kept and counted towards a regulated fish limit, would not less fish be caught and killed? Fishermen would fill their limits more quickly (maybe not with the size and type wanted) and would not be fishing longer to catch and kill more fish? It makes you wonder if some politics aren't in play that favor the fishermen to not have to take small fish.

Another game played by the regulators in restricting the catch of certain fish species involves the use of quotas, and shutting down fishing of certain species when a very questionable process of counting caught fish determines a season's quotas for a species has been reached. I understand the way this works is any species whose quota has been reached is to be thrown overboard when caught after a quota has been reached or while fishing for other species.

A news article(69) says "Discard refers to dumping tons of dead fish overboard because the quota for that species has been filled, but the fishermen are trying to fill the quota for another. Bycatch is similar - dumping dead fish overboard that are protected from harvest or have no commercial value."

What a waste. Talk about stupid is as stupid does.

Another kind of illogical thinking is provided in a news article(70) involving land use. A parcel of land is to be developed and the owner of the land wants to keep the number of sale units down. "...the county wants...to build up to 263 homes..." on the parcel and currently "...there's only enough water and sewer capacity to serve 50 houses.", and "...the county is pushing a plan..." that "...is financially unrealistic." The reason for the county's position is indicated to be the need for more low cost units; however, the county has provided no realistic way to maintain quality of home ownership and living, and is pushing to force the landowner to dream up a way to put up and service a bunch of back to back houses. The developer raises the point while "houses spread over five to eight acres each - are hardly affordable to most..." his "...mover-upper subdivision...would open the housing market in town because the up-and-comers' former houses would become vacant."

It looks like quality of living, open space, and the ability to move up in this country ideas are to play second fiddle to cramming people into crowded subdivisions. It looks like the unpredictable and unaccountable growth police are becoming even more unpredictable.

Are you getting the idea from these examples how the Fourth Branch of Government is affecting and controlling our lives? Hopefully this information will wake some folks up to what is going on.

The end of the beginning.

TAKINGS

Included in inappropriate actions by a Fourth branch of Government is the taking of private property without giving just compensation. This taking can occur through regulatory excesses, subtle actions that devalue property, and directly.

I reference you to a news story done by Fox News called "Vanishing Freedoms" which provides an overview of some examples of regulatory and taking abuses in the Western and Midwestern United States. This video illustrates a rare instance by the media where a good job of investigative and factual reporting has been done that really tells the story as I have lived and seen it.

Examples of taking methods and situations are provided in the following information.

The process of designating privately owned lands for potential acquisition for public trust purposes such as parks, conservation areas, wildlife habitat areas, and wilderness areas routinely results in inverse condemnation and a taking of private property value. Takings through inverse condemnation occur when there is no compensation for lost property values due to added restrictions on development and other uses that come with public trust designations. A designated property's potential uses are directly limited due to designation for future purchase or condemnation. Protections and limitations applied to public trust lands are automatically applied to private lands designated for direct purchase. Private lands designated to end up next to public trust lands are stigmatized by the protections and limitations required to maintain adjacent public trust values. The end result is that potential buyers can not ignore the known and potential limitations and restrictions created by such designations.

Knowingly and maybe naively, the Fourth Branches of Government and conservancy groups often team up to subtly obtain properties without giving just compensation. Once designations have been applied, it is hard to argue that limitations on use do not exist on designated private properties, and you can argue that such limitations reduce a property's value. In-turn, this argument justifies offering and paying less to acquire lands through outright purchase or eminent domain procedures.

An example of inverse condemnation is provided by a past project that designated and mapped lands for future state park acquisition near Fort Bragg, California. The involved private property was stigmatized as only having a potential use as parkland. The parkland designation created real and potential limitations and restrictions on development applicable to the involved properties, and potential buyers considered these restrictions and limitation as a reason to reduce involved property values.

The governmental practice of pre-designation of lands wanted for parks acquisition purposes can routinely be seen applied across the country.

Internet report(71) mentions "Feds may submit to Congress a list of private lands and water to be acquired, by condemnation if necessary."

A internet article(72) reports a three million acre park is being put together in Maine.

An E-mail report(73) states a two million acre Federal Greenline is being promoted in the Northeastern United States.

In these last two mentioned projects, the United States Forest Service is mapping areas including private lands most important for endangered and threatened plant and other species, having the potential to be recreation areas, and areas involving protection of water resources. In promoting the Greenline, it was stated people's homes are the final insult to land.

There is no reason to believe these two governmental designations in Maine and the Northeastern United States will not lead to reduced private property values.

The ways courts and Fourth Branches of Government with some enviros team up to take lands is illustrated in two 2004 AG ALERT Newsletter articles(274)(275).

The first article describes the New London, Connecticut situation reviewed by the Supreme Court that caught national attention. In this situation, the town of "...New London...exercising its power of domain to take waterfront property from private property owners...", and then "...give it to a private commercial entity that plans to develop it into a waterfront hotel, office space, (other) luxury homes and other retail businesses." This will be done in the name of redevelopment and to increase tax income to the city. The Supreme Court ruled in favor of the city which showed how private landowners are continually losing the ability to hold the Fourth Branch of Government accountable for damage done to them.

While the second article did not receive national attention, it provides another example of how governmental groups use eminent domain to take private property. In this article, it appears the courts will decide if a Joint Powers Authority group formed by Yolo County, California "…may use its power of domain to take…privately owned…17,300 acre ranch …and transfer it to public ownership." "The government officials say they want to maintain the status quo by keeping the land in agriculture and preserving the existing water rights." It appears "15,900 acres of the land…" is leased to "…rice farmers.", and "The Yolo County Farm Bureau…" wants "…farming to continue on the land,…" It appears the county's offer of $50 million for the land was rejected, and since the county "…is forbidden from participating in closed bids…" which the landowners want to do, "County officials say the county has no choice but to exercise its power of eminent domain." The "public good" being served is never explained, and the basis for using $50 million dollars of tax money to put more land into the Public Trust largess looks questionable.

For years, eminent domain has been inappropriately used to take private property for questionable environmental reasons, and without fear of recrimination, it seems the Fourth Branches of Government are finding more questionable ways to flex the eminent domain muscle and to take more private property.

Another method of taking private property that does not get much notice involves the closure or restriction of access to private properties surrounded by public trust lands being administered by the Fourth Branches of Government.

While there are regulations and laws requiring access be provided, the Fourth Branches of Government routinely apply many unnecessary and unjustified permit and environmental review requirements that can effectively block use of legally provided access to private properties. Environmental, archaeological, wildlife, and other species studies can be required to be done to the satisfaction of the regulators. Road maintenance and construction work can be required as determined needed by the regulators. Limitations on road use due to weather conditions and species' protection requirements can be applied as determined needed by the regulators. Species, environmental, and archaeological limitations can be determined by the regulators to be significant enough to not allow any use of a simple 4x4, four-wheel drive road. Often the cost of all the studies, road work, and limitations make obtaining access permits impossible or not worth doing.

As with most regulatory permit processes, private landowners needing access across public lands have little to no recourse if they lose an access fight with the regulators. This leverage by the regulators is routinely used to force sale of private lands often at reduced prices to the government.

The Fourth Cometh

This chapter focuses on who and what makes up a Fourth branch of Government, and shows we are all being controlled in many ways by an unaccountable governmental group. Numerous examples are provided to show how this group's excesses are affecting all of us. This group of regulators in conjunction with enviro protectionists are being allowed to shut-down natural resource use to the detriment of rural communities and this country.

Our system of laws and regulations has served us well to this point in time, and lord knows it would lead to chaos to change the basic way we make rules and regulations. However, if something is not done to stop the creation of unclear laws open to multiple and changing interpretations and a better job of requiring regulators to be accountable for regulatory abuses is not done, there is a world of hurt on its way. I see the problem of having no effective way to hold the Fourth Branch of Government accountable getting worse, and collectively as a group, the Fourth Branch of Government is getting or already has gotten as powerful as the other three branches of government.

There are other unaccountable government problems that I would have liked to discuss in this book, but there is just too much to cover at this time. As a warning, I provide the following two main areas of concern needing some attention.

First, there is a simple problem of an environmental regulatory cancer growing in California, and if groups outside of California to not get directly involved in stopping the development of many inappropriate regulations, the cancer is going to spread across this country.

Secondly, there is a Fifth Branch of Government already in play called the United Nations. This world government through UNESCO and some world heritage treaties has already been given control of some sovereign United States territory, and through another arrangement, United States armed forces can be forced to fight as directed by the United Nations. A radio show(271) provides an indication of how the United Nations gives an illusion of protecting human rights by saying the United Nations declares people have the right to freedom, religion, etc.; however, these rights can not be exercised if they interfere with stated goals of the United Nations. This sounds like a bunch of unelected bureaucrats unaccountable to no one can make goals that sovereign nations are expected to follow even if it is not in the best interest of their people.

Do you still think you can avoid being adversely affected or taken to task by the Fourth Branch of Government? Dream on baby, the regulation and the regulator designed to get you is just around the corner.

The wolf is coming for the frogs (ranchers, farmers, private landowners, fishermen, rural communities, producers, businesses, and yes, even the general public) all sitting in a pot of water over a flame relaxing, laying back, and letting the water in the pot get hotter and hotter as some members of the Fourth and Fifth Branches of Government in co-operation with many enviros turn up the flames of inappropriate regulations.

Hoooooooowwwwwwwwwwlllllllll! Here comes the wolf.

REGULATIONS AND REGULATORS RUNNING AMUCK
ENDANGERED SPECIES ACT (ESA)

Chapter Three

During my professional career I have seen when the Endangered Species Act (ESA) and other federal regulations have been correctly and effectively applied and when they haven't.

My experience with ESA and other federal regulations has found there are numerous changes needed in how ESA and other federal regulations are applied. There needs to be more oversight, peer review to assure authorized regulations are properly followed. Many federal recommendations and requirements are not appropriately supported by time tested peer reviewed science, site specific facts, experienced professional input, logic, and common sense.

WHO'S THE BOSS?

There are different situations involving the Fourth Branches of Government that raise the question "Who's the Boss". A couple situations are as follows.

Over the years, I have seen how very unclear and hard to enforce rules and regulations protecting species are frequently misapplied by California's state agencies. State regulators routinely require ESA survey and protection work to be done when a proper reading of ESA shows the work is not required.

Federal regulators routinely go along with state interpretations and misapplication of the ESA by remaining silent or doing little to correct such misapplications.

Without being out front and easily noticeable, federal agencies became heavily involved in state permits on the west coast during the beginning of the northern spotted owl fiasco. Federal involvement has continued to the current time, and now also includes coho salmon protection and total maximum daily load (TMDL) Environmental Protection Agency (EPA) water quality permit processes.

By directly telling state regulatory bodies such as the Board of Forestry that they have to apply specific federally developed guidelines in state permits, there should be little doubt that federal agencies are influencing what is required in state permits.

My experiences with California's permit processes has found state permits are handled a lot differently when the feds are involved, and not accepting federal recommended permit requirements in state permits has resulted in delayed permit approval and in disapproved permits.

I am no lawyer, but when legitimate federal issues have not been substantiated according to federal regulations, state permits should not have to incorporate federal species protection requirements.

Another slant on "Who's the Boss" is provided by news article(74) headlined "Whooo's in charge?" This article provides information on a workshop meeting involving a bunch of owl experts and wildlife managers. During the meeting it was discovered that "An effort by the California Academy of Sciences to collect barred owls on the Klamath National Forest-which Fish and Wildlife is using as a de facto removal experiment-angered conservationists and timber owners at the meeting. They said this was the first they'd heard of it." A meeting participant said "I think it's a shame the service proceeds with this basically ignoring us,…"

This little incident brings out a "Who's the Boss" problem found among members of the Fourth Branch of Government, and highlights how multiple accountability problems exist between agencies and within agencies handling ESA regulations. There appears to be a lack of co-ordinated peer review and oversight in how the northern spotted owl is being handled, and it seems this issue is going in all kinds of directions.

The poor handling of the spotted owl situation and resulting confusion is more fully discussed later in this chapter.

REGULATORY AUTHORITY RUNNING AMUCK

Testimony(75) by an experienced fishery biologist at hearings regarding the Klamath River and Klamath Basin situation stated "Many of the mistakes made by the U.S. Fish and Wildlife Service during this year could have been avoided through a proper peer review of the agencies' actions."

Internet report(76) describes remarks given to Commonwealth Club regarding "The greatest challenge facing mankind is the challenge of distinguishing reality from fantasy, truth from propaganda." "…environmentalism…" is an example of this challenge, and "…environmentalism needs to be absolutely based in objective and verifiable science, it needs to be rational,…it needs to be flexible,…and it needs to be apolitical." "...if we allow science to become politicized, then we are lost." "We need an organization that will be ruthless about acquiring verifiable results..., and will make everybody...honest fast." "How will we manage to get environmentalism ...back to scientific discipline? There's a simple answer: we must institute far more stringent requirements for what constitutes knowledge...", and get ride of "...politicized so-called facts that..." are "...falsehoods..." and "...simply aren't true..." that more and more groups are..." knowingly "...putting out..."

Many examples exist involving many different species which show how the ESA process is being used to stop projects and being misapplied by public agencies. Some examples are as follows:

Northern Spotted Owl (NSO) Fiasco
A Long, Sad Story about Spotted Owls and Questionable Application of the ESA

The NSO situation starting in the early 1990s is a well known publicized situation where many thought proper processes were followed. Society of American Foresters (SAF) newsletter(77) quotes "...editors of the Washington Post in 1994..." saying "...Northwest Forest Plan..." is "...a good proposal...scientifically based...would likely save the threatened species-most famously the northern spotted owl - and the forest ecosystem of whose health the species are the emblem."

Sadly what looked like a good plan has turned into a fiasco. Short-cuts and a lack of peer review did not allow for a fully informed decision to be made regarding the northern spotted owl. In reaching this conclusion, I have relied on the following listed information which is a summary of what I have visually observed in the field and seen documented.

In the beginning, original NSO ESA petition information was flawed and inadequate.

Problems started with the myth that spotted owls needed old-growth timber habitats to survive which was the narrow opinion of a few biologists. This myth became accepted as gospel, and owl surveys were concentrated in old-growth timber areas.

Due to enviro and lawsuit pressures, not enough time was allowed to make a fully informed listing decision. Surveying and field testing in wildlands not containing old-growth timber stands was not done, and spotted owls found outside old-growth timbered habitats were casually dismissed as nonviable, surplus owls. Biologists allowed to lead the investigations were not held accountable for deviating from proper survey and review procedures. Short cuts were taken, and adequate field testing of provided information was not done.

As things went along, it was found ESA processes do not provide for timely correction when species' situations change.

Survey and field review information available shortly after determination of listing showing much higher owl populations could not be used to change the listing. ESA regulations require a long study period before a de-listing process can be started, and all kinds of excuses are being provided why the NSO can not be de-listed.

To further strengthen their position on protecting spotted owl populations, the supposed experts have split the hard to distinguish different spotted owl populations into three different populations (Northern, California, and Mexican). This reduced population numbers per spotted owl species which helped to justify the need to have separate protection requirements for each spotted owl population.

Interestingly enough in California, spotted owls on one side of a major highway are said to be a different species population than the ones on the other side of the highway. Although the habitats on each side of the highway are the same, spotted owl habitats on one side of the highway are treated differently than the habitats on the opposite side of the highway. Go figure!

There seems to be many real world examples of NSO habitat conditions that additionally refute the thinking behind the NSO listing.

On one large block (over 25,000 acres) of heavily harvested industrial timber lands with no old-growth near Covelo, California, NSO territories were found to blanket the ownership and to be overlapping. At the same time, NSOs could not be found or were a rarity in the neighboring National Forest Public lands which contained old-growth timber.

On Jackson State Forest in Mendocino County, California which contains an advanced aged young-growth redwood/fir timber stand that has been routinely harvested and thinned, owl surveys have found, NSO nesting in the forest is heaviest on the periphery of the forest where neighboring lands have been more heavily logged and have a younger stand age.

On Simpson Timber Company and other redwood/fir mixed clearcut and selectively harvested lands along the northwest coast of California, NSO populations have been found to be heavier and more dense than found in old-growth stands in the area.

While a lot of damage to timber based rural communities has already been done, maybe the following numerous accounts from various people shows the truth is slowly coming out. Hopefully the potential for future damage can be reduced.

Internet report(78) has a Plumas County Supervisor (from California) saying "We know now that our analysis of the Forest Service procedures as "Junk Science" was as correct in 1990, as it is being proven today…" What if Forest Service "…scientists…had reviewed available data without bias?" Could we "…have avoided the loss of over 175 mills, devastation to rural communities in California and the Pacific Northwest, the suicides that were attributed to the loss of jobs, and the socio/economic loss for thousands of rural families."?

Letter to the editor(79) by a retired Forest Supervisor of the Kootenai National Forest states Forest Service leadership problems can be traced back to "…the selection of people to lead the Forest Service who were never natural resource managers and were never expected to be." The one in charge "…who led the effort to prepare the Spotted owl Management Plan, and implemented it, in the Pacific Northwest… demonstrated his lack of competence as a leader, and his lack of credibility as a scientist…"

This forest supervisor mentions how he had contacts with spotted owls "…adjacent to clearcuts that were under five years old…", and participated with research on owls with "…electronic devices…located …on the bottom crown branches of second- or third-growth Douglas-fir trees…" As additionally verified by other information provided in this book, this supervisor concluded owls like to be near clearcuts "…because of the forage base…" and "…the old growth myth." about owls preferring old-growth timber habitats was just that, a myth.

The letter goes on to mention "…the mindset of wildlife biologists and their commitment to agendas, rather than to science,…" as demonstrated by uncovered improper actions regarding "…the lynx, grizzly bear, and suckerfish…"

The letter additionally reports that "The annual timber sale volume…in the Northern Region of the Forest Service…has declined from about 1.1 billion (1,100,000,000) board feet in 1987 to only 170.2 million (170,200,000) board feet in 2001…on 25 million acres and 15 national forests." This represents an almost 85% reduction in harvest and a lot of economic upheaval based on flawed thinking.

News article(80) describes how "Just 12 years ago, we thought that the Northern Spotted Owl was dependent on old-growth redwood. We now know that the Northern Spotted Owl needs some nesting structure, densely shaded nesting and roosting habitat, and some thinned or cleared area conducive to wood rats for foraging, and otherwise thrives in a young redwood forest." Based on what I and others have experienced and learned, this description of what is required in NSO habitats in the redwood region makes a lot of sense.

News article(81) has state park employee saying "...fire may have a positive effect on...northern spotted owl..." who foraged "...more on the Chapman Ranch (more open ground) than in old-growth stands - a situation that may change now that much of the understory has been cleared by the fire,..."

In another situation, it is interesting and kind of fun to watch the biologists getting caught in their own spin as they present factual spotted owl habitat information that does not support their originally pushed ideas that spotted owls could not exist outside old-growth habitats. In their zeal to fight the Bush thinning and fire prevention plans and the possible removal of some big trees, protectionist thinking biologists are attacking the idea that fires hurt spotted owl habitat, and the Bush plan to thin and remove some big trees to reduce fire danger is not needed to protect the spotted owl.

A news article(82) has "...wildlife biologists inside and outside the Forest Service..." saying California spotted "...owl habitat destroyed by wildfires..." is "...flourishing and occupied by the rare birds." One biologist said "...fire appears to be more of a maintenance mechanism that a destructive force for owl habitat,..." Another biologist says "...majority of..." burned owl habitats reviewed are "...green and beautiful,..."

The biologists' apparent goal in the articles is to stop the salvage logging in previously designated burned spotted owl habitats by telling how the burned areas still have green trees, obviously not as many as before the fire, but enough to support spotted owls. "...the 9th U.S. Circuit Court of Appeals in San Francisco granted a temporary injunction halting a salvage logging operation based in part on... photographs...submitted to show the site was mostly alive,..."

Putting the fire and salvage logging argument aside, the information presented by these biologists most definitely describes how the owl is doing fine in burned areas where fire is prone to create holes in the canopy and forest cover, open and bare areas under the canopy, and overall disturb and change the forested landscape. The biologists do not go the next step and describe how spotted owls like disturbance and the increased prey base. What the biologists do describe as acceptable owl habitat is definitely not heavy old-growth timber habitat. They indirectly say owls will utilize disturbed habitats similar to those created by thinning and selective timber harvest operations.

To summarize, the referenced news article(82) directly and indirectly says properly done survey, sampling, and study work is showing, diverse and disturbed areas such as harvested and burned areas with adequate nesting structure have the potential to produce and maintain spotted owl populations.

I wonder how long it will take the protectionist biologists to discover how their factual site specific review and push to stop salvage logging is undoing the promoted thinking that the best spotted owl habitat is undisturbed old-growth timber stands. It is interesting what application of proper scientific review can provide.

Keep the facts coming. I love it!

Currently the NSO status is an information file bursting with owl information and no one really making an effort to de-list the NSO.

It has been proven that a much higher population of NSOs exists than was acknowledged at the time of listing. The so-called experts say the higher number of NSOs is not enough to de-list NSOs, and it has become obvious that the ESA de-listing process requires a higher level of proof than does a listing.

Despite ESA regulations requiring a recovery plan be put in place, as of June first of 2004 and years after NSO listing, a recovery plan has not been put in place. Despite ESA regulations requiring it to be done, de-listing goals which include population numbers and habitat requirements that would allow the NSO to be de-listed have not been put in place.

To maybe get things off the dime, news article(84) indicates someone has forced "The U.S. Fish and Wildlife Service (USF&W)..." to hire "...a private contractor to help determine whether the northern spotted owl and marbled murrelet should keep their federal protection as threatened species." USF&W spokesperson said "There's a ton of data out there,..." "...president of the American Forest Resource Council said 'We need a fair look at what's going on in these populations,'...", and while "...the people at Fish and Wildlife have dedicated their lives specifically to studying these populations...Perhaps they've gained a bias from the work they've done..." This independent review has the enviros and some in the USF&W nervous and saying "...the agency's biologists are the most knowledgeable on the issue.", and "For them to farm out this review seems...they don't want to get the answer that their (USF&W) scientists give them." That may be right! The USF&W has had an awful lot of time; been given an awful lot of information; and has shown little to no progress. Maybe it is time to let unbiased professionals take a crack at doing a fair, honest, unbiased, professional review.

It is time some one took charge and stopped the B.S.

News article(85) describes how "…485 other mills around the West have gone out of business since the 1980s because of a combination of recession…; sharp reductions in national forest logging to protect habitat for the northern spotted owl…salmon…" and other species, and because "Too many restrictions were placed on harvesting timber,…" "U.S. Forest Service economist said…The U.S. position in the global economy is shifting around…", and calls it "…an unintended consequence of the spotted owl (and I add other restrictive factors). It (and other restrictive factors) drove up (log) prices…", and "We made ourselves uncompetitive in world markets. Then it shifted. Places like Russia could import into Baltimore."

While the Forest Service fella is on the right track, I do not believe he sees the total picture showing how our infrastructure is being lost and how this country is becoming more and more an importing nation due to restrictions on production of natural resource products. The importation problem is discussed in more detail in Chapter 10.

Mr. Benjamin Stout has written a book "THE NORTHERN SPOTTED OWL" which provides more historical and factual information than you want to know about the misguided approach to protection of the owl and the damage that has been done to Oregon and to the Pacific Northwest.

ENTER THE BARRED OWL

News article(86) shows faulty northern spotted owl thinking is still being applied. This article is headlined "Northern spotted owl still declining" This information "…appears to be a blow to timber industry…" The headline and opening comments of the article would lead you to believe timber harvesting is causing the demise of the northern spotted owl; however, the real cause of the decline as stated in the article is "…incursions by the more aggressive barred owl, a native of Eastern Canada that has moved into Washington, and the loss of forests to insect infestations on the east slope of the Cascade Range in Washington,…" Is it possible, what is happening to the northern spotted owl is nothing more than a haphazard evolutionary process being run by Mother Nature, and man is trying to interfere with a natural evolutionary process. Additional Times Standard news articles(87)(88)(89) and USFWS (United States Fish and Wildlife Service) Press Release(90) further describe how the barred Owl is replacing the northern spotted owl.

The mentioned USFWS Press Release(90) references a Final Report on the Northern Spotted Owl and one of the news articles(89) headlined "Old growth up, but spotted owls down under plan" raise some other interesting questions. The news article says despite all the additional old-growth that has been set aside and created "...the amount of old growth forest is up but northern spotted owl populations are down and with no clear reason why, scientists reported..." "Many of the impacts were different than predicted,..." In my review of the referenced report, I found indications that increased old-growth has not been a big help to the northern spotted owl. The referenced report also made some interesting observations regarding the barred owl. It seems the barred owl likes more open old-growth timber stands and the northern spotted owl seems to do better than the barred owl in more heavy structured (more dense) forest stands. The spotted owl experts and the biologists running the show are quoted as saying "...monitoring revealed no evidence to justify departing from the current strategy of maintaining larger blocks of habitat (meaning old-growth habitats of course, of course) across the region,..."

LET'S SEE NOW, WHAT IS THE ANTIDOTAL INFORMATION TELLING US

1. Spotted owl prey populations have routinely been found to be more dense in non-old-growth areas and in areas associated with disturbance and timber harvest activity. Due to the routinely more abundant prey base found in these areas, this makes sense. It is also logical to believe more food means more reproductive activity.

2. Despite current information that demonstrates otherwise, many so-called experts still cling to the idea that NSOs need old-growth timbered territories. Current information indicates the low prey base routinely found in old-growth timbered stands is a reason for the original determination that NSOs needed 2,000 to 3,000 acres of acceptable habitat. Hopefully, the new information will eventually prevail and the push for unnecessarily large habitat areas will go away.

3. Recent information indicates barred owls may do better in old-growth areas.

4. Recent information indicates spotted owls can do better in non-old-growth timbered areas.

5. The barred owl is quickly taking out the spotted owl.

6. Biologists and others want to interfere with a possibly natural evolutionary process and want to retain and protect the spotted owl.

I and I assume others would like to have the biologists be more open in discussing the provided factual and antidotal information on NSO habitat preferences and ways active forest management can help NSOs. As illustrated in the Society of American Foresters (SAF) newsletter article(77), there seems to be an effort to not give all NSO information equal play. The referenced article says "Northern spotted owl populations have continued to decline...probably because of the lingering effects of past harvests (they are still beating up on timber harvesting), displacement by the barred owl, and other factors." By not openly recognizing and identifying limited food sources as being a key problem for NSOs, the so-called experts are ignoring ways to help NSOs survive.

When you connect all the dots, it sounds to me, a layman, a program to maintain and enhance the spotted owl would involve utilizing properly done timber harvesting and would not focus so much on maintaining old-growth habitats which the barred owl seems to prefer. Such a program would involve creating habitats preferred by the spotted owl's prey base. An increased prey base should mean increased spotted owl populations which may provide the spotted owl with the ability to more effectively compete with the barred owl. Such a program may provide a partial solution to a decline in spotted owls and a forest insect and potential fire problem that exists on the east slope of the Cascade Range in Washington State.

Of course, outright elimination or neutering of some barred owls would also help the northern spotted owl.

For various reasons, it seems the so-called experts which are part of the Fourth Branch of Government are being allowed to ignore documented and logical site specific information supporting pro-active ways to help the declining spotted owl populations. The resistance shown by many biologists and others to letting humans apply direct population control techniques to a wild species is a real stumbling block. Acknowledgment, that active forest management including timber harvesting may be a means to helping spotted owls, would raise questions about the ideas that have been promoted to date. Of course, we can not forget that promoting a change in how we handle the spotted owl situation would mean some loss of face for the so-called experts, and their power to control what is happening would be diminished.

Who am I, to use logic and common sense in questioning the sacred, questionable northern spotted owl protection program being run by the so-called experts?

Away we go, often blindly following and accepting without questioning.

As one owl sits in the cold dark forest, he says to another owl

Boy am I pooped and out of hoots!

I am down to skin and bones,
just covered 5,000 acres of old-growth timber,
and can't find a rat.

Do you know how to cut down a tree or start a fire;
so, we can get the rats to move back in?

I sure miss the good ol' days,
When those two legged critters with the hard hats were around
cutting down trees;
disturbing things;
creating food for the wood rats;
and the wood rats were producing like crazy

Now the only two legged critters we see try to sound like us,
bring us a little mouse once in awhile,
and do those funny oohs, ahs, and monkey sounds.

It is down right embarrassing how they treat us and keep staring at us.

Many other examples exist which illustrate how the ESA and other regulatory processes are being misused and misapplied by enviros and public agencies.

TMDL - EPA process

The TMDL - EPA process has required developed of numerical watershed standards lacking a site specific basis, peer review, and adequate consideration of natural background levels of involved factors such as sedimentation, and a state implementation process is now being developed where these standards lacking a good factual basis are going to have to be fulfilled. An attempt by California's Water Quality Agency to insert TMDL requirements into timber harvest permits prior to state authorization was squelched; however, prior to being squelched, many landowners, especially small landowners, through pressures involving the need to get their timber harvest permits approved, had already incorporated many unauthorized TMDL regulatory requirements into their harvest plans.

The TMDL - EPA process is more fully discussed in Chapter 2.

San Rafael (California) tunnel stalled

News article(91) describes how "...two threatened plant species has stalled plans for a pedestrian, horse and bicycle tunnel under Lucas Valley Road." "...as much as $150,000 for an environmental impact report..." will be needed, and project is on hold until impact report is done and all mitigations determined. This shows how no matter when discovered, two rare plants are all it takes to stop a project.

Salt Lake City (Utah) $235 million highway project stopped

News article(92) describes how "...highway that would unsnarl a major commuter bottleneck..." is "...stopped by federal appeals court...", because of "...Great Salt Lake..." wetland "...that is protected for migratory waterfowl." Despite "...ideas from local planning documents dating back to 1962..." and "...formal...public...comment on environmental studies in 1998 and 2000..." project was stopped. You would think all the bases and needed environmental review would have been covered in over fifty years of review, but noooooo!

Environmentalists trying to block Colombia River channel deepening project

News article(93) has "...Northwest Environmental Advocates..." going "...to court to try to block $136 million government project to deepen...shipping channel...three feet...", because "...dredging would devastate salmon habitat...,...harm wildlife...,...and worsen erosion." "The National Oceanic and Atmospheric Administration's (NOAA) fisheries agency (understood to be formerly called National Marine Fisheries Service

(NMFS)) approved the Army Corps of Engineer's project in 2002.", and "Federal scientists...concluded...two runs of salmon...and...sea lions..." would not be "...jeopardized." You'd think the pro-environmental National Oceanic Atmospheric Administration would not be called into question about saving anything, but go figure.

Anadromous fish and their habitats and a NMFS out of control

Review and regulatory handling of ESA listed anadromous fish species has followed the same pattern as the Northern Spotted Owl and has the same failings. Again, despite regulations requiring it to be done, as of June first of 2004 federal government has not properly determined population or habitat goals (population numbers, miles stream, or otherwise) for delisting anadromous fish species.

ESA process involving Coho salmon and other fishery issues has allowed National Marine Fisheries Service (NMFS or NOAA), to become involved in the California timber harvest permit process.

A letter(94) to California Board of Forestry from NMFS states "...NMFS...will utilize...standards and guidelines..." involving "...Federally listed...coho, steelhead, and Chinook...salmon...when selectively reviewing all future...Timber Harvest Plans (THPs)." Accompanying this letter is 21 pages of internally developed requirements that have not been authorized by the state of California to be applied in timber harvest plans. Application of these requirements is required in order to "...develop a short-term (<10 years) HCP and associated section 10(a)(1)(B) permit in accordance with the Endangered species Act of 1973, as amended." While NMFS states more rules are coming and kind of indicates it is the state's choice to apply their proposed guidelines, there is an obvious veiled threat that if NMFS ideas are not applied through the state's timber harvest plan approval process there will be a violation of the ESA. The result has been NMFS's direct and active involvement in preharvest inspections of timber harvest permit applications outside federal review and approval procedures including written requests from NMFS for application of regulatory requirements based on the internally developed NMFS guidelines. A review of actual THP records shows timber harvest permit approval has been withheld until NMFS's requested requirements or NMFS's concerns have been incorporated into the THP permit. This all illustrates how NMFS is directly involved in applying internally developed federal regulations without following federal regulatory procedures and inappropriately participating in a state permit process.

NMFS employees have demonstrated a lack of experience and knowledge needed to properly handle actual field situations involving fishery issues. The mentioned guidelines and routinely proposed requirements show a lack of peer review and proper application of scientific principles.

The lack of understanding of the real world is illustrated by NMFS's constant push for no disturbance in watercourse protection areas, and the desire for conifers to be established and grown in these areas. If not already in place, conifer establishment and growth is limited in the heavily vegetated, more productive watercourse protection areas. In these areas, nonconifer vegetation usually captures and holds the site and does not allow conifers to become established and to put on growth. Without mineral soil, sunlight, and reduced vegetative competition which is created through disturbance, current conditions remain in-place (brush, hardwoods, no conifers), and there will be less and less conifers over time as existing conifer trees struggle along, fall over, and are not replaced.

An actual field situation involving damage caused by NMFS's inexperience and lack of peer reviewed decisions is provided in a news article(95). In the news article, a "…project aims to slow the erosion of Rowdy Creek's banks and improve fish habitat.", and "…is funded by federal grants, so the U.S. Army Corps of Engineers must consult with fisheries service (NMFS) before it is approved." "The plan to divert water around the project site while equipment worked in the streambed was upended when a fisheries consultant (NMFS) went against…local (California) Fish and Game Warden, among others. The consultant ordered …water not be diverted, making contractor work from steam bank with a silt screen downstream to catch sediment." This required "…400 feet of asphalt road in Rowdy Creek Mobile Park…" to be dug up, and "20 50 year old trees…" to be cut down. "Three days into the project…fisheries service changed its mind, saying…do what was originally proposed." Mobile Park owner says "…site…looks like a bombed war site…" and "…many of the trees…his parents planted 50 years ago have been cut down,…" "…silt barrier is causing "…dirty water…" to get into the Smith River which is known for its clarity and fish runs and into an area "…where residents pipe water from the (Rowdy) creek,…" "Fish and Game warden…said that the fisheries service (NMFS) is inexperienced in dealing with projects like this one. They did not have the ability to make a decent suggestion.", and "…a citation would have been issued to the contractor…" if the fishery service had not been involved. A county supervisor summed up NMFS lack of expertise and accountability by saying "...There's no common sense at all going in the whole madness with (the fisheries service). It's not just this project,...it's projects all over the five-county area."

Another situation involving a California county official not being happy with NMFS's actions is illustrated in a California Licensed Forester's Newsletter article(96). This article describes how "A plan was developed...by state and federal agencies to trap some of the Green Valley coho...which are the only significant group of Coho...population surveys...the past nine years have found...in the 1,485-square-mile Russian River watershed...and bring them into a captive breeding program at the Warm Springs Dam Fish Hatchery." It is not known why (maybe the wild fish against hatchery fish argument got in the way), "...But the proposal fell apart...because of delays at National Marine Fisheries Service in issuing needed permits, and because of debate among biologists about the hatchery program." "...chairman of Sonoma County Board of Supervisors...said...it is borderline criminal what NMFS (National Marine Fisheries Service) has allowed to happen..." and "They fumbled away an opportunity...to do something to save this animal and we let it wiggle through our fingers."

California Licensed Forester's Newsletter(97) provides another example where NMFS questionable actions have resulted in damage to private property. Based on instructions from NMFS, Monterey County Department of Public Works work "...done nearly every year...cutting a channel from...lagoon to the sea..." was not finished. NMFS required "...artificial channel be cut no lower than 9.7 feet above sea level—and that the lagoon be allowed to rise to that level before flowing to the ocean." It is interesting to note this requirement"...wasn't based on listening to... weather report and all the talk about heavy surf, strong winds and high tide,..." and "...wasn't based on specific studies of the Carmel River, but on basic knowledge of trout biology..." It would also be interesting to know how trout biology resulted in a requirement that called for construction to a tenth of a foot.

The NMFS requirement was applied to "...not... breach the Lagoon too early..." because "The juvenile steelhead trout—a threatened species—may not be ready to enter the sea and cutting through prematurely (as apparently has been done for years) could kill them."

Overnight "...colossal waves and an unusually high tide (which as mentioned before were predicted)... refilled the artificial channel..." and "...only way to prevent flooding would be to cut a new channel." which "...public works supervisor...said..." was now "...too dangerous..." to do.

"By 10 a.m., the lagoon was at 11.5 feet and still rising." "…incident command post…" was set up, and all kinds of public agency and landowner effort was employed to handle the flooding situation. A supervisor said "We had a meeting two months ago to set up the procedures for breaking the lagoon this year…and we were assured by the wildlife experts that the people who lived around the lagoon wouldn't be in danger." The NMFS expert who came up with what was done said "…that's the risk you take when you build…within the 100-year flood plain…" In the end "…county workers bulldozed a channel to release the flooded lagoon waters to the ocean without getting permission from the federal government."

The situation of multiple agencies deciding what to do occurs on a frequent basis, and landowners and permitees are often caught in the middle. At times, it involves the inexperienced dueling with the inexperienced, and at times as in the discussed Rowdy Creek project, inexperienced unqualified governmental people are allowed to override input from truly knowledgeable and experienced professionals. In my dealing with California regulations involving geological, silvicultural, and common sense matters, I have had many experiences involving water quality folks overstepping their authority and levels of expertise, and I have seen the system let their incorrect and unsubstantiated input override input from more qualified and more experienced professionals. I have been amused by some of the really good arguments I have witnessed between government officials.

To cap things off regarding NMFS, there is a Clinton type "what does "is" mean?" story associated with NMFS. In California Board of Forestry board meeting minutes(98), a discussion between a board member and a NFMS spokesperson about what was being said in a NMFS report went as follows: Board member asked "…if NMFS attributed any difference in the wording of "likely," "would", or "reasonable certainty"." NMFS spokesperson said "…likely to result" is used interchangeably with "would"." How many of you would consider something as "likely to occur" as something that "would" for sure occur. Interesting how the Fourth Branch of Government and some politicians are allowed to get away with twisting the meaning of words isn't it?

It can be said permitees are often put in the following position:

Ours is not to do as historically proven and instructed by qualified professionals

But

To do as naive, inexperienced regulators say wonder why, pray, and duck

ENTER INCREDULOUS ACTIONS

The following two true stories illustrate some of the warped thinking that has permeated the ranks of the regulators.

In the first story a simple act of getting water to water roads and construction areas is involved. Watering of roads and work areas to hold soil or dirt sediments in place (to slow the creation of fine dust particles that can wash off when it rains) is a regulatory requirement applied by many governmental agencies to development, timber harvesting, mining, construction, and other soil disturbance operations.

You can't just back a water truck up to a waterhole or stream and get water. This simple operation has been turned into a big and often costly part of many projects due to need to obtain additional permits and constructing elaborate and not so elaborate sources of water without affecting various species and the environment. If you do not get the necessary permits, do the required environmental review, get regulators involved, and do what regulators say to do, you can get fined, penalized, and jail time.

In this story, a simple solution to a lot of problems was to get approval to dig a simple hole in an area like a gravel bar adjacent to a stream and let it fill with water. In this way, the stream was not affected, fish and other species in the stream were not affected, and an additional wet area was created for various aquatic species to use. Problems solved and everyone wins. Wrong!

The first year of use went okay, but second year of use did not. Contractor who went to the work and cost of building the waterhole came back to use the waterhole the next year, and the regulators said the waterhole was now a wet area and could not be disturbed. How do you think the contractor felt after he had gone to extra work to build the waterhole, had done the right thing, and had tried to get along. I can tell you his blood pressure caused a very heated discussion to occur, and the incentive for the contractor to do extra regarding reduction of environmental impacts and to work with the regulators in the future was pushed south.

In another incident involving collection of water from a watercourse, a large fire was in progress. Signs directing fire equipment were all over the place, aircraft (helicopters, planes) were flying overhead, and water trucks were lined up to get water out of a stream. The lead water truck was getting water out of a stream when a water quality regulator slides to a stop in front of the loaded water truck and gets out of his vehicle saying "What do you think you are doing?" The water truck operator says he's getting water for the fire. "You could hurt the fish getting that water, and I am not moving my vehicle", says the water quality regulator. The driver is getting just a little mad and tells the regulator move his vehicle or he's driving over it. Smaller vehicle is not moved, and water truck operator starts up his truck and starts to move when the regulator gives in and moves his vehicle. The water truck operator gets on his radio and calls the governmental fire boss. The driver tells the fire boss he better get down here (take his attention away from the fire and probably more important things), because someone is stopping them from getting needed water, and he (the water truck driver) may be going to jail. The fire boss comes down, chews out the water quality regulator, and things get back to business.

In this water truck and fire story, who really knows what the delay in water caused. Maybe just a few extra acres got burned which can environmentally be a bad thing; or, maybe the cost of fighting the fire was increased. I am sure the fire boss could provide information on how the potential for risk to the firefighters was increased.

Now, you might think this water truck story is a one time incident by an overzealous regulator with too much power, but this only illustrates a tip of the iceberg.

There is probably no greater example of the problems associated with how the ESA is being applied regarding endangered fish habitats than what happened regarding the deaths of four firefighters in the Thirty Mile Okanogan National Forest Fire in July of 2001. Internet report(99) provides the following story.

- Fire was contained by Hot Shot crew who requested helicopter water drop at 5:30 AM.
- Young fire crew arrived at 9:00 AM, and were told helicopter could not be used, because the Chewuch River contained endangered fish.
- At 12:08, dispatch office ordered the helicopter; however, they wanted to get permission from the district to dip into the river.

- Dispatch office could not reach anyone at the district with authority to give approval. Fire Manager and biologist were meeting to approve an exemption. Intra-agency team required to approve exemption did not convene until 12:00 PM.
- (The crew) were told that (the Chewuch River) was a protected water source and they needed to go through channels to use this water source.
- First load of water was dumped on fire around 3:00 PM after fire was out of control.
- Fire crew had no avenue for escape and fled to river where they deployed survival tents.
- Four firefighters died.

While this whole incident demonstrates some other very basic mistakes not involved with species protection, I leave it to the reader to decide if fighting fire should be hampered by having to convene a committee every time river water and a species of concern is involved. I know how I feel.

The kind of warped, out-of-line thinking provided by these stories does not occur everyday, but because there is no practical and effective way to hold members of the Fourth Branches of Government accountable for improper actions, you can expect the demonstrated thinking to cause more damage in the future.

MAKING HUMANS NO BETTER THAN THE SMALLEST SPECIES

WILL SPECIES PROTECTION TAKE PRECEDENT OVER HUMANS UNDER THE ENDANGERED SPECIES ACT?

As demonstrated in a news article(42) which discusses humans like other animals in a zoo in London, England, there is a movement by fellow humans to bring concern for human health and welfare to the level of the smallest species. Humans in the "…Human Zoo…sunned themselves on a rock ledge, clad in bathing suits and pinned on fig leaves." Those viewing the Human Zoo said "Seeing people in different environment, among other animals…teaches members of the public that the human is just another primate." "A lot of people think humans are above other animals,…" "When they see humans as animals, here, it kind of reminds us that we're not that special." "This exhibit made us come to the zoo. Humans are animals too."

Isn't it interesting how the human ability to live a better life than an animal is taken for granted and stupidly renounced. To those humans who wish to revert to living like animals, I say have at it, but when the fleas start to bite and the miserable living conditions get to you, do not come crying to humans working to make things better for human kind.

There are many ways we humans are looking the other way when it comes to the welfare and health of human kind. One of these ways involves West Nile disease. Due to the severity of this disease, a major media and regulatory effort to combat this disease is getting around.

A University of California Publication(52) mentions many species are being hurt by the West Nile virus. "West Nile Virus has killed the widest range and greatest number of wildlife species ever recorded in North America; ranging from cold-blooded bullfrogs to high-metabolism hummingbirds, from bats to elephants (assumably in zoos)." "The US Center for Disease Control has logged over 240 species with known mortalities,…"

As mentioned in one news article(83) "…80 percent of those bitten by mosquitoes with West Nile Virus will not get sick. Of the rest, most will get flu-like symptoms. Less than 1 percent of the people infected with West Nile Virus will become severely ill…" An agricultural newsletter article(113) puts a more serious spin on the disease by saying "In 2004, the virus was detected among wild birds, sentinel chickens, horses or humans in all California counties." In 2004, California had "…540 confirmed equine cases. More than 40 percent of those horses died or were euthanized." This same article says "Birds serve as the primary reservoir for harboring the disease. After feeding on infected birds, mosquitoes transmit the disease to humans and horses." A veterinarian says "We continue to urge horse owners to vaccinate against West Nile virus." While vaccination will not protect all horses, it will protect a "…high percentage…" People "…living in rural areas and those who spend a lot of time outdoors are especially vulnerable to contracting the infection."

Since no really knows if they are part of the 20% that are susceptible, everyone will have to abide by the promoted prevention program which says humans are on their own to avoid mosquitoes. One news article(115) outlines what those in charge are suggesting be done "…avoid mosquitoes, using repellant whenever you are outdoors and not letting puddles collect in flower pots, wading pools (I guess put no water in pools for wading) or other spots where mosquitoes can breed.

While eliminating small breeding locations can't hurt, ask yourself if this effort is really going to do much to eliminate mosquito populations. The multitude of large bodies of standing water in this country are going to continue chugging along turning out masses of mosquitoes, and telling the public to watch out for themselves isn't going to do much to reduce exposure to the West Nile virus.

Other things are being done, but it is doubtful these things will be allowed to do much good. In a news article(157), California Governor's "...revised budget includes $12 million in extra funding for existing mosquito control programs." Another news article(164) has one public official saying "...he has a mandate from the state to carry out mosquito control program that includes the possible use of pesticides...", and "...anti-pesticide demonstrators-carrying signs..." are saying "There are no Safe Poisons" and "Your Pesticides Poison Our Land, Air, Water". Per another news article(171), "The program to control disease-carrying mosquitoes also includes the state's (California) first aerial spraying...fog of sweet-smelling pesticide...over an urban area in more than 20 years." It will be interesting to see how long the urbanites will allow the spraying to be done to kill a few mosquitoes while the mosquitoes and birds are doing their thing in rural areas.

This information shows humans and many species are being put at risk, and a lot of money and good will is being expended to questionably prevent the disease.

With this background, you would think every effort to avoid promoting the disease would be at play; however, enter the ESA ferry shrimp, and vernal pool production efforts. Per a November, 2004 news article(172), there is a shallow pool recovery program in place where federal wildlife regulators are going to spend $2.1 billion (plan not yet budgeted but dollars to come from federal, state, local, and private sources) in a 1,500,000 acre plan area with 683,000 to 740,000 acres of designated critical habitat. The plan is suppose to be "...voluntary with no cost or effect on property owners unless they choose to participate", and ESA regulations preserving pool areas will be applied. In addition to the direct cost of protecting pools, one news article(173) is headlined "Saving seasonal pools translates to $1 billion in economic costs" "...over 20 years..." "...in lost development opportunities...,...transportation costs...", and "...cost to the new University of California, Merced." due to pool protection requirements. An earlier dated article(174) says "More than 136,000 acres of unique seasonal pools need no critical habitat designation..." and "...would be redundant to protect the four species of freshwater shrimp and 11 plants that survive only in shallow seasonal pools..." The 136,000 acres consist of "...42,914 acres..."

of "…national wildlife refuges or by a fish hatchery; 70,204 are on military bases; 644 acres are tribal land; 12,373 acres are in state wildlife areas or ecological reserves; and 10,224 acres are covered by habitat conservation plans."

It is not clear how all this vernal pool stuff will turn out, but a letter to the editor(175) brings us all back to the real world by saying "Those gorgeous vernal pools may also possess the potential…for breeding the species of mosquitoes that can spread the (West Nile) virus." "Once again, nature and man could be out of harmony."

Right now it appears the Fourth Branch of Government is stumbling around spending a lot of taxpayer money ineffectively fighting mosquitoes, and the politically correct pressures are pushing to spend more taxpayer money to protect and maintain mosquito breeding areas.

So, here we are with a dilemma routinely faced by society today. Do we apply ESA to the detriment of humans and many other species as wanted by many enviro thinking folks and let the human part of the equation be ignored; or, do we do what we can to protect humans?

Where do you stand on this matter?

WAYS TO IMPROVE ENVIRONMENTAL SPECIES ACT (ESA) LISTING PROCESS

As already discussed:

- Decisions to list a species need to be based on adequate site specific information.

- All input needs to be peer reviewed by field experienced professionals, biologists, and scientists.

These two ideas are reinforced by the Supreme Court of the United States in a "Scientific Evidence Rule"(100) that says "…trial judge, pursuant to Rule 104(a)…under Rule 701…, must make a assessment of …underlying reasoning or methodology…" as to being "…scientifically valid and properly applied to the facts at issue. Many considerations will bear on the inquiry, including whether the theory or techniques in question can be (and has been) tested, whether it has been subjected to peer review and publication, its potential error rate, and the existence of maintenance of standards controlling its operation, and whether it has attracted widespread acceptance within a relevant scientific community."

A lot of pseudo science is being allowed to float around and be utilized without adequate testing and peer review as described required by the Supreme Court. This pseudo science is routinely and inappropriately used to make ESA and other environmental regulatory decisions.

A news article(101) outlines how the ESA review process failed regarding the Truckee barberry plant. Per "Fish and Wildlife Service…A small shrub… Truckee barberry…once thought to be so rare it only grew on a 280 yard stretch of flood plain along the Truckee River isn't unique after all,…", because it "…isn't distinct from a…barberry found widely from Southern California into Canada and east to the Great Plains,…" This barberry was removed "…from the federal Endangered Species List."

It is interesting how a plant species that is so widely distributed could even be considered for listing, much less go through all the listing process and not be questioned by any public agencies.

I suspect the use of fringe habitat thinking got in the way where a few plants or any species for that matter exists on the edge of acceptable habitat and are considered a rarity, and some enthusiastic entity or person takes on the crusade to protect the species which other regulators willingly accommodate. This type of problem involving species protection in marginal habitat areas or in islands of acceptable habitats when the species population is really wide spread or plentiful routinely occurs. Especially in regards to plant species, my experiences have found a thorough search to verify if a species is really low in numbers and really threatened or endangered is the exception versus the norm. This lack of adequate collection of site specific information is causing a lot of unjustified and unnecessary regulatory restrictions involving the production and use of many natural resources.

The problem of where to draw the line regarding fringe populations and a listing of a species is well documented regarding the marbled murrelet, and a news article(102) outlines the problem. Site specific information is available which says the murrelets "…are numerous (930,000) in Alaska and Canada…But in the three Northwest states, they number only 21,000." The bird uses "…almost exclusively large, mossy branches typically found on old-growth trees to nest." in the lower Northwest states, and this has resulted in the push to leave old-growth for the bird in the lower Northwest states. It is interesting how the Fish and Wildlife state the habitat in California in some pretty big trees is "…perhaps marginal - old-growth murrelet habitat…", and the acceptable habitat in Alaska and Canada which has much smaller trees and a lot of murrelets, is not acceptable habitat in the lower three states. In any case, the marbled murrelet situation illustrates how a species with a larger overall population can be listed for protection and operations in marginal habitat are routinely prohibited whether justified or not.

The attempt to protect and maintain every species low in numbers in every fringe area as is being done in California and other regional areas is causing a lot of chaos and restrictions on the production of natural resource products, and in the end, Mother Nature and the natural selection process may make all the effort meaningless.

Additional ideas and food for thought regarding ESA peer review processes:

1. More input is needed from field experienced professionals who have practical experience in how species interact with disturbances and/or human activities and in how species really react in a wildland situation. The ESA peer review committee routinely lacks needed perspective on the total picture and on the real world.

2. All legitimate information, presented in a clear and professional manner, that can be supported by the site specific facts, should be included in the ESA review process. If this is done, any entity (single farmer, landowner, professional) with relevant information would have a chance to be heard, and a more factual and thorough review would occur.

3. Routinely there is a lack of adequate information during the initial review of a listing petition, and a time delay option needs to be available to the peer review committee to allow collection of the information needed to make a fully informed decision.

4. If any entity provides information that establishes a "reasonable doubt" as determined to be legitimate "reasonable doubt" by the peer review committee, the peer review committee should be able to issue a nondetermination decision and be able to delay the decision process until a fully informed decision can be made. Right now, it seems only the scientific and academic community, generally limited to a few people, is allowed to participate in the process. This limited group seems to routinely concentrate on collecting negative information structured to support a pro-listing position. Anti-listing information is not routinely available for review until late in the game. The use of "reasonable

doubt" to delay a decision until the "reasonable doubt" is factually eliminated would allow time for any entity to catch-up and to get missing legitimate and useful information into the review process.

If a "reasonable doubt" option is made available to the peer review committee, the committee can then list specific things that need to be done and can designate one federal agency to do needed follow-up work. The committee should be able to utilize private consultants; thereby, avoiding some of the cozy governmental relationships with some consulting groups that are not doing a proper job. The ability to use private consultants would eliminate some of the inefficiencies and foot dragging that occurs in many public agencies.

5. The peer review committee should be allowed to establish temporary recovery goals and targets such as population numbers and habitat acreages which can be modified as more information is provided. Right now recovery targets are not being put in place, and establishment of a goal even if it is temporary would provide some impetus for all those involved to get on the stick and get something done. An annual review of progress, would help to weed out any folks not doing their job.

6. As disturbance can be beneficial to many species, the benefits of disturbance activities should be part of any review, and one peer review committee chore should be to provide recommendations on how to manage for these benefits. The purely scientific and/or academic community generally do not understand the benefits of managed disturbance, and this is an area where an experienced field person on the peer review committee could be very useful.

7. The ESA review process should include more effort in determining if a species' population loss is an unavoidable evolutionary or natural process (vegetational changes, climate changes, uncorrectable predator problem, dominant species over a weaker species, changing watercourse flows due to earth movements, etc.). If manipulation of habitats by nature and/or man is not a significant contributor to and/or will not prevent the decline of a species, why list a species and cause unnecessary and costly disruptions to people and rural communities.

8. As part of any species review, the peer review committee should consider how a species population can be restored through correctly applied and controlled reproductive processes. Understanding and helping such processes to function better could result in the production of healthy species in larger numbers than could be produced in the wild. In some cases, these processes may be the only real hope for survival of some species such as has been illustrated by the condor program.

It is hard to understand why there is so much resistance to properly done, controlled reproduction of a species (plant and animal). The wild habitat and natural reproduction processes take a long time to replace and build species populations, and if left to just Mother Nature, there is a good chance that adequate population increases will never occur for many species. Waiting for species to recover by only using wild processes can, has, and is resulting in unnecessary damage to people, businesses, and rural communities. Let capitalism and private enterprise get involved, and you will have more of any species than you want.

If changes are not made in how the ESA and other federal regulations are being applied, there is going to be less and less incentive for landowners to work with federal regulators. A couple news articles(103)(104) mention how ESA use of "…best available data is too vague…", lacks "…sound science provisions…", and needs "…to demand empirical or peer-reviewed standards." "…Endangered Species Act's critical habitat provisions…put the needs of bark beetles and fish over humans.", and "…Act has provoked nuisance lawsuits by environmental groups out for financial gain, and pitted the government against farmers and homeowners." "…the law gives landowners an incentive to destroy species habitat in order to rid themselves of the burden of having to deal with the act's onerous (and I would add many unsupported and unjustified) regulations."

**Off like a herd of turtles, blindly, in a cloud of dust,
towards the cliff we go.**

PROTECTING THEM TO DEATH

ROADS GONE/NO ACCESS/NO MANAGEMENT/ NO DISTURBANCE
Leads to
NO DIVERSITY/NO CONIFERS/ NO LWD/NO FOOD
Which leads to
NO FISH/NO WILDLIFE

Chapter Four

In the world of environmental and species' protection, there is an ever-changing battle over what is right. Johnny-come-lately ideas are easily accepted without having stood the test of time and scientific peer review. Due to political and public perception pressures, regulatory decisions are routinely made based on emotion and feeling it is better to be conservative and careful. While being careful is not a bad thing, this type of thinking is often carried too far.

While environmental science and general information on the birds and the bees is in its infancy compared to other sciences, there are some basics that apply.

When current knowledge about species and their habitats is seriously and factually reviewed, it has to be acknowledged that every species has needs fitting a certain space and time in vegetative growth cycles that occur across the landscape. If the landscape is not allowed to cycle through all naturally occurring vegetative progressions, it is inevitable that some species will be inhibited and maybe prevented from existing.

A resident of Virginia illustrates the need for all phases of vegetative growth and habitats in an internet report(105) that mentions "In 1935, 90% of the (Jefferson National) forest was early successional habitat..." created by "...The chestnut blight..." "Fifty years ago, grouse were one of the most common bird species on the Jefferson Forest." with "...plenty of neo-tropicals and even bobwhite quail." "...woodcock... used to be common on the Jefferson - they do breed here in Virginia by-the-way, but they are now…in dire straits…rare in the Forest…" "These species "…need early successional habitat…"

Disturbance is a natural part of life and Mother Nature. Disturbance can cause bad things to happen, and it can also cause good things to happen.

Diversity does not exist without disturbance, and true diversity is a mixture of vegetation and habitats across the landscape.

Without disturbance, the natural trend is for a there to be a vegetative monoculture across the land.

Having a monoculture of only one vegetative cover type whether it is the tundra in Alaska or an old-growth forest does not fit all needs for all species. Some species like fringe areas, some species like openings and grasslands, some species like post fire habitats, some species like old-growth forests, and on and on.

Magazine article(106) re-states how different species need different habitats and real diversity is a mixture of all kinds of habitats. "A powerline…swath clear of trees that is often more than 100 feet wide…" may not be preferred by "…martin, fisher, squirrels, porcupines, ruffed grouse, canopy nesting songbirds and others…" who like some tree cover. "Edge habitat is especially valuable for many species.", and "…a power line right-of-way can benefit song birds,… rabbits, quail, cotten rats, meadow voles, woodchucks, goldfinchs, towhees, song sparrows, indigo buntings, marsh hawks,…and other edge species…" "…certain other wildlife can increase where grasslands, shrub lands and other early successional habitats…" have been created in the process of replacing the removed forest.

Proper, management that provides continually changing vegetative cover types produces a greater variety of habitats and services a larger number of species.

A report(107) describes how different species react to different levels of forest density and how heavy density is not always a good thing. The Forest Service says "…reduced understory cover following precommercial thinning temporarily reduces the local habitat quality of snowshoe hares, the primary prey of lynx."; however, "Recent research in Maine has shown that precommercially thinned stands continue to support snowshoe hares at densities greater than those found in other types of forests."

"No management" and preservation philosophies do not promote real diversity and only provide habitats for some species some of the time.

Logic and a lot of factual data says more food begets larger species' populations, and the amount of available food controls the size of species populations. I have personally observed this relationship in the field.

Over time, different vegetation provides different types of food, and without disturbance, the cycle of vegetative change will not produce the variety and quantity of food the land is capable of producing. Certain trees produce needles that provide food for the red tree vole, and this food base can disappear as forests mature. Areas with younger vegetation and brush can produce more rodents preferred by some species than deep dark forests. Fire and heavy forest removal allows new vegetative shoots to grow which provides desired browse by deer and other species.

Obviously humans, including Native Americans, have done many things which have caused impacts to the environment. Repeated burning has been done to remove forests and create better grazing, hunting, and growing conditions to help feed families and the world. Rivers have been dammed to provide water, electrical power, and flood control in order to provide a better way of life for humans and to build nations. Land has been cleared and hillsides re-sculptured to accommodate homes and towns.

A success story involving humans, wildlife, proper use of natural resources, and maintaining a rural way of life is illustrated in a news article(108). In this article written by a member of Alaska's native population, it is said "…the Prudhoe Bay experience…has been good for Alaska Natives. It has not ruined the land or harmed wildlife…the caribou herd that migrates through the Prudhoe bay area is healthier than it has ever been, now numbering nine times its population in 1974." "Our (Native Alaskan) instincts told us that oil development and migrating caribou herds would not mix" "Today we have to admit that the industry has succeeded in taking the oil from the ground without dislocation the wildlife or ruining the land." This type of story "…may not sell a lot of newspapers or generate donations to the Sierra Club, but people who care about the fate of Native Americans and the environment should know…" about "…the Prudhoe Bay experience…"

History, science, and our eyes tell us everything in nature is changing and nothing remains static, and existing vegetative conditions and species use will change over time. Except in some rare climax conditions, attempts to lock-up and preserve existing conditions and species uses is doomed to failure.

Preservationist "no management" thinking is detrimental to many undeveloped countries. In a few countries, humans have reached the point where they think they have the luxury and option to lock up natural resources at the expense of food and shelter, but there are many more countries that do not have this option. In many undeveloped countries, natural resources need to be fully utilized to provide a better life for humans, and the worldwide need for food and natural resources makes the preservationist agenda unrealistic and an unwise choice for many.

QUESTIONABLE SPECIES PROTECTION
DRIVES QUESTIONABLE REGULATORY THINKING

Environmental and regulatory protection ideas are influenced by a varied mix of confusing and often unsupportable species protection concerns. The list of species and habitats requiring protection and associated protection requirements are a moving target that changes daily, weekly, monthly, and yearly.

Without proper study and review, many species are lackadaisically and inappropriately added to special protection lists. Those advocating protections are given a lot of leeway in justifying their case for protection, and routinely unjustified protection requirements go unchallenged. Once a concern for protecting a species has been established, it is extremely difficult to rebut this concern.

One thing that has always seemed out-of-line is the routine attempt to require permitees and landowners to maintain existing species habitats that are the result of proposed project activity. Already provided information demonstrates how disturbance allows the vegetative cycle to properly service a larger number of species. Additionally, when existing habitat and species use over the years is the result of a project activity such as timber harvesting or growing a crop, why change what has been happening? Doesn't this situation indicate the critters now found in the project area like what has been happening; otherwise, why would they keep coming back or stay on the project area? In the real world, change can be mandatory in order to keep having what you now have.

Examples of questionable and often unsupportable mitigation requirements which have ties back to species protection are as follows:

1. **Increasing restrictions based on negative reporting and unclear end results are pushing landowners away from helping species.** Regulatory and biological communities are doing little to develop obtainable and easy to understand incentives and species habitat goals. Such goals would give landowners an incentive to more actively participate in habitat enhancement work. Why aren't regulatory and

biological folks working harder to provide benefits to landowners for doing a good job?

When landowners create and maintain habitats wanted by certain species, and target species move-in to utilize provided habitats, routinely the result is more species protection restrictions. Where is the incentive to create and maintain wanted habitats if the result is to be more restrictions?

2. **The infamous California Department of Fish and Game 1970s debris removal program damaged the general health of hundreds of miles of watercourses by having all woody materials removed, and inappropriate messing with watercourses is continuing.** What happened under this debris removal program is a prime example of governmental abuse of power and authority and protecting species to their death.

When the decision was made to remove woody debris from watercourses, the four basic ingredients that were not properly applied in making this decision are as follows:

1. Factual site specific information.
2. Time tested peer reviewed proven science.
3. Adequate verification and peer review by experienced field professionals.
4. Logic and common sense.

The idea anything put into the water was bad and had to come out dominated the thinking. It did not matter if woody debris was present before or after timber operations. It all had to be removed.

While it was a noble idea to eliminate existing and potential fish barriers, field application of debris removal got out of hand and evolved into elimination of theorized blockages and bank erosion problems.

The general public, fishery groups (who wanted work), politicians, Fourth Branches of Government, and media sources bought into stream cleaning programs, and taxpayer funded debris removal projects were created and promoted in areas not being harvested.

Hundreds of miles of streams were cleaned and turned into sluice-boxes in many locations. Obvious site specific information, such as wood floats and fish swim under it, wood helps stabilize watercourses, wood helps in the process of aquatic food production, wood traps and holds sediments, and the biggest trout were usually caught by log jams where they had protective cover, was ignored.

Regulations and practice of requiring debris removal from streams went unchallenged for years. California's northern neighbors (Oregon and Washington) knew better, but were ignored. The logical and common sensical knowledge being promoted north of the Mason-Dixon line (the California and Oregon state line which California state officials can't seem to find the time to cross) finally seeped into the minds of the people in California's Fourth Branch of Government, and the damaging removal of woody debris was stopped.

While restoration work can be a noble effort, the jury is still out on how much good expenditures of millions of taxpayer dollars is going to do. A lot of unnecessary and questionably beneficial road crossing, sediment manipulation, and woody debris work in watercourses is being done just because bond and taxpayer money has been allocated to do the work.

Under the guise of stream restoration work, regulators and a new bunch of pseudo experts are again finding ways to mess with an unpredictable Mother Nature, and this second-guessing has the potential to set healing processes back and make things worse. Routinely debris and sediments being removed are doing no real harm, and involved work routinely opens and destabilizes watercourses that are basically healed or on the mend. Short term accelerated sediment caused by new work has the potential to be more damaging than slow-occurring and possibly nondetrimental problem the experts may be trying to correct. Based on this new thinking, regulatory requirements are also being inappropriately developed and applied.

Regulations and restrictions have been put in place that require privately owned trees to be permanently left untouched and value taken from landowners for woody debris recruitment purposes. It is hoped that these leave trees will eventually fall in ways that beneficially help watercourses. It has been acknowledged that this requirement is also an attempt to correct past regulatory and governmental actions that improperly removed woody debris from watercourses.

A lot of speculation, not proven fact, went into development of leave tree regulations, and a lot of site specific information indicates many trees required to be left will not provide wanted benefits. As potential woody debris recruitment trees haphazardly fall, some trees will never reach a watercourse, and as trees near watercourses naturally fall, roots will be forcibly pulled and torn out of the ground causing sedimentation and channel stability problems.

Unjustified, abusive woody debris regulatory requirements have provided a double whammy for owners of private timber. These owners were first inappropriately forced to pay for removal of woody debris from watercourses, and now without adequate justification and factual basis, many landowners are forced to leave valuable trees in resolving a woody debris problem they did not create.

You would think you had heard it all; then, along comes a new twist provided by a Fish and Wildlife district fish biologist in a news article(109). When discussing the Klamath River, this biologist says a recent "...fish kill is indicative of a highly manipulated system. Dams, historical use of log rafts-bark continues to decompose on the river bottom, treatment plant effluent, farming, dredging, and hydropower operations all may affect the area,..." Interesting how logging was left off the list, but the real kicker was the concern over bark probably deposited in the early part of the nineteenth century. If almost century old bark in a debris deficient river is a problem, why do we want more bark put into streams that comes with large woody debris now required to be left to fall in streams. Before we get too excited about making regulations and doing things to strip bark from potential large woody debris, someone needs to be taken to the school of reality. When the real world is applied, what this biologist says makes little sense, and provides an example of how illogical and poorly based information gets spread around.

Serious open-minded review finds more disincentives to recruitment of large woody debris (LWD) than incentives. There should be more effort to promote and obtain placement of LWD in streams, and anyway humans can help the process along should be promoted. The general rule should be to allow placement of stumps and trees into streams any time it can be done without obvious detrimental impacts. Why not eliminate regulations that require removal of accidental, nondetrimental depositions of LWD, and replace them with regulations that require any tree placed in a stream be left in the stream? This would be no different than what Mother Nature is going to do.

The old practice of trashing streams by filling them with woody debris is gone, and for those who still think those accidentally placing trees in a stream need to be punished, they can rest easier knowing a valuable tree has been donated towards bettering the environment.

94

3. **Pseudo scientific thinking is inappropriately pushing no disturbance in everchanging and expanding watercourse protection zones (WLPZs).** Many think no disturbance near watercourses is a good thing. Sediment movement into watercourses will be slowed, and species habitats will be enhanced. While sediment movement will obviously be slowed, and existing habitats will remain unchanged for awhile, is the end result really a good thing?

When factual field conditions and time tested peer reviewed information is reviewed, the "no disturbance" thinking is not headed to a good place.

In the real world, conifer establishment and growth which it seems everyone wants requires sunlight, mineral soil, and reduced vegetative competition. Little to no disturbance in WLPZs results in less mineral soil, less sunlight, more nonconifer vegetative competition, and over time less conifers in WLPZ areas. No disturbance provides site conditions more favorable to brush and hardwood species which allows brush and hardwood species to out compete conifers and to routinely dominate the site.

Fish and other aquatic species do better in diverse streamside habitat conditions, and unchanging, undisturbed watercourse areas is not good for all species.

In the overall scheme of things, the idea sedimentation from properly conducted operations adversely affects watercourses is not true. The natural processes of erosion provide sedimentation quantities that far far far exceed that contributed by properly conducted operations. A properly conducted operation involves reduced and controlled equipment entry into WLPZs, and although conifer establishment and growth may be restricted, routinely required stabilization procedures such as grass seeding and straw mulching on disturbed soil areas makes sedimentation concerns even more insignificant.

4. **Questionable handling of sudden oak death to protect oaks and other vegetative species is in play and creates a lot of questions.** Could the tanoak tree, which for years has been considered an unwanted weed species, become a protected tree? Burning, chemical treatments, harvesting, digging stumps out, you name it has been done for years to eradicate this tree. Now a disease called Sudden Oak Death (SOD) has arrived in California. Depending how you look at it, this could be a good thing as it kills tanoak; or, a bad thing in that it affects and kills other

species of oak which the "Save Oaks in California" movement finds objectionable.

The regulators have taken control of the situation and their solution has been to throw money at research and to put in place a lot of regulatory restrictions on the harvest and use of host species which may carry the disease. While this sounds like the correct approach to handling the disease, a closer simple, logical review of the situation raises questions.

By being in wide spread pockets from Oregon into California, SOD appears to already be out of the box, can not be controlled, and is part of a larger ongoing natural process. A news article(114) mentions SOD was found in "...two Southern California nurseries..." At a forester's meeting, it was mentioned SOD is now found in 20 different states.

In Oregon the control process has involved vegetative removal and burning.

In California, regulations are quietly being considered such as debarking Douglas-fir and redwood logs and washing vehicles. Regulations now in place involve firewood transport only by permit in closed containers, and movement of host materials outside infected areas is prohibited. The news article(114) goes on to mention California nurseries were brought into the regulatory web when they "...were ordered...not to ship dozens of plant species until they have been found free of...sudden oak death (SOD)...fungus-like infection..." Since SOD regulations have been selectively applied since "...2001...in 12 Northern California counties...", and SOD was "...first...at a nursery...in an area of Marin County where the disease is common.", it makes you wonder why the nurseries are so late to the party, and why the timber industry was the first and basically only industry to be regulated for a long time.

If you step back and look at what is known, efforts to attack SOD and prevent spread have appeared inadequate and sometimes half-hearted. In California, removal and burning is not promoted, and very little seems to be done in infected Marin County's influential, well-to-do communities which have environmental leanings and political clout. It seems the regulators and academic folks want to spend money researching SOD and regulating those who do not have the ability to resist while other routine causes of spread such as people, tourists, motorbikes, general public, wildland users, and wildlife are given a pass.

Since SOD has already left the barn and spread is not being fully controlled, trees will continue to die. It appears those in charge will continue to spend a lot of tax money researching the SOD problem and be allowed to selectively applying regulations without any consequences for inappropriate actions.

Supposedly a Save the Redwoods League representative said a diverse genetic pool of affected species will allow resistant plants to survive if things are left to natural processes. Since SOD is naturally eliminating genetically inferior trees, maybe SOD should be considered part of a natural selection process, and everyone should just let it run its course?

Another interesting thought involves the tanoak tree. Will this disease cause the tanoak tree, which has been considered a nuisance and weed for years, to die back to a point it is considered a threatened species, and if this happens will all the protections and restrictions for a threatened species be applied?

I raise this question, because as illustrated in news article(116) regarding the pikeminnow squawfish one person's pest can become another's endangered species nemesis. "Squawfish are...the voracious predator of salmon and other river Critters...facing the...Eel River.", and the "...pikeminnow species in the Colorado River is endangered, and affects management of the dams on the river."

"The California Department of Fish and Game (DFG)..." has been trying all kinds of ways to eliminate squawfish in the Eel River including "...blasting them with dynamite cord, netting them and spearing them.", and there is even a fishing derby with no bag limits and a reward for who catches the most, smallest, and largest. If the Colorado squawfish is the same as the Eel River squawfish, is it possible a good eradication job in the Eel River could result in an endangered status for the squawfish in the Eel River as now in place on the Colorado?

If you want to have some fun just ask the question **"Can human's do things to improve and help Mother Nature make things better for wildlife and the environment?"** The answer provided by the person being asked tells you a lot about the mindset of that person regarding environmental issues and use of natural resources by humans.

Those adamantly opposed to human interaction with species are ignoring what happens in the real world, and often naively and selfishly hinder human activities that are in the best interest of many species.

WAYS HUMANS CAN HELP

There are many who prefer to preserve existing habitats and do not want humans to interfere with Mother Nature; however, without disturbance, a cycle of changing habitats and food production does not occur.

In general it can be said, new vegetative shoots that grow after a fire or other disturbance provide browse desired by deer and other species. A news article(121) outlines how "On Six Rivers (National Forest), burning bear grass..." provides "...young bear grass that comes up after a fire..." that "...is good elk forage..." and "...it's also the key material used in...basket making." by "...native Americans."

Although many biologists won't admit it, timber management activities such as tree thinning and even clearcutting provide benefits for a lot of species. Introduction of sunlight will cause a lot of good things to happen. Areas with younger vegetation and brush are able to produce more rodents and prey than deep dark forests.

As already mentioned earlier in this chapter a report(107) states "...precommercially thinned stands continue to support snowshoe hares at densities greater than those found in other types of forests...the primary prey of lynx."

A magazine report(110) illustrates how heavy disturbance can be good for wild species when it says "Maine's forests were cut hard in the 1980s to salvage timber from the spruce budworm epidemic. As the forests grew back, they provided habitat for snowshoe hare: plenty of food for lynx and fishers." The mentioned spruce bug problem parallels the bug killed timber and fire problems in the west, and the problem in the west could be handled just like the spruce bug problem was handled. Salvage logging could provide environmental and species benefits while reducing fire risk.

News article(122) mentions how humans created a problem, and then found a way to correct the problem and make things even better for eagles and other raptors. Eagles (and other falcon type birds) that are "...fond of roosting in...poles...were being electrocuted when they touched powerlines and metal contacts." "...poles..." are being replaced "...with ones that have at least five feet between contact points..." In addition, extension devices have been placed on poles above the wires, and these extension devices are being used for roosting and feeding observation which helps the birds more easily observe and obtain food.

The bald eagle resurgence across the lower forty eight states provides another example of how humans and Mother Nature worked together to produce good results. While humans may have contributed to the loss of bald eagles in the lower 48 states, it has been humans who have shown they can turn things around and bring a species back. A news article(123) says "...they're (eagles) found in every one of the lower 48 states..." While I have heard some people call species' populations handled by humans as trash species, I do not see many speaking out too loudly against this bald eagle success story.

News article(125) demonstrates how humans can help peregrine falcons. In "...Minnesota...at a power plant...the first known peregrine falcon to nest at a power plant...was killed in a territorial battle with another (peregrine) falcon..." While it is too bad Mother Nature can be so cruel, this incident shows artificial peregrine falcon nests can work and more than one falcon will find them attractive enough to fight over. I say lets build more nests and get the nests placed where peregrines can use them.

While the enviros and anti-human crowd will say the condor wouldn't be having problems if it wasn't for humans, logic tells us Mother Nature and natural selection processes have played a big part in what has happened to the condor. For sure, the condor story would be over if humans had not gone to a lot of effort and cost to save this struggling species. It seems the efforts to save the condor are working as indicated by news article(126) which says it is believed "...three pairs of the giant birds have produced eggs in the wild and a fourth pair is expected to produce one soon,..." "The California condor population now includes 90 birds living in the wild in California, Arizona and Mexico's Baja California, and 125 in captivity at..." zoos and research centers. This sounds like a success story where human interaction has been a good thing.

The constant barrage of blaming humans for conflicts that occur between humans and wild species is routinely not supported by what happens in the real world. The potential for losing funding and controlling wild species research and regulatory processes provides a lot of incentive for those reaping the benefits to not let conflicts die by solving problems and applying effective population control techniques.

HERE WILD FISHY FISHY

A prime example of resistance to having humans help Mother Nature involves replenishing reduced fish populations. The Fourth Branches of Government are strongly promoting the idea that if a fish is not wild (untouched by man), it is inferior and needs to be eliminated.

This idea is being used to justify elimination of fish enhancement projects such as hatcheries and instream rearing projects. There is an ugly story regarding this matter that is not being told to the public. Starting in 1999 and 2000, stories, about hatcheries being shutdown and fish eggs, small fish, and returning salmon being destroyed, have seeped out all along the west coast. The silence from the Fourth Branches of Government regarding hatchery closings is glaringly noticeable.

One undated, partial news report(130) states "The Coleman National Fish Hatchery on the Sacramento River at Anderson (California) has killed 343,596 baby chinook salmon...", and "...the state's Nimbus Fish Hatchery on the American River has destroyed 2.2 million fall-run salmon eggs." The report goes on to say "No one wants to do this, said...spokes-woman from U.S. Fish and Wildlife Service..."; however, per this report someone has made the decision that "...the river can support only so many fish (funny thing to say when everyone says fish populations are down), and hatchery-bred salmon are being sacrificed for the sake of the relatively few wild chinook spawning naturally on the rivers."

A report(131) outlines what happened at Fall Creek Hatchery on the Alsea River "...where ODFW (Oregon Department of Fish and Wildlife) killed (clubbed) 6,000 hatchery coho (because they were determined genetically inferior) to save 108 so called "wild" fish with fins intact..." This report mentions how "...Colombia River Inter-Tribal Fish Commission... were forced to court...to keep ODFW from killing 350 Chinook and 700 steelhead returning to the Imnaha River after their long journey to the ocean and back. ODFW's "reasoning" was the salmon lacked acceptable genetic characteristics." The report says it would be a good idea to raise all fish to have these fish's genetics as it appears they were physically strong by being able to run the gauntlet to the ocean and back. The report mentions how low fish numbers can mean more taxpayer dollars for those pushing restoration and fish population enhancement projects which indicates other motives for eliminating hatchery programs may be in play.

Another report(132) states "Fish clubbing to proceed" "The Oregon Department of Fish and Wildlife intends to...use clubs and electricity to euthanize tens of thousands of surplus (meaning not wild??????) hatchery salmon." "...fish clubbing on the Alsea River..." involved returning adult salmon that cost thousands of dollars to raise. What a waste and bunch of stupidity to not just shut the return spillway, and let unwanted returning adult fish go breed in the wild as many have been allowed to do in the past.

News article(133) provides a questionable and unsupportable argument that is being used against hatchery programs. "NOAA Fisheries Northwest Regional Director...federal agency in charge of restoring salmon (heaven help us)...said...Hatchery fish will not be considered a substitute (why not?) for existing naturally spawning runs..." even though according to "...fisheries biologists...hatchery fish make up about 80 percent of Pacific salmon populations." NOAA director sounds defiant as he goes on to say "For those who were thinking that putting fish in concrete would provide an easy way out, this plainly says that won't be acceptable (to who????)." While concrete ponds and poor hatchery practices have not always produced perfect fish, past problems have been eliminated, and despite the attitude provided by the NOAA director, which mirrors a lot of the thinking by those in control of the salmon restoration programs, there are many fish rearing success stories out there.

I have personally been involved with local hatchery programs that utilized predator protection and continuous natural feeding programs, and I have seen these programs produce a bigger and healthier fish than could be produced in the wild. By being bigger, the instream reared fish have a better chance of avoiding predators and making it to the ocean.

A recent Oregon judge's decision to consider hatchery fish the same as wild fish has sparked review of fishery programs and to question why only wild fish can be used to replenish salmon stocks. Hatchery and wild fish have reproduced together for years, and hatchery produced fish are physically and genetically indistinguishable from wild fish. The judge's decision was a logical one and put some common sense back into the fish issue.

A September tenth, 2001 United States District Court for the District of Oregon made a decision which included the following determinations. "...the NMF's listing decision is arbitrary and capricious, because the Oregon Coast ESU (Evolutionary Significant Unit) includes both "hatchery spawned" and "naturally spawned" coho salmon, but the agency's listing decision arbitrarily excludes "hatchery spawned" coho. Consequently the listing decision is unlawful." "...ESA recognizes that conservation of listed species may be facilitated by artificial means." "The Hatchery Policy interprets the ESA as requiring NMFS to focus on its recovery efforts on "natural populations"...", and ESA and this policy can be interpreted "...that artificial propagation may represent a potential method to conserve listed salmon species when the propagated fish are determined similar to the listed natural population in genetic, phenotype, and life history traits, and in habitat use characteristics (which definitely includes hatchery fish)." Court finds "...NMFS August 10, 1998 listing decision...invalid because it relied on factors upon which Congress did not intend the NMFS to rely." "...NMFS...makes improper distinctions...by excluding hatchery coho populations from listing protection even though they are determined to be part of the same DPS (distinct population segment) as natural coho populations." To me this can mean the killing of returning coho hatchery salmon by ODFW is a violation of ESA. "It is undisputed that "hatchery spawned" coho may account for as much as 87% of the naturally spawning coho in the Oregon coast ESU. In addition, hatchery spawned and natural coho are the same species...and interbreed when mature..." and "...NMFS considers progeny of hatchery fish...born in the wild as "naturally spawned" coho that deserve listing protection." "Thus, the NMFS listing decision creates the unusual circumstance of two genetically identical coho salmon swimming side by side in the same stream, but only one receives ESA protection while the other does not. The distinction is arbitrary." In short, hatchery fish which are the same genetically and physically as so-called wild fish are not to be given different consideration when determining their status for listing purposes.

In a news article(139) "Conservationists, fishing groups, and Indian tribes are asking a federal judge to stop the Bonneville Power Administration's plan to reduce the amount of water spilled over Columbia and Snake River hydroelectric dams to help young salmon migrate to the ocean." Every time I read about the ongoing argument about how much water to release from dams for migrating salmon and compare it to the anti-dam arguments by the same groups promoting water releases, I think of how everyone has forgotten the obvious. The water they are arguing about is winter water lost to the oceans before dams were ever built. How did salmon ever manage in the past when dammed water did not exist, and if you eliminate the dams as wanted by many, where you going to get the water that just has to be stored for controlled release to help migrating salmon?

A 2003 opinion article(141) titled "A shortsighted focus on allegedly lethal dams" provides an example of how everything good is being played down by those in charge. This article plays up "...25 lost fish out of the more than 45,000 that made it successfully up stream on a single day..." "News headlines from the Oregonian 'Salmon jam up at dam's ladder' and 'Biologists unsure of reason for fatal tangle'..." are a "...a strangely negative way to announce the glad tidings: This is the third (or is it the fourth - I've lost count) consecutive annual record-setting run of homecoming mature salmon...bound upstream to their spawning grounds and overtaxing the fish ladders in the process." "One would have thought that everybody ...would have reason to be cheery about..." all the fish. "Where is the bad news...?" "We should...get over the romantic notion that it is possible or desirable to reconstruct the rivers to resemble what Lewis and Clark saw 200 years ago."

Darn, 25 out of 45,000 fish were lost!

IGNORING THE OBVIOUS

To ignore and fight legitimate successful ways proven to increase fish populations and to only depend on Mother Nature and a low wild fish population to build fish stocks, borders on being ludicrous.

A news article(142) provides some insight on what can happen if you leave it to Mother Nature and her devices to increase fish populations.

State regulators suddenly "...ban...nontribal fishermen (as opposed to native Americans)..." from "...killing...or whack 'em on the head and take 'em home for dinner...wild steelhead in the rivers of the Olympic Peninsula (Washington state)..." Native Americans will still be allowed to catch steelhead and even sell them commercially. This has been done to reduce fish losses from fishing by having the steelhead caught by nontribal folks "...put...gently back in the river..." "...even here, where sparse population and the protections of the Olympic National Park help preserve fish habitat (deep, dark, old-growth forests), the wild runs are well below their historic heights." While this has "Many locals seething..." in a "...beat-up timber town that looks to steelhead-related tourism to ease some of the economic pain caused by the dramatic logging cutbacks of a decade ago,..." This article shows how fish populations are dropping in deep, dark, and protected old-growth areas ruled by Mother Nature which are suppose to provide premier fish rearing habitats.

It does not make sense that the best way to have large fish populations is to only utilize low wild fish populations and to not provide some stability in the haphazard wild conditions thrown at fish by Mother Nature.

If more fish are wanted, what is wrong with helping the process at any point in the process? What is wrong correcting past mistakes and properly duplicating successful instream reproduction processes? Is an anthropologically created fish (one whose creation is influenced by man) really a zoo animal as stated in a naively written newspaper's editorial(143).

If hatchery fish look, smell, and taste the same as wild fish, and in some ways are even better than wild fish, why are members of the Fourth Branch of Government allowed to kill successful properly run hatchery programs? Proven science, logic, and common sense tells us hatcheries with higher fertility and survival rates can produce more fish than wild conditions, and with the ability to utilize a superior gene pool and control rearing conditions, hatcheries can produce a larger fish that can out-compete wild fish. If you can artificially produce a larger and healthier fish "population" that has a greater ability to make it in the wild; make it past all the predators (not to mention providing better feed for the predators); make it to the ocean: and make it back to spawn, why not do it?

Leaving the chore of replenishing fish populations to Mother Nature is a haphazard crap shoot. Is the goal to produce more and larger fish or not? Are there ulterior motives at play?

Who made the decision "only" wild fish in wild haphazard conditions are to be used to replenish fish populations? There are many reasons why those promoting the wild fish "only" approach are pushing a loser, and before more damage is done, those pushing this thinking need to held accountable.

Do we continue down the wild fish only road that shuts off water per news article(144) to areas like Methow, Washington, denies water when requested by firefighters as discussed in Chapter three, spends hundreds of thousands of dollars on questionable restoration projects, unjustifiably restricts and increases costs for natural resource use operations, and unnecessarily withholds water from farmers and other wildlife?

CHOMP! CHOMP!

Some biologists have learned that an open range land condition is preferable to a brushland condition, and livestock use can enhance habitats for many species and keep rangelands as rangelands by simply not allowing brush species to take over. A news article(148) headlined "Grazing-for-wildlife project gets underway" addresses the question "Can grazing cows...help wildlife?" "The cattle are just being used as a tool..." to keep plants from becoming a "...tangle of ever-more dense vegetation..." As happened in the past when cattle were removed from "...damp, fertile bottomlands...", plants "...soon choked the area, changing the habitat for the wetland critters who lived there." This type of historical factual information known by experienced ranchers and farmers is being forgotten. Some biologists believe livestock use hurts species, and they object to what the study in the article is telling them, but they are finding it hard to rebut the facts.

The previously mentioned article(148) shows co-operation based on good science can accomplish a lot. Producers of natural resource products are generally an easy going bunch (ranchers, farmers, small landowners) who would rather do the right thing and get-a-long with everyone; however, they have been soured by how badly they have been treated by regulators. This article shows a few regulators realize use of science, site specific facts, logic, and common sense in co-operation with the producers of natural resource products is a better way to go.

DISINCENTIVES TO HELPING WILDLIFE

Environmental damage and pessimistic ideas dominate the thinking behind natural resource decisions. A pessimistic focus on environmental damage is resulting in a flood of negative reports and more and more restrictive regulations that inhibit use of natural resources. Negative information abounds, and examples of doing the right thing and healthy conditions are overlooked or purposely ignored.

Not acknowledging and rewarding landowners for doing good things kills the incentive for landowners to participate in species enhancement work and to hold-on to open space lands.

Input at late fall 2003 California hearings on current Coho recovery plan being developed by California Department of Fish and Game outlines the process of putting disincentives in place. Little recognition is being given to extra voluntary landowner efforts already in play, decisions are being made based on outdated and inadequate research data, little recognition is being given to agricultural and forestry practices that benefit fish habitats, more unsupported regulatory restrictions are being proposed, and impacts of predation and ocean conditions are being ignored.

Offers or bribes to landowners by governmental agencies with taxpayer money to do studies and wildlife projects are being meet with skepticism by many landowners. Public projects routinely come with governmental strings that interfere with a landowner's business. Many landowners are finding free grant money can have a down-side and is not so "free".

WHAT IS GOOD FOR THE GOOSE
IS NOT NECESSARILY GOOD FOR THE GANDER

CITY FOLKS DO NOT KNOW WHAT RURAL FOLKS ARE GOING THROUGH

If species protection restrictions being applied to rural folks were equally applied to urban folks, there would be more sympathy for what is happening to rural folks.

I will use an exaggerated but real world example involving peregine falcon protection to show how a double standard exists and to show why urban folks would not stand for peregine falcon protection requirements being imposed on rural folks.

A typical timber harvest operation covers a large area, and contact with a known peregine falcon nesting location would be small to none; however, the regulatory requirements found in 2003 California Forest Practice Rules under Article 9 would be fully applied. These regulations are summarized as follows.

1. A minimum buffer zone of ten acres out to over 40 acres if determined needed to avoid a take of the species.
2. Within up to ten acres of the buffer area, activities will be restricted as needed to protect the nesting habitat.
3. Critical period is February 1 to April 1 if nesting is occurring and extended to July 15 if young are in the nest. During this period, no activities are allowed in the buffer zone except for road use if governing regulatory agency determines peregines have shown a tolerance to such activity.
4. Any loud, disturbing activity such as created by helicopters is not allowed within a half mile of the nest.

In cities where the pigeon and other predator food base is plentiful, peregine falcons can be found in habitats created by humans. Our example involves peregine falcons who like to nest on bare rocklike surfaces such as ledges of skyscrapers.

When applying peregine falcon protection requirements to the city situation, we find the following:

106

1. In using the ten acre minimum buffer, we find the minimum buffer area requires a diameter of over 740 feet or more than two football fields. Conservatively in a city big enough to have skyscrapers, two large city blocks and portions of adjacent city blocks would be involved.

2. With nests high on the buildings, there are not too many activities that would affect nesting; however, whoever is nearest the nest will have to watch opening windows, window cleaning will need to be curtailed, loud activities of all kinds will need to be controlled, and lighting will have to be restricted.

3. Use of the streets by vehicles and probably pedestrians, all road maintenance work, and all building construction and maintenance activities will need to be stopped between February 1 to April 1 if nesting is occurring and extended to July 15 if young are in the nest until the involved regulatory agency determines peregrines have shown a tolerance to such activities.

4. No overflight by traffic, emergency, and police helicopters and other similar distractions may occur within a half mile of the nest.

5. These requirements will apply to all nests in the city and are required to be applied to each nest area until each nest area has been determined abandoned for a consecutive five year period.

This falcon example shows how regulators selectively chose where to apply species protection and selectively enforce species protection regulations. Regulators routinely avoid situations that would cause them and the restrictions to be called into question. It is easy to require the producers of natural resources, a minority group, to provide excessive protections for some species; because, these folks lack the means to fight unnecessary and unsupported restrictions and operational requirements.

While cities are not the wide open spaces, they provide habitat conditions and a food base similar to wild conditions. In contrast to some of their country cousins, citified peregrine falcons seem to be doing pretty well; however, because city falcons are interacting with humans and humans are providing wanted habitat in the form of skyscrapers, many biologists and enviros do not like this arrangement. Many advocating species protections seem to prefer unpredictable, chaotic existence in the wild, and there is a preference for locking-up habitats and hoping target species will find ways to survive without help from humans.

Another example of selective application of excessive protective measures not supported by factual information and authorized regulations involves the osprey fish hawk.

This hawk adapts very readily to human activities and human presence, and it is routinely seen in urban settings and people's backyards. The stories of osprey nests in folks' backyards and ospreys adapting to human presence go on and on and on. While fishing on beaches in the Fort Bragg, California area, osprey have come down and taken surfish from me and my kids. During a visit to a Boise Hawks baseball game in Boise, Idaho, I observed ospreys tending a nest during nesting season. This nest was located on top of a light pole which was overlooking a crowd of three thousand people, and the nest was located around thirty feet, right over the crowd. During timber harvesting operations I and many timber operators routinely worked in the vicinity of osprey nests, and we modified operations to slowly approach the nests while allowing ospreys to adapt to our activities. This approach to handling the osprey worked very well. We even had one situation where the loggers had to shoo young osprey out of the road every morning, because they would be in the road dusting themselves with road dust.

During my involvement with the osprey, it was declared to be a species of concern. It was not labeled threatened or endangered, but by god, it needed special protection; so, a long review was conducted, and a political compromise regulatory package which went beyond factual protection requirements was developed. This regulatory package contained buffer zones and various nest protections including the requirement that buffer zones were to be five acres and never more than eighteen acres in extreme cases. The regulations (Title 14, California Code of Regulations Subchapters 4, 5, and 6 Forest District Rules, Article 9 Wildlife Protection Practices, 919.3, 939.3, 959.3 Specific Requirements for Protection of Nest Sites, (b) (5), Osprey species) were put into play, and we all went about our business making things work.

Then the California Department of Fish and Game (DFG) on their own without any formal hearing review decided to push protections beyond that required by authorized regulations. While authorized five acre buffers are roughly 260 lineal feet in radius and extreme eighteen acre buffer areas are roughly 500 foot in radius, the new expanded buffer radius required by the DFG is 1,320 feet or a quarter mile. The DFG's expanded buffer protection area now encompasses approximately one hundred and twenty-five acres.

The argument for larger buffers says osprey's who have not adapted to human activity will be chased off nests and more easily disturbed. This thinking is correct to a point, but this concern was addressed in developing the existing buffer limits, and the added buffer protection is overkill. The DFG says osprey that have adapted can be treated differently; however, this spin is just spin, because exceptions to the quarter mile buffer requirement can not be found. In addition to the damage done to landowners, the reality is that a quarter mile of protection buffer creates even more of a barrier to ospreys adapting to human activities. The added isolation means there is less chance of ospreys experiencing contact with humans, and isolated birds actually become more susceptible to being disturbed and damaged by human activity. Maybe this nervous osprey is what the DFG wants to have; so, they can continue to say the osprey needs to be protected.

The Boise Hawks baseball fans better hope the DFG thinking does not get to Idaho; or, their baseball field and a large part of Boise will become unusable buffer area for ospreys.

To me, it looks like osprey allowed to adapt to human activities like the Boise osprey have a better chance of being around a lot longer than their isolated nervous cousins.

If given a chance, most species seem to adapt to human activities and changes in habitat, and this ability to adapt should be more of a consideration when developing species protection requirements. Some enviros and biologists resist doing this, and many simply say wild species that adapt to human presence are trash species and do not deserve to be called wild species. While many species protectionists write-off species that adapt to human presence, they still push for applying full protection requirements when these so-called trash species are encountered.

There will always be some special habitats that need to be maintained as much as possible in their current condition; but, the obsession to find and retain all potential species of concern and all involved potential habitats can unjustifiably harm species and owners of open space lands.

FIELD EXPERIENCE AND A LITTLE COMMON SENSE GOES A LONG WAYS

The following story provided by the internet(149) is a humorous illustration of how regulatory thinking has gone fruity when compared to what is happening in the real world.

This story starts with a letter to a landowner from Land and Water Management Division a part of the Michigan Department of Environmental

Quality which says the landowner put in two unauthorized wood debris dams in violation of some environmental laws. Dam failure has occurred causing downstream problems. The landowner is ordered to cease dam activities and to restore the involved stream to a free flowing condition by a certain date. The landowner is to notify the regulatory body when the restoration work is done; so, it can be site inspected. Failure to comply may result in elevated enforcement action.

The letter was sent to the wrong landowner.

The legal landowner did reply and a summary of the reply is as follows:

A couple of beavers were the ones who built and are maintaining the dams, and while not authorized to do so, they might be offended that their skillful use of natural building materials was called debris. The beavers probably do not know they need a permit. Are all beavers in the state required to get permits, and if so, please provide copies of such permits. Are the beavers entitled to legal representation, and if so, they are financially destitute and will need the State to provide them with a dam lawyer. Any damage done by the dams is a natural event and the responsibility of the State. If you want the stream restored, please contact the beavers, and as they do not understand English, be sure they know their rights. If your dam department finds these dams to be inherently hazardous and truly not permitted in this state, it seems you are interfering with the rights of beavers. Since beavers will be under the dam ice as of your due date for completing restoration work, why wait until the due date to take action?

Regarding another environmental quality health problem in the area, the bears are actually defecating in our woods, and if you are going to investigate the beaver dam, watch your step. You should be persecuting the defecating bears and leave the beavers alone.

"Being unable to comply with your dam request, and being unable to contact you on your dam answering machine, I am sending this response to your day office via another governmental organization - the dam USPS. Maybe some day it will get there."

Don't you just love it!

POPULATION CONTROL - NOT!
WILDLIFE AND HUMAN CONFLICTS

There are many other examples of questionable governmental actions and questions about how the government is managing wild species. There is a need to recognize and better understand problems created by exploding wildlife populations.

Fish predators have become a problem, and predator damage to fish stocks is routinely ignored as a main factor in the decline of fish stocks. Squawfish, lampreys, fish ducks, herons, osprey, water snakes, terns, and on and on all take a big chunk out of the fishery. Fishermen drag seals holding hooked salmon up to their boats and fight seals for salmon caught in the ocean and lower reaches of many rivers. Seals have been reported to take one bite out of a salmon and them move on to kill other salmon in the same way. A 2005 news article(269) mentions "About 40 sea lions hanging around fish ladders…at the Booneville Dam… have eaten an estimated 1,100 salmon so far this year, amounting to about 4 percent of the returns to date in a spring Chinook run that is shaping up to be one of the smallest on record." Squawfish, lampreys, fish ducks, herons, osprey, water snakes, terns, and on and on all take a big chunk out of the fishery." As illustrated by photo one provided in center of this book, seal populations are exploding, and a lot of seals eat a lot of fish.

OF COURSE WE ALL HAVE ACKNOWLEDGED THE FISH PREDATOR PROBLEM, AND WE ARE DOING ALL THAT CAN BE DONE TO MINIMIZE THE PROBLEM

NOT!!!!

So-called fishery experts have shown little to no concern over adverse impacts to fisheries by seal populations, and there has been zero effort at managing seal populations.

A conservative visual count (not including seals hidden in the shadows and hard to visually identify) finds over 1,500 seals in photo one. Assuming 1,500 seals each eat one fish a day for 365 days, 547,500 fish are taken every year by this group of seals. This amount of fish is equivalent to 42 percent of the highest salmon catch in California's recorded salmon catch history, and this seal pocket only represents one of many seal pockets on the west coast. Is it any wonder fish populations on the west coast are dropping?

Of course, the experts know best, and predators are not a significant problem for salmon and other fish populations. I wonder if these experts are interested in buying a bridge in Brooklyn?

A news article(150) says "Squawfish are...the voracious predator of salmon and other river critters...facing the...Eel River." The "...pikeminnow species in the Colorado River is endangered and affects management of the dams on the river." "The California Department of Fish and Game (DFG)..." has been trying all kinds of ways to eliminate squawfish in the Eel River including "...blasting them with dynamite cord, netting them and spearing them.", and as important as this predator is to the anadromous fishery issue, the so-called experts after all this time can not agree and have not learned how to control squawfish populations. The referenced article states "Two fisheries agencies squared off. The National Marine Fisheries Service insisted a cut in the diversion (to the Russian River) would be better for salmon who need more habitat. Fish and Game, however, argued that more water would just mean more pikeminnow." This is an interesting mix of ideas, because it is the DFG who routinely pushes for more dammed water for salmon, and in this incidence, they want less water to supposedly make it tougher on the squawfish. It looks like both so-called fishery experts are guessing as neither public agency seems to support their position with site specific facts. Words and theory provide perceptions and positions to argue from, but in this case, hard work and factual data seem to be lacking.

While I am for predator control, I have to stop and wonder when I hear proposed ideas such as that proposed in a news story(151). The article discusses how Caspian terns (a bird) are "...eating millions of young salmon migrating to the ocean..." "Researchers estimated terns on Rice Island (from just one island) devoured 11 million salmon and steelhead smolts in 1998 - a big chunk of the 95 million (one, just one, predator species got just under 12 percent of this salmon run) to make it as far downstream as the Columbia River estuary. After moving to East Sand Island..." they only consumed 4.5 million smolts. ONLY 4.5 million smolts.

The proposed solution is to spend "...$2.7 million ...shrinking the sandy expanses favored by the birds for nesting..." while "...creating seven new nesting areas in Washington, Oregon and California..." This is suppose to squeeze the tern off "...a Columbia River Island in hopes they find new nesting grounds as far away as San Francisco Bay..."

Two point seven million dollars is a lot of money to spend on an "in hopes" theory that has a lot of unanswered questions. Will the terns really go elsewhere to nest? How do you physically shrink sandy expanses while avoiding major environmental impacts on the area and species already there? Since the number of terns is not suppose to change and the terns still have to eat, what will the terns eat to make up for the salmon they are supposedly not going to consume? Since just moving the birds around does not change their intake, could the tern problem just be moved to areas with more critical fishery problems such as California? If this theory works and there are endangered plovers using the sandy areas being eliminated, wouldn't displaced homeless plovers just move-in and stress habitats south of the Columbia River? Finally, how will they keep Mother Nature from unshrinking the shrunk areas?

These stories demonstrate how the Fourth Branches of Government routinely do some pretty questionable things that show an apparent lack of common sense, and shows how regulators, biologists, and pseudo scientists need to be held more accountable for their actions.

There appears to be an unspoken rule among the biologists, regulators, and many enviros to not discuss and much less control fish predator populations. With the expressed desire to bring back anadromous fish populations, the lack of concern about legitimate ways to control fish predator populations and the small amount of effort that goes into controlling these populations is additionally hard to understand. Because they have promoted protection of predator species for so long, protecting these species has become the Holy Grail for many, and to change their spin at this time would cause a loss of credibility. Many predators are cute, cuddly, and exciting, and a lot of research money and power comes with protecting them.

Species population problems also include mountain lions, bears, deer, coyotes, geese, ducks, and many other species. While human activity and encroachment into habitats is partly to blame for some conflicts between humans, increasing species populations are also to blame. Overcrowding is forcing many critters into residential areas and population centers, and some animals like lions are learning to look at domestic animals and humans as a source of food.

While the human and species conflict problems routinely get discussed in rural areas, those with the authority and ability to do something about managing species seem to ignore or play down these conflicts.

Regulators and biologists are defensive and protective when it comes to wild species, and they routinely push the protection of humans under the table. Hunting restrictions, protectionist regulations, and media pressures have reduced most animal contacts with humans and their domesticated animals to one where nothing happens or the humans run away. This lack of adversarial contact between humans and many species is causing many species to lose their fear of humans and their domestic animals, and there is less and less incentive for animals to fear humans.

While cozying up to animals may sound nice, there is a down-side. Aggressive behavior puts wild species in a position to be taken down, and humans, especially kids, who do not learn the unpredictable and aggressive side of wild animals inappropriately put themselves in harms way. The wrong approach can get humans injured, killed, and eaten.

A story that comes to mind illustrates how everyone, especially kids, need to understand all animals are unpredictable and potentially harmful. This story involves a grown man who befriended a little buck deer while living in an isolated hot spring type resort. When the man did not show-up in the fall, some folks went looking for him. Upon arriving at the resort, these folks found a young hard horn buck in the rut with pieces of cloth stuck in his horns and pieces of the man scattered all over the resort area. This story illustrates you can get cozy, but you better always respect what any animal can do to you.

Mountain lion here! Mountain lion there! Lion here! Lion there! Lion here, there, everywhere! We better get out of here!

Despite the biologists, regulators, and media playing down a growing lion problem, media provided facts say otherwise.

The lion problem has really came to fruition in California where the lion is protected statewide. Lion damage to pets and humans is becoming a routine occurrence, and lion contacts are a growing problem. Per a news article(152) despite the protection ban, "...700 pumas have..." had to still be "...killed over the past decade for threatening or harming people."

It seems wildlife experts and public fish, game, wildlife, and park agencies are doing more to protect lions than to provide for human safety. Distributed information pushes the idea humans can easily avoid an attack and lions are not something to fear. My experiences and collected information tells me a lot of the public, wildlife experts, and public fish, game, wildlife, and park agencies are living in denial of what is really happening. Some things have been repeatedly said for so long regarding protecting lions and their habitats that many now accept these things as gospel. With the potential to lose some credibility, maybe pro-lion folks are having a hard time acknowledging they need to modify some positions they have taken.

DFG seems to play down the lion and human conflict problem by saying "only" fifteen lion attacks on humans and lion conflicts have occurred since 1890 in California(166). For DFG to play down a legitimate problem is a disservice to the public, and I assume folks attacked by a mountain lion think their experience was more than a minor incident.

Relatives, like my great uncle, who as a kid had to kill a lion with his twenty-two while guarding a herd of turkeys, hunted bears and lions in northwestern California, and these relatives could probably list more than fifteen lion encounters among themselves.

Secondly, because lions do a good job of hiding and staying out of sight, many lion incidents probably occurred that were never observed by humans, and many livestock and domestic animals killed by lions were probably never listed as lion kills.

In comparing my limited data for a seven month period in 2004 with DFG data, supposedly seven of the fifteen reported attacks since 1890(166) have occurred in the last ten years, and attacks are escalating with seven close encounters and multiple sightings in residential areas over a seven month period.

Additionally, who in his right mind wants to put themselves through the scrutiny that would come from reporting a purposeful or accidental killing of a protected species?

To deny there is a growing lion and human conflict problem beyond human encroachment into wildland areas goes against logic and information that says otherwise.

The idea is promoted that large tracts of set-aside areas are needed to maintain lion populations, and lions do not adapt well to human presence; yet, multiple sightings around populated areas indicate lions are easily adapting to the presence of humans. There are stories where lions like to get real close and to eat you up. News article(152) has a researcher saying "What surprised me the most is the degree of adaptability to what I consider to be high human activity in puma habitat,..." where "...there were literally hundreds to a thousand people living in the (research) area." Please note, the researcher calls areas with a lot of people lion habitat areas and not human habitat areas.

Isn't it logical to think escalating lion sightings are due to an increasing lion population that pushes lions out of prime areas as stated in a previously mentioned news article(170). In this article the DFG says "Mountain lions are likely being spotted in increasingly urban areas because they are being pushed out of prime wild areas by larger lions."

One news article(163) has a DFG official saying "There are between 4,000 and 6,000 mountain lions in California, and there are probably more today that there were a decade ago. Young, especially male, lions tend to get booted from the best cougar real estate, When the prime lands are full, the lions spread out into less desirable areas,...", and "Sometimes that means they're pushed into neighborhoods on the edges of wildlands."

Another news article(170) has DFG additionally saying "The (lion) sightings are pouring in. People in McKinleyville, Fieldbrook, Samoa (surrounded by water and beach areas), Scotia, Cutten, Fortuna and nearly every other suburban or urban area in Humboldt County have seen the big cats." "...cougars have been sighted in increasingly unusual places." such as "...young, thin female lion...at the corner of V Street and Samoa Boulevard in Arcata." "...near there two weeks ago...another lion killed two goats..." and "...was...killed by the U.S. Department of Agriculture's Wildlife Services." "It has been illegal to hunt mountain lions in California since...the mid-1980s.", and "...Fish and Game generally doesn't do anything about a lion unless it's acting aggressive or has killed a pet or livestock." Note how something bad has to happen to get the experts to do anything pro-active.

Kitty cats are nice, but too many big ones are resulting in a lot of hurt.

Coyotes are finding it easy to adapt to humans, and they find humans are very helpful by providing their dogs, cats, and other pets to supplement their diets. News article(180) says "Zoologists estimate half a million coyotes live in California (alone),..." near and in "...Los Angeles...,...Marin County...,...San Francisco...", San Diego, and all over the state. "Throughout Los Angeles small pets are frequently taken..." and "...eaten..." "In areas where predation on pets has been documented, cats and small dogs should not be left out after dark." In news article dated 1/5/04, "...San Joaquin County Animal Control estimated...the mauling death of three pet emus whose dismembered corpses were discovered...in a field...was unmistakably the work of a coyote." Emus are not all that small, and I have heard of small children being menaced by coyotes. There is little reason to not include coyotes on the list of wild species needing population control.

"Groups push Feds to protect bloodsucking lampreys" is the headline for a news article(181). "Lamprey are fish (are really more like eels)...with jawless, toothed mouths...that suck blood and tissue from other fish..." and kill fish like trout and young salmon. "American Indians on the Klamath and Trinity rivers catch lampreys for food..." It is interesting to see the groups supporting protection of the lamprey (Center for Biological Diversity, Environmental Protection Information Center, Friends of the Eel, Native Fish Society, Northwest Environmental Center, Oregon Natural Resources

Council, Washington trout, and various Native American groups) are also the groups pushing for increasing fish and salmon populations. Talk about conflicting interests; or, is this just a case of hollering for protection for the sake of having more regulations?

As a sidenote, I can remember reading articles in elementary school back in the early fifties that described how lamprey populations had gotten so big that the fish populations in the Great Lakes were in danger of being wiped out.

A radio spot I recently heard mentions the folks in the United Kingdom (Great Britain, England) are questioning another species protection program involving buzzards. It seems buzzards are considered an endangered species, and because they are no longer low in numbers and are killing other birds, some folks want to "off" them. Although not low in numbers and not considered threatened or endangered, I understand buzzards are also protected in the United States, because they clean up dead animals and the like. As shown in a buzzard cartoon, it sounds like the buzzards in England are tired of waiting for things to die and are killing things to eat.

Bear here! Bear there! Here a bear! There a bear! Here, there a bear! Yeh gads, bears everywhere!

From my experiences in rural areas, I have observed evidence of more bears than in the past. I have seen hundreds of trees eaten and destroyed by bears, and hunting information, population study information, and other antidotal information seems to scream bear populations are increasing.

Even eastern United States bear populations are rebounding as indicated in two 2003 news articles(188)(189) when they say "New Jersy (NEW JERSY!!) holds first bear hunt in 33 years...to reduce a bear population that has swelled across northwestern New Jersy...to an estimated 3,200...bears." The human conflicts are outlined in one article when "...state wildlife agency..." says "Bears have broken into 58 homes in New Jersy this year,..." and "...fifty bears have been hit by vehicles. Bears have also killed livestock,...bloodied a few people...", and "...have killed eight people over the past three years in North America..." The poor bear and bad human story is provided in another news article(190). "Leaving out trash or other food can result in bears being killed by wildlife authorities who consider them a problem or a danger. Everyone wants to own their share of the Big Sky. But there's an inherent responsibility that goes with that, said...regional wildlife manager for Montana Department of Fish, Wildlife and Parks."

The party line of those involved with managing bear populations and human conflict problems repeatedly say human encroachment into bear habitats is shrinking available bear habitat and human encroachment is forcing bears into conflicts with humans. The fish and game folks say over and over and over how garbage messes and other conflicts with bears (tearing into garages, tearing up fruit trees, breaking into houses, eating pets, and even bothering and harming humans) are the fault of humans for encroaching on bears' habitat.

While human encroachment is part of the problem, the possibility that high bear populations force bears into populated areas is not included in the party line promoted by biologists and regulators.

It seems even factual information provided by the so-called bear experts contradicts the party line's push to blame humans. News article(194) says Two "Wildlife Conservation Society..." folks say their "...study...debunked assumptions that the bear population was booming." Now watch closely how they inadvertently dispel the idea that the bear and human problems are due to humans encroaching into bear habitat by saying the referenced study "...found bears were moving from the mountains to neighborhoods (note: the bears are moving not the humans), leading to increased conflicts and more bear deaths." The article blames these bear deaths on bad human practices.

The party line thinking is being used to justify ordinances that punish humans for not doing more to eliminate conflicts with bears. While attempts to keep bears out of garbage may sometimes work, there is no way to keep bears from garbage all the time. Due to the impossibility of keeping bears out of garbage, ordinances will have to be selectively applied and inappropriate citations will occur.

Whoops, it looks like bears like humans for more than their garbage. A Los Angeles news article(326) describes how "A 140-pound bear wandered into a suburban neighborhood and took a dip in a swimming pool...", and the article was accompanied by a picture of a content looking bear holding onto the side of a swimming pool. Bear bumped "...into doors and windows before taking a few swims...", and children were pulled out of the pool when the bear got in. Of course this was the fault of humans that the bear came into the suburban area, and we will need to make ordinances that require humans to bear proof swimming pools. The homeowner made this sound like a harmless adventure with a bear, but I wonder how the homeowner would feel if one of the kids had been hurt.

News article(195) brings out problems with an ordinance approach. A resident "...fired at a bear after the animal crashed through his front door while he slept ...at...Lodge...near Reno(Nevada)." "...biologist for Nevada Division of Wildlife..." investigated the incident and "...found unprotected trash bags around the lodge…" "He said Washoe County's failure to enact an ordinance requiring bear-proof containers is partly to blame for such incidents." Now if I have this right, this biologist thinks some kind of bear-proof container will stop bears from coming around, and fines or other punishment should be given to residents who don't use whatever the regulators dream up as being bear-proof. Boy does this biologist need some real world education about bears.

My personnel experiences with bears and garbage has involved bears ripping off my garage door and chewing holes in boarded up windows trying to get to my garbage; so, I wonder just what the regulators have in mind that will do more than I have to stop bears. If the bears want to get into something, they will, and some silly bear proof container won't stop them.

Based on my experiences and a little logic and common sense, I have to ask "what makes biologists think taking garbage and a source of food away is going to stop bears from ripping into people's homes as described in the Washoe County news article?" Isn't it logical to think the harder you make it for the bears to get food the harder they will work at getting food. An increasing bear population is going to make bears more desperate and aggressive in their hunt for food, and instead of reducing their push for food, things are going to get worse.

With more and more bears coming into long and well established human inhabited areas and no significant loss of adjacent bear habitat, the fish and game folks need to do more to fulfill their responsibility to manage species populations, and they should be held directly responsible for inaction on their part. It is only a matter of time before something serious happens such as a youngster or other human getting hurt or killed by a bear in their backyard. Where repeated reporting of aggressive behavior has occurred, damaged parties should be able to bring lawsuits against any public agency that has refused to pro-actively eliminate the potential for damage, injury, or death.

Obviously, when a bear is killed, the problem is solved for that one bear, but this approach is not solving the overall conflict problem. Once a trait of easy food around humans is learned, there is little reason to believe this trait will be unlearned, and capturing and moving bears to unpopulated areas just delays their unavoidable return to areas inhabited by humans.

Fish and game folks of all kinds continue saying the way to handle bears is to not do things to attract them to you (as if this is something humans generally like to do), stand tall, and play dead or don't move. The one instruction I really like is the one to not move or play dead. I have read and heard about folks who tried the docile playing possum trick, and while this may have worked for some, other folks have paid a high price for using this advice. Some playing dead have been bitten in the head, clawed, torn-up, and drug off. Some even died and were eaten.

Over my many years in the woods, I have encountered a lot of bears, and these encounters usually went as follows:

See bear.
See bear run away.

One time things went a little differently during a cruise tallying timber.

I see Bear
I expect bear to run away
Whoops!
Oh Sheet!
Bear is running towards me!
I look at big boulders and no climbable trees all around me.
I decide getting high in all my heavy and bulky rain gear is not possible.
Out of options and feeling kind of silly,
I pulled out my trusty little pocket knife and faced the coming bear.

Bear with fire in its eyes gets to within 20 feet, stops, then turns away.
I turn to get away, but take a look back to be sure bear is going the other way.
Bear sees me turn, probably thinks I am running away, comes at me again.

With even more easily seen rippling muscles and fire in its eyes,
bear gets within 10 feet.
I tell the bear what I think of him.

Bear lets out a good growl, turns, and bails down the hill.
This time I make sure bear is going away.
I let out a sigh of relief and get the hell out of there.

Have you ever had a bear get perturbed and come at you? Well this story shows I have, and standing tall is not easy to do. It is not natural for humans to stand their ground like I did, and I only did it because I was out of options. While it worked for me, I believe I was lucky the bear was not a large one about my size at 240 pounds, and I guess I looked big enough to give him a tussle. I was lucky, because even 240 pound bears can tear a person up pretty good, and I sometimes wonder what would have happened if the bear was bigger and in an unstoppable really bad mood.

For damn sure, laying on the ground playing dead could have made me dead. To avoid the same unprotected situation, I obtained a concealed weapons permit and now, when I am in the woods, I pack a gun.

I heard about a naturalist and his wife who had been around bears for a long time and supposedly knew what to do (stand tall, lay and be docile, and supposedly did all the things the fish and game folks say to do), and they were found torn to shreds by bears.

I see things getting pretty warped with a lot of potential for unjustified things happening to humans and landowners. The following three "SAD" stories bring up bear issues including the cuddling and protecting bears to the detriment of humans. Ignoring an exploding bear population and labeling humans as the villains in bear and human conflicts is not going to lead to a practical and effective solution. Sadly, many people have come to believe species interests are more important than human safety.

News article(196) is headlined "Three bears killed". These "...bears have been damaging property...in the neighborhood for the past two weeks." Police and state game wardens were involved in the shooting of the bears. Letters of objection to the killing of the bears are represented by a Letter to the Editor(197). This letter stated "We knew these bears. Days before, they had eaten apples from our neighbor's tree (note neighbor's tree, not their tree) and accomplished a lot of sniffing. Local dogs barked and barked. This did not have much impact on the bears. I imagine the bears have met a lot of dogs in their travels. They certainly were not impressed nor threatened by them." "We heard that the bears had mauled a dog, and had been shot. Did the dog attack the bears? In my mind, they must have because the bears showed no interest in dogs in many visits to us." "A female bear is going to protect her cubs." "I care that three bears died because we shoved them out of their habitat (Note how "WE" shoved them out of their habitat and forced them to come into a well and long time established town), and then killed them when they did something any of us would do, protect our cubs."

In reviewing this story, we see how a lot of the general public has accepted the spin promoted by biologists and regulators.

Further review of this story shows a couple other things.

Bears are losing a fear of man and animals. Bears are allowed to roam, unbothered in our neighborhoods. They are cute and fun to watch as long as they do not bother "US", and it is okay if they do something bad to our neighbors. By routinely doing nothing about bears roaming around in our neighborhoods, humans are helping to promote the potential for more and more conflicts between bears and humans. Mother bears teach younger bears what they learn, and if there is easy food to be had, you can bet the young bears will be taught where and how to go get it.

The letter to the editor points out the danger from a mother bear wanting to protect her cubs. This is an excellent point which shows wild animals are unpredictable and should not be taken lightly. Without a change in thinking and more active management of bear populations, it is only a matter of time before some mother bear is put in the position of protecting a cub and some human pays the price for allowing bears a free ride. How cute and cuddy will the bear next door look after it mauls a child?

Another bear and human conflict story is provided by four other news articles(198)(199)(200)(201).

In this story, homeowners of a "...Lake Tahoe area..." home that was "...clearly owned by bear lovers..." as illustrated by bear things around the home such as a bear bust. Damage involved "...ripping furniture, defecating on the floor,...furniture was tossed about, cabinets were broken and electrical wiring and heating ducts were destroyed." Using a high estimate, "...$100,000 worth of damage..." to the west shore home was done, and the bear was found still sleeping under the home.

This story goes on to show how easily unknowledgeable lay folks can unwittingly get caught in an unclear regulatory and public misperception mess surrounding management of wild species.

"...executive director of Lake Tahoe's BEAR League, said she offered to remove the animals...", and the homeowners said the executive director "...found only one bear under the house and advised them to leave it alone..." as "...the bear would return or not be able to survive on its own if scared outside..." In short the so-called bear expert, told the homeowners to live with the bear damage and the bear living in their house.

The homeowners "...had no idea what to do,...". With no realistic and practical options provided by the so-called bear expert and apparently the California Department of Fish and Game (CDFG), they "...obtained a depredation permit from the state to kill one bear..." They "...hired three licensed hunters, who fatally shot a mother bear and her two cubs..." "The hunters told authorities that the bears charged them, forcing them to kill all three."

The so-called executive director, bear expert "...said the permit only allowed for the shooting of one bear, and she is seeking legal action against the…" landowners and hunters. She said "(We hope to win) a conviction against these cold-bloodied killers,…" CDFG "…submitted the incident report to the Placer County Deputy District Attorney…"who began investigating the case last week." "…CDFG officials stress, the agency is not suggesting a crime occurred."

The homeowners are being put through hell for very questionable reasons including having to suffer unjustified vandalism and harassment. The home owners have received "…phone calls and letters expressing anger over the shootings…" The phone calls and letters contained "…death and arson threats.", and "…500 calls in three days following the incident from outraged people as far away as Maine, some vowing to get even." were received. The homeowners "…consulted an attorney regarding the calls, but were told callers were protected under First Amendment free speech rights and there was nothing they could legally do." I do not think much of the local law enforcement folks and the contacted attorney for not finding a way to help these folks. "Vandals caused more than $2,000 damage to the homeowners home.", and "…owners think someone unhappy over the killings could be responsible." All this is causing the homeowners to consider "…selling the Tahoe-area vacation home…"

Bear stories abound in the Tahoe area, and include "…breaking into cars, walking into houses, and swiping pies off windowsills." Bears have literally come out of the woods for the easy pickings in subdivisions circling the alpine lake." "A 2003 study of black bears in the Tahoe basin found they had limited their range from 150 square miles to residential neighborhoods; didn't hibernate as long, or at all, because they could Dumpster-dive all winter; and they are much fatter than average bears."

Let's see, because of bad, bad humans, bears are fatter (meaning healthier?????) and instead of staying in their natural habitat, they have voluntarily elected to enter habitats occupied by humans. Sounds like the bears are doing pretty well despite the bad, bad humans.

Let's see now. Bears cause a lot of damage. Helpless homeowners are damaged and threatened with legal and physical actions. Public agencies do not step-up and help landowners. Misperceptions and harmful thinking is promoted. Unaccountable regulatory groups have the ability to inappropriately harass people. A major cause for bear problems is ignored, and bears continue to cause a lot of damage.

Quite a story, hey what?

Now for the last and saddest story about cuddly bears and bear mismanagement. A news article(202) tells how "A grizzly bear attacked and killed a woman jogging on a popular hiking trail near…Canmore, Alberta…just days after authorities moved the animal from another neighborhood for threatening humans…" "The bear was relocated after approaching…" a "…resident…", and it "…was tranquilized, fitted with a radio collar and flown by helicopter to a…National park." "Fish and wildlife officers…shot and killed the animal."

It was later determined it was the dead lady's fault for being where the bear could get her. "The trail…" she was on "…had been subject to a voluntary closure since April to protect a corridor designed to allow wildlife, including cougars and bears to move between habitats." An Alberta Wilderness Association says "We've kept on pushing and pushing until the wildlife has been squeezed out,…" See, the bear shares no blame.

This botched mishandling and human death should make the involved Fish and Wildlife Service officers feel real good.

These kinds of bad happenings do not seem to bother advocates for protecting wildlife as they continue to push for more wildlife corridors near populated areas. They "…have fought for wildlife corridors on the outskirts of the community of 13,000 where resort gold courses and mountain chalets have expanded into prime (prime mind you) wildlife habitat." Once the corridors are in place with their invisible barriers, everything will be fine as wildife will stay in their designated space and humans will not be bothered in their designated space.

The only thing missing in this warped thinking is putting bells on people as suggested in Idaho and watching for bells in bear poop.

Just how many bears do we need?

At some stage we have to say enough is enough.

Isn't it time to control and manage bear populations instead of just letting them reproduce at will?

Why do biologists and regulators continue to ignore what looks so obvious?

In the past, species population control was random and based on trying to improve human conditions. Predators were eliminated due to threats to livestock and humans. Hunting and fishing was driven by the need for food. Insects and bugs were eliminated to increase crop yields and reduce human health problems. Despite some undesirable results, these controls did help make things better for humans.

While protective regulations, different lifestyles, and enviros have changed the way things are done, species populations still need to be controlled and managed. Those with the responsibility to develop effective and practical population control management plans are dropping the ball. They do not actively try to control and manage populations at acceptable environmental levels, and their approach to handling species populations is to simply "help the critters do their thing and deal with the consequences later".

Some enviros, biologists, and regulators have an agenda that resists actively controlling some species populations. E-mail report(73) describing the need for a two million acre Greenline idea and species protection in the northeastern United States gives an insight to what some protectionists really feel with the statement that "...people's homes are the final insult to the land."

Why aren't stories of exploding wildlife populations told to the public? Are some ulterior motives in play? The knowledge that many species populations are sustaining and increasing contradicts a lot of what many enviros, regulators, and biologists promote. Perpetuating the idea a species needs protection and restoration provides a basis for more funding and enforcement dollars and strengthens the ability to manipulate regulatory requirements.

It is time for those professing to be wildlife experts to start doing their jobs and to start actually managing wildlife populations. Those handling species populations need to take some lessons from knowledgeable livestock producers who understand the real world of population control.

The constant drum beat that humans have to do all the work in solving species and human conflict problems is really getting old. If seriously pursued with an open mind, practical and effective management and control of species populations can be as lucrative and self-fulfilling as the one-sided protect species approach. It should feel good to be a part of building and maintaining healthy species populations and eliminating adversarial problems between humans and animals.

The majority of wildlife biologists, regulators, and folks who push to protect wild animals at the expense of human safety are ignoring the obvious. Without pro-active control of wild animal populations, conflicts with lions, bears, coyotes, deer and many other supposedly benign critters will get worse and will result in injuries and death for domestic animals and humans. Species will unnecessarily be put in harms way when humans are forced to protect their interests, themselves, and their families. In protecting their interests, themselves, and their families, many humans will unintentionally and sometimes purposefully be forced to break unclear and hard to understand regulations, and many humans will unjustifiably be cited, fined, arrested, and in general harassed by regulators.

Handling species populations is made simple by the folks in the United Kingdom (Great Britain). A radio spot report(215) outlined a problem involving how rudi (spelling????) ducks migrate to Spain where they mate with the white headed duck, an endangered species, and this mating is causing contamination of the white headed duck's population. The solution to the problem presented in the news spot was to kill the rudi duck buggers. Now, I do not know if I believe what I heard or not, but for sure, whether they do or do not manage to kill "all" the buggers, it looks like the rudi duck has a good chance of becoming endangered in the U.K.

MUCKING AROUND WITH MOTHER NATURE
IS RE-INTRODUCING SPECIES A GOOD THING?

Re-introduction of protected species into Rural America is a wolf in sheep's clothing. While downplayed as not a big deal, increasing populations of re-introduced predator species will unavoidably occur, and these increasing predator populations will cause livestock losses, human injury, and human death.

In the current real world of species protection, restrictions on human activities is unavoidable, and re-introduction of protected species just results in restrictions sooner than later. Activities that will potentially harass and interfere with protected species and their habitats such as herding, grazing, mining, timber harvesting, and recreational activities have a high potential for being restricted.

A news article(216) touches on the issue of interference with protected species habitats and movements. A lawsuit that said "...efforts to haze or capture bison that leave...Yellowstone National Park...were adversely affecting nearby bald eagles,..." was dismissed. Although this case was dismissed, I can easily see how this thinking will eventually be applied to hazing and other control efforts associated with human activities and the handling of livestock in areas containing introduced protected species. Conflicts and restrictions involving re-introduced grizzlies and wolves are already occurring, and there are no signs that regulators and enviros are going to stop their push to restrict human and livestock activity in expanding ranges of protected species.

As illustrated by the bison hazing story, there is more and more effort by enviros to drop the bar when it comes to restricting human activities around various species. As outline in another news article(217), "...harassment means any act that disturbs or has the potential to disturb a marine mammal or marine mammal stock in the wild by causing disruption of biologically significant behaviors including, but not limited to, surfacing, migration, breeding, care of young, predator avoidance, defense or feeding to a point where such behavioral patterns are significantly altered." The enviros do not think this definition does enough, and they are gaining ground in their push for looser use of the harassment standard.

"Environmental groups sued the Navy in federal court...saying the sonar tests harmed or were responsible for the deaths of mammals...", and "U.S. Magistrate...in San Francisco...curtailed...the geographic areas where the Navy could conduct the underwater sound tests."

You airplane pilots and I guess anyone who takes to the air better look out for the bird harassment police as described in news article(218). "Salinas helicopter pilot ...stands accused by the federal government of buzzing bevies of beleaguered birds at Big Sur with his whirlybird." The pilot "...demurred...when asked whether he was aiming for...43 common murres, a threatened species..." when they flushed while helicopter "...was used to televise...18th annual Big Sur International Marathon..." Helicopter was also utilized "...to insure the runners' safety..." and "...to spot injured runners..." "...helicopters had been used at the event since 1994..., because cell-phone reception is spotty along the route. The aircraft has a birds-eye view and can immediately report to emergency officials..." Helicopter pilot "...has been ordered to appear before U.S. Magistrate...in San Jose..." which must be where the pilot demurred.

Hummmmmm! If harassment of endangered birds is such a big deal along the run's route, I wonder how you are going to keep runners and other human activity from bothering the endangered birds during future beach runs? Should the run be stopped all together? Quite a quandary, hey what?

I wonder what will happen when someone kills an endangered species while in flight? Obviously such a thing routinely happens as mentioned in Letter to the Editor(219). "History is full of accidents and incidents resulting from aircraft bird strikes." Regarding development of wetlands and water fowl habitat near any airport, the letter said "Our country spends millions of dollars each year in bird mitigation efforts at airports..." "Why spend taxpayer dollars now to create a hazard...?" As our skies fill with more and more things that can hit, hurt, kill, and harass birds, it is obvious regulators will not be far behind doing what they can to harass the humans who are harassing flying species.

A lower and lower harassment standard has the potential to adversely affect everyone. The regulators are now able to interfere with how people conduct their every day lives when protected species move-in next door. Bird feeders are coming under scrutiny, and use of the barbie when cooking hamburgers may be next. The dog police could become very busy if any dog in the woods is determined to be a potential source of harassment. Plover concerns are already restricting dog activity on beaches, and human presence has been labeled bad for species like the osprey during nesting periods. Imagine what will happen as wolves, grizzlies, red legged frogs, tiger salamanders, and all kinds of protected species are found in ever expanding areas. Already recreational activity is being shut-down, natural resource production is being curtailed, human activities once thought benign have become grounds for infraction and misdemeanor citations, and fire access and firefighting activity (building fire trails and using river water) is being curtailed and prohibited.

With harassment restrictions being applied to national defense efforts and to use of river water for fighting fire, it appears the rest of us do not stand much chance holding off the harassment police.

As illustrated in internet report(220), rural folks are being harassed in how they use their backyards and how they manage their livestock. This internet report tells how "...Defenders of Wildlife (DOW)...partnered with...Fish and Wildlife Service (FWS)...", and DOW agreed to "...pay for damage and compensate ranchers (for stock losses)." There has been an arbitrary change in thinking, and "DOW recently sent a letter to a ranch family in Montana..." that "...lose sheep to grizzly bears..." The letter said "...they (DOW) have decided to refine the terms of our Grizzly Bear Compensation Trust..." as "...there are some places where it simply does not make sense to encourage sheep grazing...", and "DOW will no longer pay compensation for sheep depredation by grizzly bears..." on some public lands. This example shows how the rural folks are being jacked around by those with the power to do so, and the spin that re-introducing species like wolves and grizzly bears will not be a problem is misleading, false, and not realistic.

Wolves are being re-introduced into western states, and news article(221) mentions "...guidelines for dealing with wolves that may migrate from Yellowstone National Park and Idaho where they were released in the 1990s." May migrate? Of course, they will migrate. What is there to stop them? Isn't the intent to increase the population, and when the population increases, it has to branch out in the search for food. "The prospect of wild wolves in Colorado for the first time since the mid-1930s horrifies some Coloradans..." "Ranchers fear the loss of livestock and grazing right on public land if the federally protected animals once again wander the state." Activities interfering with wolf activities such as grazing and herding livestock could be considered harassment and stopped. It is amusing how many folks expect you to believe wolf populations will not increase and spread outside some boundaries drawn on a map. They seem to assume wolves can read and will voluntarily not cross some invisible boundary shown on a map.

At this point, a joke by an Idaho spokesman regarding the introduction of grizzlies into the western states is in order. As I remember, this joke went as follows.

At a meeting, residents expressed concerns about grizzlies attacking humans, especially young kids. The idea was presented that making noise such as that provided by putting bells on kids might be a good idea. Another resident asked what would happen to rogue and bad bears? After a long winded explanation that provided no practical answer, the person trying to dodge the questions said "telling a bad bear from the good ones is pretty hard to do". At this comment, another resident spoke up and said "telling the bad bears from the good ones will be no problem, because all you have to do is look for bells in the bear poop.

ACCENTUATING THE NEGATIVE

Over the course of my life when reviewing problems and issues, I have developed a process of finding the good and the bad in any problem or issue. I then figure out how to correct the bad and how to improve on the good. If I am in a position to actually work on the problem or the issue, I roll my sleeves up and work to improve and make things better. When new and better thinking and information comes along that can be substantiated and verified, I use it, but if this thinking and information looks questionable or can not be substantiated, I avoid using it until I can substantiate and verify it. Why do the enviros, regulators, and their accomplices, the media, not do the same?

I routinely see environmental protection activities promoted by enviros, regulators, and media which concentrate on the negative while ignoring the positive. By this I mean, there is a concentrated focus on what has gone wrong, and not on the positive that has occurred. Preservation is promoted and management of our wildlands is played up as a necessary evil. A concentrated focus on eliminating perceived bad things mixed with the ability of protectionist thinking folks to influence environmental protection decisions often results in throwing the baby out with the bath water just to stop having polluted water.

Three examples where enviros, regulators, and media emphasis the negative and promote eliminating the good are:

- The push to only use wild fish to build fish populations and to eliminate other acceptable ways to raise fish.

- Elimination of road access needed to prevent waste, damage, injury, and death due to fire, disease, and insects.

- Not recognizing the importance of disturbance in the overall scheme of things and preventing proper application of disturbance to make things better for species and humans.

The enviros' and media's fixation on eliminating the good and accentuating the negative is not just confined to wildland situations.

The SUV issue provides an example where the good is routinely ignored. Assuming less human injury is a desired goal, an honest look at accident statistics should find less injuries occur in larger, stouter vehicles such as larger SUVs and pick-up trucks. Additionally, increased control provided by four wheel drive SUVs in bad conditions should be a plus. Instead of working to understand and eliminate gas usage and small SUV accident problems, there seems to be a push to eliminate all SUVs and to ignore the good provided by SUVs.

A book titled "The Bias Against Guns" by John R. Lott, Jr. demonstrates with factual numbers how access to guns for defensive reasons has protected far, far more people from harm than have been hurt due to inappropriate gun use. Again, I assume it is an overall good thing for individuals and society to have less people harmed because guns are available to law abiding people versus a situation where only criminals have guns. Why is there more emphasis on the fewer bad incidents with guns and hardy any recognition of the good that occurs? Why isn't there more emphasis on enforcing existing gun laws that are not adequately applied versus the continual drum beat for more gun laws and less guns?

The list goes on and on and on about things the enviros, regulators, and the media work to eliminate that could improve species and human conditions. Humans could accomplish a lot more by accentuating the good instead of accentuating the negative.

Go figure?

BEING SMART

Unfortunately many regulators and enviros are not smart and can not stand to just butt out. They push to apply unproven science and ideas through governmental taxpayer supported programs and through required mitigations in governmental permits. They keep making and applying poor laws based on pseudo science and political pressure that are causing damage to species and their habitats, to our natural resources, and to our rural communities.

There is a need to recognize and understand natural sedimentation, vegetative, and stability processes, and humans need to do a better job of picking and choosing when and where to help Mother Nature. There is little humans can do to stop and change many natural processes, and in many situations when damage has occurred, it is can be better to stand back and let Mother Nature do her healing without interfering. A lot of wasted tax money and effort would be saved if humans exercised more patience and took the time to apply time tested proven peer reviewed science and site specific facts in a logical and common sensical manner. Time does heal, and often humans can do more by doing nothing.

THE FOLLY OF THE BROKEN HEARING AND PETITION PROCESSES

Chapter Five

At board, commission, and committees levels of government, the hearing, appeal, and petition processes used in developing, applying, and enforcing new regulations are routinely ineffective and broken.

Boards, commissions, and committees, who are part of the Fourth Branch of Government, routinely do not apply legislated laws and regulations as intended by higher levels of government, and a lack of accountability oversight by legislatures and other higher levels of government allows serious failings in hearing and regulatory processes to go unabated. These regulatory groups pretty well do as they wish in handling hearing and regulatory matters.

Because member qualifications are loosely applied, influenced by political favoritism, and routinely do not require members to be experienced and knowledgeable, regulatory boards, commissions, and committees contain many members that are not qualified to be making the decisions they are making. This is especially true regarding general public members.

On many boards, commissions, and committees, there is suppose to be no potential for financial gain by members. Because experienced professionals, ranchers, landowners, and farmers are considered eligible to financially benefit from regulatory group actions, they are routinely considered ineligible to be members of these groups. This restriction on use of knowledgeable and experienced producers of natural resource products really aggravates the problem of regulatory groups routinely mishandling natural resource issues.

If an issue does come up which might remotely result in a member getting a financial benefit, that board, commission, or committee member is suppose to withdraw themselves from any discussion or involvement in the involved issue. This again limits the potential for knowledgeable input.

The trade-off of eliminating experienced and knowledgeable people in order to avoid potential self-interest conflicts is resulting in a lot of poor and often damaging laws and regulations.

With all the restrictions on really knowledgeable people being members of boards, commissions, and committees, membership in these groups generally defaults to existing or past regulators, lay persons, and academic folks. The domination by these types of members often results in regulatory actions based on personal bias, enviro leanings, and erroneous viewpoints.

When you get right down to it, it is a rarity to find any board, commission, or committee member that does not have some bias about issues being reviewed; however, it seems the process used to select and appoint members turns a blind-eye to this problem. I have even seen this blind-eye applied in order to purposely have certain biased viewpoints placed on a board, commission, or committee.

To further slant the outcome of board, commission, and committee actions, there are protocols and regulations that limit how these regulatory bodies can obtain and handle information. In many situations, regulatory group members can not freely discuss issues among themselves, and members are restricted in how they can obtain and discuss issues with others outside their regulatory group.

These restrictions provide staff and involved regulatory agencies the opportunity to more tightly influence and control informational input and to get their opinions and ideas a front row seat at public hearings.

Boards, commissions, and committees resist and routinely kill regulatory ideas not created by them or their staffs. Human Nature causes all of us to work at not losing control and to resist change. When those closest to us are involved, the tendency is to protect and support them. Regulatory bodies are no different. When boards, commissions, and committees are confronted with ideas or actions that might affect them or their buddies, they routinely use their slight of hand and shuffling abilities to bury and lose such ideas or actions in the bureaucratic cloud that surrounds them. The simple act of assigning a petition for regulatory change to a committee can be as good as killing the petition.

The public hearing processes routinely do not allow for all relevant site specific factual information, time tested and peer reviewed science, experienced professional input, logic, and common sense to be heard. A disproportionate amount of time is spent listening to a lot of questionable information provided by public agencies and staff members. Other input at hearings is routinely limited to three or five minute verbal presentations which are inadequate to expound on any specific point or issue. Most written input disappears into a black hole where it is lost and not utilized. Many hearings are a long way from areas being affected by hearing issues, and because travel costs, financial limitations, and job requirements prevent a lot of experienced and knowledgeable professionals and affected people from attending, a lot of useful and pertinent information is not heard.

In short, board, commission, and committee hearing processes have a lot of problems and do not function in a way that allows fully informed and proper decisions to occur.

A real life story which brings together how boards lacking real world experience can put in place inappropriate and unsubstantiated regulations involves a personnel experience of mine. The story goes like this:

As a supposedly green, upstart forester of I estimate around 10 years of field experience, I gave testimony at a California Board of Forestry (BOF) hearing. I explained how the new proposed watercourse and lake protection zone (WLPZ) rule being proposed for use in the California Coastal Zone would result in the loss of conifer trees in the WLPZ. I described how these buffer zones would slowly revert to being covered by low level, brushy vegetative cover. In the middle of my testimony, the Board Chairman, a well respected forester with a strong academic background and associated with the School of Forestry at U.C. Berkley, said I couldn't say what I was saying. Having been confronted by my peer, whom I respected, and told I could not say what I was saying, I had to hesitate. I quickly reviewed in my mind what I had experienced and I had to decide if what I was saying was proper, correct, and supportable. I continued my testimony by saying, based on my experience, what I had said was correct, and I could support what I had said. A little discussion occurred, and over the course of the hearing, my input was quickly and quietly disregarded by the board.

Later, over my professional life, I saw my testimony before the BOF repeatedly verified as I saw conifer trees struggle to survive and exist under applied Coastal Zone WLPZ regulations. These regulations did not allow for the creation of sunlight, mineral soil, and reduced vegetative competition which is required for conifers to establish themselves, to grow at reasonable rates, and to survive.

The thinking behind the Coastal Zone WLPZ regulations has now spread to other rules and regulations, and real world examples are all over the place which show an unintended reduction of conifers in WLPZs.

An example of the power, control, and slight-of-hand abilities wielded by staffs is illustrated in an opinion article(222) which covers the release of the infamous "...interim report of...commission... appointed to investigate the 9/11 attacks...by the commission's runaway staff,..." "...the staff's (and I emphasize "staff's") sweeping...twisted...conclusion was soon disavowed by both commission chairman..." "...that there was never any evidence of a link between Iraq and al-Qaida." The chairmen said "Yes...no question...there...were...contacts between Al-Qaida and Iraq..." The chairmen "...allowed themselves to be jerked around by a manipulative staff." One chairman stated "Members do not get involved in staff reports." Say what? Does the commission staff just do as it pleases?

The article goes on to explain what the commission has to do to correct things, but no mention is provided explaining how staff members were reprimanded or punished for their inappropriate and damaging misconduct. The article clearly shows damage did occur due to unprofessional and uncontrolled misconduct by the involved staff. From the lack of information about how the 9/11 staff members were handled, it is easy to assume "if" the staff was taken to the woodshed they were not harshly reprimanded or punished.

To further demonstrate how the staff and various boards and commissions control the hearing and public input processes, I have provided a listing of hearing notice and agenda and meeting requirements prepared by a California Water Board's staff. In reviewing this information, put yourself in the place of someone (member of the public, average landowner, professional, contractor, and so on) who wants to give constructive input on a proposed Water Quality (WQ) regulation. How would you react to the many listed requirements, road blocks, and hurdles that need to be overcome in order to give input at a WQ hearing?

A listing of some WQ hearing input requirements are as follows:

1. Written material is required to be submitted by a certain date. While this is a reasonable requirement and required by certain regulatory requirements, the staff is not very generous in giving adequate time to provide written input materials.

An example of routinely allowed, short period of time given to provide written input is demonstrated in a hearing notice I received. This notice was mailed April 24, 2003 and received a couple days later. It contained a May first, 2003 due date for written input materials. This gave maybe four days to prepare and deliver input. If a weekend and closed offices were involved, there may have been less than four days provided to accomplish the involved task.

2. The time allowed for oral comment is severely limited. These limitations routinely make attendance at public hearings a waste of time and money.

One notice I received stated, "Speakers should plan to deliver their oral comments within 3 minutes." In another notice I received, "Unless otherwise specified in the public notice for a specific item, the Board wishes to limit oral presentations from all parties (dischargers, staff, governmental agencies, the public, etc.) to 0.5 hour maximum per party, but may limit testimony to 3 minutes or less per party depending on time constraints."

As appropriate, permitees or recipients of violations are generally given more time to speak but it is rare that anyone other than regulatory agencies get to have .5 hour to speak. Generally, oral presentations by individuals and other affected public members are forcibly limited to three minutes. When time gets short, expect public comment periods to be reduced to less than three minutes or to just be cut-off.

3. "If the submitted written material is more than 5 pages or contains foldouts, color graphics, maps, etc., 20 copies must be submitted for distribution to the Board members and staff." Technical issues involving studies and site specific information can not realistically be provided on five pages; so, twenty copies are routinely needed.

While this may save the government some time and cost, the costly requirement to provide so many copies causes a lot of pertinent information to not be copied and provided to the WQ board.

Be advised, fulfilling the 20 copy requirement is not a guarantee that the board will review all the provided information. I know of one instance where nine boxes of information were provided at a hearing. WQ simply decided too much information was involved, and they did not want to utilize the provided information in making required hearing decisions. So much for a fair and impartial hearing review.

4. Speaker cards have to be filled out. This is a reasonable requirement; however, I have seen staff determine the order of speakers, and speakers are not always called on a first come first to speak basis

5. As illustrated by the following quoted hearing requirements, things can really get complicated and confusing for those wanting to give input at water quality hearings. A careful read of these hearing requirements will still leave many with a lot of questions.

Quoted requirement 1. "Please note that some items on the agenda may have been previously noticed with earlier deadlines for submitting written comments. In those cases the earlier deadlines apply."

Quoted requirement 2. "Note C, attached to this notice, contains a description of the hearing procedures that will be followed by the Board. Hearings before the Board are normally conducted using procedures that do not include cross-examination. Parties requesting use of more formal procedures must do so in accord with the directions in Note C." "Cross-examination may be allowed by the Board Chair as necessary for the Board to evaluate the credibility of factual evidence or in the opinions of the experts."

Shortened version of this requirements is as follows: Discussions with the board and staff at hearings needed to clarify and resolve questions and confusing items will only occur if the board wants it to be done.

Quoted requirement 3. "Items may be taken out of order at the discretion of the chairman."

This requirement is telling everyone that really has a desire to give testimony on an agenda item or wants to know the hearing results for an agenda item they better plan on attending the whole hearing. Overnight stays may be required. The ability of boards and staff to move agendas around is a definite disadvantage for the small people.

Quoted requirement 4. "The Board reserves the right to refuse to accept any late submitted written materials, absent a proper showing that information is available which was not available at the time the written materials were submitted."

Short version of this requirement is as follows: If you know of additional pertinent information or a better way to present information after the written input deadline, the board will decide if it will be considered or not considered.

Quoted requirement 5. "Testimony or comments that are not reasonably relevant, or that are repetitious, will be excluded."

Short version of this requirement is as follows: The Board will decide what is relevant or needs to be considered.

While there needs to be procedural requirements to provide for orderly hearings, this provided WQ hearing notice information shows how hard it can be for a publicly involved person to abide by all the rules and requirements. Hearing input seems to be purposely limited and made confusing, complicated, and one-sided.

Staffs have control over the make-up of hearing notices and agendas, how rules are applied, how proposed rules are written and presented, and how all input is handled. When it comes to input being recognized and utilized, there has to be a lot of blind faith that hearing input provided through staffs will get to the members of involved boards, commissions, committees, and legislators.

Think about it. How much public input and factual information that does not originate from staff and closely associated public agencies do you really think gets utilized in the development of our many laws and regulations? Who do you think really influences the make up of our many laws and regulations?

The current folly of attempting to use petition processes is illustrated by how a petition was handled which I presented to the California Board of Forestry (BOF). The petition simply required Timber Harvest Plan (THP) permit forms to be filed when received by the California Department of Forestry (CDF) as required by existing approved and authorized regulations. The petition required any discretionary questions raised during filing review to be identified and resolved during other applicable permit review and approval procedures. Sounds pretty simple doesn't it.

The BOF ended up killing the petition.

THP permits continued being returned to permitees for unjustified and unauthorized reasons. The THP permit filing process continued being a discretionary review process which is applied according to constantly changing, internally developed California Department of Forestry (CDF) guidelines not found in authorized regulations. These guidelines are inappropriately structured to accommodate various legal opinions and sister agency concerns. Many reasons given for returning THP permits can not be resolved without field review, and THP review can not start until the THP permit form is accepted for filing.

The California Board of Forestry (BOF) and the CDF have acknowledged there is no authorized regulatory avenue of appeal available for inappropriate return of a THP permit during the filing process. Obviously, the CDF has unbridled control over how they apply the THP permit filing process, and permitees are dead in the water if the CDF for any reason does not want to file a THP permit form.

The petition process does provide a way to expose boards, commissions, and committees to inappropriate actions by the Fourth Branches of Government.

For the good it did, the THP permit filing petition resulted in a good hearing of the involved issues and exposed CDF's inappropriate use of discretion in accepting permits for filing.

It was unfortunate that the BOF chose to delay and parlay the issue until it was worn out and forgotten, and in so doing, demonstrated their ability to not confront inappropriate actions by themselves and the CDF. Without reducing regulatory and environmental protections, the BOF ignored an opportunity to act within its authority to correct a wrong and to provide some badly needed regulatory relief to timber landowners and producers of timber products.

Based on my memory, past actions by the California Board of Forestry (BOF) can be used to further demonstrate how petition and appeal processes are dysfunctional. I have been an active professional through the full life of the current California harvest plan review and approval process, and during this period many, many petitions and THP appeals have been sent to the BOF. A quick and informal file review finds no appeals that have been upheld by the BOF, and I can remember no petitions requiring productive regulatory change that have been accepted by the BOF. If you leave out the confusing Redwood National Park and timber harvest plan fiasco, I can remember only one appeal situation where the BOF upheld an appeal of a THP that was rejected by the CDF.

The standard cope-out reason used by the BOF when denying THP appeals is to simply take the position "not enough information has been provided in the THP to make a fully informed decision". For years, the BOF has repeatedly used this position to weasel out of acknowledging inappropriate CDF actions and to not responsibly work towards solutions to regulatory problems.

Who can argue with the need for more information which leaves those appealing inappropriate regulatory actions standing there with their mouths open saying "…but…but…but…this is not right.

My review of past board actions finds the BOF has rejected an overwhelming majority of appeals and petitions brought before it. If we believe the BOF has been unbiased in their rulings, then we have to believe, at great expense and exposure to loss of investment, an overwhelming majority of folks brought unsupportable and losing positions before the BOF. I believe THP permitees and other involved professionals are smarter than this record indicates.

I believe the BOF record of denying petitions and appeals demonstrates how most boards, commissions, and committees handle appeals and petitions. This also demonstrates how boards, commissions, and committees support and protect the actions of their staffs and the other members of the Fourth Branch of Government.

The hearings on wildland fire control before the House Resources Subcommittee on Forests provide another example of how needed input and the obvious eludes the members of committees. These subcommittee hearings showed how development of a factual site specific understanding of an issue can get lost in a lot of socio-economic and political mumbo jumbo that is presented in a random, disjointed, confusing, unfactual, and biased manner.

This subcommittee tried to mix fact with political correctness, and except for some grandstanding, the subcommittee accomplished little. How to do needed fire prevention work can be defined if it is discussed and done by accountable, experienced, and knowledgeable professionals. It is not a politicians' job with input from laypersons to make specific prescriptive decisions regarding site specific factors. Every piece of ground requires different treatment, and the attempt to find a one size fits all politically correct, silver bullet is doomed to failure.

Chapter Seventeen provides a more detailed discussion of the wildfire situation.

There are many so-called workshops, fact finding meetings, and hearing processes where a lot of money is spent to develop a lot of touchy feely ideas instead of making a serious effort at developing workable ideas based on factual information.

A news article(223) describes how money is being spent on such a venture. In this article, harbor and county officials are going to review a consultant developed harbor revitalization plan. This plan has already cost someone some dollars, and more dollars may be spent to hire a group called "Humboldt State University's Institute for the Study of Alternate Dispute Resolution…" to "…lead a so-called interactive visioning exercise…" Say what? The future of the involved harbor and community is to be based on what comes out of this type of meeting?

Another news article(224) describes how a group is working on how to spend "…$1.3 million…mental health money…next year…" Using an assumably paid facilitator, "…fifty attendees…" meet "…to gain a clear picture of what a working system looks like." "The top vote-getter was 'respectful engagement'" This really sounds like a good use of public employees' time and salaries doesn't it? They'll have that $1.3 million dollars spent in no time learning to have 'respectful engagement' meetings.

As these two groups interactively vision away, I wish them all a lot of luck in doing the right thing. They are going to need it.

JUST THE FACTS PLEASE

If you could get boards, commissions, and committees to change, the basic solution to eliminating unclear laws, multiple rule interpretation problems, and inappropriate application of regulations is to make the playing field level for all participants. If applied, the following suggested actions can help provide a level playing field.

1. Require all new regulations to be based on experienced field professional input, site specific factual information, time tested and peer reviewed science, logic, and common sense.

2. Require all regulations to be clearly understandable and to not be open to multiple interpretations. To accomplish this, adequate review before implementation by experienced field professionals is mandatory.

3. Apply oversight on how the rules are being interpreted and applied. To have effective oversight, blind checks on how rules and regulations are being applied in the field are mandatory. Current lack of oversight and accountability when the rules are misinterpreted and misapplied is allowing regulatory abuses to continue.

4. Public agencies should be required to standardize rule interpretations and to provide adequate "infield" training on how the rules are to be applied. Hastily thrown together crowded room training sessions that leave multiple questions unanswered are not going to get the job done.

5. Peer review groups consisting of experienced field professionals need to be put into the field to monitor how rules are being applied. These groups are to make and send reports containing pertinent comments and recommendations back to involved boards, commissions, and committees.

LOOK AWAY! LOOK AWAY! LOOK AWAY!

The boards, commissions, and committees, part of the Fourth Branch of Government, have shown a lack of concern over the ineffectiveness of the hearing processes. Their lack of effort in acknowledging the referenced problems illustrates how they have little interest in correcting things, and there seems to be little incentive for them to change.

While the many provided public hearing problems indicate California probably has the worst public hearing situation in the nation, California's problems are not unique to California. I believe the described problems are inherent in all boards, commissions, and committees across the country.

The problem of board, commission, and committee decisions not being based on experienced field professional input, site specific factual information, time tested and peer reviewed science, logic, and common sense needs to be discussed and resisted on a national level. Not being more upfront in discussing and attacking this problem has helped to create the mess we now have in California, and lord knows, without some outside help at the California level, there is no holding the line in California.

It has been a long and frustrating experience for me in learning how boards, commissions, and committees have made the petition and public hearing processes dysfunctional and a waste of time. While participation in provided governmental review processes has to occur to avoid complete shutdown of natural resource use, there sure is little incentive to spend your time and money participating.

FAULTY LEGALESE

Chapter Six

Many will say court action is the way to handle governmental abuse and to resolve environmental issues. When this approach is examined, it is obvious there are many problems with using this approach, and judicial review through the courts is not a cure-all.

The judicial review processes are supposed to be controlled by a blind lady holding a scale that tips towards the preponderance of factual evidence. This should mean the scales would tip towards the proper use of our resources and towards just compensation when a taking occurs. To the contrary, the judicial review processes have been effectively used by protectionist eviros and some governmental bodies to shutdown the use of natural resources and to take private property without just compensation. I consider the judicial court system lower than the Supreme Court to be part of an unaccountable Fourth Branch of Government as more fully discussed in Chapter Two.

I have had enough experience in dealing with the judicial processes and environmental matters to conclude judicial determinations routinely do little to eliminate governmental abuse problems, and routinely do not provide for proper resolution of environmental matters. I say this for the following reasons:

1. Court decisions are routinely not based on the most accurate information. Environmental law and environmental sciences are in their infancy, and the type of information allowed into the judicial process is routinely not site specific, time tested, or peer reviewed. The inability of the lawyers and judges to determine what information is right and what information is wrong, lets all kinds of information to be thrown into the pot. Routinely the desire to have some information, any information on which to base a decision allows unproven ideas and confusing information into the judicial review process. Layman judges and jurors are tasked to figure out what is right and wrong and to attempt to make proper decisions based on inadequate information. Judicial decisions based on garbage information results in judicial garbage.

2. Due to a lack of expertise and knowledge involving environmental issues, judges and jurors routinely make determinations they are not qualified to make. This lack of expertise and knowledge causes judges and juries to be biased towards conservative and restrictive thinking and to push towards erring on the side of being careful. This promotes a trend towards inappropriately restricting the use of natural resources at the expense of those producing natural resource products.

3. Judicial determinations are often very unclear and hard to understand, and they often create more confusion than they eliminate.

4. Any positive results from court action are generally short-lived, because they are ignored, not enforced, or circumvented over time.

5. There is no practical way to rebut biased judicial decisions. Except when complicated and costly appeal procedures are attempted, which may or may not be accepted for review by higher courts, biased decisions based on biased justifications are routinely allowed to stand.

6. Due to lack of clarity in many environmental laws, there is the potential for judges and juries to make their judicial decisions based on inappropriate and incorrect interpretations of regulatory requirements. Introduction of inappropriate and incorrect interpretations of regulatory requirements can be intentional or unintentional. In a court room situation, there is routinely no one qualified to question and correct inappropriately presented regulatory information. Additionally, there is no easy answer for this problem, because, even professionals applying these same laws in the field are having trouble determining how they should be interpreted and applied.

7. Push to use old existing case law gets in the way of developing proper court decisions. My experiences with the court system have lead me to believe the legal community will do everything it can to use old case law before considering use of new factual information that may create new law. The judicial processes and the ones running these processes, the lawyers and judges, push for their decisions to be supported by old case law, and site specific facts and time tested peer reviewed science are given a lesser priority than old case law in making judicial decisions.

Lawyers and judges like to control things, and they are obviously trained and educated in the law and legal matters. It is understandable that in their practice of the law they insist on working with information they understand and can control, and it is no surprise they are laymen when it comes to real world environmental matters. To them, the mixture of unknowns and variables involved with environmental issues and regulations provides a very uncontrollable scenario which probably really freaks them out.

PROBLEMS WITH USE OF OLD CASE LAW

Obviously, what has been decided regarding similar issues in the past provides a sound basis for making current decisions. WRONG!!!!! Routinely this is not true especially regarding environmental law.

A short list of problems associated with heavy reliance on old or existing case law in determining environmental issues as experienced by me are as follows.

First, the short history of environmental case law has not allowed enough judicial scrutiny to occur. Peer review and historical verification of judicial determinations is lacking.

Second, erroneous information and decisions exist in old case law. Improper decisions and improper information previously accepted by the courts is allowed to stand. The legal community and the judicial process resist acknowledging past judicial errors and formally nullifying improper decisions. The resistance to use of new factual information and resistance to creation of new law, limits the ability to correct erroneous information and decisions in old law.

Third, existing case law contains a lot of unjustified bias against the use of natural resources.

Fourth, except in long lasting high pro-file cases like the O.J. Simpson trial, time limits during judicial review processes do not allow for enough time to rebut and correct improper or inadequate information problems found in existing case law.

Fifth, the small number of environmental determinations makes it hard to find support among existing case law for situations involving site specific factors. To build support for a position involving site specific factors using just old case law, remotely connected court decisions have to be inappropriately twisted and forced into some kind of logical argument. This results in more poorly supported and routinely improper precedents that are later improperly used to support other poorly supported and routinely improper precedents.

An example of unjustified and illogical case law that has done a lot of damage is illustrated in a lawsuit understood filed April 26, 2002 by California Farm Bureau Federation, (California) Cattlemen's Association, and Pacific Legal Foundation against United States Army Corp of Engineers (Corps) and United States Environmental Protection Agency (EPA). "The Ninth Circuit ruled that the Corps did have jurisdiction over deep plowing...under section 404 jurisdiction...of the Clean Water Act...which require permits for those activities that "discharge" or "add" a "pollutant" from a "point source" into waters of the United States." "Deep plowing loosens and mixes virtually in place - the compacted soils to a depth of four to six feet. It breaks through the hard soil to allow the percolation of irrigation water." This definition of plowing looks logical to me, and is something we have all seen done by farmers and gardeners all over this country. "The Corps concluded...plowing is subject to Section 404 control because it causes the addition of a pollutant (dirt) from a point source (plow) into navigable waters (somewhere distant as involved ranch is described as having seasonal streams, normally dry, seasonally wet ranch land which pretty well describes most farmland in this country) at specified disposal sites (the plowed ranch land)."

Despite the illogical reasoning, lack of site specific basis, and lack of real world applicability of the Corps interpretation of Section 404, the Ninth Circuit Court went along with the Corp's warped thinking, and made new law that will require farmers to get an unnecessary and unjustified Section 404 permit that can take "...well over a year to get..." which will adversely affect "...approximately 43,000 California farm families (and their means of likelihoods and ability to hold onto their lands as open space lands) who grow over 250 kinds of crops."

A federal law is involved in this court's decision which means this court's inappropriate decision could be used to force all the farmers in this country to get 404 permits. The part of Section 404 that states "...normal farming and ranching activities such as plowing" which do not convert an area of water "into a use to which it was not previously subject." are to be exempt has been ignored.

Does anyone seriously believe Congress ever intended Section 404 to be applied to plowing a dry field, because an unmeasureable amount of dirt might very slowly migrate over land by some unidentified means for substantial distances to an undefined watercourse? This is how Section 404 is being applied by the Corps, EPA, and Ninth Circuit Court, and this application of the law is wrong for many reasons.

This unintended application of Section 404 demonstrates how layman courts are making uninformed and unknowledgeable decisions they should not be making. This judicial decision shows a bias in the judicial processes against use of natural resources and illustrates how Fourth Branches of Government can get away with abusing their authority.

Because this Section 404 situation really looks a little odd, I would almost bet this whole matter started over a confrontation between a landowner and a regulator which left the regulator with a bent nose. Because they can, the regulator probably then took the matter to higher levels until the matter ended up in the Ninth Circuit Court.

UNCONTROLLABLE JUDICIAL POWER

The power welded by judges to directly and indirectly influence judicial decisions can not be effectively challenged or controlled. There is no practical way to hold layman judges accountable for inappropriate determinations. It is hard and usually impossible to remove judges from the bench who are acting inappropriately, outside their legal authority. Once they are on the bench, judges can pretty well do whatever they want without fear of penalty or reprimand.

This situation has allowed many improper decisions to be made and to stand over time.

Judicial decisions can be all over the place, and the basis for decisions can change from judge to judge. The inability to control improper judicial conduct or to hold judges accountable allows the legal process to be twisted towards the thinking of any judge controlling a situation. Multiple and varied judicial determinations come from built-in bias as illustrated in many judicial decisions that unjustly restrict the use of natural resources. The fickle nature of the court system is illustrated by the varied judicial handling of the Boy Scouts, and the circus debate over this organization being a religious organization or a private organization.

A news article(225) illustrates the power held by layman judges. The article illustrates how a judge can hold the economic well being of a timber company, various contractors, and a local community in his hands. The article shows a judge does not have to fully explain and justify the basis for his decisions. While the judge in the article did not enjoin or shutdown a bunch of timber harvest plan permits, it is not clear if the judge provided a decision based on the merits of the case, on the adverse economic consequences of a shutdown, or on his personal feelings.

Additionally, this article illustrates how a bias towards conservative thinking affects the actions of layman judges, and provides an example of why a layman judicial process should not be utilized in making decisions involving scientific and site specific information. The article indicates the judge believes the involved company's "...logging had degraded water quality, caused flooding and damaged fish populations..." which was not conclusively proven. The article additionally has the judge indicating the listed bad effects from the logging "...could occur on timber operations not subject to the special guidelines..." being applied by the involved timber company. The article shows the judge has preconceived ideas that any state approved harvest permit could result in degraded water quality, flooding, and damaged fish populations. This expressed thinking shows how the involved judge has not done his homework. It is obvious the judge does not know the state will not allow timber harvest operations to be conducted unless all potential detrimental impacts are mitigated to a level of insignificance.

Another example showing why the layman legal processes and layman judges should not be involved in making decisions involving scientific and site specific information is provided in another news article(226). The article mentions a judge believes treating logging operations in a site specific manner (which to me as an experienced professional is "in a factual manner") "lessens protection for watersheds..." Per the article, what the judge has done by his ruling is to say it is better to require use of the current, one-size fits all regulatory prescriptions even if they do fit the site-specific situation. The truth and facts be damned, full speed ahead and apply regulatory requirements developed in far off, non site specific locations which are heavily influenced by inexperienced lay persons as described in this book.

As illustrated in a news article (227), judges are continuing to halt logging of older trees. The article is headlined "Judge rules against Forest Service on old-growth timber sales". The article states "The Northwest Forest Plan set aside 6.9 million acres of old-growth and younger trees in large blocks where commercial logging was prohibited to protect habitat for the northern spotted owls and other species. These reserves amount to 28 percent of the 24.5 million acres of national forest west of the Cascade Range in Washington, Oregon, and Northern California. Environmentalists continue to fight to save small blocks of big trees..." "...150 timber sales..." are potentially affected by this decision.

149

This article illustrates how a judge in conjunction with the enviro community can take and twist questionable public input and confusing laws and regulations to provide a basis for ignoring long term agreements and approved land management plans.

The examples are plentiful that show judicial authority inappropriately controlling natural resource use to the detriment of rural communities. A 2004 Action Alert(228) by California Licensed Foresters Association describes how Jackson State Forest, a state run forest has been shut down by judicial actions and a layman judge. The forest has been run by the state according to very stringent harvest requirements based on accepted timber sustain yield principles, and all the remaining old-growth on the forest has been put into protected preserves. Under this management scheme, this forest has been providing jobs and other benefits for years.

The enviros are not satisfied. They are now "...campaigning for preservation of "older" second growth stands." which some have illogically called "virgin" second-growth stands. The confusion created by many unclear and questionable cumulative impacts analysis regulations with the help of laymen judges, is helping the enviros to win the judicial battles. Instead of keeping good producing young-growth timber lands producing for the benefit of all, this story shows how the environmentalists are able to shutdown these lands for their own selfish reasons. Per a news article(229), an attorney for the enviros said "We have many options open to us to stop the logging,..." which speaks volumes to the attitude of the enviros and how easily the judicial review processes can be manipulated to stop even the best prepared and best intended use of natural resources.

There is no end in sight to the judicial squabbles involving this state forest which has curtailed and restricted the state forest's timber sale program. The potential to contribute around $10,000,000 dollars annually to help the state's budget crisis has been denied the people of California, and the associated loss of jobs and economic benefits will continue to hurt the affected rural community.

Even when landowners win, they lose as demonstrated in an internet report(313) describing a situation involving an Idaho ranch family. While the United States Ninth District Court ruled "...environmental plaintiffs must present actual evidence that a species is likely to be harmed..." to get an injunction, and in my words, the court ruled lack of past harm indicates future harm is unlikely. Even though they won in the end, the involved family had to go through a bad time and suffer losses to get a final court decision. The issue involved "diverting water from Otter Creek and killing bull trout...to irrigate alfalfa pastures for livestock." The enviros "...presented no evidence that the bull trout were being harmed..." and no one could identify any damaged bull trout since the start of diversion in 1961. It took full court review to come to the court's decision, and along the way, the involved family was ordered "...to stop diverting water to the family ranch...", and they were "...forced to buy about 100 tons of hay per year to make up for the loss of irrigation water for the past three years."

This Idaho ranch situation involved "An antigrazing, environmental activist group, the Idaho Watersheds Project,...claiming the family was violating the ESA (Environmental Species Act)...". This group's aim was "...to shut off water use..." and "...force the family into bankruptcy and off their land." For this family, "...like other citizens in Idaho and across the west, the Endangered Species Act has brought nothing but despair, hardship, and lawsuits. Instead of restoring fish, the ESA has been used by environmental groups to hurt people who work the land for a living,..." said a Pacific Legal Foundation spokesperson.

These stories show how the enviros have been able to use judicial processes to unjustly and selfishly shutdown sales and use of natural resources on public trust lands to the detriment of many, many other rural communities. The enviro groups are able to use unclear laws open to multiple interpretations and the layman judicial review processes to their advantage in achieving their protectionist goals. The judicial processes for reasons already described routinely find in favor of such groups, and these groups are routinely able to stop development and activities they do not like. The slant in their favor has additionally resulted in making lawsuits a lucrative way for such groups to obtain funding for other projects and for themselves.

Has anyone heard of the Our Children's Earth Foundation? I hadn't until I read a news article(230) which says this group is "...one of three groups that filed..." lawsuit "...against the U.S. Environmental Protection Agency, claiming...water permits for nearly two dozen oil drilling platforms..." have not been updated, and "...we're living with a much more polluted ocean as a result." This group is mentioned to show there is no end to the number and kind of environmental groups that know how to use the judicial processes to further their self-interests.

Judicial processes can produce some pretty weird and unsupported decisions.

A news article(231) describes where a judge determined lack of fog drip information was enough to ban logging on 13 acres. The article is headlined

"Fog drip plays role in halting logging" and quotes a spokesperson who says "Now the CDF has to take into account fog-drip in water scarce areas..." The article says numerous studies were cited to show redwoods can trap ocean fog and condense it into water which then seeps onto the forest floor and into underground aquifers. If any one seriously believes fog drip collected by redwood trees creates more water in wells and underground aquifers than removal of trees which pump water out of the ground, then I want to see if these folks would like to buy a bridge in Brooklyn. This situation illustrates how layman judges and the judicial processes can make any decision they want based on the flimsiest of information.

Per a news article(232), a federal appeals court of three judges ruled an area ravaged by fire near Lake Tahoe cannot be logged. The article says the U. S Forest Service wanted to remove trees to avoid dead trees falling "...haphazardly across the forest..." creating a "...campfire effect, as brush and new growth comes up underneath..." and to avoid increasing fuel loads and potential for a large fire. The article says the ruling centers around consideration for the "...California spotted owl and other environmental concerns." although "The government does not classify the California spotted owl as endangered or threatened." This story shows how layman judges can make decisions based on questionable environmental reasons that go against experienced professional opinion; even though, their decision may end up causing a lot of fire and environmental damage.

As illustrated in a news article(233), the expertise of judges has no bounds when it comes to environmental matters. In this article the ninth U.S. Circuit Court of Appeals will decide if the National Park officials determine the right "...number of people who can use the Merced River and area surrounding it without causing environmental harm." Good luck with the layman judges making a factual, unbiased decision.

Water issues involving various fish species are routinely being decided by layman judges as illustrated in a news article(234). In this article "...federal court agreed with the Natural Resources Defense Council, and found Bureau of Reclamation...violated state law by not letting enough water down the San Joaquin (River in California)...to keep fish alive." The "...Friant Dam..." water "...transformed...a region characterized by hot, dry summers...into an energy and irrigation powerhouse that now feeds some of the country's highest grossing agricultural land.", and this judge has the say on what happens to "...the number one and number two ag counties in the country..." When the ramifications for the involved rural area and the food production base of this country are considered, the cost of possibly helping some fish could be big depending how this matter is resolved.

The use of the judicial processes by enviro groups to restrict growth and business development is further illustrated in another news article(235). In this article, a spokesperson for an eviro leaning group stated that Calpine, who wanted to place a lignified natural gas terminal on Humboldt Bay would most likely be sued over the project. Enviros said "No matter where you put this facility it will be challenged every step of the way." This enviro attitude is presented despite the main industry keeping the harbor going, the handling of natural resource products, being in decline. Without new industries, the harbor has a good chance of dying.

The result of the Calpine situation was "Calpine pulls the plug" as headlined in a news article(236). The Calpine story illustrates how the enviro no-growth folks play the game by destroying credibility, creating confusion, and causing delay. They have been doing this for years and winning. Producers of natural resource products and politicians, repeatedly do not directly confront the credibility of opposing enviro information, and instead, they routinely play a losing appeasement game. Maybe Calpine didn't have truth on their side, and needed to call it quits. We'll never know.

The following listed Times Standard, Press Democrat, Buckeye Association Newsletter, and San Francisco Chronicle news articles shows a variety of issues that are handled by judiciary processes and routinely by layman judges.

A news article(237) describes how Sierra Club along with an activist group called the San Luis Obispo Mothers for peace has sued the Bush administration over security risks at California's Diablo Canyon nuclear power plant. This situation involves a real interesting mix of people and self-interests, and this situation illustrates the power and financial ability of the Sierra Club to branch out into all kinds of issues.

Two news articles(238)(230) mention the opening of 8.8 million acres of North Slope outside wildlife refuge for oil, gas hunt which I am sure environmentalists are lining up to stop through use of lawsuits.

Various associated articles(240) describe how layman judges are reviewing a decision by the Bush administration to open 330,000 acres (3 percent) of Alaska's Tongass 9,300,000 acre forest to logging.

A news article(241) has environmentalists suing two California regional water quality boards and the California State Water Resources Control Board over waivers for logging on private lands.

A news article(242) mentions 72,000 acres of land administered by the Bureau of Land Management in Colorado has been leased for oil and gas development which enviros and other groups believe should be locked up as wilderness.

A news article(243) has California Department of Justice getting involved in a fence dispute with a landowner, a city, and the California Coastal Commission. While this seems to be a small matter over a fence, I can tell you this simple fence matter has become very complicated, been going on for a long long time, and has cost the involved parties including various forms of taxpayer funded groups a lot of money. Ah, the beauty of our judicial and regulatory processes.

In two articles(244)(245), two California water agencies are filing $500 million taking claim against the U.S. Bureau of Reclamation for failing to deliver 37.5 million gallons a year from New Melones Dam. Much of the water was used to meet state and federal environmental regulations on salinity and federally protected fish in the Sacramento-San Joaquin Delta in California. Farmers in the Klamath Basin along the California-Oregon border are seeking $100 million for water the Bureau of Reclamation used to protect endangered suckers and coho salmon in another suit. A judge awarded $26 million to farmers in Kern and Tulare counties (California) for water given to two rare fish. One judge simply said "...the government is certainly free to protect the fish under the Endangered Species Act, but it must pay to do so,..." Take note that the involved judges and public agencies are playing around, giving away taxpayer dollars which could be considered nothing more than unauthorized and unbudgeted restoration dollars. Protecting these few fish in just these three cases is going to cost the taxpayers .626 billion dollars.

Landowner Association Newsletter article(246) describes how "The Pacific Legal Foundation has filed a lawsuit on behalf of Barnum Timber Company (a family and individually owned company)...against the State (California) Water Resources Control Board ...seeking to invalidate the listing of Redwood Creek as an impaired water body under section 303(d) of the federal Clean Water Act." "...re-listing of Redwood Creek was not supported by the evidence in the extensive public record..., fish...sampling...has shown that anadromous salmonids are reproducing in Redwood Creek..." in numbers "...amongst the highest ever recorded in the Pacific Northwest...," and "...all available literature and other information regarding the historic conditions of Redwood Creek..." has provided "...compelling evidence..." for not listing Redwood Creek. This lawsuit has occurred, because the original impaired water body listing could not be supported by factual information, and the water board has ignored volumes of provided factual information that supports de-listing.

As mentioned throughout this book, site specific facts are routinely ignored by the Fourth Branches of Government, and the Redwood Creek situation provides another example of how this is occurring.

Whether the ability for enviro and protectionist groups to use the judicial processes to advance their goals is a good thing, or not, will eventually be decided by society and historians. In my opinion, using the judicial processes as they are being used by enviro and protectionist groups is causing unnecessary and routinely unjustified cost and damage, and there are better ways to make the decisions that are being made.

TAKINGS

Judicial determinations are routinely not providing just compensation for private lands taken for environmental reasons. The determination of loss of value by a taking is a complicated matter requiring expert input. Adequate compensation for partial takings and loss of value due to inverse condemnation routinely does not occur. Layman judges and jurors are making decisions they are not qualified to make. The judicial process is routinely putting out slanted and improper determinations.

This section focuses on judicial involvement in taking situations. For information regarding takings created by Fourth Branch of Government and conservancy groups, please refer to Chapters Two and Seven.

After factual information has been gathered, there is routinely disagreement on how much is enough in providing just compensation when private property is taken; hence, the need for judicial review in making such determinations.

Taking situations take on many forms, and a recent judgment involving a governmental taking of water for endangered species discussed in a news article(247) illustrates how complicated and abusive takings can be. The government "...between 1992 and 1994..." withheld "...billions of gallons (of water) from farmers in California's Kern and Tulare counties." in an effort to protect threatened fish species. As mentioned in the article, the governmental practice of controlling water for the protection of fish species is widespread with water having been "...diverted from farmers in 2001" "...along the California-Oregon border..."; "...in California, where courts have halted diversions of water..." for environmental reasons; "...in Methow

Valley in Washington state...U.S. Forest Service plans" "...to close irrigation ditches..."; "...in New Mexico, the Bureau of Reclamation is seeking court approval to take water from farmers and cities..."

As illustrated in this article, there is an attitude among governmental agencies that they should have the right under the Endangered Species Act to take water for species' use whenever they determine it is warranted, and when water is taken for species' use, they believe there should not be compensation for damage or loss incurred by private property owners or human beings. With the taking of water mentioned in the article having occurred around a decade ago, the ruling that the government must compensate the farmers $26,000,000 for taking their water has been long in coming, and this story illustrates how resolution of taking cases can take a long time.

If the referenced water compensation ruling survives appeal procedures, it will be a rarity among environmental rulings. I have found most parties who incur damage and loss from having to provide protection for species can not afford the cost and time needed to get just compensation through the courts. For this reason and the reasons already discussed, it is rare to see a ruling that requires the government to provide just compensation for takings or losses incurred by others for species protection.

Another judicial rarity is illustrated by an opinion(248) issued by the Ninth Circuit Court out of Arizona which was argued and submitted March Fourteenth, 2001. Cattle grazing permits were involved. In the opinion, the Fish and Wildlife Service was found to have acted in an arbitrary and capricious manner by issuing Incidental Take Statements imposing terms and conditions on land use permits, where there either was no evidence that the endangered species existed on the land or no evidence that a take would occur if the permits were issued. In the body of the case write-up it is stated absent proven need for a habitat in an area and absent the presence of a species "...there is no evidence that Congress intended to allow Fish and Wildlife Service to regulate any parcel of land that is merely capable of supporting a protected species." "It would be improper to force (permittees) to prove that the species does not exist on the permitted area...because it would require (permittees) to meet the burden statutorily imposed on the agency, and because it would be requiring it to prove a negative."

Sounds like what the Ninth Circuit Court determined should not be done is the way things are done in California. In California, permitees are routinely required to prove species absence or lack of habitat for species of concern in a permit area; or, when absence is not proven, mitigations must be applied to protect potential habitat for the involved species. Too bad California permittees can't get in front of the referenced Ninth Circuit Court to get some relief.

It was surprising to find the mention of another case in the body of the referenced court decision(248) that said "Other courts similarly have found that an activity may constitute "harm" even though the harm is indirect and prospective, see e.g., Greenpeace v. Nat'l Marine Fisheries Serv., 106 F. Supp.2d 1066 (W.D. Wash. 2000) (finding that Alaskan fisheries' operations may constitute a taking of the Stellar sea lion because the fisheries are catching fish normally eaten by the sea lion)". This case is a real scary one if it is allowed to be applied anywhere a resource is used that might also be eaten or utilized by a species of concern. This case also illustrates a weakness and inappropriateness of using old case law in place of site specific facts, proven science, logic, and common sense.

A news article(249) shows how a city government and the judicial system can team-up to twist the interpretation of a supposedly clearly understood law to take private property. The article states "Under a state law that allows governments to seize land designated as "urbanized and blighted,..." California City (actual city name) was given permission by a court "...to take more than 700 acres from (multiple) private landowners, paying..." for the land. It is debated by the landowners that the sale price was a fair price and some landowners say "...land...must be worth much more than what the city offered." Land is to be used for an "...auto testing track..." by Hyundai that is hoped to "...bring a wealth of property taxes for a struggling town,..." Sale area is "...anything but "urbanized"...lies 100 miles north of Los Angeles set amid a lonely expanse of Mojave Desert dotted with Joshua trees and scrub brush." One owner of 20 acres said the land is "...pristine and hardly anybody's out there and there's no tracks or anything..." "And it's been like that for hundreds of years." "Environmentalists have filed suit to stop ongoing construction because "...the project could destroy land that is home to the threatened Mojave ground squirrel and desert tortoise. Hyundai said it is protecting and relocating the species, and they hired President Clinton's former secretary of the Interior Department to win permits for the project."

This situation raises all kinds of interesting things.

President Clinton's former secretary of the Interior Department was in the middle of the spotted owl deal. While in this position, he sure didn't show a lot of concern for communities adversely affect by species protection requirements, and I believe he would have resisted destroying habitat and moving any species around as a way of protecting them. What has changed President Clinton's former Secretary of the Interior Department's thinking?

Media slant appears to be for the project and for taking private property for private industrial use. The taking of private property without justification is nothing new in the game of species protection, but taking private property for private industry use is a new twist and sets a troublesome precedent in applying a new law. Why the seemingly obvious change in media thinking?

If the enviro lawsuit results in designation of some lands as needed habitat for certain listed species, loss of private property values and inverse condemnation will occur. Future uses of private properties adjacent to designated species' protection areas and on properties within designated species' protection areas will be restricted by species' protection requirements. Such restrictions will reduce the number and kind of potential purchasers for the involved properties.

This is a case where all kinds of worlds and issues collide (private property rights, taking of private property without just compensation, inappropriate use of laws, poor layman court decisions, questionable enviro and species protection, different societal needs, possible use of political clout, media taking an unusual position).

With a recent 2005 Supreme Court decision(250), the ability of courts to let the Fourth Branches of Government take private property for questionable reasons has been strengthened. "Cities may bulldoze people's homes to make way for shopping malls or other private development..." the court gave "...local governments broad power to seize private property to generate tax revenue." Do we still live in the United States? In this ruling, eminent domain and "...the Fifth Amendment, which allows government to take private property if the land is for public use,..." was broadly interpreted to mean the promise of "...more jobs and revenue." Justice Stevens said "Promoting economic development is a traditional and long accepted function of government.", and local officials are better positioned than federal judges to decide what is best for the local community." Boy, will this ruling open the door to all kinds of abusive actions by local Fourth Branches of Government.

In summary, regarding environmental issues, the legal judicial processes can be called a crap shoot which is weighted against private landowners and producers of natural resource products. The truth gets watered down and routinely lost in cases involving environmental issues. Decisions are more often than not based on who out-lawyers who, and who can provide the most environmental friendly, moral high ground position to laymen judges and juries.

As time moves along, the situation gets worse and worse as more and more biased environmental case law is developed. The lawyers promoting natural resource use, who do not understand how to use site specific facts and scientifically proven information and persist in using old case law, continue to lose. The legal processes make it harder and harder for site specific facts and scientifically proven information to get into the record and be used to make proper decisions. As incorrect accepted legal opinion is used over and over again to support and create more incorrect court decisions, the hole gets deeper and deeper. Incorrect case decisions are not rebutted or corrected and are allowed to become accepted legal opinion. Legislators and other governing bodies use the incorrectly developed legal opinions to make more unjustified and inappropriate laws. Bad law begets more bad law

Due to built-in bias and resistance to change, there is no incentive for changing how judicial processes work. These processes have shown themselves to routinely not be a reliable and practical way to handle governmental abuse, properly resolve environmental issues, and provide just compensation for the taking of private property.

My main purpose in listing problems with our judicial processes is to point out we should not naively believe these processes always provide the right answers. There is a need to understand the abuses and the limitations that are occurring within judicial review processes and by this Fourth Branch of Government.

Despite having put our legal judicial system down, I acknowledge use of this system is unavoidable for this country to function. Having no choice, away we go, following into the land of legalese. As we go along, it is up to all of us to recognize the obstacles and weaknesses inherent in the system of judicial review and to find ways to overcome and live with these obstacles and weaknesses.

I heard a speaker once capsulize the problems with the legal system as follows:

Precedent is more important than truth
Procedure is more important than bringing out the truth

BYE BYE DOLLARS

Chapter Seven

A conversion of privately held open space lands into uses other than the production of natural resource products is causing an erosion of economic support for rural communities.

The problem of changing open space land use and corresponding loss of privately owned open space land has not gone unnoticed. Some meddling and fussing to stop the conversions and loss of private ownership has occurred; however, those with the wherewithal to put needed changes in place have been part of the problem. They are not listening to rural landowners, ranchers, and farmers who are living the reasons for the problem. These folks are saying they need regulatory relief, and they are being ignored.

When privately owned open space lands are not able to produce enough income to compete with other highest and best land use values, these lands are sold to those not dependent on an income from the land.

When open space lands are converted from producing natural resource products, income needed to feed economies supporting and maintaining rural communities is lost.

Six factors causing conversions to occur are as follows:

1. The constant frenzy to purchase privately owned open space land and put it into protected areas such as wilderness, wildlife preserves, and parks is causing a loss of income producing lands. With a lot of money and a willingness to pay top dollar, nonprofit groups and the taxpayers are charging ahead and setting aside more and more lands.

With shrinking incomes from the land, it is hard for private landowners to ignore the high prices being paid for public trust purposes.

When logic and temptation win out and open space lands are sold to taxpayers and non-profit groups, the economic base of rural communities is eroded in two ways.

Income production is reduced, because many purchases are made with the intent to limit use of resources. Routinely perceived species' and habitat protection takes precedence over production of natural resource products, and it should be obvious how creation of protected areas reduces production of income.

Local tax revenues are reduced. This loss is often not noticed right away. Transfer of lands to public trust ownership routinely results in a direct tax loss when these lands are dropped from property tax rolls. A drop in local incomes and business means a reduction in various other tax revenues. This all reduces the pool of dollars available for schools, fire control, public roads, law enforcement, and many other local services.

Editorial(251) recognizes the problem by saying "...the endless acquisition of land by the government is a strategy that can be destructive."

A reading of two news articles(252)(253) covering the Grizzley Creek land sale provides one example of the high prices ($18,200,000) paid for single species protection. It is mentioned that Proposition 40 "...a parks, clean air and clear water fund." money can be used to acquire more land and timber near the sale area, and there is no indication voters are going to stop approving more and more bond money for similar purposes into the future.

The comment in one article(252) "We just think it is time to do it..." illustrates an unbridled ability many governmental agencies and controlling boards have in spending large sums of taxpayer money as they see fit.

The rest of the story and questions not mentioned in the Grizzley Creek sale articles are as follows.

Prior to the sale, excessive regulatory restrictions and legal pressures by the state and the environmental community resulted in severe timber harvest limitations. As referenced in the news articles, the marbled murrelet and old-growth habitats were the primary issues behind the restrictions, and these restrictions were causing an underutilization of resources such as timber on the sale area.

The timber harvesting restrictions placed Pacific Lumber in the position many landowners are finding themselves, where economically the best course of action is to not hold onto the land for resource income producing purposes. Newspaper article(254) highlights the regulatory restrictions problem by saying "farmers and ranchers—under burgeoning regulations and harsh marketplace realities, are increasingly under pressure to sell their lands."

The sale area is intended to be held as a preserve to protect the marbled murrelet and old-growth conifer habitats. Under these constraints, the sale area resources are never intended to be used to produce natural resource products.

The sale area's contribution to the local economy from tourism will be zilch. Species' protection restrictions and inaccessibility of the sale area due to steep topography, hard to traverse ground, and heavy vegetative cover will prohibit recreational use to a hardy few on very small portions of the sale area.

The news editorial(255) raises questions about the use of voter approved bond funds. Why are Proposition 40 funds being used for direct land purchases? How does a fund designed to "...replace culverts that block migrating fish from reaching spawning grounds." become a land acquisition program for nonfish uses? Apparently Proposition 40's fund was designed to do a lot more than has been mentioned in the editorial. I wonder if the voters really understood everything intended to be done under Proposition 40 when they voted to approve it? I wonder if Proposition 40 is being applied as intended by the voters?

The affected rural community had little to no involvement in the decision process and sale arrangements involved with the Grizzley Creek sale. A news article(253) provides a benign comment from the local Humboldt Taxpayers League that said "...wasn't familiar with the particular purchase...the league is in general concerned about taking property off the tax rolls..." This comment illustrates how the local folks are not trying very hard to learn and fully understand the impacts of such land sales.

While it looks like Pacific Lumber Company came out whole on the referenced deal, it appears the affected rural community will lose some of its economic support base and will not come out ahead.

Another article(257) illustrates the continual push to set aside more and more land in public trust ownership in a wilderness bill "...to ensure...2 million acres of California land and more than 300 miles of the state's rivers...will remain pristine for future generations." This particular article involves 100,915,000 acres in a state that is already over half in public ownership per California's Forest and Range Assessment Project 2003 Report. The mentioned proposed wilderness bill will "...permanently grant the strongest possible level of federal protection..." to the involved land which means very very very very limited use while "...banning development, logging, off-road vehicles, mountain biking, and new mining and cattle grazing..." The article fails to mention that there will be many restrictions and limitations to public recreational and visitation use for species and environmental protection reasons.

The thirst to tie up rural lands and resources does not stop at lands end. A news article(258) says there is a plan "...to create 1,100-mile necklace of coastal marine reserves..." along California's coast line. This plan "...could put up to a fifth of state coastal waters off-limits to fishing..." Putting this much area off limits to fishing has to hurt rural areas that depend on fishing.

Rural communities are starting to realize there are adverse impacts to having large amounts of publicly managed land within their area of economic support. As stated in a news article(259) "...outright purchase of land has increasingly become a matter of controversy ...notably in Del Norte County, where some three-quarters of the land is publicly owned." "Together the state and federal governments...(county and other governmental agencies not included)...own about 550,000 acres of Humboldt's..." acreage which is listed as 2,293 million acres by California's Forest and Range Assessment Project 2003 Report. "Boards of supervisors in both counties have expressed concerns over the loss of property tax revenue."

To those who say more Public Trust Lands means more tourism, governmental payroll, and governmental contract dollars, I say show examples of where these dollars have for the long term saved the day. To the contrary, I find over and over and over again where wilderness and park acquisition situations have not produced enough tourism and government program dollars to replace the economic void left when the production of natural resource products was stopped. Also, keep in mind governmental payroll and contract dollars at any time can be taken away and used for other purposes.

The more land they buy the less they let the public use.

While protection of park and wilderness values and species' habitats is important, unexpected and unjustified access restrictions are being placed on wilderness areas, heritage park lands, historical monuments, and park lands. For various reasons and because they can, public agency folks are not developing a lot of existing Public Trust Land, and all kinds of physical barriers are being put up restricting access to public lands. A lot of Public Trust Land is even being placed off limits to horses and hiking use, and existing road access is routinely being eliminated into many historical recreational areas.

As roads are eliminated and access is restricted, only a select few, the hardy and physically capable, are able to access our public lands. Senior citizens, disabled folks, and small young people are being denied access. If you look closely, you will probably find, like most of us, you are one of the ones now unable to access many public lands.

Many promised benefits from tourism dollars are proving to be false promises.

Public officials are continually asking for money to maintain and develop parks. It is well advertised that there is not enough taxpayer money (county, state, federal, and otherwise) available to develop all the lands already purchased for park and recreational uses. In the push to buy up more lands for parks, the fact large amounts of existing park lands lay fallow and unused is hushed up.

A guest opinion article(260) summarizes what is happening by saying "While our government is buying up private land, we are increasingly being kept out of it." "…often without warning and often without a legitimate explanation."

An internet report(105) by a resident of Virginia describes how many current policies are hurting many citizens and their enjoyment of the outdoors. When commenting on a proposed plan for the Jefferson National Forest, this Virginia resident says "One of the greatest deficiencies of the Plan is that it does not address the recreational use and needs of the average American citizen…Your Plan focuses on the recreational wants of the young…Your plan makes very little allowance for those of us that want to get off the paved roads, away from the crowds…" which requires in your plan to "…hike or backpack two or more miles." "…the Plan has a strong recreational bias against the following people: the old, the middle-aged, the infirm, the non-runners, the non-hikers, the obese, the full-figured, the gray-haired…" "With its template to decommission roads, to eliminate future road building, to further restrict access, the Plan is tailored to the recreational wants and abilities of a very minor portion of our citizenry: the young and the strong."

In California, the budget crunch has been used as an excuse to unexpectedly close off and shutdown historically used recreation areas that contribute tourism dollars to local economies.

Photos 2 & 3 in center of this book show California State Park's closure of a low maintenance access road leading to a good rocked parking area. While under Cal Trans Highway department ownership, this access road was open to public use for many years without any problems. The parking area and road provide easy and safe access to a public beach area located just off the edge of the closed road. As of the end of the summer in 2004, this access road was still closed forcing users of the public beach area to park on a busy highway and to walk across the busy highway to access the public beach area. How much effort and cost does it really take to maintain and keep open a short section of paved road and a well rocked parking area?

I personally know of a situation where Cal Trans blocked access to property they acquired which was historically accessible by vehicles. This access provided a unique ocean front experience to those less capable of getting around. Now only those capable of handling a good physical walk can access the ocean frontage area.

Unjustified closures of California state parks for budget reasons are highlighted in news articles, and it appears park department folks may be using closures to put pressure on the politicians to provide more money for park uses. Gimme! Gimme! Gimmie!

The following information indicates the real unspoken goal behind restricting access to many public lands is to prevent any human use of the land. When you are prohibited from riding, walking, or simply entering onto Public Trust Lands that are not part of some very very special critical species' habitat, how can there be any doubt about the motives driving those applying the restrictions.

The author of an article(260) does a good job outlining and listing many of the questions and arguments being made by those on both sides of the access issues. "…we are losing ground to walk on…", "…we"…adapt to restrictions that make some sort of horse sense…", restrictions are being based on questionable human impacts, and unjustified restrictions are turning allies for using public lands into anti-governmental advocates.

Another news article(262) which describes "…a bike trail project, stalled more than a decade by insufficient funds and wildlife concerns…" illustrates the increasing conflicts between wanted recreational uses of the forest and questionable species' protection requirements. "The trail…designed to reduce air pollution…might have to follow roads in some places to avoid conflicts with…goshawks, owl, and osprey nesting habitat." The pro-trail folks are "…hoping…to find…a route…within the trees rather than…down… roads…" Maybe there is a legitimate concern for a nest situation; but, the species mentioned are low on the regulatory list of concerns, and a decade long delay for wildlife protection reasons seems just a little out of line.

Letter to the Editor(263) says "Even equestrian groups have felt the sting of extreme green groups who have sued to ban horse packing in wilderness areas."

Letter to the Editor dated(264) says "As a member of the Wilderness Society…I am…concerned about the challenges that Wilderness Designations bring to… public lands…including access for firefighting, emergency rescue, trail maintenance and recreation." "Studies have shown that…Mountain cyclists…have similar levels of impact on trails as do hikers and horseback riders.", and "…Wilderness legislation now threatens to kick them off trails in California that they have built, ridden, maintained and shared with other users."

Letter to the Editor(265) says "Department of Public Works told me at a meeting, the disabled shouldn't be on the beach at night! You could have heard a pin drop!"

News article(266) says "Snowmobiling ban overturned by judge…in Yellowstone and Grand Teton national parks…nearly two months after they were put in place." "It was not immediately clear…what rules would be in effect for the 2005 season." I can see where too many snowmobiles in one place could need some control; however, it is questionable that such activity on top of snow that protects the ground until it melts away is a significant environmental problem.

A sad thing about all this is that without proper justification protectionist groups with the help of the Fourth Branch of Government have the ability to apply and make questionable access restrictions stick.

It is also interesting how access restriction problems and single use of the land ideas have not been emphasized and brought out into the open by the press and media.

Simply put, having more parks does not automatically mean more dollars into the local community.

While it is a good thing for any landowner to be able to sell his land without undue and inappropriate outside interference, converting privately owned open space land into Public Trust ownership reduces production of income and tax revenues needed to support rural communities.

Ask the folks in the town of Orick, California what happened to them. Chapter Eight describes the devastating impacts the creation of the Redwood National Park had on the town of Orick.

2.   On many open space lands, the income producing capacity is reduced by conservation easements that underutilize, limit, and stop use of natural resources.

While I have reviewed and worked with conservation easements, I am not a lawyer; so, take what I say about conservation easements with a grain of salt.

Conservation easements have become a major player in reducing the amount of resources and open space land that contribute to the economic base in rural communities. While resource use is allowed and landowners are provided a way to hold onto some rights, restrictions on resource use are routinely applied. Easement restrictions can involve no-use buffer areas, below carrying capacity requirements for livestock, and restricting timber harvest levels to less than sustainable levels. Such restrictions on resource use results in reduced income producing capacity and a reduction of dollars into the local economy.

My understanding of how conservation easements are routinely handled is as follows:

- Private landowner sells to another party or parties the right to own and control uses of property as defined in conservation easement agreements.

- There may be a middle man holder of conservation easements such as some kind of public trust group or governmental agency. These holding parties routinely get compensated for their part in the process. Such compensation may be a set payment; or, provided through increases in easement re-sale value; or, both. Taxpayers seem to be very generous in settling with middlemen holders of easements.

- In the end, these easements frequently end up in public ownership. Based on current market values, bond money and other taxpayer money is often used to buy these easements and to pay the landowner for lost income and lost real estate values.

Conservation easement contractual law has for all practical purposes newly arrived on the scene, and any involved parties can make an easement say whatever they want it to say. A conservation easement is a long term commitment put into contract form involving land and natural resources which has been given the name of conservation easement. Except for some existing tax and other regulatory requirements and standard legal requirements regarding contracts, there is no magical formula to be applied or list of requirements that must be followed.

Some basic things that need to be considered when developing a conservation easement are as follows:

a. All involved parties should utilize competent professionals (lawyer, forester, accountant, biologist, etc.). As a landowner if you try doing an agreement without professional help, you have a good chance of having other parties to the agreement take advantage of you.

- Many decisions involving very technical matters will need to be researched and reviewed.
- Many unfamiliar terms only understood by competent professionals will be tossed around.
- Careful development and understanding of wording used in the easement is required.
- Interpretations and those interpreting easements will change over time
- Regulations and those interpreting regulations will change over time
- Vegetation and site specific conditions will change over time
- Etc.

b. Be sure you clearly understand and want the goals of the easement, and be sure these goals are clearly described and easy for others to understand:
- Why doing the easement?
- Is the easement going to do what you want?
- Are the goals doable?
- Do you want to control future use(s) and treatments?
- What are the immediate economic concerns (release tied-up capitol, tax consequences, etc.)
- What kind of easement options are physically and financially available to landowner?
- What other holders to rights are involved? (Are mineral, timber, rights-of way, and other deeds and agreements involved, and if so, how do these need to be handled?)
- Does road access and management access situation fit agreement goals? (Are new roads going to be needed, how will property uses be allowed to continue, etc.?)
- A **BIG, BIG** ETC.

c. Easement creates a partnership - Holder of easement ends up with a say in management and use decisions on involved property. Landowner no longer has final and only say.

- Final easement holder identity and relationship needs to be known (Will original partner, trust, conservancy, government agency, be final holder of agreement? Is agreement assignable?)
- Are there administrative, maintenance, and management requirements tied to the agreement? (Is holder of easement to be paid money to service agreement or to fulfill requirements listed in the agreement? Is monitoring to be done and if yes, what kind and how is monitoring to be done? How much is to be paid and how often are payments to be made for the work? Where will money for cost payments come from? etc.)?
- Who is responsible for what (tax payments, management activities, monitoring work, road maintenance, etc.)?

d. What base information is needed?
- Before and after, or if you do and if you don't, information needed for valuation of total subject. In order to answer a lot of questions and to make needed decisions, an appraisal of values before easement and after easement will be needed.
- Timber inventory
- Legal owner(s) identity and legal description of property
- Current site specific conditions (vegetative cover, etc.)
- Current regulatory requirements
- Big Etc.

e. Just what is landowner giving up?
- This needs to be clearly defined and understood; so, dollar values can be assigned, and property owners can fully understand what they are buying into.

Some PROS and CONS from my perspective on conservation easements.

PRO
- Releases tied-up capitol for other uses
- Controls future treatments and uses of land and resources
- May provide for favorable tax consequences

CON
- Easement requirements involve review and mutual acceptance of management and other activities by all parties to an easement.

169

This will delay implementation of such activities, and there is potential for conflicts galore between the parties to an easement (partners, easement holder(s) and original owner(s)).

- Unavoidable changing interpretations of easement requirements and restrictions will occur over time (legal system and just human nature will not let original understandings remain unchanged).
- Current and future sale values will be reduced due to restrictions and liens placed on involved property and its resources.

THEY ALL LOVE THE MONEY

The whole process of holding, re-selling, and maintaining conservation easements has become a very lucrative business for many nonprofit and trust groups. Easements routinely contain maintenance instructions which assure easement requirements are fulfilled. Routinely holders of easements or other chosen contractors are hired and paid to oversee the application of maintenance requirements. Holding, re-sale, and maintenance arrangements seem to get little attention or public scrutiny.

Funding for conservation easements and easement maintenance agreements does not seem to be in short supply. There seems to be no end to bond money and non-profit donations available for acquiring and maintaining conservation easements.

The process of public entities acquiring resource income producing lands through a middle man process such as a conservation easement is outlined in a news article(267). In this article a private timber company "...has agreed to sell the land to the Trust for Public Lands (a privately funded middle man holding group which could be any privately or publicly funded group). More than $1,700,000 is needed to purchase the forest (land)." "California Transportation Commission has recommended funding for Arcata's $375,000 grant application towards purchase of..." the land. "Financing for the grant would come from the state's Environmental Enhancement and Mitigation Program (EEMP) which is overseen and run by the California Transportation Commission." Prioritization is such that automatic funding is expected if the state's fiscal crisis does not eliminate the "...$5,000,000 currently allocated to EEMP grants..." "The land would be added to the Arcata Community Forest." and management of the land is be handled by the Arcata Community Forest which "...will insure that this tract remains in forest cover for the long term."

What is happening under this sale and holding process does not seem to directly involve a conservation easement agreement, but the procedures and path to sale to a public agency appear to be similar or the same. When everything is sorted out, it appears Trust for Public Lands is to pay $1,700,000 to Sierra Pacific; the sale is finalized to a holding entity; the Trust for Public Lands is to be the primary holder or owner of the property (or easement in the case of an easement) until it is again sold to another public body such as the EEMP where operations will be overseen and run by the California Transportation Commission and Arcata. Arcata City is buying into the land by getting $375,000 of grant money through a Cal Trans process that provides money for such purchases. In the end, a public agency or multiple public agency arrangement involving Arcata City is to end up owning and managing the forest.

Some background information that is worth knowing is as follows. The land to be sold is near and adjacent to a community where a lot of the community members do not like timber harvesting, and an existing approved timber harvest plan on the sale property has met a lot of resistance. The land is high quality producing redwood timberland which can produce good returns if managed as timber producing land, and timber companies generally want to hang onto such lands. The resistance by the local community to timber harvesting was a strong incentive for the landowner to sell the land, and the resistance to timber harvesting probably influenced the final sale price.

While the Arcata Community Forest gets kudos for harvesting and selling some timber despite local resistance to such timber harvesting, community and city council resistance to timber harvesting has lead to an ultraconservative approach regarding the levels of harvest allowed on the Arcata Community Forest. There is a lot of pressure to only use the forest for preservation and recreational uses. Although the timber harvest funds are happily spent by the City of Arcata, there is repeated resistance and outcry every time a harvest is proposed on the community forest.

All kinds of questions come up regarding current and future affects from this sale arrangement. Is this another example of high producing timberland being forced into public ownership where it returns less to the local community? Was there adequate review of benefits versus adverse impacts regarding the local community? Will the mixed funding arrangement result in some kind of shared management and ownership of the sale parcel between the mentioned two owners, Trust for Public Lands and Arcata Community Forest? What is the connection between the EEMP a California

Transportation Commission and the Trust for Public Lands? What and how much does the Trust for Public Lands get out of the arrangement? Is there not a conflict with using funds from Cal Trans (a state highway construction and maintenance body) to purchase land and timber that will be used for local community forest purposes? How does this expenditure of funds fit into being a Cal Trans project or into what was intended by the voters regarding use of the EEMP grant monies? Is the $1,700,000 needed to purchase the property properly being handled through a shuffling of funds from one taxpayer funded entity to another taxpayer funded entity?

With application of a more aggressive but environmentally sound harvest schedule, the sale parcel has the potential to economically return more to the local community than will result from sale to the trust and the involved public agencies.

The local tax base is adversely affected when conservation easements restrict use of natural resources. Restrictions on land use and the potential for less income provide the basis for reducing land value assessments for land tax purposes. Also, generation of less income and business revenues results in less tax revenues. This all results in less tax revenue available for schools, fire control, public roads, law enforcement, and many other local services.

The impact to a local economy by individual conservation easements may go unnoticed; however, cumulatively multiple conservation easements can significantly erode the economic base supporting rural communities.

There needs to be a better understanding of the adverse impacts caused by putting conservation easements in place.

Enviro conservation groups say they are becoming aware of the problems facing rural landowners and rural communities as mentioned in news article(259) and editorial(251). It is stated that public land trust groups need "...to come up with different approaches to conservation not just acquisition.", and it is critical to "...work with landowners on a voluntary basis to protect their land." The editorial continues these thoughts when it says "...It is vital for landowners to consider ways to keep their land in production, and crucial for the public to help them do it."

To these comments, I can only say beware of the messenger, because there might be a wolf in sheep's clothing involved. The mention of voluntary landowner actions and different approaches to conservation can be a smoke screen to hide a major goal of protectionist thinking people, which is to reduce use of the land and resources.

172

As already stated, many landowners are being put in the position where economically they can not hold onto the land as resource income producing land, and they need all the options they can get to hold onto their lands. Conservation easements can provide a way to sell the rights to some uses and to obtain funds needed to hang onto a property. I suppose something is better than nothing, but there is a "Beware Sign" that comes with any conservation easement arrangement.

There is also a need to more closely check that tax dollars used to purchase and service conservation easements are being spent as intended by the voters.

For more discussion on conservation easements and their impact on landowners, please refer to Chapters Two and Six.

3. Various regulatory permit processes result in reduced returns from open space income producing lands. Regulatory restrictions increase operational costs, reduce operational efficiencies, reduce production levels, and reduce returns on produced natural resource products. Reduced returns on natural resource products makes the land less valuable to potential buyers as income producing lands. The slow to change legal processes have yet to fully recognize the extent of this quiet, hidden taking of value from landowners.

a. Unjustified and unnecessary operational requirements are routinely placed on operations producing natural resource products.

Equipment is often inappropriately limited in where and how it can be used. Unnecessary size and type equipment limitations can result in forced use of underpowered equipment. Such limitations can often result in reduced efficiency and production. Sometimes poorly understood restrictions and requirements result in unintended environmental damage.

I have learned the quality of a job is not driven so much by the equipment being used as it is by the abilities of the equipment operator. Many regulators have not learned this simple real world lesson.

An example of an unnecessary equipment restriction occurs when helicopters are required to harvest timber, and use of existing roads and lower costing equipment could easily do the job in an environmentally acceptable manner.

When regulators require smaller, frequently underpowered machines to be used to skid logs, unnecessary damage routinely occurs. Smaller machines are often not able to handle and control logs as well as larger machines. Extra skid trips and reduced control over the logs routinely results in extra soil disturbance and more damage to residual vegetation such as leave trees.

There is a push to eliminate road use just for the sake of having less roads. This is often a pennywise and pound foolish way of thinking, and it is routinely smarter to retain and maintain existing roads.

Roads provide access for management, ranching, and fire control purposes, and more cost and effort is required to get the job done when there is a lack of easy road access. Restricting and eliminating access routinely results in increased loss of livestock and agricultural crops when they can not be properly tended and protected from predators and the elements. Losses due to fire, insects, and disease are routinely higher when access is limited.

Many restrictions on road use are not justified and the practice of "putting to bed" existing roads by pulling stabilized banks and making roads unusable is being overused and creates future access problems. Future access needs routinely require many roads "put to bed" to be re-opened and re-built, and re-building requires duplication of construction costs and unnecessarily disturbing designated road areas over and over and over again. It often makes little sense to spend time and money destroying and eliminating roads, and then spending time and money re-building them.

Just for the sake of moving road use further from watercourses, new roads are routinely required to be built higher up on steeper slopes where stability problems are more likely to occur. Even when usable stable roads exist on lower gentler slopes subject to less stability and erosion problems, use of these roads is routinely restricted.

Regulators do a lot of second-guessing about Mother Nature and what is best for unstable land situations. Such second-guessing routinely generates requirements to re-enter and disturb nonproblem stabilized and healed areas. Re-entry of any kind loosens healed and stablized soils, and until a new healing process can take place, loose soils erode merrily away. Old hidden unstable conditions are often re-activated when old unstable areas are re-opened. Messing with old unstable areas creates unnecessary erosion and can result in a more unstable condition than existed before re-entry.

Regulators routinely require operators to "mess where they shouldn't oughta be a messing", and landowners routinely end up with damaged property, exacerbated maintenance problems, and direct value losses.

Regulatory operational limitations can result in unnecessary environmental damage, reduced income returns, and lower land values.

b. Without a site specific basis, many regulatory limits are placed on quantities of natural resources products that can be produced.

Regulations routinely require a reduction in harvestable timber levels when such reduction is not needed to maintain timber growth or to provide watershed and other wanted protections. Livestock herd limitations are inappropriately being applied to resolve unproven water quality problems. Many regulatory restrictions reducing resource use are being put in place which lack a site specific and scientific basis.

Unjustified limits on production simply means unjustified reduction in income to landowners.

Refer to Chapter Three which outlines how and why regulatory abuses are occurring.

c. Mixed in the regulatory scheme is the application of many kinds of unjustified sensitive species protection requirements.

Without proper scientific review and justification, the list of sensitive species being protected is getting longer and longer and longer. Regulatory protections are being applied to species that are no-where near rare, endangered, or threatened.

As provided by many examples in this book, low-on-the-food-chain regulators without adequate peer review and oversight are allowed to create and put in place a lot of sensitive species' protection requirements. Many of these protection requirements are required to remain in place for long periods of time, and some appear to have no end.

In combination with unpredictable weather and physical field limitations, species' protection requirements have restricted many management, harvest, and road activities to being done during very short periods in any given year. Routinely the work does not get done in the short allotted period, and when this happens, the work may have to be delayed a year or more. Routinely natural resource producers have to just suffer losses from not getting done.

The ability to train and hold experienced people to operate equipment and to do specialized work is routinely complicated by odd timing and shortness of allowed operational periods. When available, trained people are paid extra to keep them around during and between jobs, but routinely untrained people just passing through have to be utilized. The lack of ability to have and hold trained employees routinely results in all kinds of extra costs from improperly done work, reduced efficiency, extra required supervision, increased safety problems and unintended damage to equipment, resources, and people.

On top of operational period problems, the producers of natural resource products are left to the mercy of the markets available to them at the time harvest operations are allowed to occur.

Species' protection requirements are taking land out of production, limiting use of resources, and increasing operating costs for indefinite periods of time. Less use of resources means a reduction in near term income. To potential buyers of lands used to produce natural resource products, species' protection requirements indicate a reduced potential for income from the land, and offers to purchase open space lands are reduced accordingly.

Please refer to Chapters Three, Four, and Nineteen for more discussion about regulatory and species protection abuses.

The addition of restrictive regulatory requirements and the chaos and instability they cause in natural resource product markets seems to have no end. Those making a living from the production of natural resources and the rural communities dependent on the production of natural resources have been on a roller coaster ride for a very long time.

In the early 1990s without adequate peer and scientific review, the Fourth Branches of Government went wild and applied all kinds of species and environmental protection requirements to all kinds of natural resource production operations. Along with a lot of restrictions for various environmental reasons, protection requirements involving the northern spotted owl and various anadromous fish species were put in place. These restrictions combined to severely restrict the production of many natural resource products.

In my opinion, it needs to be noted that the referenced 1990s' regulatory problems were not driven so much by new legislation. They were mostly driven by improper and abusive application of existing unclear laws and by application of unauthorized internally developed guidelines.

What happened in the 1990s, was tough on all kinds of landowners and rural folks trying to make a living, trying to hold onto to their open space lands, and trying to keep living the rural way of life.

The following relative graph of lumber futures demonstrates how chaotic timber product prices were in the early 1990s when reliability of timber supply was also jumping all over the place. All kinds of new regulatory restrictions were creating all kinds of uncertainties about permits and ability to harvest timber.

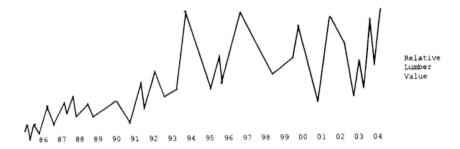

Relative
Lumber
Value

d. Permit review and approval processes have become very costly, and once permit restrictions and requirements are put in place, they seem to stay with the land.

Permit review and approval processes are rigged. Regulators have pretty much free reign in approving or denying permits, and backing from higher levels allows regulators to basically require anything they want in permits. Permitees have little choice but to play a permit approval game that utilizes standards and sideboards controlled by the regulators.

In this game, the regulators are the referees, and they seem to start off with the assumption that whatever permitees want to do will cause environmental damage. The burden of proof that no damage will occur is heavily if not entirely placed on the shoulders of the permitees. This means permitees must expend a large effort and a lot of money to collect all kinds of data. This data is used in trying to answer all possible questions and resolve all environmental issues, justified or not, presented to them by the regulators. Routinely a lot of data required to be collected by the regulators is never utilized.

It is standard practice to not require regulators to perform to the same level or to the same standards as the permitees. Restriction requirements requested by regulators routinely lack adequate explanation and justification, and attempts to require regulators to be more professional are mostly ignored by those at higher levels of authority.

An example of unbridled handling of permits is provided by Total Maximum Daily Load (TMDL) regulations that are being developed for designated impaired watersheds all over this country by the Environmental Protection Agency. These regulations are going to give water quality agencies all kinds of ways to apply regulatory restrictions on producers of natural resource products. Thousands of dollars will have to be expended in preparing management plans and in fulfilling water quality permit requirements. Refer to Chapter Two for a more complete discussion of how water quality regulations are being applied in California.

As in the case of operational limitations, permit requirements directly increase costs, reduce operational efficiency, reduce production levels, and reduce returns to producers of natural resources. Potential buyers keep track of what permit requirements are doing to bottom line figures, and they reduce purchase offers for lands used to produce natural resource products accordingly.

As illustrated by California appraisals routinely discounting timber values by 30% or more due to regulatory restrictions, regulatory restrictions have changed how open space lands are valued. Regulatory restrictions have caused income from lands producing natural resource products to drop, and this drop has caused a lot of open space land to be converted to other uses.

More cost and less production means lower return and lower open space land values.

4. Privately owned open space lands producing natural resource products are being converted to higher valued uses such as actual and speculated residential use. The production of natural resource products is not considered the highest and best use on many open space lands, and the higher valued uses are winning the day.

Larger residential use parcels do produce some income from the production of natural resource products; however, the income generated is small in the scheme of things, and these parcels can not realistically be considered viable income producing units.

Residential use can result in increased tax revenues for local economies; however, these increased revenues are routinely eaten up by increased service requirement costs involving fire suppression, public road maintenance, adverse environmental impact restoration work, and increased law enforcement coverage.

Residential uses are causing many watershed and environmental problems as outlined in an editorial(251). The editorial lists problems caused by residential use on open space lands by saying "…threat of subdivision…which fragments wildlife habitat, requires roads which often end up poorly maintained, and stress ground- and stream-water resources needed for fish and other animals." and humans.

The bottom line is higher residential use land values are hard to ignore, and they are causing a lot of open space land to be sold and converted to lands not being managed for the purpose of producing natural resource products.

5. Existing Public Trust Lands such as our National Forests are quietly being converted from income producing lands to taxpayer subsidized units. As this shutdown occurs, these lands are contributing less and less to supporting rural communities. Additionally, this is causing a loss of infrastructure and markets needed to keep producers of natural resources going. Supporting businesses are finding it hard to make a go of it, and they are leaving rural communities.

In the name of protecting the environment, wildlife habitats, fishery resources, and old-growth forests, restrictions are inappropriately being applied to timber harvesting, oil and mineral exploration, livestock grazing, and recreational use. Many areas are being locked up where no resources can be used to produce natural resource products. Many recreational activities such as off-road vehicle use, horseback riding, mountain biking, snowmobiling, motorskiing, and even hiking is being restricted and eliminated in areas previously used for these recreational activities. Reduction in access for the physically limited is occurring on many Public Trust Lands.

While the problem of restrictions on recreational uses and production of natural resources on Public Trust Lands has been fully discussed at the beginning of this chapter, it is again worth mentioning. For years, production of natural resource products and recreational activities on long existing Public Trust Lands has provided the main economic supports for many rural communities, and the ongoing shutdown of these uses is more than just a loss of potential economic benefits. The inability to utilize Public Trust Lands cuts hard into the infrastructure that has been built up over the years, and the loss of this infrastructure, hurts all the other producers of natural resource products. As the sawmills, contractors, grocery stores, and other needed infrastructure and support facilities go, so goes the ability to keep equipment repaired and operating, so goes contractors needed to do the work, so goes a place to sell natural resource products, so goes a way to make a living, so goes food and schools, and so goes a way of life.

Except for some local recognition about what is happening, these changes are going relatively unnoticed by the general public. While protecting the environment, species habitats, and wildland values has merit in the right places, there seems to be an unstoppable appetite by governmental and enviro folks to tie up and restrict uses on more and more land. A lot of what is happening is weakly supported and not justified.

"...the Giant (and the word **Giant** needs to be emphasized) Sequoia (National) Monument..." designation by President Clinton as mentioned in a news article(1) provides an example of applying unjustified restrictions because "he could" on "...327,769 acres..." of land already controlled by governmental agencies. This monument designation was done under the Antiquities Act, and there was a lack of public input and scientific review in making this designation. Prior to the monument designation, this land was mostly National Forest Land used for multiple use purposes, and monument designation will result in restricting and eliminating many historical uses.

The real focus of concern and reason for establishing the monument to protect the "...sequoia groves..." that "...account for about 20,000 acres, or roughly 6 percent, of the total monument." What was the reason for including the other over 300,000 acres in the monument designation?

Like many Clinton actions, the monument designations will look good for him, and in his isolated and far off location, he will experience no real adverse impacts or repercussions. This can not be said for the rural communities affected by this irresponsible action. The news article portrays a plan for the monument that will serve all, but a reading of the plan and monument restrictions finds the land will produce less income and rural economic support will be reduced.

The shutdown of long time existing Public Trust Lands goes to the throat of rural communities that have built an economy and life around use of these lands. This shutdown is the cruelest blow of all by the Fourth Branch of Government.

6. Many things are happening to drive producers of natural resource products away from rural communities.

As demonstrated by the spotted owl fiasco and the shut-down of the timber industry in many rural communities, there are social problems involved with a change from a hard working, rural way of life to whatever follows. This change has resulted in the expenditure of many taxpayer dollars to handle problems such as alcoholism, job retraining, feeding the hungry, and re-locating people. These problems drive people away and obviously put a strain on already limited rural community resources.

When incomes and land values are forced down, many owning open space lands do not have the resources and ability to stick around and be part of a dying community.

A newspaper article(272) adds to the information outlined in the provided six factors by saying "A robust real estate market helped push Humboldt County's property assessments over $7,000,000,000" which sounds good until the impacts such as added service costs and higher residential land prices are considered. The residential gains go to cover added service costs, and the higher residential land values create pressures to sell lower valued open space lands into residential use. The article goes on to say "...county officials indicate the timber industry faced with downsizing and mill closures continues to ask for property reassessments." These reassessments are resulting in reduced tax revenues to the county as the article goes on to say "Pacific Lumber Co.'s annual property taxes paid to the county have dropped by an estimated $800,000 over the past year..." Removal of resource producing income lands from the tax rolls through sales to public agencies is a part of the reassessment process which is reducing the amount of taxes paid to the county. County costs are going up for "...routine repairs and maintenance..." which includes road repairs and maintenance in residential areas. The Redwood Park impact is mentioned in the article as "...the federal government still owes the county some $6,000,000 in payments associated with a 1979 Redwood National Park expansion." which illustrates the failure of park expansions to fulfill promised economic benefits.

Problems and cost factors facing producers of natural resource products are further outlined in a news article(273) which states "...North Coast landowners today face real threats from development, rising costs and...estate taxes...Losing farm and timberlands to development and taxes and taking working land out of production is one of the major perils to the North Coast's rural economy and character."

A news editorial(251) presents information on past losses of some income producing lands and the potential for future losses. The editorial states "between 1991 and 1997, the U.S. Census of Agriculture found that the number of full-time farms in the county (Humboldt) dropped 13 percent, and the number of acres on working farms fell 13,000 acres to 584,538." "A survey produced by Ben Morehead and sponsored by Humboldt County Farm Bureau and Humboldt State University found 40 percent of farmers and ranchers don't have an heir to continue their operations. Nearly half are nearing retirement-representing more than 100,000 acres- may sell their land within 15 years."

Another news article(276) has "...Broward County, Fla...officials..." saying the county "...has lost 62,000 acres of agricultural land to development since 1972, and has only 7,600 acres left. There the land-preservation tax break has not slowed development an iota." The focus of this article was to show how developers are able to take advantage of attempts to preserve open space lands, and provided information on how these attempts were failing. This article re-enforces the ideas that development is going to happen and can not be stopped if the economic incentive for holding the lands in an open space condition is not maintained.

REALITIES FOR THOSE WHO LIVE OFF THE LAND

Income can come from production and use of the natural resources such as grass, timber, minerals, wildlife, and other uses of the land. Grass begets livestock for sale, timber and minerals provide direct monies, and wildlife and the land provide for various kinds of recreational revenues.

Real life expenses that need to be covered include the following items:

1. Taxes - income, land taxes, workers compensation, social security, medicare, fire district, school district, sales tax, payroll, fuel, inheritance.
2. Insurance - health, vehicle, operational, liability, personal injury, and property damage.
3. Financial obligations - mortgage, loans, payrolls.
4. Equipment and operational costs.
5. Conformance to regulatory and permit mitigation requirements.
6. Security and trespass concerns.
7. Family needs including food, shelter, and kids education.

Increasingly tougher regulatory restrictions are causing lower harvest levels and increased operational costs.

Operational expenses and the fickle markets are routinely taking a larger and larger bite out of produced income.

The continuing push to reduce use of our natural resources and the resulting inability to produce a livable income is making private ownership of open space a losing proposition.

When acceptable levels of income from the land are no longer possible, the incentive and ability to hold onto the land is lost.

A lot of rural landowners, farmers and ranchers, do not live a wealthy and easy life, and hanging onto their land in an open space condition generally means just "Getting By". "Getting By" generally means just enough income is produced from the land to meet expenses and provide for family needs. Routinely the income from the land falls short of needs, and income from outside sources such as investments, outside jobs, and inheritances is required to "Get By".

With an uncertain future in the resource markets and an ever-changing regulatory situation, the incentive to hold onto the land and live a "Getting By" life style is wearing thin. The obvious incentive for most rural landowners who work the land is to sell the land at the best market price available, and move on to a less complicated, simpler, more financially secure life.

For various reasons, the sale of their land for many rural landowners is a choice of last resort. There are some that will continue to fight the "Getting By" way of life to the end; because, they believe in the way of life provided by the rural life style. My hat is off to those that remain.

In summary, income producing lands are being lost in rural communities, and this loss is resulting in a silent reduction in the economies and tax bases needed to support and maintain rural communities. Increasing restrictions on access and use of Public Trust Lands is making them into nonincome producing, tax subsidized units that do not contribute to maintaining rural communities. Privately held open space lands producing natural resource products can not compete with higher valued uses such as residential and public trust uses.

By not effectively stopping the loss of income producing lands, we are saying bye bye to dollars needed to support rural communities.

A news editorial(251) asks "What will Humboldt become? A Del Norte County, with some 75 percent of land in government ownership? A Marin County, where land has been swallowed in the course of development?"

It appears the answer to this editorial's questions for Humboldt County and the rest of Rural America is "Yep"!

A CASTLE FOR A SMALL TOWN

Chapter Eight

There once was a thriving little town in the Redwoods of California which bustled with activity. Large old-growth redwood tree forests existed north, south, and east of the town on public park lands and on private lands. The parks were state owned parks which were visited regularly by tourists. Timber harvesting on private lands was a booming activity in the Orick area. Being located on a main highway 101, greyhound buses and tourists passed through Orick on the way to the parks, and the restaurants, grocery stores, and gas stations catered to the tourists and the loggers. A few fishermen and sellers of driftwood and burylwood had shops and woodlots along the highway. The motels were kept busy. Life was good.

This country's politicians and proponents of a Redwood National Park (RNP) decided they wanted more redwood land to be in public park ownership even though most of the majestic and best old and big trees were already in state parks. They got what they wanted. The taxpayers bought up a lot of the local private forest land, old and young, big and small trees, and a bunch of cutover land which contained a lot of small, Oregon seed source trees. Thus was created what is understood to be the most expensive and least visited National Park in the country.

With a lot of the local timber, old and young, being tied up in the new park preserve, many loggers were forced to go away, and with less timber available to be milled, the local sawmill curtailed operations to a lower production level which utilized less employees. The National Park Service promised a big visitor count and said returns from increased tourism will offset economic loss from reduced timber harvest and milling activity. The park folks promised big things for Orick.

To head off local economy loss impacts, millions of taxpayers dollars were thrown into the area. Laid off timber and sawmill workers directly received without any strings attached pay-off money based on their estimated wage and salary losses for many years after creation of the national park. A questionably needed 101 highway by-pass project around the state parks was constructed with tax dollars, and local and nonlocal contractors were employed to do the construction work. This highway project was later identified as the reason for sedimentation and environmental damage to local watercourses, and tax dollars were again put into play working on watercourse restoration projects. Millions and millions of taxpayer dollars are spent and are continuing to be spent on putting roads to bed which involves tearing up stable and unstable roads and newly established trees inside and outside the park.

Other subtle hidden costs and expenditure of tax dollars were put into play. Special restrictions were placed on all activities in a special buffer zone around the park which required expenditure of tax dollars and public agency time in reviewing permit activity in the buffer zone. Buffer zone restrictions increased operating costs on private land operations in the buffer zone. The putting-roads-to-bed projects reduced needed access for fire control and other management activities, and the loss of access for these purposes increased the cost to fight fire and conduct management activities and increased the potential for more damage due to fire. Other park projects involved using taxpayers' money to fall, kill, and leave to rot trees determined to not be acceptable park trees, because they came from considered unnatural, nonlocal seed sources such as nearby Oregon. Tax money was and is being spent to burn and kill young Douglas-fir trees that are naturally seeding-in under true oak tree stands.

It is amazing all the ways the National Park Service invented and is inventing to spend budgeted and unbudgeted taxpayer dollars.

As time passes by, local fishermen and sellers of driftwood and burylwood continue their battle with the National Park Service over beach access and use of driftwood. The remaining survivors continue to cater to the few tourists that stop by. The highway is now lined with old buildings, some occupied and some vacant, and sellers of driftwood and burylwood continue trying to make a living. Motels, restaurants, gas stations, and schools have long faded into the sunset. What's left of the local Chamber of Commerce has said to the National Park Service "please do not help us anymore".

Orick's problems are exasperated as other governmental agencies work at causing problems for the town. As reported in a news article(278), Orick is protected by levees built in the late 1960s after bad floods in 1964. The county is responsible for maintaining the levees, but this maintenance has been hard and costly to accomplish. Vegetation control has been hampered by the banned use of herbicide spraying for salmon protection reasons. Tightening of gravel mining regulations has hindered removal of excess gravels to make the levees handle more and higher water flows. Despite "The maintenance of the levee..." being "...essential for the health and safety of residents in Orick.", required U.S. Army Corps of Engineers permit needed for levee work "...has been in the works since 2000 - and corps has yet to issue that permit."

The Orick area's frustration with governmental agencies is further illustrated in a Letter to the Editor(279) involving removal of a two year old, junked car near Redwood Park's boundary which "...sits upside down, slowly leaching contaminates into the riparian plain." Contact with the Redwood Park and California Department of Fish and Game has not resulted in removal of the junked car, and the author of the letter shows his frustration by saying this "...illustrates a larger problem vis-avis the community of Orick and the local, state, and federal entities.", and the letter suggests a new slogan for the RNP Visitors Center should be, "Welcome to the junkyard gateway to the most expensive National Park in America."

In a time of budget shortfalls and not enough money and staff to maintain and open trail access and park facilities, comes the idea to build a large Redwood National Park office complex in the middle of the small town. The office is touted as a good thing which will bring people into the town. The locals are split as to this being a good idea, but the locals have little say anyway. The large office is built and stands like a castle among the remaining buildings, many boarded up and vacant, and among the piles of driftwood and burylwood. One local's opinion of the new office is expressed in a Letter to the Editor(280), and in this letter the writer states "...the enormity of the building was definitely overkill for the center of Orick..." "...lawn in the front is probably three feet tall...", and "Someone said they are going for a natural look" which can be assumed to mean never cutting the grass.

A follow-up local letter to the editor, mentions the grass is still not mowed by the office.

Production of natural resource products, the town's past main source of economic support continues to decline. The producers of wood products are down to sporadic milling activity and a few sellers of driftwood and burylwood. Despite regulatory restrictions and fickle markets, the local rancher types are still hanging-on, but they will soon succumb to the power of developers dollars or taxpayer dollars as income return to the land continues to drop.

However, all will not be lost, because the town does have a castle.

This little story is based on what really happened to a little town in a little area in a little part of the country in the redwoods. The National Park Service office stands sometimes untended as a glaring monument to unaccountable governmental power and the demise of Rural America. Some folks feel the castle office means Orick is on the come back trail. Could this castle be the big thing promised by the park folks? Only time will tell, but for sure, the comeback trail is going to be a long one if the idea is to get back to where the town was before the Redwood National Park.

Refer to photos 4, 5, 6, and 7 in center of book to see castle and town remnants

With the castle, will the little town return to the days of old? Will the old buildings around the office get a new coat of paint and come to life? Will businesses re-open? Will cows fly?

A SHORT STORY
"THE LAST BALE"
THIS SHORT STORY ILLUSTRATES THE PROBLEMS
FACING RURAL LANDOWNERS

Chapter Nine

John, a rancher, sits sipping his last cup of coffee at 5:00 AM and gets ready to start another day working the ranch that has been in his family for years. Through use and sale of the natural resources on the ranch, grass and timber, and by John and his wife working outside jobs, life has been pretty good for him and his family, but things are starting to fall apart. John is thinking about the coming year.

The timber market is down this year and the cost of obtaining a state approved harvest plan is going up to over $40,000. The cost of hooting for owls and hiring required professionals such as registered professional foresters, geologists, and archaeologists is increasing. Increasing harvest plan restrictions are increasing the cost of moving the logs and fulfilling mitigation requirements, and a lot of ranch timber value is being placed off limits. This all means more trees will have to be cut to pay for the harvest plan and to get the annually needed income to cover family and ranch costs. With regulatory and species restrictions increasing and regulatory interpretations constantly changing, obtaining a harvest plan and getting logs moving is becoming a questionable procedure that is rarely accomplished in time for the generally higher spring log markets. It is getting harder and harder to know how to understand and to satisfy what is wanted by the public agencies controlling the review and approval processes. The number of involved agencies seems to be increasing and now includes the California Department of Forestry, Water Quality, Department of Fish and Game, National Marine Fisheries, Federal Fish and Wildlife, and various other local, state, and federal agencies. A new name cropped up the other day, the Environmental Protection Agency or EPA, that John hasn't had to deal with before.

The only mill left in the local market area is finding logs coming over the bar to be a more reliable and better overall source of logs than the costly local logs. Sixty percent of this mill's supply came over the bar last year. The other nearest mill is 150 miles away which greatly adds to the haul costs and means less return to John. The places to sell logs are dwindling and so is the price.

Hopefully beef prices will be good this year to help pick up the slack; however, there is this thing called an Implementation Plan being created by Water Quality to control Total Maximum Daily Loads involving sediment, woody debris, temperature, and other things in streams that by word of mouth John heard needs to be prepared for cattle operations and use of any access roads on the ranch.

From information provided by the County Farm Advisor, the process for getting this plan looks pretty vague, and the cost of this plan is an unknown. All kinds of professional contractors and specialists can be involved depending on what Water Quality agency and their guidelines called the "Bible" requires to be put in these plans. In the mean time the cows have got to graze and the roads have to be traveled. John hopes he can figure all this out before he violates some regulations in the list of undefined and unclear regulations he has been handed to try and figure out. The last thing he needs is some kind of monetary fine this year.

John takes another sip of coffee, and thinks about how all this is leading to a triple whammy situation for him and his family.

Right off, the extra costs and the lower markets are reducing the income from timber and cattle; so, the ranch's contribution to family income is dropping. It is obvious that the use of natural resources is not being promoted, and the opposite is happening. Use of natural resources is being restricted and the production of these resources is being made more and more costly throughout the whole community. Other ranchers, farmers, and timberland owners are in the same boat as John as cost go up and markets shrink.

With the main economic base being taken away, there is nothing to keep the rural economy going. Supplemental jobs needed by John and his wife are being lost. Work at the mill, with logging contractors, other ranchers, and at the grocery store are in high demand and hard to get. The number of government jobs are being reduced as use of forest resources is reduced. The government forest positions are being limited to specialists, restricted by allocation quotas, or are low paying labor intensive type jobs. John and his wife do not have the ability to raise a family, work the ranch, and attempt to train for the specialized jobs; and, John questions his physical ability to handle the labor intensive, low paying jobs which won't bring in enough to cover their needs anyway.

John is really bothered by the third whammy. How will his kids ever be able to make a go of it. With no reliable source of income in the local area, they will have no chance to stay in the local area, and much less, be able to hold onto the ranch when he gets too old.

There has been talk of Hi-tech industries and tourism picking up the slack, but his doesn't make sense to John. With all the rural communities being affected and all the other areas better suited to Hi-tech and tourism, why would anyone bring these economies to their remote community. Access is poor which will create high operational and product costs. The resistance to any growth ideas has been increasing, and new businesses have found it hard to get established in the area. Land zoning restrictions which restrict land use to natural resource uses such as timber production and agricultural uses have basically eliminated the availability of any site large enough to support that needed by any major industry. Tourism seems to mainly provide low paying jobs; so, there is no replacement for the higher paying production and natural resource type jobs. It seems out of town folks from all over, including out of country, grab up these type of jobs. Government jobs are not available, and why should the taxpayers have to or want to keep their community alive? John kicks back and wonders who is kidding who.

There was some kind of meeting down at the Grange Hall the other night about some new regulations and the impact on the community. With the kids' sports, family business, and the long days, John just couldn't and didn't want to spend his time at a meeting where no one really listens anyway.

The last time John got involved and let some government folks onto the ranch, reports were written about how bad things were. Added watercourse and species protection requirements included in the reports forced 30 percent of his ranch timber be left untouched, and he had to reduce livestock grazing. This really bothered John; because, he thought he was doing a good job of selecting how his timber was harvested, and the land was well vegetated with forage plants. He had been abiding by all the regulations and advice he had been given. The problems the report listed and some things advocated by the governmental professionals did not make sense to John. He remembers how as a kid he could catch his best fish around the log jams, and how the jam and woody debris removal done by the Fish and Game and required by regulation in the 70s resulted in the elimination of a lot of the deeper pools and hiding places for the fish. Based on what he was being told, the ranch was showing signs of getting better. More fish were being seen, and despite the many no fishing regulations, the kids were able to slip around and catch fish where as a kid he had never caught them before. Although the return of the mountain lion was hurting the deer herd and was a questionable benefit, all kinds of wildlife was showing up all over the ranch.

There was talk of free government money to correct the problems listed in the report. John stops his thoughts and reflects on the idea of free government money which is actually his and others tax money, and his head starts to swim. The free money came with some strings. Use of this money required all kinds of follow-up inspections and monitoring costs and involvement with the government people. All reports and collected information would be public information and available to anyone who requested to see it. It did not seem to be a good idea to let anyone and everyone in the world have access to ranch business and other private matters.

Based on his past experiences, being around those government folks anymore than you have to does not seem to be a good idea.

There was talk of a conservation easement. This would mean someone else would become a partner and have a say in running the ranch. The ranch income would be reduced and there would be more involvement with outsiders. There are some county assessor's saying re-assessment to higher values and taxes is required when a conservation easement is put in place. While there would be more money in the bank to smooth out money problems, would it be enough? The current regulatory and zoning restrictions on the ranch would require significant appraisal discounts regarding development values, and the conservation easement value might not be equal to the actual reduction in value that would occur. It might turn out that the overall value of the ranch in the long run would be more without having a conservation easement in place. This conservation easement idea would take more thought and understanding before John could buy into it.

All this thinking slowly brings back to John, the high offer recently made by a developer fella for the ranch. John knows the kids and the grand folks would be mad if he sold the ranch, but wouldn't that solve a lot of problems. His wife would support him in a decision to sell, because she knows what they are going through. His medical and health insurance costs are going through the roof.

It is really bothersome and frustrating having to dig up money to cover insurance premium costs for health, vehicle, liability, and general ranch operation policies. It would be so easy to leave all the concerns over ranch taxes, equipment and operational costs, regulatory problems, and ranching problems behind. Things like a previously proposed $6 per acre fire protection tax considered by the state which would be a major blow would no longer be a source of worry. The penny pinching to hold onto the ranch would go away, the grand folks financial problems could be eliminated, the kids educational needs would be covered, and the long work days and worries would be lifted from his shoulders. The ideals that involve working with the land and its resources to keep a community and a way of life he loves alive are wearing thin for John.

As John sips the last of his coffee and looks out over the hay field behind the barn, he wonders what species or regulatory protection will be next. As he heads out to cut the hay field and feels the warmth of the early morning sunrise, the best part of the day, he wonders how much longer he will be able to cut and bale the hay on this field, and how much longer the way of life he has known all his life will be allowed to exist.

Food for thought: What would you do if you were John? Continue the fight to be able to graze a few cows and/or to be able to harvest a few trees; or, sit back and have a lucrative mountain estate. This story is being repeated thousands of times in California and across the western United States. There may be no stopping what is happening, but if better clarity and accountability was required of the regulators, the impacts of change could be made a lot less severe. To do nothing, means the eventual end of ownership of open space lands by nonindstrial private individual and family interests who are ranchers, farmers, and timberland owners. In combination with the opposition to the use of natural resources, the loss of this ownership group will lead to the end of many rural communities and a way of life.

Disclaimer: Any resemblance to a real John and described situation is purely co-incidental. Any semblance to reality is intended.

HI HO! HI HO!
IMPORTATION IS ACOMING

Chapter Ten

If not already here, the potential for this country becoming dependent on importing the majority of needed resources (food, gravels, minerals, timber, cattle, oil) and basic natural resource products (food, clothing, shoes, household goods) is coming closer everyday.

Due to the continually changing and often abusive regulatory situation, all the variables provided by Mother Nature, land set-asides, changing markets, and changing landowner goals, the domestic production of needed natural resource products is dropping. With need for natural resource products remaining the same or increasing and with increasing production costs, market prices are going up. Increasing market prices create the opportunity for world wide importers with lower regulatory restrictions and lower production costs to enter this country's markets and to directly compete with this country's domestic producers.

While not necessarily all bad, the increasing import situation requires incountry producers to adjust supply and prices according to world markets. The import situation causes problems when incountry producers are undercut and unable to compete due to unequal constraints.

The reduction in use of natural resources due to importation, regulation, and set-asides is causing a loss of materials needed to maintain infrastructure (sawmills, food processing plants, textile plants, clothing manufacturing facilities) used to produce natural resource products. This situation is spelling the end of economic supports for rural communities, and this country's dependence on others for basic needs is increasing.

Over regulation and an unaccountable Fourth Branch of Government are playing a major part in what is happening.

The following listed news stories illustrate how wide spread import competition has become for the producers of natural resource products.

A news article(281) illustrates how the importation of food materials is affecting rural farmers all over this country. This article outlines how olive growers are in competition with countries like Spain and Morocco. The article says farmers do not want subsidies. They just want a level playing field. Knowing all the regulations that apply to operations in California and in this country, it would be interesting to know if a reduction in unnecessary regulation and environmental requirements would help this situation.

Another news article(282) tells more about the loss of food markets to importers. The article refers to growing trend by consumers for cheap vegetables. The article mentions "...struggling with finding legal inexpensive workers, with rising costs of worker's compensation insurance, and the general increase in input costs." The article says "...vegetable imports went up by 7 percent in the first 10 months of 2003-a trend that may be elbowing U.S. farmers out of production..." "...some farmers are clearly losing their grip on domestic markets." The article specifically mentions independent tomato farmers as becoming nonexistent and year round imports from Mexico and Canadian greenhouses are adding to the squeeze. Sixty-six percent of world's garlic market is mentioned as coming from China. In 1999 there were 36,000 acres of asparagus fields in California, and this acreage is now down to 24,000. Thirty percent of asparagus consumed in this country in 1990 was foreign and 65 percent of asparagus now consumed comes from abroad, mainly from Peru and Mexico. Asparagus farmers are plowing under whole fields of asparagus because harvest costs could not be recovered through harvest and sale.

Another thought not mentioned in this article involves how high prices for domestically produced goods may be a bigger problem than the lower prices for imported vegetables. While higher prices may sound good for domestic farmers, the higher the price charged by domestic producers, the more room there is for importers to fit into domestic markets. With their lower regulatory restrictions and lower costs, importers can pay more and more to ship products longer and longer distances and still have an acceptable margin of return.

Importation of some food products has become so common, domestic prices being paid to ranchers and farmers are easily influenced by the world supply situation. A news article(283) mentions how "...the discovery of mad cow in Canada last year drove up demand for local beef, resulting in record-high cattle prices,..." I wonder if Hillary got in on this cattle deal? While this was a plus for domestic cattle producers, price changes do not always go up, and as mentioned in this chapter and found by my review, world supply changes are pushing domestic product prices down more often than up. Another news article(284) mentions how "California is a big producer of powdered milk products and the import of milk protein concentrate from overseas has pushed much of that off the market." and a primary cause "...for the low dairy prices..." is "...international competition."

Another news article(285) discusses the changing farm food markets in this country as "San Diego farmers urge purchase of locally grown and fresh-picked crops". While the article focuses on a co-op type venture, the article mentions how farms are "...surrounded by multimillion-dollar homes..." and the struggle to preserve agriculture in the area is an ongoing battle. There is a need for "People to understand that agriculture is important to the local economy and become advocates,...otherwise we'll be regulated out of existence."

A news article(286) provides another example of how world supply can easily affect domestic natural resource product markets. "...Oriented strand board, or OSB...(wood) sheathing..." reached historic price (high). This "...increase is attributed to wildfires that have destroyed thousands of acres of timberland in British Columbia and interrupted logging operations." Again, this is a plus for areas with OSB manufacturing plants; however, OSB is only a part of the business and landowner group that produces and handles wood products, and imports are having a major impact and routinely depressing returns to those producing other timber products in this country.

Internet report(287) mentions "...Brady, Texas... ranchers who raise goats for angora wool are victims of low prices and competition from New Zealand and Argentina." "Foreign potash and uranium are now cheaper than New Mexico's, and Australian wool is cheaper than that produced in Brady..." "In part because of competition from Latin America, the copper mining that has stalled in Arizona and New Mexico might never return." "Canadian potash is increasingly competitive..." "There is more oil out there, but further exploration is costly and industry faces competition not just from Saudi Arabia but from Kazakhstan, Tajikistan and Uzebekistan." and a whole bunch of other countries. "High...cotton...production in countries like China has led to oversupply and plunging prices.", and "For farmers in Pima, Arizona, and Bartow, Georgia, cotton prices have sunk to 30-year lows."

A news report(288) says "Peach imports have increased from one million to three million cases in the past three years." and "Peach imports from Greece and Spain...with subsidies supplied by the European Union, allowing foreign farmers to offer prices..." that "...have caused direct competition with U.S. farmers." "California peach growers...are ripping out peach trees...to offset a glut as they compete with foreign growers."

Even flower growers are being affected as mentioned in a news article(289). The number of flower growers in California have dwindled due to foreign competition or sale of valuable coastal properties to developers.

The article says "The flower industry decline is part of America losing its ability to be a producer nation." Many growers can not compete with countries like Colombia, Ecuador, Costa Rica, and the Netherlands. Foreign growers share of the domestic market was 45 percent ten years ago, and foreign growers have 70 percent of the cut flower market in 2002. "Domestic growers face increasing costs for labor, energy, and water along with strict environmental regulations." Some growers are turning to producing different products such as herbs, watercress, mint, and flowers not easily provided by foreign producers. Some just succumb to the high prices developers are paying for their high valued land, go out of business, and hopefully enjoy the good life with their land sale dollars.

While there is a resistance to fish farming in this country, the rest of the world is going ahead full speed with the idea, and the world markets are having a major impact on the price of fish products and the domestic fishing industry. A news article(290) says "Nearly a third of the world's food fish now are farmed, an industry that quadrupled (and is going to get a lot bigger) in size between 1985 and 2000." While this article says "...aquaculture..." is "...never going to replace natural fisheries...", my quick review has found there is an expanding aquaculture industry happening all over the world, and news article(291) says "Only 2 percent of the market today is wild salmon." A couple other news articles(292)(293) mention fish coming from Canada, Norway, Scotland, Faroe islands, and Chile "...which produces 81 percent of the 206 million pounds of farmed fish consumed in the United States."

All kinds of fish food producers are being affected by import competition as illustrated by a news article(294) about catfish and shrimp imports. Vietnam is importing catfish to this country, and in one instance captured 20 percent of the market. Per a Texas Shrimp Association spokesperson, "They're (Vietnam) totally flooding our (shrimp) market." Forest Gump might have not done so well with his shrimp operation if there had been the current level of foreign competition.

Because the world aquaculture industry is unstoppable, some rural communities are going to be sorry they have resisted efforts to get this industry going in this country. The aquaculture industry is here to stay and could provide some economic stability for rural communities.

The continuous loss of natural resource product producers is illustrated by the following news articles. The numbers provided in one news article(295) shows 90,000 farms were lost from 1997 to 2002 in this country. Another news article(296) shows 8,282 farms were lost from 1997 to 2002 in California. A third news article(297) states "87,000 acres of timber, dairy, and ranch lands were lost between 1992 and 1997 to rural subdivisions, and the number of full time farms dropped 13 percent according to U.S. Census of Agriculture statistics." While competition from imports is not the only reason for these losses, the increasing level and wide spread effect of importation indicates a lot of folks and businesses are being driven away from being producers of natural resource products.

Foreign import problem is not unique to any one area of this country.

In the little corner of the world called Humboldt County, the rich timber resource and other agricultural resources are slowly being idled by inappropriate state and federal regulatory actions and by market conditions. Humboldt county used to produce logs from private and federal timber lands to many, many local mills, to mills out of the county, and to overseas locations. In 2001, this county per County Agricultural Adviser information produced 190,571,200 board feet of logs and imported 99,785,000 board feet logs for use in a few remaining mills. Compared to historical usage numbers, the level of total log usage is way down and the percentage of log usage from imported logs is way up.

Some might say a slow down was inevitable because of overcutting, the end of the old-growth volumes, or poor management, but the facts speak otherwise. The most recent timber inventory information from the U.S. Forest Service Pacific Northwest Inventory office in Portland in a letter dated April 19, 2004 shows Humboldt County timberlands outside the thousands of acres of federal, state, and county parks and wilderness areas in the county have a standing timber inventory of 26,488,000,000 (26.488 billion) board feet of conifer timber. Additionally this letter says the standing timber is annually growing an additional 768,000,000 (.768 billion) board feet of conifer timber. This means the reported 190,571,200 (.19 billion) board feet that local mills utilize annually is less than 25% of the amount of timber grown annually on lands available to be harvested in Humboldt County. These numbers show local mill usage is far far below the amount of locally grown timber, and the timber resource is far far from being depleted or overcut. The underutilization of the timber resource combined with the need to import timber to keep the few remaining mills going shows there are reasons other than a overcut, poorly managed, and depleted forest situation causing the slow down in log production and increase in importation of logs in Humboldt County.

It has to be acknowledged that the importation of logs through Humboldt Bay has provided some economic pluses for Humboldt County. Local contractors and harbor employees are being utilized which adds to the local economy, and local mills are kept going. As mentioned in a 2003 news article(298), the timber industry in the area is "...now dependent on out-of-area logs..." to remain viable; so, without imports, some mill capacity would be idled.

While importation of logs does some good and is a necessity right now, a closer look finds the importation of logs to the Humboldt County area could be a short term fix. There are signs and rumors that more regulatory restrictions, land set-asides, and market conditions will not allow current milling capacity to be maintained. Even with log imports, the remaining mills are having trouble getting an adequate log supply, and rising business costs and imports of manufactured wood products are causing even more trouble.

A news article(299) states a Humboldt State University Department of Economics report says "...Lumber-based manufacturing..." which generates about 60% of Humboldt County's manufacturing jobs "...plummeted 15 percent..." from January 1994 through November of 2003.

Overall in California, importation of wood products and alternate products are replacing much of California's need for California grown and manufactured wood products. As verified by multiple other informational sources, a news article(300) dated April 21,2004 says while California grows "...80 percent of what..." California needs, California is not cutting what is grown and "California imports 80 percent of their wood,..." Another 2004 newspaper article(301) has a statement that 70 percent of the wood used in California is imported.

I do not know where the "California produces 80% of California's wood needs" information comes from, but my research found this information to understate the amount of timber growth in California. California Forest and Range Assessment Project (FRAP) 2003 Assessment Report says total 2001 annual wood usage was 5,035,000,000 board feet of lumber plus some pulpwood and other types of fiber usage, and California Timber Commission, a Montana source, and United State Department of Agriculture (USDA) General Technical Report PNW-GTR-615 dated July 2004 says based on governmental continuous forestry inventory work that California grows 5,012,600,000 board feet on nonreserved lands (lands other than state and federal parks, wilderness areas, etc.) The 5,012,600,000 board feet growth number does not include what is grown on Public trust Lands which make up around fifty percent of the state's land base. To summarize, this information says wood usage is 5,035,000,000 board feet and timber growth on only private lands is 5,012,600,000 board feet.

Both news article and other informational sources show California is a heavy importer of needed wood, and despite the ability of the state to produce more than enough wood to fulfill its usage needs, California is experiencing a shrinking wood producing infrastructure and reducing returns to timberland owners. It is getting easier and cheaper to bring the widgets (wood products) to California than it is to make the widgets in California.

A fall 2003 Newsletter article by Northern California Chapter of the Society of American Foresters shows adjacent county to Humboldt County, Mendocino County, is illustrating the same downward use of timber resources for the same reasons as Humboldt County. "Harvests from Mendocino County have been falling sharply since 1996, when harvests... were nearly three times what they were in 2002." "...decline is due to...small landowners can't afford... harvest plans...", and "...even with an approved plan, many landowners...have to harvest...heavily...to recover plan costs." A "...vast majority of wood...use in California..." is now imported. For personal reasons and "...handsome profits by selling of the family forest ...to be converted to non-forest uses...", the amount of timber resource available to be harvested is being reduced.

A real life example of how regulatory and other restrictions are reducing use of natural resources and production infrastructure in this country is provided in a 2004 news article(85). A mill owner in "Prineville, Oregon...went offshore building a sawmill in Lithuania to process wood from Russia, imported lumber from South America and New Zealand, and investing in port facilities in Russian Far East." The mill owner even with "...70,000 acres..." of privately owned timberland was like "...485 other mills around the West..." that "...have gone out of business (in this country) since the 1980s because of a combination of recession...; sharp reductions in national forest logging to protect habitat for the northern spotted owl...salmon..." and other species"; and because "Too many restrictions were placed on harvesting timber,..." "U.S. Forest Service economist said...The U.S. position in the global economy is shifting around...", and calls it "...an unintended consequence of the spotted owl (and I add other restrictive factors). It (and other restrictive factors) drove up (log) prices...", and "We made ourselves uncompetitive in world markets. Then it shifted. Places like Russia could import into Baltimore." While the Forest Service fella is on the right track, I do not believe he still sees the total picture how our infrastructure is being lost and how this country is becoming more and more an importing nation due to restrictions on production of natural resource products. "Canada dominates U.S. imports, accounting for 19.4

million board feet of the total 21.2 billion board feet…, Europe including Lithuania, provides 904 million board feet, Latin America 712 million board feet, and New Zealand 203 million board feet…" with imports "…from Russia and Lithuania growing." As other mills' production capacity leaves this country, so goes this country's increased dependence on imports from other countries.

A news article(6) which discusses regulatory problems for businesses provides an example of how regulatory restrictions and harassment problems can force all kinds of industries out of the country. "The Holy Yashis…star client…Yakima…grew to a certain point and said: 'We're out of here. We need to compete on a global level and we need to manufacture product that can go into stores and sell for $99. We can't do that in Humboldt County (California).' And so a part of their business moved to Mexico…and…Humboldt County's…going 'Oh my God, they just shipped all their jobs out of Humboldt County,' But that's reality." "…are we developing a community we can't afford to live in or produce things from? Obviously Yakima said, 'We can't - we need to move out of Humboldt County (and California) to be competitive in the world.'

The restrictions on use and production of natural resources is having a direct affect on another key component of the economic base in Humboldt County which is use of the Humboldt Bay deep water harbor. As illustrated in 2003 newspaper articles(304), Humboldt harbor faces a questionable future, and this questionable future no doubt applies to a lot of other areas in this country. The referenced side by side 2003 news articles illustrate the conflicting views about Humboldt harbor's future. These articles show the local pulp mill being auctioned off and in trouble, describe how one of the area's largest timber companies may have its timber harvest operations stopped by a lawsuit and a judge, and provide a U.S. Senator's I believe misguided comments on how things are looking up for the harbor.

These articles raise the question, who is kidding who? It appears the blind are leading the blind, and the light bulbs are all turned off.

The following provided news articles and discussion illustrates what routinely happens all over this country when new businesses attempt to locate in many rural communities. These articles illustrate the kind of resistance that can even occur before all the studies, plans, and facts are known.

In 2003, Calpine approached the community around Humboldt Bay about putting an LNG (Liquid Natural Gas) storage facility on the bay. Boy did the anti-growth folks come out.

News article(306) says "…Environmental Protection Information Center told Calpine that it would most likely be sued over the project." "No matter where you put this facility it will be challenged every step of the way,…"

It is worth noting that the main proposed plan site is in an area that has included industrial activities including two pulp mills and export facilities for years, and this site is across the bay from residential areas and the town of Eureka. Visual and operational impacts to the community are rather small or the same in comparison to what was originally in the area of the proposed plant site.

A news article(310) discusses another town meeting at another city on Humboldt Bay. This article quotes the mayor as saying "…one of his goals for 2004 is to get Calpine out of town." "I find myself constantly frustrated that Calpine is still in town,…"

A third news article(312) quotes a spokesperson from the Northcoast Environmental Center as saying "Beware of Calpine bearing gifts.' "What disappoints me is that there are so many people in Humboldt County hiding behind feasibility rather than saying this is a bad idea for Humboldt Bay."

A news article(315) points out problems for fisherman and other users of the harbor due to security restrictions and physical maneuvering and harbor access delays when large LNG ships are in the harbor.

A review of all the anti-Calpine information indicates the main problems that needed to be resolved were some harbor traffic problems and the potential for damage from an explosion which needed to be understood and eliminated as a concern. If these two items could not be resolved and there was a legitimate safety issue, then the project should have been terminated for these reasons; however, things did not get that far.

The Calpine story ends like a lot of other such decisions now days without a factual determination. As loudly and clearly stated in a news headline, "Calpine pulls the plug". The accompanying news article(236) says Calpine was run-off. While all the objections thrown at the LNG idea may have been rebuttable, we will never know. Like most producers of natural resource products and politicians, Calpine did not directly confront the credibility of opposing information.

Generally producers of natural resource products and politicians play the appeasement game, but Calpine didn't even go that far. They may have wisely said they had enough of Humboldt County. Maybe Calpine didn't have truth on their side and needed to call it quits. Since the truth and site specific situation never got to be discussed, we'll never know.

The Calpine story illustrates how the enviro no-growth folks play the game of destroying credibility, creating confusion, and causing delay. They been doing this for years and winning, and in the case of Calpine on the bay, they won another one.

Someone has to produce and pay the bills, and it is going to take more than a constant barrage of negative thinking to get the job done. Some things are going to have to give way to accommodate needed change.

While there is no one single factor that is causing the loss of farms and the loss of domestic natural resource markets to suppliers of imports, there is one constant theme that runs through all the provided stories. This one theme is the increased cost to operate and produce natural resource products in this country, and this extra cost is not helping the domestic producers stay competitive with importers. Foreign importers have lower labor costs, and do not have to deal with things like this country's workman compensation insurance cost problem.

As mentioned earlier in this chapter, rising domestic market prices are making it easier for foreign competition to compete in the domestic markets. The higher the cost of a product, the more the product comes within the range of the importer to compete. As product prices increase, there is more and more room for an overseas producer with lower production costs and lower regulatory costs to cover the shipping costs to this country and still make an acceptable return.

A guest opinion article(318) provides a very telling story about how overpriced some of our domestic products have become. In this article, a women having a hard time making ends meet needs to buy shoes for her 12 year old son whose shoes had holes and hurt his feet. American made shoes were costing $50 which she could not afford. She found a factory outlet store selling shoes made overseas, and bought a fine leather pair of shoes for $24 dollars which made the boys face light up. From this story I got the impression something such as over regulation, human greed, selfish hoarding of our resources, and maybe some politically correct protectionist thinking is making American products overly expensive.

By not directly confronting the causes for American products being unjustifiably overpriced, the producers of this country are creating the ability for imports to compete with their products and are causing their own demise. You can only add extras onto the price for a product so far until the consumer stops paying the high asking price and goes elsewhere.

This shoe story illustrates another point that needs to be understood. We do not want to completely isolate ourselves from participation in the world markets. Tariffs and other disincentives to imports may be short term fixes for this country's producers, but in the long run, could hurt this country's ability to produce and be a major player in the world markets. As the shoe story illustrates, competition is good for the consumer, and we need to be continually reminded to check why our domestic product is not competitive with the world market. Such checks remind us there is no justification for saddling our producers of natural resource products with unnecessary and inappropriate regulations and to put them at a cost and price disadvantage with the rest of the world.

Hoarding our resources and losing the infrastructure needed to produce natural resource products will adversely affect this country and unwisely make this country dependent on others in the long run. An example of being at the mercy of import materials and the world market was provided by a 2004 radio report(319) which stated housing construction was being held up due to lack of inability to obtain foundation concrete. This report stated a lot of this country's base concrete material is now imported, and as also heard mentioned in other news items, a lot of the world's concrete supply is being diverted to China. This illustrates how uncontrollable and unpredictable import markets can be and how easily our country can be adversely affected when there is a lot of dependence on importing simple base materials like concrete.

In reviewing all the information and ideas about importation, I see a pattern of change that is leading to an imbalance that looks bad for this country.

The world markets **"for now"** seem more than willing to supply this country's natural resource needs, and domestic markets are already heavily influenced by world market supply and price swings. As illustrated by all the many products (food, tools, radios, cars, and on and on and on) already coming into this country from overseas, the maturing world is continually learning how to make the widget and ship it to this country. As is happening with oil, I can see where it is only a matter of time before the supply of natural resources needed to maintain what is left of this country's production infrastructure is going to come hard and be costly. The world's natural resources will still be in play, but as our production infrastructure shrinks, there will be less and less reasons for imported resources to come our way.

As the world becomes a smaller place and wanted products become easier and cheaper to make, incountry owners of manufacturing facilities are going to realize it makes sense to move their facilities out of country and closer to cheaper resources and cheaper labor. As this type of thinking increases, out-of-country competitors will more easily invade this country's markets, and as is now happening, the infrastructure needed to produce wanted products will slowly disappear in this country.

The environmental consequences of not utilizing our natural resources and our productive natural resource base and replacing our available resources with imported materials and products is not often discussed. Importation of needed natural resource materials and widgets made from natural resource products generally means getting these things from places that do not have a lot of concern about how the materials are obtained and produced, and is leading to increased world wide environmental impacts. Article in a Newsletter(320) describes how "...UC Berkeley Professor...research shows that for every 100 acres of (California) forestland...(or) 33-50 acres of coastal redwood forest (land)...we set aside..., we cause the extinction of or significantly move forward the timetable for extinction of one species somewhere else in the world."

While this all describes a complicated tangled mess, there are some simple basics that can be understood. As the use of natural resources and associated production infrastructure goes away, which looks likely at this point, what is going to replace these two creators of wealth and economic supports? Are hi-tech and information industries, tourism, and yankee ingenuity suppose to be the answer? A couple news articles(321)(322) say "...Indian (India) leaders... marketing their country as a global technology hub." and "...promoting the economic benefits of migrating technology jobs to low-wage workers in the developing world." "...Americans have been complacent about the loss of technology jobs to overseas workers since the trend began in the late 1990s." "Hundreds of Sonoma County workers will lose their jobs when...County's largest medical manufacturing company...will make its vascular devices or stents in Mexico and Ireland." It appears our hold on the hi-tech information industries and advanced technological production infrastructure is slipping away, and I do not see how a steady diet of tourism is going to pay the bills. Yankee ingenuity will go a long way, but can not do it all. While our country is strong and will be strong for a long time, I see this strength as having come from a balance of natural resource use, a healthy and solid production infrastructure, a competitive hi-tech and information industry, and a mix of other economic drivers. Our country has lost a lot of needed balance, and I do not see any real effort to get it back.

GREENSPAN, OH GREENSPAN
IS NO ONE THINKING AHEAD?

While I am definitely an amateur economist, there are some things that come to mind while listening to Mr. Greenspan discuss how world market competition has lead to a better life on the whole for those who participate in the Global market situation. I heard him acknowledge competition has hurt some, and I have provided examples of this hurt in this chapter. When I put the whole picture together, I can see a cycle of production and return that produces the worldwide goods mentioned by Mr. Greenspan. In simple terms, the cycle is use of natural resources which provides materials needed to support a production infrastructure that produces goods for the world wide market. In turn, the producers receive the means to obtain housing, food, medical services, and access to all the good things in life.

During Mr. Greenspan's presentation to a legislative hearing, I heard a governmental representative complain many citizens could not afford their own homes and adequate medical care with a pitch that global competition was not a good thing for them. It occurred to me that the citizens being discussed were mainly in the producer and working class of this country such as the rural communities, and a major reason these folks were having to do without was because they could not or were not participating in the larger world market process to provide for their needs. Instead of blaming the world market situation for their troubles, I could see where the blame should be re-directed towards what was preventing them from participating in the world market process. This thinking brought me full circle back to one reason these folks did not have jobs and were not allowed or could not participate in the world market. This reason was the loss of using natural resources and the loss of product producing infrastructure using these resources. The world market situation was not the evil that was hurting these folks; but rather, the internal decisions being made in this country that were eliminating their means to participate in the world market process and in obtaining the means to the good life.

I can see how this country is participating less and less in the full cycle that drives the world market situation. I see our country headed towards only participating in the world market portion of the cycle which is a drain and not a supplier of return to the producers and citizens of in this country.

If you look closely at what is happening to rural communities, you will see a shut down of natural resource use, a loss of production infrastructure, and increased importation of world wide products. This is causing life in rural communities to get tougher and tougher which is routinely ending in the elimination of many rural communities. What is happening to rural communities mimics what is slowing happening all over this country.

Importation can provide some economic pluses (dock worker wages, use of local contractors such as truckers, provides competition that keeps consumer prices in-line); however, a logical look at the situation finds a heavy dependence on imported materials will lead to bad things for this country and the world. There are a lot of benefits from keeping domestic producers of natural resource products going.

The overall problem of how bad science and unaccountable regulatory abuse is shutting down use of our natural resources, destroying our rural communities, and hurting our country is not being presented in a clear and unavoidable way. There is a lack of discussion about the long term implications of land management decisions not being based on site specific facts and peer reviewed scientific ideas, and about the unaccountable Fourth Branch of Government's misapplication of the multitude of unclear regulations. Various professionals, foresters, land managers, and others who can see the coming problem, being good professionals, nibble around the edges and complain a lot in a gentlemanly way, but by being satisfied to sit by and be reactive instead of pro-active, they do little to change where we are headed.

If importation of needed natural resources (and preservation of ours) and eventually importation of wanted widgets is what society wants, then the old saying "Be careful of what you wish for, because you might get it" is very applicable. By providing markets for world products while increasing environmental impacts, shutting done use of our natural resources may be a mixed bonus and an environmental curse for the rest of the world. For us, shutting down use of our natural resources for sure means problems for us.

Internet report(323) sums up some of what is headed our way. "…land being purchased by Ted Turner types and conservation groups…is being restricted in future use by conservation easements…" and "…moving from private to state control…" "…main threats are political decision making, bias against management, and poor environmental outcomes…" An illustration of what could be coming was illustrated by a person who said while on tour "…in England. In a countryside where manufacturing plants were deserted, a beautiful highway was being dozed, and…tour guide…" said this was happening because "…it did not meet the European Community standards…" Tour guide "…said, at the time of WWII we could feed our people and arm our nation. Now… we can do neither and we are a service industry to Europe." Has what happened to England to be this country's destiny as we shut down Rural America and the use of natural resources and build a dependence on importing our raw material needs?

A NEEDED KICK IN THE SHINS
(A FOCUS ON THE RURAL FOLKS - DARN THEM ALL)

Rural folks are among the best people in this world

Loggers, ranchers, miners, farmers, fishermen, and on

Love them all

But everyone of then needs a kick in the shins for letting the rural way of life slip away to the detriment of themselves, their families, and this nation. Without putting up a good fight, they are letting regulators and populous areas take away the rural way of life as we now know it.

Force the truth to be heard; or, sit back and lose it all.

Chapter Eleven

The people in this country have become complacent about what has made this nation strong, and this complacency has lead to a loss of initiative to do what is needed to hold onto what we have. This is no more evident than in Rural America.

We are very well-off. We live a darn good life or have the opportunity to live a darn good life.

Despite constant media coverage and the coming computer age which gives us the ability and knowledge to know what is happening, most of us find little reason to think our good life is in any danger. Few spend time and effort to learn what is happening to take our good life away, and even less of us actively work to protect our way of life.

In the past as in the Great Depression, the basic need to obtain food and shelter kept the population focused on actively holding onto what they had and to actively work at making things better. Today the basics such as food and shelter are taken for granted, and while we enjoy a lot of leisure and free time, we rarely utilize much of this time in protecting our good life.

Many enviros and many in the general public are meddlers affecting our way of life. These meddlers outnumber the few trying to protect what we have. Due to government handouts and other means, most meddlers do not have to worry about basic needs such as food and shelter, and they seem to have a lot of time and resources for meddling. Many meddlers have the desire to do good, but an awful lot meddle just to fill leisure time, join the crowd, or have a party. Routinely meddlers do not do their homework, and their uninformed meddling creates confusion and politically correct pressures that routinely causes factual information to be watered down and ignored.

Rural America is made up of what I would call producers (farmers, miners, ranchers, loggers), and for various reasons they are complacent in letting the meddlers take away their rural way of life.

These rural folks work hard and think they have little time to participate in the regulatory processes that are controlling and changing their rural way of life.

Except for a couple individuals who occasionally do something, the rural folks rarely exhibit real backbone and commitment to fighting illegitimate environmental concerns and abusive regulatory actions. The "I am going to hang on to what I got for as long as I can" attitude dictates the actions of many rural folks. Routinely, many capitulate to inappropriate regulatory demands in the hope their losses will be minimized and things will get better. "If it interferes with my comfort level I am not going to get involved" thinking permeates the rural communities.

Many in this group have let a feeling of guilt dominate their actions. They routinely roll over without a fight when criticized by the enviros and by what some call the "Environmental Brain Trust".

All foresters, loggers, ranchers, farmers, related associations, and community members need to be lined up and kicked in the shins to wake them up. These folks need to re-think what they are doing. By not taking the time and effort to learn and fight what is coming, these folks are putting themselves in a position to lose it all. The regulators and enviros are winning, and they have no reason to back off.

The rural folks are letting themselves be divided into groups sometimes called stakeholders which makes it easier for the regulators and enviros to handle and take them down. By not combining their efforts and developing a stronger common interest position, timber, fishery, farming, mining, ranching, landowners, and various recreational groups are fighting their battles from a weaker minority position.

For a long time, the Native Americans did as the rural folks are doing. They sat back and took the abuse. It took awhile, but the Native Americans finally found ways to fight back, and they developed a strategy and morally supportable message to use in changing their situation. Collectively the Native Americans have created and promoted a simple and consistent picture of being downtrodden, abused, and one with nature. While not always true,

Photo referenced in Chapter 4 of seal pocket near Klamath River, California in September, 1993

Photo 1

Photos referenced in Chapter 7 showing closure by California State Parks at low maintenance and paved access road leading to a good rocked parking area during California's budget crunch.

Photos 2 & 3

HERE STANDS ORICK'S CASTLE
Compliments of U.S. Taxpayer as referenced in Chapter 8.

Photo 4

ORICK LEFTOVERS as referenced in Chapter 8.
A closed restaurant symbolizes Orick's loss. A town that once supported a theater now has a blank marquee. A look down main street shows the remnants.

Photos 5, 6, & 7

Oh where, Oh where, has the river gone?????

Eel river traverses through the middle of the tents in the provided pictures.
Could there be impacts to the Eel River that need to be addressed and
mitigated?
Do birds fly?

As referenced in Chapter 14, do you think a little preference might be in
play?

Photo 8

As referenced in Chapter 14, the critters, plants, and bugs just might be getting squished while some regulators look the other way.

Photo 9

THIS IS NEW FORESTRY
(Chapter 16)

"New Forestry" likes the colors red and grey in a young "New Forestry" Forest.

Photo(s) 10

THIS IS NEW FORESTRY
(Chapter 16)
"New Forestry" likes bug infested true firs (top) and bear damaged redwoods (bottom).

"New Forestry" advocates may say they do not want bad tree conditions; however, what they advocate requires bad tree conditions.

Photo(s) 11

THIS IS NEW FORESTRY
(Chapter 16)
Multiple canopy levels, snags, and big trees.

Photo(s) 12

THIS IS NEW FORESTRY
(Chapter 16)
The look of "New Forestry" in Idaho.

Acres and acres, miles and miles, of dead and dying trees mixed with thrifty and not so thrifty live trees.

Photo(s) 13

THIS IS NEW FORESTRY
(Chapter 16)
A most desired "New Forestry" tree.
Gnarled, twisted, limby, stunted, dead, rotten, defective, diseased, bug infested, black, brown, gray, white, dead, deformed, tall, large, and old tree.

Photo 14

CANOE FIRE: Wary residents not out of the woods yet

Photos by KENT PORTER / The Press Demo

Renee Henault, a firefighter with the California Department of Forestry in Santa Clara, on Saturday uses dirt to cool down a snag that dropped over the fire line of the Canoe Fire in Humboldt County. As of Saturday, the fire was 40 percent contained.

Salmon Creek escapes, so far

As mentioned in Chapter 17, this news photo by Kent Porter of Press Democrat newspaper shows how old-growth fires are intense, unsafe, and burn hot.

Photo 15

Untreated timbered area after heavy burn near Weaverville, California as mentioned in Chapter 17.

Photo(s) 16

More of the untreated burned area near Weaverville, California
(Chapter 17)

Photo(s) 17

More of the untreated burned area near Weaverville, California
(Chapter 17)

Photo 18

the message they have promoted provides them with a politically correct and moral high ground position that has proven to be a winner.

The producers of natural resource products and rural folks need to take a lesson from the Native Americans. They need to stop squabbling among themselves and recognize who is the real enemy. They need to use some imagination and develop a single, stronger, and morally supportable message and to fight back.

This country can not run without the use of natural resources, and as the use of this country's natural resources dries up, the economic support for rural communities disappears. As rural communities disappear and change, many of life's better qualities and production of natural resource products disappears to the detriment of this country.

HOW DID WE GET HERE/THE POLITICS OF THE SITUATION

Facts and the truth have become less and less important in the running of this country.

In the past even for the producers of natural resource products, being politically active provided some control over regulatory processes. While financial contributions still open a lot of doors, natural resource dollars do not seem to be able to buy as much and can not seem to compete in today's political markets. Like with a fickle lover, long lasting commitments by a politician are a rarity in today's world. When it no longer comfortably fits the needs of a politician, the contributor can be left holding an empty bag.

The media and politically correct thinking has gained a major foot-hold in the political processes. Perception is reality, and the politicians follow the lead provided by the media and politically correct thinking. Even donations of money can not win the day if strong enough politically correct pressure is applied.

What is happening all over the country can be illustrated by what has happened in the small world of California timber harvesting regulation. Starting in the 1970s, timber harvesting regulation in California was completely overhauled, and has been undergoing an overhaul every year since.

Early in the game, the Fourth Branches of Government were held accountable by the legislature and others. Time tested and peer reviewed science, site specific facts, logic, and common sense were utilized through use of District Technical Advisory Committees (DTACs). Timber money also appeared to have some influence in the legislature.

As the California timber harvesting rule making process proceeded, it was thought the hearing process would allow science and field experience to be the basis for regulatory wording. This was not the case. DTACs were eliminated. Input was taken but routinely ignored, and many rules subject to multiple interpretations were created without considering all the facts and scientific information. Experienced regulators and field professionals, including me, still believed it was possible to work together in overcoming regulatory interpretation problems in the field.

Things did work for awhile until the environmental community found it could take complicated rules and regulations to court and get an inexperienced, layman court system to make decisions that helped their cause.

The timber people thought this was okay; because, surely justice and science would prevail. Wrong! As discussed in Chapter Six, the judicial review processes in many ways actually make things worse.

A recent article(226) in a local paper illustrates how layman judges have further confused things. This article describes how a judge believes treating logging operations in a site specific manner (which to me as an experienced professional is "in a factual manner") "lessens protection for watersheds..." Per the article, what the judge has done by his ruling is to say it is better to require use of the current, one-size fits all regulatory prescriptions even if they do fit the site-specific situation. The truth and facts be damned, full speed ahead and apply regulatory requirements developed in far off, non site specific locations which are heavily influenced by inexperienced lay persons as described in Chapter Five.

Along the way, the media had their own agenda. The media played to the emotion of the moment and promoted ideas of their choosing. Media reporting reflected inadequate review and a collection of unproven information and misinformation.

While the rural community, timberland owners, and field professionals acknowledge sometimes quite loudly to themselves that there are problems with the regulatory processes, there is a lack of will to provide time and financial resources needed to bring about needed corrections. There is a fear confrontation will make things worse, and many choose to hold back with the hope things will not get worse for themselves and their families.

Some rebuttal efforts by the rural community, timberland owners, and field professionals has involved use of costly experts and professionals lacking field experience, and some theories and facts have been thrown to the public. A lot of what the general public has seen is too technical and confusing for them to understand, and some information is just plain not reviewed in a favorable light by the general public.

The California timber harvest regulation story is being repeated all over this country as the Fourth Branches of government, media, legislatures, and meddling public are allowed to capture control of public thought regarding natural resource issues. The producers of natural resource products and the rural communities have not made a commitment, financially and personally, to confront what is happening, and they are losing the battle.

ARE THEY NO-SHOWS OR JUST LATE TO THE PARTY

The ones leading the fight for a reasonable handling of wildland and environmental issues have been large landowners and various professional, landowner, and industry groups. Except for a few hard to recognize successes, the continually worsening situation indicates these folks have not pursued a winning course of action.

It appears for various reasons the resource oriented brotherhood and a thing called the "Environmental Brain Trust" has been willing to accept compromise and not rock the boat. There has been a focus on working with the ones at the top of the regulatory heap and pursuing a strategy that favors political and high level solutions. They have used a "can't we all get along" approach in an attempt to not alienate the Fourth Branch of Government.

The focus on those at the top of the regulatory pack has generated no real desire by these top people to do the right thing. Those at the top, supervisors and various boards, committees, and commissions, routinely are kept from needed information; or, they selectively chose what they want to hear. Staffs and lower level employees restrict flow of information about problem situations, and surrounding loud political and public misperception noise drowns out real world information.

Without some pressure, those at the top are routinely going to avoid getting involved if they believe it is not in their best interest or in the best interest of their governing body.

The rural folks are basically leaderless. The professional, landowner, and industry representatives are not effectively networking and pooling their ideas and resources. No one is showing the troops a winning way to counter the politically correct and damaging regulatory activities, and the so-called leaders have everyone playing a mostly defensive game plan which includes sitting around complaining and doing nothing really productive. Have another cocktail.

The practice of friendly arguments between advocacy and association groups and regulators at hearings and then having meetings over lunch, dinner, or cocktails for a friendly get together isn't solving many problems. Instead of pushing to make problems go away, there seems to be more done to perpetuate problems and retain the need for association services.

Less productive and routinely inappropriate and misguided public relations efforts, politically correctness, and legalese are promoted, and input from experienced field professionals has been given a secondary role.

Experienced field professionals are the backbone of natural resource use in this country, and there has been a reluctance to fight the rapidly increasing unjustified everyday problems and liabilities being experienced by these professionals. Professional newsletters and magazines promote many regulatory ideas and incorrect practices that have not stood peer review and the test of time. This promotion is creating all kinds of liability and regulatory obstacles for professionals in the field, and inappropriately has supported giving many pseudo experts leadership roles in land management decisions.

While simply requiring everyone in the regulatory processes to be accountable and act professionally would go a long way in resolving many regulatory problems, this simple thought has for very questionable reasons fallen on deaf ears and has been resisted by all sides of the fence. The track record of the associations and those running things for the producers of natural resource products and the rural folks shows a losing game plan which has not even been able to hold the line.

Maybe the independent nature of rural folks is getting in the way. Maybe pride of authorship, fear of losing control, and fear of controversy which may cause more work for the paid representatives is keeping the so-called leaders from working together and being more effective.

Being timid and defensive has not been getting the job done.

RUDDERLESS LEADERS

FORESTERS WHEEEERRRRREEEEE ARRRREEEE YOU?

Who should be lead "Land Managers"?

The title "Land Manager" says it all. A true land manager is required to be involved in all things that affect land management decisions. In making land management decisions, a field professional can not avoid putting his or her reputation on the line whenever performing any land management activity. Forester's work requires they have the ability to handle land management activities, tax work, estate planning, land productivity, educational skills, appraisals, maintenance of open space, all forms of regulation, species protection, politics, and people.

Due to the continually changing regulatory situation, all the variables provided by Mother Nature, changing markets, future unknowns, and changing landowner goals, land managers are never going to have it easy in making many educated decisions.

What is required of a land manager makes it impossible for any one person or profession to do the job alone; however, I believe for successful management to occur there needs to a single leader and final decision maker. Experienced professionals know soliciting needed information is a must before making decisions; however, letting all those providing input to be involved in a final decision can be a recipe for delay and disaster.

The management by committee approach being applied in the spotted owl issue and on the National Forests provides examples of failing multi-discipline management schemes. In these two management examples, the leadership role has been relegated to many inexperienced and unqualified pseudo experts and pseudo ideas that have not been time tested, peer reviewed, and scientifically proven. This gathering of inexperienced and unproven thinking is being utilized by a multi-tasking decision process that is routinely resulting in delays and lost benefits. These two management situations provide good examples of what not to do, and they are more fully discussed elsewhere in this book.

It is said foresters' principal purpose is to grow and harvest trees, and this purpose may conflict with environmental protection and many of society's wildland goals. For this reason, foresters need to back-off and play second fiddle to other ologists.

To this, I say hogwash.

Especially in California, foresters can lose their livelihoods if they violate environmental laws, and professional foresters have gone out of their way to do what society wants. To bad too many people have not been exposed to the level of professionalism practiced by professional foresters, and too many people still think a forester's principal purpose is firefighting, being a park ranger, or being a lookout in a fire lookout tower.

Of all the professionals involved with land management decisions, including the Johnny-come-lately ologists, forester's are the best trained and most experienced in handling what is expected of lead land managers. For years and years foresters have handled land management activities, tax work, estate planning, land productivity, educational skills, appraisals, maintenance of open space, all forms of regulation, species protection, politics, and people. Land management is what foresters have always done.

For sure, foresters have been around for a long, long time, and much, much longer than the other ologists who are just starting to learn what land management is all about.

While I believe foresters are the best ones to be lead land managers, they do have one failing. Leadership has to be earned, and most foresters have not illustrated the desire and need to use them as lead land managers. Foresters have been comfortable backing away from the leadership role and letting others define what they do.

When controversial environmental issues or regulatory problems are being discussed, foresters shun the spotlight. Routinely they do not confront those with theories and ideas not based on time tested peer reviewed science, site specific facts, truth, logic, common sense.

Having been there and played the same loser's game, I know why foresters often let themselves be pushed aside. Like most foresters, I routinely was not in a position to stand up to wrongful thinking and wrongful actions. Having a family to support and other financial commitments, makes you not want to put yourself in a position that might cost you your job or your capacity to earn a living. Realities of life do get in the way.

As in the case of most professionals, the potential for criticism or being found at fault causes foresters to back off. Foresters have been hit over the head so much about perceived bad things they do that many have developed an inferiority complex. In reacting defensively to criticism, foresters routinely fall on their own sword and supply information for others to use against them. Foresters routinely just give in and do as they are told in the hope they can avoid criticism, they will be considered good people, and they will not have to shoulder all the responsibility for perceived bad things.

So, what should a forester do?

DO THE FOLLOWING

YOU WON'T MAKE SOME FAIR WEATHER FRIENDS AND YOU
WON'T PLEASE EVERYONE

BUT

IT WILL SET YOU FREE

-

BASE YOUR DECISIONS

ON

LOGIC
COMMON SENSE
AND
SITE SPECIFIC FACTS
(THE TRUTH)

-

SUPPORT OTHER PROFESSIONAL ACTION AND PROFESSIONAL
INPUT THAT DOES THE SAME
IT'S WORKING FOR ME AND I SLEEP GOOD AT NIGHT

The way foresters act has additionally been re-enforced by a lack of support from the resource producing community and forestry professional groups. Associations and so-called leaders of natural resource use have been absent in fighting the rapidly increasing unjustified everyday problems and liabilities experienced by field professionals who are the backbone of natural resource use in this country. Some foresters have stepped up to protect landowners and client interests and goals, and they have been left alone to swing in the breeze.

It is a rare forester that wants to be a martyr and alone in a fight.

This reluctance to get involved in resolving field professionals' problems is illustrated by unsupportable politically correct comments in newsletters that promote many ideas that have not stood peer review and the test of time. These comments routinely reflect badly on the profession and do not reflect the real world.

Not doing more to protect field professionals and their livelihoods and to promote experienced professionals as lead land managers in all fields of land management (appraisal, planning, silviculture, and operational activities) is creating problems for producers of natural resource products and rural communities. Experienced professionals are becoming less and less relevant. The decision processes involving natural resource use is becoming rudderless as multiple experts and resource disciplines muddle around with decision processes. Without a central leader, decisions needed to keep resource use going will continue to be chaotic and more and more unproductive.

It is going to take a major effort by all the resource user and producer groups to keep the experienced professional in the lead land manager's position.

I believe foresters are the ones most qualified to fill lead manager positions, but they are going to have to do a better job proving they have the desire and ability to handle the position. They need to stop back-peddling and not be afraid to confront wrongful ideas and thinking. This will show they are leaders and not followers. If foresters collectively do this, they have a better shot at being given the lead land manager's position and being supported in this position.

It's a use it or lose it situation for foresters.

IDEAS AND INFO IS NEEDED TO ENERGIZE THE TROOPS

There needs to be more effort in educating the rural folks and making them knowledgeable advocates.

Granted there is a need to educate the masses, and a lot of effort and expense has gone into targeting public relation efforts towards the more heavily populated areas; however, the realities of the situation are making conversion of the masses through simple public relation efforts an impossible task.

Those being targeted are the more educated and professional folks who already have the knowledge and resources to sort out and understand the issues, and most of them have probably already made up their mind about wildland issues. The discovery of E-mails, faxes, and other means of quick flow of information has provided a lazy man's way to again connect with the more educated and professional folks, but how many of the voting and affected working folks do you think are being energized by this approach?

It is easy to say everyone is responsible to do their own homework and get involved on their own, but we can all see how this approach is failing. A

218

personal, forceful touch like a kick in the shins is routinely needed to energize some folks.

Respectful and professional confrontation on many small fronts using supportable and truthful arguments can generate a lot of free positive press and can create some building blocks to support needed change. Such an approach also creates some excitement and stimulates interest in getting involved. I hope we have not reached the point where we are afraid of stimulating discussion with the truth, because we are afraid of a fight over the truth.

I believe the main base of support is the rural communities and the working folks in all areas. It seems doing more to get these folks energized and working together to make the Fourth Branch of Government accountable for inappropriate actions would yield all kinds of benefits. It seems little is being done to educate these folks and make them aware of what is happening to them. Some of these folks are hungry for information, and there is a lack of distribution of factual information and ideas to working folks and the rural communities. Because they are not helped to understand the issues, they do not know how they are personally affected and how to easily participate. All they see is a losing effort, and they are not stimulated to participate. No one wants to continually play on a losing team and to sit the bench all the time.

There seems to be a lack of co-ordination and networking among groups of similar regulatory interests such as landowners, agricultural producers, labor unions, and other related professional groups. This lack of co-ordination and networking reduces the effectiveness of these groups. Relevant information does not seem to get distributed in a timely manner, and opportunities for combining information into more co-hesive and co-ordinated messages are routinely lost.

It seems individual associations are trying to hard to do all things for all people on all issues, and limited resources and people are not being concentrated where it will do the most good.

There needs to be more effort to spread information that others understand, find interesting, and worth passing on to others. The Fox News' "Vanishing Freedom" program on governmental land set asides and lock-ups, the elimination of hatchery fish by clubbing returning fish and elimination of fish hatcheries, the "Not In My Backyard (NIMBY)" problem and how the global forests are being affected by the restrictions on the use of natural resources being promoted in this country, and a video by American Investigator with Marc Morano showing how pseudo science and inappropriate eviro thinking is hurting people in third world countries are examples of information that needs to be spread around. Refer to end of

Chapter Twelve for information on obtaining the listed videos, and refer to Chapter Four for more information on the unnecessary and wasteful killing of viable, healthy hatchery fish.

People need to know how they will be affected by the Environmental Protection Agency's (EPA) Total Maximum Daily Load(TMDL) program that is discussed in Chapter Two.

National Marine Fishery Service (NMFS), National Oceanic Atmospheric Agency (NOAA), and Fish and Wildlife Service (F&WS) problems more fully discussed in Chapter Three need to be exposed; so, they can be effectively confronted.

The adverse impacts from conservation easements which are more fully discussed in Chapter Seven need to be better advertised.

People need to be made aware of the failings of new, untested theories and ideas involving elimination of road use, not allowing disturbance in watercourse protection buffer zones, and disturbing old stabilized slide areas.

People, especially landowners, need to know research and needed data collection does not have to be as expensive, time consuming, and complicated as a lot of pseudo experts have indicated. The idea only certain politically correct professionals can do needed work is false. The idea that good data only comes from complex and costly projects is scaring a lot of people out of doing data collection work, and routinely this thinking results in limited manpower and resources being used-up chasing unrealistic and costly windmills.

People need to know there is an emphasis on collecting negative and bad data, and the lack of collecting and using positive data is resulting in regulatory overkill and unnecessary operational restrictions. Many healthy and positive things are happening and healthy watersheds exist, but these good things are routinely ignored and go unreported. A simple, usable definition of a healthy watercourse would help to resolve many regulatory road-blocks. For some self-interest and unprofessional reasons, the so-called experts resist making even a temporary workable definition. This reluctance to make any definition indicates these folks are not qualified to make the decisions required of lead land managers.

Rural folks and producers of natural resources simply need to know how to promote and watch out for their self interests.

Landowners need to know to not participate in only collecting negative information. Why participate, only to get your hand slapped? Landowners need to know to collect all relevant information, and to be trained in using this information to press for less land use restrictions when things are going okay on their lands. There needs to be incentives for doing the right things.

If a watershed is healthy, landowners should be left alone to continue doing what has lead to a healthy situation. Why is there a need to change land use activities if things are looking good and are working okay? Why aren't achievable standards provided and rewards provided for doing the right thing? Why aren't examples of the right things provided as much as examples of unproven bad things?

Informational food for rural area folks includes the need to understand what is needed to keep their way of life alive and to give them ammunition to use in supporting the continued use of natural resources. They need to understand their rural way of life and private ownership of open space can not survive without the use of natural resources. The production of natural resource products provides the main economic support for rural communities, and the use of natural resources (farming, timber harvesting, mining, ranching) is restricted if open space lands are not retained in private ownership. While tourism and High Tech are touted as substitutes for use of natural resources, the historical data says these economies can be unreliable sources of income and routinely can not replace natural resource production dollars. High Tech sounds nice, but the things that make a rural community rural such as distance from people, not easily usable transportation facilities, lack of support facilities and distribution facilities make significant Hi-tech production unattainable without destroying the basic things that make a rural area rural. In the larger scheme of things, the loss of natural resource use and production of natural resource products results in a loss of infrastructure production facilities and an increasing dependence by this country on the rest of the world for needed resource products.

Future wars will not only be fought over oil.

HOW TO FIGHT BACK

What is happening does not have to happen.

There are ways to fight back and win.

What can be done, and what does it take?

An idealistic version of a winning game plan includes the following:

Do the right thing and apply the truth in a direct, open, smart, and professional manner. Stay on the moral high ground and on the side of truth. Do not let spin replace the good hard truth.

Base the truth on time tested and peer reviewed science, site specific facts, logic, and common sense.

When others do not do these two things, stand up and make them accountable. Commit to sticking the truth in the faces of anyone resisting the truth.

Educate more people especially in the rural communities to the truth? More informed troops would lead to more knowledgeable involvement by more people, and numbers of people, especially knowledgeable people, get the attention of politicians.

Like the enviros, do not be afraid to use a little imagination in playing the game. Quietly and patiently waiting for hearing and legislative processes to provide solutions is routinely producing losers. As the enviros have done, directly confront the Fourth Branch of Government with some out of the box imaginative thinking.

Some more realistic ways to apply these ideas are provided in Chapter 21.

An example of when to beware of regulators bearing gifts is provided by the following comments in a 1/15/02 write-up summarizing a committee's activities that was supposedly set-up to find ways to help small landowners.

"Stewardship Committee - Desperately seeking 'Process Relief for Landowners' with three prongs (all barbed)."

"STAY TUNED FOR THE FEBRUARY EPISODE OF 'COASTAL SURVIVOR' where 12 small landowners will pit their survival skills against the wiley regulators and each other. The winner gets to conduct limited harvest operations on his small tract, while the losers will be regulated to making lucrative mountain subdivisions."

PS: This committee was originally set-up by the regulators (Fourth Branch of Government) to collect input from so-called leaders and associations representing small landowners. At the start, the committee only consisted of regulators and a couple association people until a forester made the committee aware there were no small landowners on the committee. The lack of small landowners on the committee showed the wiley regulators and association representatives weren't really serious about the interests of small wildland owners.

Internet report(334) echoes my thoughts by saying "For too long, our willingness to play only defense in our confrontation with hostile agendas has resulted in a steady retreat from active resource management to a wasteful and biologically damaging no-management, no-use, lock-it-up and throw the key away approach to environmental management." With

"…reduction of property rights in resources, animals, and the environment…" being done in this country and being "…mimicked by the United Nations…", "Opposition…" to "…developing nations to manage their own resources for their own citizens…can be expected from environmental and animal rights groups whose influence of Federal and UN bureaucracies would be jeopardized by…" such independent actions.

Amen and hallelujah.

Legitimate problems need to be faced head on and resolved based on the facts. This takes some gumption. In my experiences with permit, regulatory, and enviro matters, workable long term solutions to legitimate issues require the truth and facts to be clearly presented and understood. The short cut, get-along-approach used to avoid having to do the work needed to dig out the truth and facts routinely yields short term compromises that don't last very long. It just takes the gumption to not give-in and to pro-actively participate.

Unfortunately, gumption seems to be in short supply.

FREQUENT RESULT
OF ENCOUNTERS BETWEEN
REGULATORS AND PERMITEES

Away we go,
Not knowing where we go,
But knowing we must go,
Because someone said so.

POOR POOR MISINFORMED PUBLIC

Chapter Twelve

I am sure many like me have learned to view information from public media sources with a skeptical eye and to continually question the credibility of this information. It is hard to tell which information has been juiced up to get your attention or slanted to present a biased viewpoint. Public media sources routinely sensationalize stories and push viewpoints favored by reporters or owners of the media outlets. News articles do not always support accompanying headlines, and some articles are written with so much slant you are left wondering what is the truth after reading them.

The internet can be a useful source of information, but beware of what you believe and how you use information from the internet. With anyone being able to put basically anything they want on the internet, getting credible, unslanted, unbiased, factual, and verifiable information over the internet can be a pig in the poke.

Even environmental reports and information distributed by governmental agencies contains slant and bias.

The general public never really knows the truth about many issues, and it is tough for a lay person to get good factual information. Most of us do not have the access, time, or ability to do the research needed to get to the truth. Some of us do the best we can and pick around trying to figure out the truth. Ones who work hard at finding the truth are in the minority, and the majority lazily accepts whatever comes easily from newspapers, government publications, internet, radio, and television.

Reporters and owners of the media handle information in a way that indicates they do not want to get cross-ways with those that think environmental protection is as good as mom and apple pie, and routinely media reporting of environmental issues contains a slant towards environmental protection. Chosen quotes are sensationalized and put-downs are emphasized in a way that favors environmental protection. Gloom and doom environmental news gets more play than good environmental news.

The media's knowledge of Public Speaking 101, which teaches the last thing read or heard is the best remembered, is demonstrated by the routine slant towards environmental protection at the end of environmental articles.

To give an illusion of balanced reporting, two sides of an issue and good guy, bad guy situations are routinely provided. Commonly used match-ups to portray good versus bad include republicans and loggers versus species protection, clearcutting versus fish, and corporations versus pollution controls. Even long ago European immigrants, our forefathers, are getting blamed for some current environmental problems, because they replaced "one with nature" Native Americans.

This type of reporting helps to create incorrect perceptions that generate political and public pressures to inappropriately reduce use of our natural resources. By not fully disclosing the adverse impacts from the reduction of natural resource use, the media additionally allows pressures for reduced use of natural resources to remain in place.

During interviews, reporters give the impression they want to be fair and balanced; however, final reporting often demonstrates a close mindedness and unwillingness to fully report on environmental issues. Because key points and pertinent information on issues familiar to me are routinely missing in final reports, I have to assume some information must end up on the cutting room floor. Media's focus on negative and damaging environmental situations and reduced emphasis on healthy environmental conditions indicates ulterior motives and agendas are at play.

A news article(335) provides a good insight to how a lot of the media approaches the reporting of news stories. This news article mentions how it was discovered the "60 Minutes" program had "...corporate ties to the publisher of Richard Clarke's book.", and there may be a conflict of interest because Richard Clarke's book against President Bush was discussed on a "60 Minutes" program. At the end of this news article a quote is provided that says "The idea that we have any political agenda is silly,..." "We want to make news, that is what our agenda is." This quote is interesting, because it provides a slip of the tongue that shows the news media routinely tries to make news as opposed to just reporting the news.

Another news article(336) discussing the potential San Bernadino Forest fire problem, illustrates how the media writes in a way to slant public opinion towards an enviro protectionist view point. Out of the blue, this news article ends on the thought that "The forest's problems began with 19th century logging that cleared the way for new trees to grow almost on top of each other."

There is no mention in the article how the harvested wood helped to build the local communities and to provide benefits enjoyed by these communities. The article makes it sound like growing a new forest is a bad thing.

This news article also discusses how everyone is playing catch-up in trying to get fire control work done, however, the article conveniently or naively does not emphasized how the current problems have been long in coming and are due to a lack of active management. Active management could have reduced and made manageable the fire control problem involving beetle killed trees and the tight forest condition. The problems mentioned in the article did not start when the forest started to regrow. The problems started when a "no management" approach was applied, infrastructure needed to produce and handle forest products was allowed to disappear, and Mother Nature was allowed to determine in her haphazard way what happens on our wildlands.

The idea that everything would have been hunky dory if no timber harvesting had ever been done ignores reality and all the benefits and reasons for actively managing wildlands.

SLANTED MEDIA ABOUNDS

Slanted and misleading headlines

Forest cases going cutters' way - News article(337) uses the word "cutters" which creates a picture of trees being cut down and makes it look like some bad things are going to happen. Reading the article finds the ability to thin some forests for fire protection reasons has been won in court, and the fact court cases have delayed needed fire prevention work is glossed over. The headline that should have been used to describe this story is "Fire prevention work finally gets started".

"Forest thinning OK without state review, Assembly says" - News article(338) accompanied this headline which made it sound like any timber or landowner, big and small, get to cut trees without anyone checking them out. This sounds like a bad thing. When you read the article, you find a special permit process overseen by the state forestry agency was created to help removal of vegetation in low environmental impact situations for fire prevention reasons. Allowed work included clearing vegetation around houses while allowing no work around watercourses. Existing permit processes for the same work situation were expensive and cumbersome to obtain, and the change eliminated some unnecessary regulatory obstacles that impeded fire prevention work.

New forest rules puts Appalachian Trail at risk - Accompanying news article(339) says 163 miles of the 2,174 Appalachian Trail System "...fall within the 58 million acres where the Bush administration proposed

(proposed!) lifting a ban on logging, road building and other development." Representative of "The Campaign to Protect America's Lands...said he knows of no plans to allow timbering along any of the 163 miles...", and "...according to the Appalachian Trail Conference a volunteer group...which works closely with the Forest Service in managing the trail..., Most of the trail is protected by existing forest management plans." Now lets see, less than 8% of the trail is located in a 58 million acre area that is in an area that is "proposed - not officially authorized" for some timber harvesting, and there are no known plans to harvest timber along the 163 miles of involved trail which is already protected from timber harvest activity. So what is the risk? The whole article sounds more like a nonstory about something that is set-up to not happen. I wonder if anyone has considered the benefits of opening up some of the trail area to provide some vista views, create a larger variety of wildlife to be observed, and in general add to the diversity of the trail?

Slanted Magazine article

An article in the January 27, 2003 edition of Time Magazine provides slanted reporting regarding use of natural resources in an article titled "How Bush Gets His Way on the Environment" The article starts out making no bones how the writer feels by saying "...the Administration stepped up what critics view as an all out assault on the environment..." Regarding a fire in "...Kern River in...California..." an environmentalist says "...they've been looking for an opportunity to log...and the fires have suddenly handed them a way to get around the usual restrictions." Administration "...lieutenants...have quietly focused on the regulatory route, using administrative guidance and legal loopholes..." "Judicious thinning of trees...would provide for the logging of trees as much as 30 inches in diameter (As if there is something special about a tree less than a yard in diameter. Under average growing conditions, many tree species can grow to 30 inches in diameter at chest height in less than 40 years.)..."

The article provides a picture of what looks like California coastal old-growth redwood trees which to an experienced eye appear to range from 6 feet to 10 feet and larger in diameter. A caption is provided with the picture that indicates trees like the ones shown in the picture could be harvested.

The article has critics saying "The Bush Plan..." is "...actually a veiled attempt to bypass restrictions and increase commercial logging in the U.S.'s 155 national forests." The article closes by having an environmentalist saying "I consider this my forest, not theirs." "Unfortunately…the Bush Administration doesn't appear to agree." Nor do I.

Note how the quoted environmentalist says Public Trust trees belong to him and not to all of us.

The whole article has a slant, but the picture portrayal of potentially cutting down coastal old-growth redwood trees during an inland fire salvage operation in the Kern River area of California is particularly deceiving and misleading.

So much for fair and balanced reporting.

As you can tell, I have developed a biased viewpoint regarding public media reporting of environmental issues; so, I challenge you, the reader, to do your own open-minded review of articles discussing environmental and natural resource use matters. See if you do not agree with my assessment that there is a bias towards protectionist thinking.

The media occasionally touches on environmental regulatory problems, but well researched, factual reports on unjustified environmental restrictions damaging Rural America are rare. Sedimentation problems from exploding residential road use on converted open space lands get some play, but the reasons why the conversions are happening are not fully presented. The problems with putting private land into environmentally restricted public ownership are not discussed by the media, and to the contrary, this loss of income producing land is routinely promoted by the media. The reduced production of fish, timber, livestock, farm products, and natural resources and the increasing importation of these items routinely goes unnoticed. The disappearing incentives for maintaining privately owned open space lands and economic base needed to support rural communities get relatively little play. Little serious attention is paid to the disappearance of rural communities.

A recent editorial(340) says "…the reality is that unless we're going to legalize pot, agriculture on a big scale here and elsewhere will never be what it once was." While editor did follow-up at later date and say "…reference to some future legalization of marijuana was part of a comparison to past dominance of agriculture in the county and the current situation.", these kinds of comments illustrate a lackadaisical feeling by the media towards rural community issues and possibly an unwillingness to promote the use of natural resources. Accompanying front page coverage of tree sitters protesting timber harvesting and a hemp festival, also indicated another agenda was possibly in play.

For there to be a change in how the media reports environmental issues, there is a need for them to do the following.

GET OUT INTO THE FIELD AND SEE WHAT THEY ARE TALKING ABOUT!

Getting out into the field can include attending public hearings and other forums. While a lot of good information can be provided through public meetings, not all reporters do the work needed to dig out relevant information. Public meeting reports routinely contain a slant or bias and you can not assume these reports provide a full and factual accounting of meetings. Good guy versus bad guy and environmental gloom and doom themes are commonly included in media reports on public meetings. Quotes and information from the most vocal and offensive participants at hearings are used to spice up reports, and this often slanted and untrue information can result in misleading reports. How public agencies are ignoring ways to provide regulatory relief is rarely told. How staff input routinely overrides other input is rarely told. How experienced and knowledgeable field professionals, workers, and families living and working in the rural communities are being left out of the decision making processes is rarely told. No matter how good public meeting information can be, second hand reporting of what happens at public meetings can not replace information collected from getting out into the real world.

Is it such a novel idea to go get information from those who have built a current working knowledge about the issues of concern? Some reporters will tell you they do this, but routinely when their sources of information and review are checked, you find a short list of repeatedly used people. Their sources are frequently high level and well known often senior community members or group spokespersons who have developed their own personal and political viewpoints. Many contact folks are professionally inactive or lack current experience in dealing with regulatory processes, and they are usually disconnected from what is happening in the real world.

Routinely not enough time is spent researching and writing good, factual stories. Excuses that there isn't enough time and deadlines get in the way may be valid, but they are poor excuses for not doing a good job. You would think journalistic professionalism would push reporters to do a more factual job.

As for wanting stories that stimulate interest, you can't beat the interest generated by use of natural resources, environmental issues, and impacts to communities. On a local level, interest on these issues is routinely high. If the media wants zesty stories, all they to do is get out and prime the pump.

Working at a story instead of sitting back waiting for random articles from laypeople to come their way has its rewards.

GO GET THE REAL STORY

The real story is not:

Jobs against the environment
Industry against the enviros

The real story includes:

Truth against poor and improper science
Landowners against unfounded and improper regulation
Retention of open space lands and proper use of needed natural resources

The full story includes:

1. How rural communities and the nation are being hurt by an out of control Fourth Branch of Government that is allowed to operate without being accountable for improper actions.

2. How a quagmire of regulations and regulatory processes are being created without input from experienced field professionals and without application of time tested and peer reviewed science, site specific facts, logic, and common sense.

3. How governmental employees, especially the honest and well intentioned ones, are inadequately or improperly instructed regarding the intent and limitations of the regulations they apply.

4. How government employees, especially higher level employees, are allowed to apply inappropriate interpretations of rules and regulations, unauthorized internally developed guidelines, and personal agendas without any consequences.

THE REAL RURAL AMERICA STORY THAT IS NOT BEING TOLD IN A NUTSHELL

The rural way of life as we know it:

A. Can be described as existing in lightly populated areas with a lot of open space and a sustainable economic base.
B. Was developed and built around working the land and use of natural resources.
C. Has brought us an honest day's work, some darn good people, good values to live by, pride of sacrifice, and production of needed natural resource products.
D. **Can not be maintained without the proper use of natural resources and production of natural resource products.** Production of natural resource products is the most consistent and largest economic base in rural areas.

The private ownership of open space lands can not exist or be maintained without the use of natural resources and production of natural resource products

TOURISM AND HI-TECH
THE FALSE HOPES

Tourism and High Tech have been touted as substitutes for economies provided by use of natural resources, but a close review finds the fallacy of this thinking.

I want to make it clear a war between natural resource use and other industries is not necessary, and comparisons are provided to illustrate the importance of resource based industries to Rural America. Knowing how all industries fit into the rural community picture and understanding tourism and high-tech industries can not easily replace resource based industries makes it easier to understand and resolve rural community issues.

Lord knows, rural folks need all the legal economic help they can get to keep going. Many have fallen to temptation and taken up illegal ventures to survive.

Industries not associated with natural resource use are routinely not major contributors to rural community economies. All kind of antidotal and numerical information exists which shows lost natural resource dollars are rarely replaced by tourism, hi-tech, and other legal industries' dollars.

High-tech sounds nice, but the things that make a rural community rural such as distance from people, lack of reliable communication and power, not easily usable transportation facilities, and lack of support facilities and distribution facilities routinely make hi-tech unattainable without destroying the basic things that make a rural area rural.

In rural areas where tourism is increasing and natural resource based industries are declining, news articles tell stories about young people not being able to find jobs and school enrollment going down. A news article(341) discusses the situation in the Roseburg area of Oregon. Due to new products, overseas competition, and environmental and political shutdown of timber industry, a change from high-paying timber jobs to lower paying jobs is occurring. The current situation has left little opportunity or incentive for the area's youth to stick around after they have left school. Another article dated(242) mentions a decline in school enrollment in Humboldt County, and the consensus is that lower enrollment is from young families leaving the area due to a lack of jobs. From these stories, it appears tourism and other industries are not filling the hole left by the decline in use of natural resources.

As illustrated by many recreational closures, tourism can be a fickle source of economic support.

In California, a news article(344) says, state parks are raising their annual fee from "...$67...to $110...to $115...to $120...to announced limit of $125..." This means less people will be buying annual park permits and there will be less incentive to go to parks and play tourist.

Not all protectionists see tourism as an acceptable replacement for lost natural resource use. A news article(345) says Alaskan cruise ship "...industry...has tried...to move past accusations that its big ships are hurting the lush scenery (in the water??????) and wildlife that attract..." tourists, and "...the industry has been very, very diligent in making sure that its ships have the latest technology to ensure environmental protection." If the big ships are catching heck when they spend most of their time away from land and in deeper waters, the smaller cruise ships and parties having closer and more direct contact with the vegetation and the wildlife are potential targets for being harassed and possibly shut down.

California Forest and Range Project (FRAP) 2003 Report provides a Lumber and wood products employment number in Humboldt County of around 3,400 people in 2001. Using realistic assumption that primary wood products industry (timber harvesting and logging) possibly contributes half the economic base provided by the total wood products industry which includes logging "and" manufacturing in the county and using the $442,637,587 estimate of primary wood products (log) value which reasonably represents half of the total county value in logs and higher valued finished products like lumber, it is possible that the wood products industry produces 2 x $442,637,587 or around $900,000,000 in value with 3,400 people. A news article dated 9/25/2003 mentions 6,110 were involved in producing $287,000,000 tourism dollars. This gives $900,000,000 versus $287,000,000 in an area with reduced natural resource use and increasing tourism.

A news article(346) mentions Humboldt County's timber industry employs 5,000 timber workers who make on the average about $36,000 per year. I do not believe the **"average"** annual wage for tourism jobs runs anywhere near $36,000 per year.

The higher return per employee in the wood products industry equates into higher salaries, increased benefits, and a stronger, more stable community.

If you put the saying "liars figure and figures lie" aside and apply logic and common sense, I believe you will agree that the provided comparisons logically show natural resource based industries are the main support for Rural America, and the media should spend more time and effort in promoting ways to increase the production and use of natural resources.

Occasionally some articles slip-out that discuss how the use of natural resources helps rural communities.

A news article(347) says "...Wyoming has no personal or corporate income tax and relatively low property taxes thanks to revenue for mining." This will all change if natural resource production and mining become curtailed.

An opinion article(348) says "Historically, the economic success of Humboldt County has been based on the harvesting of its natural resources..." such as "...logging...fishing...dairy...", and ranching. "...instead of seeking out and attempting to attract other new and environmentally damaging industries...efforts would be directed to restore the basic industries upon which the county was built." It is important to acknowledge that these basic industries are still sustaining the county.

A news article(349) has county supervisor saying "We've got resources here, and we've got a lot of them,..." "...he foresees the area continuing, as it always has, to rely in its natural assets, such as oysters in the bay, fish in the ocean, timber, and gravel in the rivers." I would add range and grassland to this list.

Infrastructure that processes natural resource products and production of natural resource products go hand in hand with each other. Reducing natural resource use reduces associated infrastructure, and loss of infrastructure further hurts realistic options for revitalizing rural areas.

A news article(350) mentions "Petaluma creamery to close its doors." which is "...a real loss for the community and (rural) Sonoma County agriculture. Processing plants (infrastructure), like the creamery, are critical to the survival of local agriculture,..."

A news article(352) shows what is happening in Redding, California. "Too many low wage jobs have sent Shasta County's economy spiraling downward, and economic analyst says." "The city of Redding and Shasta County need to do a better job of attracting companies to the area,..." More has to be done than getting low costing jobs provided by tourism to provide the economic support needed to maintain rural communities.

Substitute ideas for use of natural resources come in many forms, and can be pretty unrealistic and unproductive.

A news article(354) says "Rutgers University professor...and his wife..." who obviously do not understand rural communities suggest "...farming...in a swath stretching from Texas and New Mexico to Montana and North Dakota...be replaced by nature preserves and bison herds..." and this idea is part of "...the Buffalo Commons theory..." While farms, farming, and the rural towns may be on the way out, the suggestion by the Rutgers outsiders, who have a lot to learn about the rural way of life, "...have drawn the ire of many in the Great Plains." The Bufffalo theory describes how "...the region's...plight..." is occurring because "...the plains were oversettled and contend population declines are part of a trend toward a changing landscape." In short, it is being suggested the land and resources be made fallow and unused, and some kind of social and population relocation process be put into play to move people to other locations in the country. This idea smacks of impractical social engineering and ignores all the other factors causing folks to leave rural areas. I am sure the rural folks living in the Great Plains appreciate the suggestion that they are simply a mistake of history and must move because they are simply not where the theorist believe they should be.

Another news article(355) says rural folks can revert to using "...Paleotechnics..." which involves "...an array of primitive arts..." such as making "...braintanned deer hides..., antler buttons..., dogbane, plant fiber, sinew and hair..." into "...cordage..." that can become "...snares, ropes, belts, bags, and nets..." There are "...treats..." such as '...mild buzz...from...California bay trees..." and "...nuts..." Food comes from "...oak acorn mush,... roosters,...hens,...edible plant...beehive(s)..., venison (legal or illegal????)...", and "...winter garden..." with "dogbane..., broccoli, chard..." This life style is interesting and definitely utilizes natural resources. Some rural folks may chose to revert to this simple life style in order to survive in rural areas, but it is unrealistic to think this is a practical solution to maintaining an acceptable way of life.

Then as provided in another news article(356) you have some other folks saying they want to "...transplant African wildlife to the Great Plains of North America." "They...believe the relocated animals could restore biodiversity on this continent to a condition closer to what nature was like before humans overran the landscape." "...the scientists (probably pseudo scientists) believe today's animals could duplicate the natural roles played by their departed, even larger cousins—mastodons, camels, and saber-toothed tigers..." The article has someone asking "How many calves or lambs..." are needed "...to feed a family of lions for a month?"

If I have this straight, somehow a bunch of animals striving to survive will change the overall complexity and content of fields and fields of corn. I assume the plan includes confiscating large tracts of land under eminent domain or some other governmental taking of private property process; so, large pens can be built (I assume these animals will need large areas to roam) which are good enough to keep the newly imported animals from doing damage to naturally occurring species, domestic animals, and humans. Whoops, I forgot the humans will be re-located and gone.

Can you believe people are paid probably with taxpayer dollars to think-up this stuff?

These animal lovers and their far out ideas involve a restored balance in Nature which does not include humans. It is real scary to think these folks are smart and serious enough to actually convince someone somewhere to give their far out ideas a try no matter the human misery.

How would you like to wake up with an elephant in your backyard and in the middle of your clothesline? It looks like wolves are headed to the Northeastern part of the country, and if saber-toothed tigers were still around, you could bet that someone would want to turn them loose in someone's backyard.

I bet the quiet, easy-going rural folks in the Great Plains didn't know so many folks were against what they have done to the Great Plains in feeding the world. They are being told their life style is not one with Nature, and they need to be eliminated from the Great Plains.

As far-out ideas proliferate, use of natural resources continues to decline with many impacts to rural communities.

A Letter to the Editor(357) mentions how the problems facing rural communities like Humboldt County are highlighted by the "...declining (school) enrollment..." and required "...unification choices... currently affecting school districts,..."

A Newsletter(358) and internet report(359) describe how the environmental community is hurting efforts to keep rural communities going as illustrated by "...the use of lawsuits..." that have had JSDF (California's Jackson Demonstration State Forest) shut down for the last three years. "Court decisions by Mendocino Superior Court Judge...required the BOF to set aside its 2002 management plan for the forest..." This court decisions "...followed previous decision...to upgrade previous management plan before resuming logging." "The combined effect of the rulings has been to essentially shut down JSDF management for the past three years." JSDF timber harvest activities contribute in a significant way to Mendocino County's economic well-being. Restricted harvesting has a major impact on the local tax base, schools, and "...rural ambulance and hospital services..." in "Mendocino County Supervisor...district..." covering "...the JSDF/Fort Bragg area..." The loss of timber harvest from JSDF "...has cost Mendocino County about 200 jobs and significant yield tax revenue." "...county's timber harvest last year was the lowest since 1975, leaving a million dollar hole in the school budget due to loss of yield tax revenue.", and "...due to families leaving the region in search of work...schools are losing enrollment..."

This JSDF battle is not over the harvesting of old-growth and protecting unprotected values. It is an argument over how much and where young-growth (regrown trees) can be harvested in a forest where state regulators already tightly and professionally watch over all involved values.

In addition, in a time of budget deficit crisis in California, "...this shut down has cost the State of California the lost revenue from about 90 million bdft (board feet) of timber." which equates to tens of millions of badly needed state revenues.

Hope the enviros are proud of this one.

Unsupported, off-the-wall thinking is not new for enviros.

The scary part is that many use off-the-wall enviro protectionist ideas and actions to justify hindering attempts at new ways to improve rural community situations. While sometimes initiated by a legitimate wildlife and environmental concern, enviro and regulator thinking often morphs into unfounded and illogical arguments that too often smack of politics and a push for more control and power.

Efforts to put in place alternate ways to produce fish products versus depending on Mother Nature's haphazard ways routinely meet with resistance from the fishing community, enviros, and the regulators. The fishing community is losing jobs; so, their resistance is understandable. The reasons for the enviro's and regulator's resistance are more complicated and maybe a little sinister.

A news article(361) says "...our wild (fish) resources have hit a plateau (as perceived by enviros and regulators)." "So aquaculture provides a big opportunity." as "...by the year 2020, an additional 1.1 billion pounds of seafood will be needed annually to meet the growing demand." "Farm-raised fish could eventually dominate that market..." "The aquaculture industry has seen a 300 percent increase in the last two decades and has become the fastest-growing segment of U.S. agriculture production."

You would think this is good news for rural communities that could use aquaculture to help replace lost economies; however, the enviros, fishermen, and regulators seem to be doing little to promote aquaculture and are doing a whole lot to fight the use of aquaculture.

Because of the potential benefits and the world's need for food, I believe aquaculture is on the way no matter how hard some folks try to stop it. Instead of being so negative, more folks should get on board the aquaculture bandwagon and work to make it a winner by seeing things are done right.

Unfortunately getting together and making a winner does not seem to be the order of the day.

In a news article(362), a Pacific Marine Farms aquaculture project proposal at Fort Bragg, California that would "...be capable of generating two million pounds of red abaloney, 360,000 pounds of white shrimp, and 900,000 pounds of trout per year." was put in jeopardy by "...Coastal Commission..." requiring "...intake discharge pipelines be placed underground in areas of hard bottom habitat." The "...required horizontal drilling...to place the pipelines underground..." creates "...a cost of $8 million, making the project unfeasible." With Fort Bragg facing all kinds of economic losses, you would think someone would find a way to satisfy whatever coastal protection reason (possibly aesthetics?) requires use of underground pipes at a cost of up to $8 million dollars.

Excessive and unjust application of regulations is causing loss of privately owned open space lands.

An opinion article(363) shows regulation plays a big part in hurting the economies of rural communities. "...all those laws, taxes and rules businesses (and landowners) must comply with to remain legally operational - are at the dead center of any economy's depression, recession, or recovery. Overly regulated economies create high unemployment and zero growth. Loosen up a bit and things start to improve: unburden a lot and economies take off. In the pathologies of economies, regulations are the worst cancer. A new study, "The Spread of Regulations": "...demonstrates how regulations start small, metasize, and eventually consume the vital organs of healthy businesses." While many may say these are just words from another economic expert, I can say these words describe what I have seen happen regarding the shutdown of natural resource use and rural communities by environmental type regulations.

Another news article(364) mentions except for those who wish to voluntarily and legitimately preserve old-growth trees, the incentive to not harvest older trees does not exist for private landowners, because if they are not harvested, the regulators and enviros are finding ways to take them. Rancher in Sonoma County "...seeks OK to log...44-acre old-growth...redwood forest...on 600-acre parcel that has been in...family for three generations." "...conservationists (really preservationists) consider..." this stand of redwoods to be "...the largest stand of old-growth redwoods left in Sonoma County (true or not, never mind all the other old-growth redwoods already locked up elsewhere)." "...CDF (California Department of Forestry) denied... (harvest) plan (permit).", and landowner said "...I feel like the whole thing is a flat-out taking of my private property rights." The landowner is right about the taking, because I have seen this happen to timber landowners of large timber over and over and over again. Keep in mind this landowner and family husbanded their timber for three generations which shows their intentions to not overcut their lands. When it is time to reap their rewards for being conservative stewards of their resources, they are treated rudely and basically slapped in the face.

A later news article(366) provides how the rancher in Sonoma County and so many other ranchers are having to handle their regulatory and economic problems. "The 975 acre coastal ranch is on the market..." and for sale. So much for "...124 years in the same family,..." It looks like the family has decided to call it quits, and by hook and crook the regulators, enviros, and developers win another one.

Another news article(366) goes on to say "...Washington and Oregon have enjoyed an image of growth and prosperity...but...Rural areas are still struggling to crawl out of the hole created by downturns in natural resources based industries: fishing, farming, mining and timber." "Areas like Matlock... Washington..." where "...roar of logging trucks on nearby roads testifies to the main industry in the county ...that's been declining since the 1980s...haven't yet found a substitute for the family-wage jobs that logging once provided." "In Matlock, as in so many rural Western communities, everyone knows the threat of hunger is never far away. The (hunger) problem has spread throughout the West, where researchers identify a "hunger belt" stretching from New Mexico to Washington state. The (hunger) phenomenon baffled researchers when it was first documented in the 1990s (during the northern spotted owl shutdown) - poverty rates are higher in the South (where use of natural resources are not so restricted by regulation), so why do people suffer from hunger more often in the West? Now researchers point to a combination of unemployment, seasonal work, rural isolation, population growth and high cost of living..."

It is obvious to me these researchers did not fully review what has happened in rural communities; or, they could not miss listing one of the main culprits for the "hunger belt" which is the unnecessary and unjustified regulatory shut down of natural resource use. The news article itself clearly lists the economic depression in western rural areas as being due to the downturn in natural resources based industries: fishing, farming, mining and timber, but this information somehow went over the heads of the researchers when they arrived at their complicated combination of reasons for the rural community's economic and hunger problems. I am no economic expert, but history shows the rural communities were able to overcome "...seasonal work, rural isolation, population growth and high cost of living..." problems before the regulators unjustifiably restricted the use of natural resources.

A news article(367) states as advertised, doing business of any kind in California has become very costly due to regulations and taxes, and even the nonprofit recycling groups are crying and saying "For every dollar we're paying an employee we have 70 cents of additional costs, of which 30 cents is workers compensation." I know folks in business involving hazardous work such as timber falling and logging have to double employee cost numbers in order to cover all the higher wage costs such as taxes when determining negotiated and bid rates for work projects.

A variety of tax laws and permit regulations are making the production of natural resource products so costly that reduced income returns sometimes do not support continuing the production of natural resources. When this happens, privately owned open space land is sold off to other uses.

An internet report(368) mentions how "Schwarzenegger has proposed establishing THP (Timber Harvest Plan) fees in the 2004-05 State (California) Budget…" While more fees may be a way to help the state's budget deficit, these fees will just make the hole deeper for many businesses and rural communities in California.`

A news article(369) mentions how "…California Resources Secretary…said…The state should raise $10 million from new fees to cover its reviews of logging plans,…" "Timber owners already pay an average $42,954 to prepare harvest plans…" plus other state fees already in place. Department of Fish and Game (DFG) charges $800 per plan permit. In addition, required DFG stream alternation permits have fees starting at $600 and going over $1,000 per permit, and there is a proposal to double this permit's fees. Water Quality (WQ) has just put in place a fee starting at $800 per year for every year an approved harvest plan is in effect in the north coast region of California. Using state provided numbers and "Dividing the $10 million by the 555 harvest plans the state reviewed last year produces an average (California Department of Forestry) review cost of $18,000…" Adding this cost to the current plan preparation cost brings average approved plan costs to more than $60,000 per plan without including DFG and WQ permit fees. Is it any wonder "…the number of harvest plans has dropped 10 percent a year for the each of the last five years."

Please refer to the following copied Base Costs Table from Buckeye Forest Project June 2003 Report for another estimated summary listing of timber harvest plan costs in place in California as of 2003. Buckeye Association is located in Eureka, California.

APPENDIX B

Base Costs Occurring on all Timber Harvesting Plans (THP)
Note: Cost estimated at $50.00 per hour, and each column is an estimated THP Cost.

		Subject	Low	High*	Average
1.	Preliminary meeting	$0	$0	$1,000	$250
2.	Preliminary mapping and aerial photography evaluation	$250	$150	$500	$250
3.	Evaluation of problem areas	$2,000	$900	$4,000	$1,800
4.	Field Work	$5,000	$2,000	$9,000	$6,000
5.	Flagging and Marking	$4,500	$1,000	$6,000	$3,000
6.	Archaeology	$5,500	$1,500	$10,000	$3,500
7.	THP Document Preparation, Calculate Erosion Hazard rating	$4,000	$2,500	$7,500	$3,000
8.	Plan Submittal through approval by Department of Forestry	$4,000	$2,500	$9,000	$4,000
9.	Department of Fish and Game fee	$850	$850	$850	$850
10.	Department of Fish and Game watercourse grossing fee	$800	$0	$1,031	$800
11.	Spotted Owl survey and report	$3,000	$500	$10,000	$3,000
12.	Plant survey and report	$2,500	$0	$9,000	$3,000
13.	Potential additional surveys and reports		$1,000	$8,500	$3,000

Golden Eagle** $1,200
Goshawk** $1,200
Peregrine Falcon** $1,200
Osprey $1,200
Great Egret
Great Blue Heron
Marbled Murrelett
Red tree Vole
Pond Turtle
Willow Flycatcher $3,000
Long Eared Bat

14. Other potential costs:
Certified Engineering Geologist

	Subject	Low	High*	Average
Preconsultation with agency personell (each)	$2,500	$1,500	$10,000	$2,500
	$3,00	$200	$4,000	$500
TOTAL	**$45,700**	**$14,600**	**$90,381**	**$35,450**

Note: Costs listed are estimates and vary.
* Figure listed as High should not be considered a ceiling on potential costs. The number could increase depending on the number of additional surveys, various costs of surveys and related consultants.
** Costs of eagle, goshawk and falcon surveys were reduced based on combining the field work and completing portions of the field surveys and consultants at the same time. Written reports would still be separate.

In case anyone is interested, based on reasonable and conservative calculations using estimated 2004 California log market information and Douglas-fir, the most heavily harvested, middle valued tree species harvested in California, the indicated cost to a timber landowner to prepare a harvest plan including the proposed added state fee ($60,000) requires the removal of around 500 Douglas-fir trees or approximately fifty truck loads of logs. Contractor log and haul and state required forester administration costs roughly require removal of another 500 trees. This means before timber owners can expect any return for themselves from their timber, they have to remove 1,000 trees or 100 loads of logs to breakeven.

People who think timber owners are making a lot of money need to know many landowners do not even have 100 loads of logs to harvest, and many small timber owners are barely getting by. It is a mystery why more California timberland owners do not just sell out and move on.

Overcoming the obstacles being put in place to harvest timber and keep lands producing natural resource products is not easy. Willingly giving a lot of money to the tax man to fund the Fourth Branches of Government who are continually beating you over the head is not for the weak of heart.

A news article(370) outlines "...the level of pain that is being felt by dairy farmers regardless of size and location...isn't a problem only in California." "Many farmers across the country can not plan, fix broken machinery nor upgrade their facilities..." and "...they struggle to simply pay their bills."

A Newsletter article(371) describes how "...Central Valley Regional Water Quality Board...staff... proposed to revise...water quality program..." "...California Farm Bureau Federation...water resources director said...April proposal (the latest staff proposal)...monitoring and reporting costs range from $7,450 annually (with startup costs of $4,900 or $7,400) to annual costs of $14,118. The range depends on whether a particular farmer hires a consultant to take samples and has a more complex operation that would require monitoring for a larger range of pesticides." "...these costs are basically the same for farms of all sizes." For farmers and ranchers making a living off the land, an annual monitoring cost of $7,450 to $14,118 is a big bite out of anyone's annual income. Note it is staff who came up with the latest proposal and not the water board which raises the question who is running the water quality show.

In a news article(372), "...Schwarzenegger said... Agriculture is...one of the state's (California's) top three industries, supporting more than 1 million jobs and contributing nearly $28 billion to the state's economy. Protecting California agriculture is absolutely critical in rebuilding California's economy..., and yet farming is always threatened. Right now it costs too much to do business in California. Schwarzeneggar said he wants to remove some of the obstacles that make life hard for the state's farmers and asked...his workers' compensation reform initiative..." be put into place. While these are some pretty words, it is not clear the governor really understands what is happening to hurt the ranchers, farmers, and rural areas of this state. Until he actually pinpoints and acknowledges the ways unaccountable governmental actions are causing problems, I see no reason to think much change is on the way.

Due to an increasing population which is causing an increase in demand for houses, there is no way the taking of open space land for development purposes will ever stop.

Due to reduced economic returns producers of natural resource products, large tracts of farmland are being converted to other uses as illustrated in a news article(373) which says "Roseville (California) officials have received approval to annex nearly 3,200 acres of farmland...which will allow new housing construction to begin...".

Another news article(374) mentions how "The population explosion in California's cities is sending ripples deep into farm country,..." "Between 1990 and 2002, 166,364 acres of farmland in the Central Valley were paved over..." and "During those same 12 years, a total of 3.2 million acres statewide were taken out of farming..." "...some farmers are finding they can not make ends meet in an industry where the production costs are determined locally, but the prices of their product are often determined globally." "...the cost of doing business is high..." and "many...farmers sell when encroaching development has raised the price of land beyond the value of what it can produce..." "...sometimes selling is the only alternative that makes sense."

244

Another news article(375) says country's "...farm acreage continued to shrink..." as "Land devoted to farming and ranching in 2002 totaled 302.7 million acres, about 16 million acres fewer than five years ago."

This last article(376) goes on to say "The sprawling bottomland dairies and expansive hill-country ranches are giving way." as "Development creeps from the cities,..." "California has lost a quarter of its productive farmland since the mid-1960s." "...while many farmers and ranchers have deep ties to the land, they can't always turn down relatively large amounts of money offered by developers." "...estate taxes and the reality..." family members can not afford to hold onto open space lands which causes natural resource producing lands to be converted to other uses. "Preserving land outright can also take agricultural land out of production." "Rural subdivisions...mean less farmland,..." and rural "...homesteads and accompanying roads contributed the lion's share of sediment to the...Eel River." "...pressure outward into agricultural lands...drives up land prices and (along with all the regulatory hassles and costs) prompts farmers to sell and move on. Why would you want to lease a 10 acre pasture for $400 a month when you could sell it for half a million dollars?"

While this last news article(376) seemed to say a lot of things that need to be said, a careful reading of the article raises some caution flags. The regulator's answer to the loss of agricultural land involves further restricting use of natural resources and more regulations.

The article(376) said "When land is economically viable as agriculture...the conversion to other uses is lower." This statement is ever so true, but the article indicates the way to have economically viable agricultural lands is to restrict all but agricultural uses of the land. This way the temptation to sell the land for other uses will not occur, because values for other uses can not be applied to the land. Restricting uses and de-valuing the land is routinely proposed by regulators and enviros to prevent the conversion of open space lands.

County recommendations in the article "...range from creating a nonprofit land trust...to support using conservation programs...to supporting no net loss of farm, ranch and timber land..." When you understand how trusts and conservation easements work and you think like the regulators, these words really mean a reduction in use of natural resources and putting more zoning and other legal restrictions in place that will forcefully prohibit conversions. Additionally, reduced income from the land keeps conservation easements and trusts from being self-sustaining, and an infusion of taxpayer money is routinely needed to keep them going.

Be careful when the government says it wants to hep you.

Too bad the last article(376) did not build on the statement "When land is economically viable as agriculture...the conversion to other uses is lower." by simply saying one way to make agricultural lands more viable is to help them produce more. If unjustified regulatory restrictions such as bans on genetically modified organisms does not get in the way, all kinds of safe and wondrous technical and scientific ways to increase production are coming down the pike. For now, simply reducing and eliminating unnecessary and unjustified regulatory practices would do a lot to increase income returns and the ability to hold onto open space lands.

A news article(377) and editorial(378) combine to say, "Supervisors...endorsed a land stewardship group's efforts to ease regulatory burdens on landowners who cut timber as part of their ranching operations." "Ranchers, environmentalists and government agencies all attested to a looming threat in the state and Humboldt County: The likelihood that unless regulations are eased to make non-industrial logging more feasible to private landowners, the trend toward subdividing open lands will only continue." "This subdivided land often ends up in the hands of developers or illegal marijuana growers,..."

In a Newsletter(379), "...environmental organizations and fishing groups...have advocated a highly regulated solution to recovering the (Coho salmon) species." "...landowner representatives, including those from the Farm Bureau, Cattlemen's Association and California Forestry Association, have consistently told..." the regulators "...a regulatory approach won't work and will destroy the hundreds of existing voluntary efforts by landowners and watershed organizations to improve habitat." "Department of Fish and Game (DFG) staff (note reference to staff) failed to accommodate our insistence for inclusion of our (voluntary approach) option." As stated in Forest Landowner's letter to DFG and staff "...we participated in this team process in the spirit of openness and good faith, making many voluntary trips to meetings to seek a successful solution to restoring Coho habitat. We feel (know) our suggestions were largely disregarded and our efforts turned to our distinct disadvantage." A lot of good faith time, effort, and expense went into landowner option and attending and giving input at hearings and meetings. It looks like these folks learned a hard lesson about the one-sided and dysfunctional hearing processes. All their effort was blunted by the power of the Fourth Branch of Government.

PRIVATELY OWNED OPEN SPACE LANDS
TO BE OR NOT TO BE IS THE QUESTION

There are two obvious ways to maintain open space lands.

As now being promoted more and more, the government or conservation groups can take land out of private ownership and put it into taxpayer supported Public Trust set-asides. This approach underutilizes the land and restricts the use of natural resources. Adding more land to the Public Trust largess where natural resource use is being reduced and eliminated, increases the erosion of the economic base supporting rural communities. Under this approach, rural communities will continue to get smaller and smaller until they disappear.

Another approach involves increasing production of natural resource products and increasing income from the land which creates incentive to hold land in an open space condition. Increased yields can be obtained by promoting and not hindering properly developed and applied technology and through regulatory relief. Without sacrificing environmental protections, regulatory relief can be provided by requiring the Fourth Branches of Government to be more professional in applying authorized regulations. Being more professional involves using time tested and peer reviewed science, site specific information, input from experienced professionals, logic, and common sense in developing and applying regulations and eliminating many unnecessary and unjustified regulations.

Is it time for rural communities to go?

Everyone says they want to maintain the rural way of life and open space lands; however, when you take a good look, it seems more is being done to eliminate these things than is being done to maintain them.

Too many people are trying to construct a Rural America along the lines of Ma and Pa Kettle where the easy, simple life, being one with nature, and poverty dominate the scene. This thinking is not realistic, and an acceptable rural way of life can not be maintained with government handouts and lazy living.

Healthy rural communities and the rural way of life as we know it can not exist without working the land and using natural resources.

In exchange for the qualities provided by the rural way of life, the people in rural communities are willing to accept the hard work and insecurities provided in a rural setting. They just need a little common sense help.

The ongoing shutdown of natural resource use (farming, timber harvesting, mining, ranching, grazing, recreation) and the hoarding of our natural resources is hurting Rural America and will eventually hurt us all.

This country needs to properly utilize its natural resources to feed the demands and needs of our society. Being selfish and greedy by hoarding and locking-up our resources is increasing our dependence on the rest of the world and forcing us to pull from third world countries. Since these countries have larger environmental problems than us, there is an obvious disregard for the slogan touted by many enviros, "Think globally and act locally".

The morally right thing to do is to promote (not restrict) the proper use of natural resources.

Could it be the public media is uninformed, too lazy to see the truth, and does not know what is really going on?

Is there a way to override the misperceptions that have been enhanced by the public media?

Is there a way to get the real story to the general public?

Is there a way to pressure the ones in control to do the right thing?

Will the Lone Ranger ride again?

The "Vanishing Freedom" program provided by Fox News touched on some of the problems facing Rural America. This program did a good job focusing on the taking of property by governmental agencies to increase the Public Trust largess and to questionably protect some species. The "Vanishing Freedom" program also touched on how the Fourth Branches of government are out of control and lack accountability.

I had hoped the Fox News program was a turning point in the media ignoring the problems faced by Rural America; however, it seems the media is continuing its old ways of light and occasional coverage.

I can only hope shows such as the Rush Limbaugh, No Spin O'Reilly, and Stossel show develop an interest. I won't hold my breath until this happens, but I can dream.

If the real story does not get told and something does not change, Atlas will surely shrug, and we will again learn what it means to say "you don't know what you got until it is gone."

LIKE TO HEAR THE REST OF THE STORY????

THEN WATCH THE FOLLOWING VIDEOS

VANISHING FREEDOM BY FOX NEWS
C/O Fox News Channel
2044 Armacost Avenue
Los Angeles, CA 90025

AMAZON RAINFOREST: CLEAR–CUTTING THE MYTHS
American investigator
P.O. Box 76064
Washington DC 20013-6064

Why We Have No Salmon
(A Video)
Elimination of the Oregon Fish Hatchery Runs
By Ron Yechout
Call Liz VanLeeuwen if like to see video per flyer notice at 541-369-2544

IF YOU HAVE NOT HAD A CHANCE TO SEE THESE VIDEOS,
YOU HAVE MISSED SOME INTERESTING STUFF

IF YOU FEEL IT IS NEEDED
BEFORE VIEWING THE VIDEOS
TAKE SOME NERVE RELAXING, BLOOD PRESSURE MEDICINE
OF YOUR CHOICE

WE GET WHAT WE PREACH

Chapter Thirteen

Where have all the trees gone?
For I have been told they are all gone
Wait, what do I see?
Thousands and millions and billions of trees
From sea to shining sea
How can this be, for I have been told this can not be
I suspect like a past President, there has been some mischief afoot
By those that can

Where to start? The producers of natural resource products are in a deep, deep public relations hole. The enviros have successfully sold the idea clearcuts are the scourge of the earth, loggers cut down big trees that can never be replaced, mines tear into mother earth and pollute our rivers, farmers carelessly apply herbicides, hunters ruthlessly kill animals, and even the easy going cowboys' cows are hurting the wildlife and tearing up the creeks.

By being late to the game with money and winning public relation (PR) ideas, producers of natural resource products have fallen way behind in the public relations game. These folks routinely shoot themselves in the foot by not being upfront about many things, and PR efforts that hang onto the same old PR ideas are not doing a whole lot of good.

Damage control and defensive public relation efforts have been the order of the day. Natural resources use is defended as being a necessity, and business facts, consumer costs, and private property rights information is spread around. Some attempts are made to present producers of natural resource products as just regular folks and all around good guys. Things done to make things right have gotten some play, but these efforts are routinely nullified by enviro PR. A lot of smoke has been blown to hide perceived wrongs, and some smoke is coming back to bite.

To many of us in the field, it seems PR efforts have done little to make the PR hole smaller.

So, what can be done? Roll over and take whatever comes; or, try something different?

PR efforts could stop being so defensive. Stories of environmental benefits that are created during production of natural resource products rarely get told. Humans do many good things such as creation and maintenance of diversity which benefits wildland species that go unrecognized.

Producers of natural resource products have to be smarter, because they can not match the money and power of enviros and their allies. These folks may never have the wherewithal to change things, but they could help their cause by putting more effort into re-butting enviro mistruths. This would force the enviros to expend resources fighting factual information, and without a lot of expense, such confrontation would bring attention to the truth.

More effort showing foresters are lead land managers and not just park rangers would emphasize the professional handling of natural resources.

While many think it is an impossible task, changing the picture of a clearcut from one of devastation to one of rebirth, herds of deer, romping mountain lions, foraging spotted owls, and increasing fish populations would open a lot of eyes.

THE DISCONNECT

Public relation efforts targeting population centers may not be connecting with the folks and may not be the smartest use of limited PR resources. While expensive PR specialists say this is the way to go, the lack of noticeable results indicates they may not know everything.

Old PR messages using hard to understand business facts, consumer costs, and private property rights are still in play, and at great expense, this information has been put into classy looking PR packages. Beautiful flyers, pamphlets, brochures, handouts, and short television and radio spots are being used.

The well read, educated, and professional public may give PR information a serious look; but, because these folks have the ability to do their own research and make their own decisions, nice looking PR information is probably not going to change their minds about environmental issues.

This leaves the average folks as the real target for PR efforts. I assume the pretty flyers, pamphlets, and radio and television spots do some good, but are these PR packages really stimulating average folks into caring about pro-resource use problems? Beautiful, eye-catching wildland scenes may catch the eye, but accompanying complicated, wordy, and uninspiring messages could turn average folks off. A lot of people probably see beautiful wildland scenes as areas that have to be destroyed in order to produce natural resource products. Handouts at fairs and other public gatherings and short television and radio spots are quickly forgotten and replaced by everyday struggles. The folks in the populated areas are still able to buy what they need without much trouble from some store, and a lot of them do not own land or understand landowners' problems. What obvious connection makes the folks in the cities care about what happens to those in some far off rural area who want to tear up beautiful landscapes?

One way to overcome the complacency of city folks, especially homeowners, to rural folks' problems may be to show they have similar regulatory problems. Bringing similar regulator problems into the open might create some very useful connections.

The producers of natural resource products and the rural folks do not have a label that resonates with average Americans. As hard as they have tried, producers of natural resource products and rural folks have not been given the "environmentalist" and "conservationist" labels.

A factually correct name (or label) for producers of natural resource products is needed to help build a morally acceptable identity among the general public. Like so many that have tried, I am at a loss in trying to come up with a simple, winning label that paints the producers of natural resources as the real stewards of the land and real creators of wildlife habitats. Since it is their job, it is time for the high priced PR folks to earn their money by coming up with such a label.

In the mean time, a main support group, the rural folks, who are being adversely affected by the shutdown of natural resource use, are not being fully utilized. These folks talk among themselves, like a preacher talking to the choir, but little is done to educate and energize them into doing pro-active things. By not getting the same information distributed to the populated areas, rural communities are being left out of the information loop. This disconnect is not helping the rural folks understand what is happening. Without information and direction, a potentially valuable group with the most to lose or gain, the rural communities, are being left to drift in the wind.

Many including rural folks are disconnected from the real world. Because of so much anti-resource use propaganda and little effort showing the benefits, many believe use of natural resources is a necessary but bitter thing we do to survive. Those who think for themselves probably look at the nice looking PR packages with a lot of skepticism. When healthy unharvested corn fields or heavily forested areas are viewed by unknowledgeable viewers, I doubt many think about needed resource products and environmental benefits provided by harvesting these areas. If the issue of harvesting is brought up, more than likely a thought of a clearcut, a dead bird, or a plowed and eroded field crosses the mind.

By being afraid to rock the boat, maybe cause more anger, create a backlash that might lead to more adverse regulatory impacts; or, maybe just due to guilt from past land use abuses, no one has really challenged the idea that use of natural resources has to result in adverse impacts to the environment. Some chosen and good looking before and after use of the land pictures are spread around, but captions are rarely provided that describe the many good things that are happening. Little to nothing is said about harvest disturbance creating habitat diversity which allows more species to use the landscape, and PR protocol seems to forbid any mentioning how increasing sunlight in the right places means more tree growth and more food for aquatic species.

Until there is a major effort to change how folks have been programmed to think, the perception that natural resource use has to adversely affect the environment will not go away.

A Sacramento Bee Editorial(380) provides a real world example of slanted and incorrect ingrained thinking and failure to educate the public, the media, and the politicians to what happens under current regulations. The editorial outlines the need for California's governor to veto SB 810 which is a bill that gives the Water Quality agency the ability to turn down timber harvest plan permits without providing justification.

This editorial correctly points out the California Department of Forestry and Board of Forestry now oversee permit review and approval processes, and the Water Quality agency has all kinds of input and control over water quality issues during the review and approval of timber harvest plan permits. The editorial further outlines how having two agencies with equal powers over a permitting process can be confusing, problematic, and environmentally bad for California and other world environments.

The editorial says we need the wood; so, we have to allow bad things to occur. By saying this, the editorial re-enforces the idea that timber harvesting does bad things. The editorial wrongly says the current review and approval processes allow logging activities to introduce sediment into already stressed waterways and cause detrimental water quality problems.

Anyone who understands the California timber harvest permit review and approval process knows a permit can not be approved if it will adversely affect water quality or species of concern. The California permit approval process requires environmental impacts to be mitigated to a level of insignificance. This simple permit requirement has been lost to the editor, the newspaper, the public, and the politicians.

Another example of the media showing a bias regarding natural resource producers is illustrated in another newspaper editorial(381). The editorial mentions how a pulp mill may not be pretty and produces undesirable side effects, but it must be tolerated until something better comes along. The editorial says the pulp mill is a steam-belching monstrosity, and using state of the art technology to make the pulp mill one of the most environmentally friendly pulp mills in the world seems to mean little to the editorial writer. A Letter to the Editor(382) also picks-up on the bias by rebutting the reference to a wafting stink and by questioning the basis for the bias in the editorial.

One news article(383) really illustrates disconnect between the producers of natural resources and the ones promoting rural counties in public forums. This article raises the question how a display at the state fair which shows a guy juggling while riding a unicycle and a woman playing a drum demonstrates industries to be found in a rural area like Humboldt County. This additionally raises questions about who is making decisions on how to spend limited dollars available to promote rural counties.

Maybe the PR battle is too tough to win, but some simple, straight talk with the average folks would do a lot to close the disconnect and would stimulate support for using our natural resources. It is time to stop talking to the choir and to those who have already formed an opinion. It is time to tell "all" the folks with simple straight talk what is really happening to this country's wildlands.

Until the barrage of mistruths and negative information and the credibility of the enviro thinking crowd is confronted and rebutted, I do not see any reason for the general public to change the way they think.

Attacking mistruths with good irrefutable facts would bring attention to many inappropriate policies that are adversely affecting the environment and this country. The public needs to be exposed to burned area resources being left to rot and waste away. There needs to be more said about burned areas being left to revert to brush lands which produce little and provide limited species' habitats. The story of hatchery fish being unjustifiably killed and eliminated needs more exposure.

Better packaging and distribution of the truth could do a whole lot of good.

INAPPROPRIATELY PROMOTED IDEAS AND INFORMATION

Many partial truths, inappropriate mistruths, and ideas have been preached and accepted by the general public, media, regulators, politicians, and even some pro-resource use folks. As part of a more direct and factual approach to informing the public, these partial truths, inappropriate mistruths, and ideas need to be identified and debunked.

MISGUIDED THINKING NUMBER ONE
Value that can not be removed after a regulation has been put in place but could have been removed before the regulation was put in place has not been taken from the owner of that value

It is routinely argued by enviros and many regulators that they can make a regulation that restricts use of a value, and by simply saying you can have that value back sometime into the future, a value has not been taken from you.

What do you think?

If you can't access a value until the regulators say you can, do you agree nothing has been taken from you?

This argument is routinely applied regarding restrictions involving tree harvesting. Buffers and outright prohibitions for perceived species protection and questionable timber production goals routinely prevent trees from being harvested. Because there is a perceived possibility that new trees will replace trees currently required to be left, it is believed the trees being left will become free for harvest at a later date. Cost of money over time and ability to utilize a tree's value in a better investment are both ignored.

In the real world there is no question that any value, that can not be removed after a regulation has been put in place but could have been removed before the regulation was put in place, has been taken from the owner of that value.

In California, many new timber harvest regulations have been put in place that require large existing trees to be left standing until they are replaced by new trees. It is argued that smaller trees or newly established trees will grow up and fulfill the same nitch as retained large trees, and when his happens, the retained large trees can be harvested.

Because of the way trees grow, this thinking is flawed and ignores the real world. Large trees dominating a site suck up sunlight and nutrients, and this restricts and slows small and new tree growth around them. Without a change in growing conditions such as opening of the canopy, how are small, inhibited trees ever going to catch-up and equal larger trees that are probably growing better than them?

Any logical thinking person has to see how regulations requiring retention of big trees until they are replaced by new trees does not work, and when large trees are forced to be retained, there is no question that value is taken from owners of large trees.

A news article(324) provides another example of indefinitely restricting timber harvest and effectively taking value from a landowner. "A small family owned company based in Monroe (Oregon)...sought permission to log...nine acres around the nest of a bald eagle, a threatened species,...After nesting season..." "...the Oregon Department of Forestry..." said no; although, "...there has been no evidence the eagle nest has been occupied in the nine years..." the landowners have owned the involved 40 acre parcel. This raises the question how they know it is a bald eagle nest; but moving on, the matter went to court. It was ruled "...regulating private property in line with public policy is not equivalent to taking a piece of property for public use..." "...the state constitution clause guaranteeing compensation when private property is taken for a public use only applies when the full economic use of the property is denied, not a portion." "...The eagle might ("might" mind you) use it (nest) in the future..."

This situation illustrates how for years chunks of value have been locked up and placed off-limits to landowners for species protection and supposedly public good reasons. As more and different species of concern move onto a property, more and more can be taken from landowners. It is like taking chunks of a person's savings account until that person is forced to take what they can out of the bank and to move-on.

To say regulatory takings for species protection are not takings is factually and logically wrong.

MISGUIDED THINKING NUMBER TWO
Humans can not produce natural resource products without damaging the environment

The constant barrage of negativism from enviros, media, and many other closed minded sources has created a mindset that environmental damage has to occur when producing natural resource products.

As discussed earlier in this chapter, things done in the production of natural resource products are not forever and the production of natural resources routinely results in good things.

Because disturbed vegetative cover grows back and disturbed land heals professionally and properly done operations only cause temporary interruption to natural processes. The making of a garden, plowing a field for planting, and harvesting a forest does not destroy the land. How quickly things grow back or heal is a function of how good a job is done. Beautiful stands of re-grown timber in areas that were literally blitzed in the past and healing of San Francisco Bay after mining siltation filled the Sacramento River, shows how even severely disturbed areas will eventually heal.

Properly managed disturbance can produce a lot of benefits. Disturbance that allows new vegetative growth can enhance the food base for many species, and this can then lead to more sex and higher reproduction rates. This has been proven true for many raptor species such as the northern spotted owl. Deer populations increase in areas of new vegetative growth which in turn helps the mountain lion populations. Openings along streams increase habitat diversity and increase food production for aquatic species, and this leads to increased fish biomass and larger fish for fishermen and predators to catch. The examples of benefits from properly managed disturbance go on and on and on.

To feel guilty and think environmental damage has to occur in order to use natural resource products is a misplaced guilt trip.

MISGUIDED THINKING NUMBER THREE
Humans can not improve on Mother Nature.

To think there is no-way humans can help improve on Mother Nature's haphazard ways, shows a misguided waste of brain power. While Mother Nature routinely does pretty good on her own, to not attempt improving upon her haphazard ways is not logical or supported by what happens in the real world.

Granted man has fouled up in many ways. California Fish and Game's program and California department of Forestry's accompanying regulatory requirements to remove debris from streams in the 1970s did untold damage to many hundreds of miles of streams in California. The damming of rivers without the foresight to provide all possible benefits (power, water, recreation, flood control) and destroying fish hatcheries is going to adversely affect a lot of species and us far into the future.

Putting the foul-ups aside, some of man's activities have been very beneficial. The ability to hold and use water lost during winter flows has allowed for more waterfowl habitat. The Colorado River is no longer the muddy torrent that it once was. Access for fire control purposes allows for the possibility of maintaining wildlife habitats in areas where explosive fuels are allowed to build. The science and methods of properly producing genetically acceptable fish populations has reached the point we can have large salmon populations if we let it happen.

Some enviros and their allies say humans should butt out. They say it is okay to burn up habitat and kill species caught in any fire, because it is a natural process, and Mother Nature will do the right thing in her haphazard way to heal and replenish burned areas.

To these folks I say you are a fool.

There is no guarantee what Mother Nature will bring back to a burned area, and humans can prevent burned forest areas from becoming nothing more than brush fields which produce little and provide limited wildlife habitat. Without help, brush fields burn over and over again perpetuating brush conditions.

The trick is to be smart and apply some foresight. We need to stop playing around with unproven pseudo "no management" thinking.

It is time to think positively and more actively manage our wildlands. We need to start applying more pro-active management based on time tested and peer reviewed science, experienced professional input, site specific facts, logic, and common sense.

There are many reasons why erroneous ideas and positions have been included in various PR efforts. Some folks lacking the expertise and education may honestly believe the distributed erroneous information will do some good. Maybe the lure of possibly being left alone to do their jobs and run their businesses has caused many professionals, associations, and landowners to go down the path of telling and promoting a few white lies and slanted truths. Various pressures created by peers, financial factors, and employers may have caused some folks to go along with presentation and promotion of erroneous ideas and information. I know I was affected by some of these pressures in the past.

There will be those that disagree with what I have to say regarding my list of routinely accepted but flawed ideas. Some will vehemently disagree with me. To those that disagree with me, I can only say my thinking is based on over 38 years of working with time tested science, site specific facts, logic, common sense, and the real world, and my comments are simply my honest straight forward opinion. I present this information with the hope some of it will be taken seriously, and it will help others make a more truthful PR product.

The enviros have learned well the lesson of short and simple to the point factual messages, and in the PR and political world, they are beating the pants off the producers of natural resources.

Perception is reality? In the absence of conflicting information, what is seen and heard is perceived to be real.

The perceptions held by the general public can be slanted by advocates from all sides of the issues. If not re-butted, political and advocacy viewpoints routinely win the day.

Pro-natural resource use advocates routinely lose the perception game.

PR messages have to be based on information that can not be challenged and overturned.

Do not get caught in a lie!

If a simple and easy to understand message is backed by time tested and peer reviewed science, site specific truthful facts, and a logical and common sensical argument, the critics of the message are put in the position of having to prove a truth to be false. When a message is forcefully defended using the truth, credibility soars, and spin and perceptions lose.

Too often experienced professionals are not included in the preparation of messages, and short cuts in preparing PR and informational messages routinely result in poor, indefensible messages.

An example of a poor PR message was provided during the fight to repeal the death tax. A bill was going to Bubba Clinton to be signed, and there was a television add supporting the bill which showed a gussed up farmer with a big new hat on a bright new $100,000(+) tractor. Dah!!!!!! The image portrayed by the rich looking farmer and an expensive tractor really helped the effort to tell the country how badly inheritance death taxes hurt the small business and rural landowners. Where was the family and small business image and picture of the real people being hurt by being taxed out of business and having to sell the farm to pay off the estate taxes?

Presentation can be everything, and messages need to be presented in a forceful direct, professional, upfront, simple to the point, truthful, unwavering, unchanging, and repetitive manner.

Audiences need to be forced to listen; so, factual messages do not get missed. If you get the audience to pay attention, the critics of your message will have to do more to re-but your message and defend their position.

Pro-natural resource use folks are routinely nonadversarial to a fault, and the credibility of the other side is routinely not put under the spotlight.

HELP AUDIENCE PARTICIPATE

The listeners need to know how they are personally involved and affected. This is a basic requirement we all learned in Public Speaking 101. Provide obtainable goals and easy ways to get involved.

There needs to be commitment to not let a message be buried and lost.

Make a pest of yourself.

When a message or position is properly supported and repeatedly presented, it can not be ignored forever.

Confronting the Fourth Branches of Government with these kinds of supported arguments and public relation messages puts pressure on the Fourth Branch of Government to be more accountable, provides for more positive free PR, and creates building blocks towards constructive change.

There is no silver bullet, and every issue requires a different collection of the facts, determination of a goal, and development of ways to achieve wanted goals.

Except for frequent omission of the truth, this outlines what the enviros have done with some imaginative and innovative thinking, and look what they have accomplished.

ACCENTUATE THE POSITIVE

PR efforts are mostly defensive on the part of natural resource producers and not enough effort is put into providing a positive slant.

There is a repeated reference to harming the land. Enviros and natural resource producers routinely say a choice has to be made to harm the land or go without needed natural resources. This is bogus thinking, and more effort needs to be done to educate others about benefits from proper management, benefits from disturbance for wildlife, and ability of Mother Nature to heal herself.

A way to develop support and information useful in promoting the use of natural resources involves asking and finding answers to questions like the following:

1. How much of this country is tied up in Public Trust governmental ownership that is off limits to development and proper use of natural resources?

2. How do regulatory restrictions promote the loss of open space?

3. Current regulations restrict or prohibit use of natural resources on how much land in the country?

4. How do land management activities co-exist and beneficially interact with fish, water, and wildlife?

5. How does Mother Nature heal herself after disturbance activities have occurred?

6. What is diversity?

7. How can land management activities such as clearcutting, which mimics Mother Nature and fire, create diversity?

8. When trees grow better in sunlight, mineral soil, and areas where vegetative competition has been reduced, what management activities promote the conditions favored by trees?

And on and on and on and on

THE ENEMY CALLED COMPLACENCY

As discussed in Chapter Eleven, all those who represent rural areas and producers of natural resources need a good kick in the shins. They could do more than they do. Those who have reached a position of authority and power who could do some good in bringing balance to what is going on and who should know better, shy away from doing what is needed.

There are many reasons for ineffective action by the so-called rural community leaders. High salaries and pensions feel good, and human nature says to not shake the boat and bring attention to yourself. The inability to unseat incumbent elected officials who are acting inappropriately creates a feeling of "what's the use". On both sides of the issues, those in control with the power believe they are untouchable, and they can do whatever they want to do. Some leaders have deluded themselves into thinking they can still play the game of politics and legislative maneuvering like their predecessors, and still do some good. Some continue to believe the broken hearing process and who wins the point and counterpoint political battle process which is controlled by the layman courts, staff people, and the Fourth Branch of Government will bring constructive results. Some live in a dream world where the enviros and regulators will meet them halfway with compromises that will last over time. The list of excuses and reasons for not getting involved and not doing more goes on and on.

The following simple illustration shows how erroneous information and a chaotic blind process is being utilized to develop and apply environmental regulations.

OFF IN A CLOUD OF DUST
THE BLIND ARE LEADING THE BLIND
LEAVING A TRAIL OF DEVASTATION
(WITH TRUTH AND EXPERIENCED PROFESSIONALS TRYING TO PREVENT THE INEVITABLE)

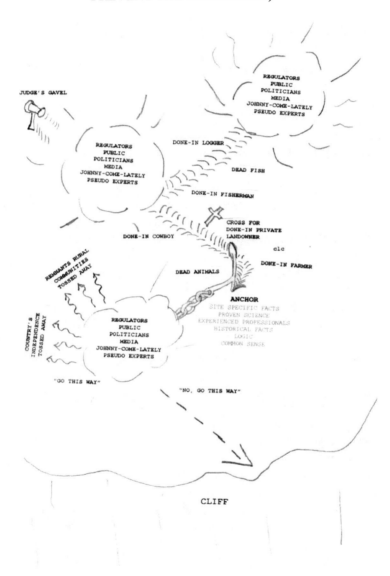

DOST THO PROTEST TO MUCH

Chapter Fourteen

The process of protesting and civil disobedience has been successfully used by those opposed to use of natural resources to sway regulators, media, political opinion, and layman courts.

Ever wonder why those wanting to use our natural resources don't use the protest route?

Obviously effective protests take time, money, and a lot of free time which hard working folks do not have.

Because they are generally ignored and given little coverage, pro-resource use folks do not often take their message directly to the media and the public. Past treatment by the media and the public has been a disappointment, and there has been little incentive to keep trying.

Even with advanced notice, the media usually ignores pro-resource use informational forums. If you want to know what it feels like to be snubbed, just tell the media they can come hear information supporting use of natural resources. Written presentation will be accepted which generally ends up in a black hole or file thirteen, but if it takes some effort and time to get information, the media is AWOL.

By not being taught how to get the most out of public forums, pro-resource use people develop messages that are routinely dull and uninspiring. The pizzazz wanted by the media is routinely missing.

When pro-resource use folks do get the gumption to protest, they don't do a very good job of preparation, and they routinely look out-of-place behind protest signs. I remember the time I went to a weird National Forest's hearing on allowable levels of harvest. The hearing was in a small backroom, and the room was packed with pro-harvest folks. Two forest officials were at the front of the room with a tape recorder and a stop watch. After providing hearing guidelines, the forest officials never spoke or answered questions. They just started the stop watch and punched the tape recorder. As people talked, the crowd held up signs and gave applause. For hours, the whole show involved a room full of people talking to themselves and holding up signs that no one of any significance ever saw. It was sad to watch what was happening in that room.

I wonder?

Does the media have something against promoting the use of natural resources?

The protectionist crowd gets a lot of attention. The hard working folks get the shaft, and those living off hard working folks with time on their hands get the royal treatment. Controversy stimulated by the enviros and their allies sells papers, and everyday real life facts are usually too dull to sell papers.

I wonder?

What would be public reaction if the media and pollsters asked protesters the following questions?

Are you taking time off your job to participate? What resources (money, welfare checks) do you have to cover living and protest expenses (travel money, room and board)? How long can you attend before you have to leave and why would you leave? What group or interest do you feel you represent or are the most closely associated with? Who (group or person) do you think has done the most to organize the protest? Ask the question and then follow-up with research and report that describes who really did organize the protest. Are you present to meet others with similar ideas or to generally meet others and make new friends? Are you present to make contact with others and learn how to plan and conduct protests?

I wonder?

Is lack of punishment, lack of consequences, and increased media attention for bad behavior encouraging protesters to get increasingly bolder and more and more violent? Are protesters being encouraged to push the boundaries of civil disobedience further and further?

Past protest results indicate the answer to these questions is yes. We all see an increasing trend of violence and damage to property and humans at protests. A logical reason for this trend is the increased media attention and not being held accountable for illegal and bad behavior. By its routine silence about applied punishments, the media helps to downplay the consequences of illegal activities.

Like any wild animal that has no fear of humans, protesters have learned there are few consequences for bad behavior and there is little reason to fear the law. While many protests may start out as parties, they usually get excessively rambunctious as the protesters get into the swing of the party mood. An atmosphere is created that causes people to want to get more and more involved. They do not want to be left out and be a party pooper. They want to contribute to what is happening. Professional protesters with a violent agenda feed and stimulate these feelings with various forms of encouragement.

I wonder?

Are protests just plain fun?

It sure looks like the "high" of being with an uncontrollable group defying authority and participating in a party atmosphere is the main reason many attend protests. "Get juiced and have at it" seems to be the motto of many protesters.

A news article(387) has "The radical Cheerleaders, a loose network of young, mostly female activists…" putting "…a new face on protest." The media gives this group a full article on page A2 with a large picture of smiling cheerleaders having a real good time. One cheerleader says "We do for our fellow activists what cheerleaders do for sports players: We get people going,…"

I wonder?

Do some attend to feel better about themselves and say they have done something about an issue? Do some have ulterior motives such as getting attention for causes, issues, or beliefs unrelated to the protest and to promote general chaos? Some attendees honestly believe in protest issues and work hard on them; but, would proper research and reporting of all the factors for attendance find this last group in the minority? Does the media give protests and protesters too much credibility and legitimacy?

I wonder?

How far will disrespectful actions be allowed to go? Are disrespectful actions during public hearings and other forums a carryover from lack of controlling such actions during protests? Will this type of activity eventually make the public hearing processes completely unworkable?

An opinion article(388) describes what is frequently happening right now, and I believe shows where things are headed. This article discusses how disrespectful and abusive activity was allowed to occur before, during, and after a public forum, and indicates how this activity disrupted and slanted the outcome of a meeting. The article's author says "Once it became clear that I supported the study process, I was booed, jeered and belittled, even as I spoke. I had not even had 15 seconds of my time before the boos started. Catcalls continued as I pressed on to share my views." This was all done "…for one purpose only; to try to intimidate me into sitting down and shutting up. Ironically, those who tried to intimidate me into silence would tell you they support free speech. Baloney." What they did "…they did…to kill free speech." "…I must take exception with how Mayor…ran the meeting." and "…for allowing the boos, jeers and catcalls to happen." "…by allowing applause and yelling, you created the environment where people thought, if it's okay to cheer…it must be okay to boo…" "Before the meeting …members of the City Council were called every name in the book. They received harassing phone calls. They were accosted in public. They received hateful letters and e-mail." "…council members were followed to the meetings." and "…had their pictures taken in public places." "…there is a pattern, a systematic effort to kill free speech: a. Before meetings, harass elected officials…; b. At the meetings, boo and jeer anyone who dares express a contrary view; c. After the meetings, practice the politics of personal destruction to belittle, harass, demean…"

This opinion article clearly shows how more and more the practice of bad behavior is spilling over into public hearing and decision making processes. Protesters are getting increasingly bolder in applying disruptive and threatening actions against ideas and issues they are fighting. The general practice of cuddling protesters by the media and the Fourth Branches of Government promotes bad behavior. By not forcefully dealing with bad and illegal behavior and by not standing up and making all abusive parties accountable for their actions, members of the Fourth Branch of Government are allowing a breakdown in public forums to occur. Playing patty cake with inappropriate harmful protest actions is leading us to a bad place.

Examples of light touch, patty cake, slap on the wrist actions against improper protest activities are provided in the following Times Standard and North Coast Journal news articles.

In a news article(389), "…federal judge warned three animal rights activists…affiliated with Stop Huntington Animal Cruelty USA…charged with stalking to refrain from advocating violence or publicizing personal information about executives who run companies that have been targets of bombing and other violent protests." Activists' actions have involved "…vandalism, stalking, computer hacking, and sending blitzes of e-mail, telephone calls and faxes to harass…" involved company. No mention of possible punishment or penalties was provided in the article. The activists "…remained free on $50,000 bond…" and "…are expected to be arraigned in a New Jersey court…later". While judge said "I will not tolerate threats to people,…", it would be interesting to know what the judge would have done if the protest activities did not involve threats to people. It will be interesting to see if any significant punishment is ever applied.

In a news article(390), San Francisco's District Attorney "…ended up dropping cases against…124 anti-war protesters…" in an attempt "…to preempt the criticism that dogged her predecessor..." involving "...2,300 demonstrators who shut down the city as the war in Iraq began." "...last year's multi-day demonstrations...cost police...$3.5 million..." 124 plus 2,300 demonstrators get light treatment and the taxpayers are out $3.5 million dollars.

Another news article(391) shows "...arson...highly flammable smoke-bomb attacks on theaters across the country...in 10 states...during contract negotiations..." which sent "...movie-goers fleeing in panic." go unpunished. "Three members of a movie projectionists' union were acquitted..." of the acts which leaves no one being punished for causing property damage, scaring a lot of people, and causing a lot of panic that could have resulted in injuries or worse.

Two news articles(392)(393) have "Earth First activist...protester...convicted...of resisting arrest...", and going "...to jail for 37 days." "...jury was hung on...trespassing charge..." which "...was later dropped." Follow-up article(394) has this activist released early "...because of good behavior..." after spending "...24 days in jail..." I wonder how many inter-city folks get 24 days for resisting arrest, get time off for good behavior, and three news articles to promote their stories.

For protesters, it is just too good to be true the way they are handled by the media and the legal system. Getting arrested is a badge of honor, illegal actions and involved issues get all kinds of praise and attention, and there is no significant punishment for illegal actions. Why would any good protester avoid confrontation and the spending of good taxpayer dollars for jury trials?

I wonder?

Do the media and Fourth Branch of Government naively or knowingly promote violent protest actions? Violate protest actions are routinely glorified and promoted in slanted media reports, and the Fourth Branch of Government routinely looks the other way.

A news article(395) helps promote one protester's agenda and self interest by giving his situation a full article with the headline "From his jail cell, radical environmentalist...says he's no terrorist". "...a veteran of anti-logging protests in Oregon...accused of firebombing logging and cement trucks..., and having links to a group of radical environmentalists viewed as terrorists by the FBI." such as the "...Earth Liberation Front (ELF)...that has claimed responsibility for scores of acts of destruction and vandalism...," this protester says "As an activist, I stand tall, I hold my head high, ...he is not a terrorist.," and is against "...the evils of corporate culture..."

Thank you media for providing an article that more strongly emphasizes this protester's ideas and the bad things being done by others like him. Why couldn't this article(395) simply been headlined "There is a price for radical environmentalism"? Instead of putting out a message of defiance which helps support a bad person and his warped cause, a truthful message could have been sent showing there are consequences for violent and unlawful actions.

I wonder?

Are the bad results from many protests going to hurt all protest movement? While some protesters are giving their lives over serious issues, others are frivolously causing damage and bad feelings over unsupportable and unclear issues. Many watching what is happening are given reasons to turn away from all protest actions. Is the frequency and frivolity of protests diminishing legitimate protesting, and do many protesters really understand the purpose of protesting? Protests are coming in all shapes and sizes with varying degrees of seriousness. Some protests have a legitimate, serious basis and some look to be done for the fun of it.

The following Times Standard and San Francisco Chronicle news articles and letters to the editor illustrate the variety of protest activities, issues, benefits, and results that are occurring.

A Letter to the Editor(396) discusses protests by out of area, nonresidential people not even affected by a new business trying to come into a community. A news article(387) has cheerleaders trying to get the folks going on an issue. Another news article(397) mentions how Haitian student is killed by a tear gas container while supporting some leader and blocking use of a hospital.

Two news articles(398)(399) have "...several hundred people..." gathering to celebrate "...the term 4/20 (or 420 depending on article)..." It is claimed the probably illegal pot-smoking event "...originated in the early 1970s at San Rafael High School (California) among a group of pot-smokers who called themselves the Waldos..." "...each year on April 20..." the Waldos have an unofficial 'tea time' for smoking marijuana (sounds like a party to me)..."

A news article(400) has "...15 people...arrested... at a rally outside..." grocery store "...when they tried to block traffic by laying down in...parking lot,..." In another article(401), "...40 people were arrested...for misdemeanors such as trespassing, obstructing and entrance or failure to disperse...during supermarket rallies in support of grocery clerks idled by a four-month strike and lockout."

A news article(402) has "...400 California State University, Sacramento students..." rallying "...against proposed cutbacks in the state's public colleges and universities."

One news article(403) has "Peace activists..." marching "...on Washington..." against "...the war in Iraq..." Another article(404) says "...11 Million marched..." in "...rally across Spain against terrorist attacks".

A news article(405) says "Protesters blocked traffic at a border bridge...to demand summer electrical subsidies...where temperatures can climb above 120 degrees..." Another article(406) describes how "Old oak moved after month of protests..." at a cost of "...about $1 million..." A news article(407) covers political "...sympathizers obstructing traffic with rocks and burning trees..." in Nicaragua.

Smiling tenants get whole article(408) covering their protest of a landlord. Another article(409) mentions a "...homeless...group..." protesting...lack of public bathrooms..." and saying "Businesses could sacrifice one parking space to have a toilet." "...city officials..." are saying "Every time we put a toilet in someone ruins it,..." and "...not to expect public toilets anytime soon because they always get trashed." The involved city has "...about 200 homeless people in (a small) town,..." which I might add is a pretty liberal thinking college town that is maybe getting what they have promoted.

A news article(410) mentions "...soldiers fired warning shots to disperse protesters...killing at least three and wounding eight...after protesters attempted to seize military vehicles..." in Beirut, Lebanon. This Lebanon protest illustrates how protests get out of hand as the protest "...started with only about 40...van and taxi drivers angry at high fuel prices...but grew to around 2,000 as word of the violence spread. After the killings, protesters stormed the Labor of Ministry...and set it on fire." Could this extreme out of control situation be an illustration of where all protest actions are headed and shows protests are going to get a lot worse before they get better?

An article(411) has "Thousands..." protesting "gay marriage". Another article(412) describes "...march... about not just abortion but sex education, funding for family planning and a host of other issues." Any protest is a good time to protest anything.

Two articles(413)(414) have "Bureau of Land Management..." giving "...Greenpeace 48 hours to dismantle summer encampment..." due to "...14-day camping limit..." and after "...group tried to disrupt logging on nearby timber sale." "...20-foot steel shipping container was used to block loggers..." Group protest represented "...a violation of trust..." regarding use of campsite. Greenpeace blocked "...second timber sale in Oregon..." with a "...bright yellow steel shipping container..." with two protesters locked inside..." "One woman perched on a pole 20 feet over the container,..." with "Another...locked to the container." In first blockage attempt "...three activists were arrested after...shipping container was used to block loggers..."

A news article(415) has "Tree sitter arrested at (Sacramento, California) Capitol...by SWAT officers for trespassing...less than three hours after campaign began." "...highway patrol officers were alerted, fire trucks with ladders arrived and chainsaw was used to cut a path through some branches. SWAT officers (didn't mess around and) cut loose...bags, sending them crashing to the ground..." with sitter following the bags "...about a half hour later." The result of this tree sit was a lot of expense for the taxpayers, diversion of public employees from more important work, and damage to an innocent tree. I never saw any media coverage and attention to the cost, damage, and sitter's punishment; however, the media provided the tree sitter a full article coverage and gave him the attention he wanted.

A news article(417) says "At least 1,000 patients were denied medical treatment Monday after hundreds of nurses and other workers walked off the job before dawn at several East Bay (California) hospitals, disgruntled by proposed layoffs that they say would cripple delivery of care." Good protest action or bad? Either way, the patients lost.

A news article(418) describes anti-GOP protests in New York involving thousands of protesters. Multiple arrests, a lot of law enforcement personnel tied up, and a lot of taxpayer dollars spent to show a lot of discord and hatred. Was it worth the effort and cost? You decide. I know what I think.

I wonder?

Is the same level of environmental concern, permit requirements, and attention applied to protest and alternate life style gatherings as is applied to general recreational activities and activities that produce natural resource products? Based on the following examples of such happenings as described in Times Standard news articles and a letter to the editor, I have to say "NO"!

An article(46) says "...a benefit concert at a nature preserve..." had an environmental member complaining "...the preserve, populated by quail, deer, and mountain lions, shouldn't be used for a concert at all."

Another article(416) has "...Rainbows..." group gathering "...in the Modoc National Forest..." with "Fort Bidwell Indian Community Council...worried diggings of latrines...would harm ancestral artifacts." "The Forest Service has budgeted $720,000 for a National Incident

Management Team to oversee this year's (Rainbow) event...", and plans for help from sheriff. Spend, spend, spend that taxpayer money.

One news article(420) describes how "...around 50,000 people on each day of..." a "...two day music festival...descended on grassy grounds of the Empire Polo Field..." in "...Indio...,...California..." While the festival was not held in a wildland environment, can you imagine the impact to surrounding desert areas from overnight camping and other illegal uses?

There is a Redwood Motorcycle Run held in the redwoods where areas along the Eel River are inundated (and I mean inundated) with back to back and side by side tents. I seriously doubt full environmental review of impacts caused by this gathering are developed and reviewed by the regulators.

There is another activity every year that creates camping impacts similar to the Redwood Motorcycle Run; however, this event called the Reggae on the Eel River has a much, much, much larger impact on the Eel River. The following letter to the editor outlines how a double standard is being applied.

Dear Editor:

Is environmental review of Eel River Reggae by Water Quality (WQ), Department of Fish and Game (DFG), National Marine Fishery (NMF), and Humboldt (County) Environmental Department conducted to the same level of scrutiny and mitigation applied to Benbow Dam and other Eel River natural resource activities? Are nonresource based activities and resource based activities handled differently?

Clean-up appears excellent, and event seems to help southern Humboldt's legal economy which needs a shot in the arm.

Check of provided file information indicates taxpayers, not permittee, pays for environmental review. List of all potentially affected species and species' survey information was not provided. WQ involvement appeared light, and NMF's input focused on benign temporary bridge.

Logic says hot weather causes heavy drinking and splashing in river; tangled tents and long portapotty lines complicate nature's call; and after dark, improper activities are unavoidable. Newspaper said rakes and shovels cleared river rocks, and use turned river murky with oily sunscreen, thin film covering surface. Around half mile of river habitat is impacted.

With over 40 times increase in E. coli counts and around 15 times increase in Streptococcus faecalis counts, 2002 Humboldt County samples show something new does get into river. Per county, salt water beach standards apply and things are okay.

California Environmental Quality Act requires all environmental impacts, no matter how benign, be disclosed and discussed. Provided environmental review information did not address all impacts, and on-site results, indicate mitigation requirements may be inadequate.

Charles L. Ciancio
8/30/04

Photos 8 & 9 in the center of the book show just how impactive the California Reggae event is to the Eel River.

Even the local businesses benefiting from the Reggae event are admitting to some downsides from the event.

In one case, a shop keeper was overheard saying how customers had to be watched closely during the Reggae Event, because the level of shoplifting went way up during the event.

In another case, some visiting folks were discussing how it might be nice to take a swim in the lake in the Eel River downstream of the event. A waitress was overheard telling them it might not be a good idea for awhile because of all the goodies that the folks at the Reggae event put into the river. In this case, strictly enforced fish protection environmental regulations and taxpayer dollars used for regulatory oversight and assumably in construction of Benbow lake for public use are wasted and put on hold by an event that is not subject to the same level of environmental scrutiny and protection.

And the beat goes on.

VANDALISM AND ECO-TERROR

Enviro vigilantes are having a field day in rural areas.

From personal knowledge, I know of an incident where spikes were purposely placed in a tree in an attempt to protest and stop a timber harvest operation. The spikes were not found until they hit a mill cut-up saw and a mill worker was badly hurt. While there was no way to identify and charge someone for putting the spikes in the trees, there was no doubt about what happened and why the spikes were in the tree.

Do the enviro goals justify damaged property and injured or dead species and people? I could go on and on about the injured worker due to the spiking of trees, but I believe the following internet report and Times Standard and The Examiner news articles provide enough reason to condemn vandalism and eco-terror as a legitimate means of protest.

A news article(421) describes how "...an elitist minority..." is "...putting forth their own agenda,...", and "Indirectly...fueling criminal acts." Some are saying "The question is how do we keep our neighborhoods unique and special?" and "It's not by bringing in big corporations." like "Starbucks..."

It appears the no growth and no new development crowd have eco-terrorists as allies. "...Starbucks opening (in Portland, Oregon) marred by vandalism..." as store had "...windows...broken by some kind of incendiary device..."

It is interesting how a simple cup of coffee has become a threat to some who believe the world is better off remaining unchanged and made up of old, deteriorating things.

Change is needed to replace old and worn out infrastructure. Nothing lasts forever, and trying to hold onto the past and force others to utilize old things hinders the ability to live a normal and comfortable life. Take a walk around San Francisco, and imagine what is going to happen when next big quake hits the old and deteriorating infrastructure and old buildings in that city. After the next quake, there will be a lot of new businesses and buildings replacing the old, and San Franciscans and the anti-new crowd will be glad for it.

It is okay to support retention of old things if you can afford to do so; however, we need to understand such actions are a luxury which a lot of places in the world can not afford.

A article(422) mentions how "An East Bay biotechnology...Emeryville (California)...company succeeded in getting a restraining order against and animal rights group...after vandalism...of a..." company "attorney's East Bay home." This illustrates how just being an employee or contractor involved with a company targeted by an enviro activist group can put your home and family in harms way.

In a news article(423), "A radical environmental group...The Earth Liberation Front...claimed responsibility...for a...Salt Lake City...lumberyard fire that caused $1.5 million in damage...saying...graffiti left at the scene..." provides "a legitimate claim of responsibility." "Authorities...said the arson had the hallmarks of an ELF attack."

An internet report(424) mentions "...an environmental group burned down a ski lodge in Vail because they thought it threatened the lynx."

Report has "…land rights activist…" saying "We basically say if you have an endangered species in your area, we are going to take your livelihood away, we're going to destroy your communities, and we're going to make it very difficult for your families to survive."

A news article(425) reports, "FBI investigators are trying to determine the motive for a bombing at the headquarters of a nutritional company…including the possibility that the small explosion was the work of animal rights activists…" Such activists in the past have "…targeted…" nutritional company's "…parent company…for doing business with…" another company "…that conducts experiments on animals." Another "…biotech company that also does business with the…" company that conducts experiments on animals "…was the victim of two pipe bombings last month." Sounds like any company with ties, distant or close, to a company doing anything the enviros do not like better watch out.

Article(426) describes how "…animal-rights activists…" are attacking one business, its partners, partners' property, and partner's family. "…vandals spray painted walls, fixtures, and electrical outlets…" and "…poured dry concrete down the drains and then left the water running, flooding restaurant and two adjacent businesses." This was done because the restaurant was involved with a "…farm, where they force-feed ducks to make the French delicacy foie gras." "…last month vandals struck…a store…" which "…was intended to showcase products from the duck farm,…" One farm partner's "…home in Marin County (California)…" was "…struck…" with "…spray painting…" saying "…murderer…", pouring acid on…car and leaving threatening videotape of his family." "Police have estimated damages from all attacks at more than $60,000." This article again shows how association with enviro targeted businesses can put your personal property and your family in harms way.

I don't know if the enviros feel the threats and damage were worth the results, but the article indicates the partners have decided "…foie gras (which the article says is a liver with extra fat that is created by force-feeding) will not be such an important part of the merchandise at a specialty foods shop…", "…the venture's focus has shifted from foie gras to other gourmet food.", "…a French scientist who specializes in foie gras production…" has been hired "…to evaluate their farm…", and "…partners have scrapped their logo, which had depicted a smiling duck."

I don't know if the farm ducks are smiling, and I don't really care if duck livers are available to eat; however, I do believe as long as there is someone who likes foie gras and there is a market for foie gras, the farm operations will continue. The ducks will still be overfed and killed for their livers, and all the eco-terrorism and vandalism will have done is to cause damage and hurt for some innocent folks.

A news article(427) tells how "The Animal Liberation Front, which the FBI has said is responsible for more than 600 animal-related crimes in the past seven years, has claimed responsibility for..." releasing "...10,000 minks...in Sultan...Washington...from cages at...Fur Farm..." "...lives of most of the (free) minks...have been far from beautiful." "...cars squashed a couple hundred..." One neighbor "...has killed 20..." because "...they have slaughtered dozens of his ducks and chickens, feasted on fingerling salmon in his creek..., bit his dog..., leapt out of the shadows and scratched his arm...," and showed "...They are brutal little guys." Minks "...often have an insatiable desire to kill and eat one another." "...ecoterrorists caused...release of 14,000 minks..." on "...an Iowa farm...in 2000..." which "The Animal Liberation Front also claimed responsibility..." Let's see the tally for these acts of liberation is a lot of dead and hurt: ducks, chickens, salmon, dogs, people; a lot of dead and starving mink; and who knows what other damage. What a wonderful thing was done by this ecoterrorism, not!

Two other news articles(428)(429) provide a story of wanting to do good; or, do they? In this article, a guy turned himself in for "...damaging or attempting to damage more than 20...high-voltage transmission towers...in California, Idaho, Oregon, and Washington." He "...is an active member in Peace and Justice Action League of Spokane (Washington)...", and he "...said his actions...were necessary to highlight critical vulnerabilities to the power infrastructure - a system that could be breached easily (by terrorists),..." Did this fella do us a favor by putting our electrical needs (hospital, etc.) at risk and exposing who knows who to being hurt or killed by failed towers to show we have an obvious weakness? What do you think? I know what I think.

Ecoterrorism ideas are spreading as illustrated in a news article(430), and why not? If you believe your cause is environmentally just, the media will support you, and there seems to be little punishment for causing damage, burning, bombing, and exposing people to being hurt. "...radical environmental groups had a busy year...From a $50 million arson at a San Diego condominium to four chickens liberated from a California egg farm,..."

Past actions by "...fronts..." have involved "...logging operations, Forest Service facilities, fur farms, slaughterhouses..." "...the groups…released…a list of actions…" that show they plan to spread "…their violent political action through the rest of the country…" outside their past focus in the "…Pacific Northwest…" "…FBI…" spokesperson says "…they are moving out around the country…" "The groups claimed responsibility for 75 actions in 2003." including "…graffiti on cars of a circus train to dirt in gas tanks to arson of condominiums (to stop urban sprawl) and firebombing of new Hummer SUVs."

The list of groups in this article(430) include Animal Liberation Front (ALF), Environmental Liberation Front (ELF), Frogs, Animal Liberation Brigade, Vegan Dumpster Militia, and Direct Action Front.

"…arrests have been few.", and lack of accountability and punishment for ecoterrorism acts can only stimulate a feeling of being untouchable and being justified in doing ecoterrorism activities.

Spokesperson for "…FBI's domestic terrorism operations…said…it was sheer dumb luck and providence that someone has not been killed."

When in the wrong, have protesters been punished and treated in a manner equivalent to the damage, injury, and cost they have caused? When you think about this question, try to think of when the legal system has applied adequate justice for legitimate wrongs by protesters. Try to think of when the media has provided articles that emphasize or at least give equal billing to the legal and damaging ramifications of wrongful actions by protesters. It is hard to think of or find examples of properly applied justice and to find follow-up articles that emphasize the down side of protest actions, isn't it?

As the public sees more and more wild and silly protest activity and as the public is more and more adversely affected, you would think support for protests would wane. The senselessness of many protests, the damage being caused, the cost of providing enforcement personnel, and the diversion of funds and enforcement personnel away from more important enforcement matters over time should turn many people away from supporting any protest actions, legitimate or not. If logic and common sense prevail which is a distant possibility, the ones enjoying the party may eventually find a lost interest in protests and waning support. Wild and silly protest parties may turn sour.

I wonder?

What would happen if the media took the Fox New's fair and balanced approached and fully reported all protest actions?

As illustrated by internet report(431), there is a large amount of people, possibly an unacknowledged majority in this country and the world, with a viewpoint opposite the anti-development and anti-use crowd. This internet report tells of protests and protestors at "...Johannesburg...Earth summit, formally known as the United Nations Summit on Sustainable Development...to criticize what they see as the sustainable poverty agenda of environmentalists..." "...United Nation's sustainable development policy, known as Agenda 21." says "Sustainable development is broadly defined as development that does not harm the environment."

"...environmentalists have inserted themselves into India's agricultural practices and opposed the use of genetically modified crops and modern chemical farming techniques in favor of more earth-friendly organic farming methods. There is definitely an arrogance on the part of these western activists..." when "...they come...and tell us how to live, they don't even understand the basic issues of farmers,..."

"The protestors – including...street vendors, traders, farmers and free-market advocates - believe the Earth summit's agenda is designed to keep developing nations from achieving economic prosperity by limiting infrastructure development that environmentalists consider to be ecologically destructive. The marchers also decried the environmentalists' push for organic farming methods in the developing world, where people are starving. That push for organic farming has condemned the residents of poor nations to backbreaking agricultural techniques...instead of giving them the technology...that would lead to higher crop yields."

"The anti-summit protesters presented a special BS award to international environmental groups for sustaining poverty..." and "...carried signs reading 'Profit Beats Poverty', 'People First', 'Trade Not Aid', 'Freedom to Farm', 'People Not Pandas', and 'Save the Earth from Sustainable Development'."

How many of you have ever heard of these protests? I know I have not seen them provided in regular media coverage. Isn't it interesting how such protests and viewpoints are given little to no play by the regular media? Could it be the majority of the media outlets have a biased agenda?

THE CIRCLE

Chapter Fifteen

The environmental community is fond of saying life is a circle. All things come from Mother Earth and return to her. Re-cycle and reuse what nature has provided us, and we will be able to treat Mother Earth better.

Re-cycling is an okay thing and should be done, but recycling is not the only circle that needs to be understood and perpetuated. Human intervention and proper management of our wildlands mixed with incentives and economic realities need to be added to the mix to allow Mother Earth to more fully provide good things for humans and all species.

As we apply the circle idea to any landscape, we need to understand as the landscape is manipulated or disturbed, things happen. Any existing landscape that meets current needs of humans and other species has been created by disturbance of some kind at some time.

Haphazard happenings such as fire create haphazard conditions. In unmanaged old-growth forests, survival of the big trees depends on how often and where Mother Nature has provided lightning and fire. Where large fuel build-up occurs, things will burn hot and streams will run putrid. Rebirth after fire can be good to haphazardly bad.

When our current knowledge about species and their habitats is seriously and factually reviewed, it has to be acknowledged that every species has needs that fit a certain space and time in the vegetative growth cycle that occurs across the landscape. If the landscape is not allowed to cycle through all naturally occurring vegetative progressions, it is inevitable that some species will be inhibited and maybe prevented from existing.

A resident of Virginia illustrates the need for all phases of vegetative growth and habitats across the landscape in an internet report(105). "In 1935, 90% of the (Jefferson National) forest was early successional habitat..." created by "...The chestnut blight...", and "Fifty years ago, grouse were one of the most common bird species on the Jefferson Forest." with "...plenty of neo-tropicals and even bobwhite quail." "...woodcock ...used to be common on the Jefferson - they do breed here in Virginia by-the-way, but they are now...in dire straits...rare in the Forest..." These species "...need early successional habitat..."

Another internet report(433) from a wildlife biologist who has given testimony in Washington says "Woods vary greatly.

Northern…southern…eastern hardwoods…western pines and firs…wet woods…steep south facing slopes…harbor different animals and plants…" When destroyed by fire or hurricane or when logged or cleared…woods slowly go back to a recognizable mix of trees, plants, and animals." "Generally they first become grassy…then brushy… then one or more intermediate tree stands will grow and decline…and mature." "…if…replanted…only a few years of grassy/brushy plants will intervene." before a forest can return.

Letting Mother Nature haphazardly developed diversity and habitats will not result in as many benefits as that provided by an active management program. If humans are allowed to intervene, better controlled and managed changes will occur in our wildlands as they cycle from disturbance and rebirth to maturity. When a landscape matures and it is time to start the process, or the circle, over again, human intervention can help the needed disturbance and re-growth to occur in a manner that is more beneficial to both humans and other species.

There is more opportunity to create, produce, and maintain society's chosen landscapes if experienced professionals are allowed to utilize their experience, proven management techniques, site specific factual information, time tested and peer reviewed science, logic, and common sense. Properly placed and maintained roads can provide access for management and fire control purposes. Re-vegetation processes and other factors such as damage due to disease and insects can be controlled. Food and economic benefits needed to maintain our rural communities and our way of life without adversely affecting the environment and species' habitats can be provided.

I had a relative that worked for one of the park services tell me a story how even the folks working in the parks interfere with natural processes in order to maintain park like qualities desired by park visitors.

Meadows are not forever. It is natural for meadows to replace lakes as the lakes fill with deposits from various vegetative and peat creation processes. It is also a natural process for trees to seed into meadows and for meadows to be replaced by forests. Disturbance can cause these processes to start over, but the amount of disturbance required to stop the reforesting of meadows is not conducive to most park uses and is generally restricted or not allowed to occur on park lands.

Meadows make for beautiful park pictures, and park visitors like to see meadows; so, park employees do things to prevent meadows from becoming forests. One way they do this is to walk around pulling up new tree seedlings, and putting the tree seedlings in a paper bag to hide what they are doing from the public. In this way, trees are prevented from taking over beautiful meadow areas.

This is interesting, because this demonstrates how nothing really remains static in our wildlands, and even in parks, it takes humans to help maintain many of the park conditions everyone thinks they are preserving and keeping unmanipulated by man.

Even the one with nature Native Americans require human help in maintaining areas as they were in the past. In a news article(327), "U. S forest officials have agreed to cut down...encroaching pine trees..." that "...have blocked the view of...Mt. Shasta..."; so, the mountain can be seen from "...a historically wide-open meadow..." used to "...dance and pray..."

Can you see how the circle can give better results with the help of proven and proper human intervention?

Can you see how we can have our cake (not adversely impacting environments) and eat it (use natural resources) too? History, my experiences, and site specific facts tell me proper use of natural resources mixed with Mother Nature's ability to heal and reproduce lets all this happen.

Maybe a story(434) provided by a liberal talk show host can help show how humans fit into the environmental picture in a good way. The story starts with an old man and a boy sitting on a porch sipping lemonade. They are looking out over a peaceful and beautiful landscape of wheat fields, forest, and really blue sky. The old man leans over and says quietly to the boy "It's all alive". Now, the old man understood what it takes to create the scene he and the boy were enjoying, but I doubt most people would understand what the old man knew. It was humans that had created the beautiful, living landscape they were viewing. When properly done, humans can take what Mother Nature provides and do some really wondrous things.

So what is preventing this wonderful picture of proper management and giving the best results for all from becoming a reality?

Murphy's Law which says if something can go wrong it will is constantly getting in the way, and Mother Nature does a lot of unpredictable things which complicate matters. While Murphy's law and Mother nature can not be predicted and totally eliminated, proper and active management can and is blunting a lot of the impacts from these two factors: something going wrong and Mother Nature.

Human greed and human nature are routinely causing problems; however, these problems are being reduced properly and sometimes improperly through regulatory and environmental pressures. Again, proper and active management can and is blunting these factors.

Ah hah!

Trying to get society to decide what it wants is probably the main road block keeping the circle from repeating itself in a smooth manner that provides the best for humans and all species. The currently pushed mentality that says lock-up and do not use our natural resources which is aided by a lot of pseudo science keeps getting in the way.

As further discussed in this book over and over and over again, the decision making processes that are determining what society wants have been taken over and are driven by the uninformed and vocal special interest groups. The political processes bow to the most vocal and media driven pressures. Those in power use the inability to hold them accountable to further their ideas and increase their power routinely to the detriment of the environment, private landowners, and rural communities. The struggle to do the right thing is not being controlled by site specific factual information, time tested and peer reviewed science, logic, and common sense.

The most vocal protectionist groups have successfully promoted the idea that human activities may have to be tolerated, but they are bad for the land. This group routinely pushes the idea that the land and Mother Nature are better off existing in a haphazard manner, and man can not improve or help Mother Nature. An open minded, scrutinizing look shows this is not true.

So, here we are. Because of the hobbles placed on human involvement and active management, the described circle can not provide the best for both humans and all species. As the resistance to making decisions based on site specific factual information, time tested and peer reviewed science, logic, and common sense, is allowed to continue, humans and all species will continue to lose out somewhere in someway.

Do we and other species settle for second best; or, do we change how landuse decisions are being made and applied; so, we can all get more out of the circle?

NEW FORESTRY

A LITTLE NEW
(PSEUDO AND UNPROVEN IDEAS)
AND
A LOT OF OLD
(OLD TREES AND DEAD THINGS)

BEAUTY IS IN THE EYE OF THE BEHOLDER

Chapter Sixteen

Many involved in environmental and wildland issues are growing enamored with a thing called "New Forestry". My interpretation of "New Forestry" goals involves developing and providing habitats for selected plant and animal species. Recreational uses, active management, and production of wood products are to be subservient to "New Forestry". "New Forestry's" forest will not consist of mostly healthy and vigorous trees, and plantation green is definitely out of place.

The recipe for "New Forestry" requires a selected mix of wildlife trees and special habitats. "New Forestry" wants a mix of trees that provide brown, red, yellow, gray, white, dead, gnarled, twisted, limby, deformed, stunted, diseased, tall, short, large, small, medium, young, old, laying on the ground, grouse slider, wolf, and occasional healthy conditions. The wanted forest is to have multistoried canopies, abundant dead woody material standing and on the ground, vertical and horizontal habitats, dying trees, and a **"few"** growing trees to perpetuate the forested appearance.

In "New Forestry", road and human use is to be de-emphasized, reduced, and in places eliminated. Human activities that manipulate vegetation but do not produce "New Forestry" conditions will be frowned upon. Removal of brush and down woody debris for fire control reasons can be a no, no.

Fire is actually an enemy of "New Forestry"; yet, "New Forestry" welcomes fire by providing the ingredients for devastating wildfire. Allowing dead and dying materials to build, limiting access, and preventing fire prevention work routinely results in uncontrollable, damaging fire.

When unavoidable fire does come, it will be hot, and dead and dying materials, standing trees, species, and all habitats can all go up in smoke.

In the West, the Fourth Branch of Government, especially Federal agencies administering Public Trust lands, are promoting "New Forestry" in a big way. The public, politicians, and media are routinely told by the Fourth Branch of Government and many pseudo experts that "New Forestry" is a good thing. This spin is allowing "New Forestry" to upstage other forest uses and needs. When funding is distributed, recreation, production of natural resource products, fire prevention work, and management favoring healthy, vigorous tree growth often lose out. On some Public Trust Lands, "New Forestry" is replacing use of natural resources, maintaining road access, and restoring burned areas to trees.

The media, pseudo experts, and the Fourth Branch of Government are not telling the full story about "New Forestry". The politicians and the public are not hearing what can happen under "New Forestry", and they are routinely not told about the benefits of alternative management options. The potential for increased loss, waste, erosion, and overall damage from fire under "New Forestry" is not getting much attention. Without a practical and effective way to hold the Fourth Branches of Government and enviros accountable, cute critters and theoretical spin are winning the day, and many management decisions are not based on all the facts and available science.

They say pictures are worth a thousand words; so, to make it easier to understand the goal of "New Forestry", a series of photos (10,11,12,13,14) are provided in the center of this book which highlights the goals of "New Forestry".

While many "New Forestry" advocates will say they want no more than a compromise, current pressures to apply New Forestry are not the result of compromise.

Compromise is suppose to involve all sides of an issue giving-in to something in exchange for something of equal value. This is not happening in the majority of confrontations between producers of natural resources and regulatory and environmental folks. The latter currently have the hammer, and without getting something equal in return, producers of natural resources are routinely having to given-in.

While past thinking did promote maximizing timber growth on forest lands and this did not result in the maintenance of some species' habitats, the application of "New Forestry" ideas has gotten out of hand. There is an absence of full and adequate peer review of the science and regulations being thrown around.

284

"New Forestry" advocates routinely ignore real world conditions and how timber harvest activities provide many species' benefits often not provided by "New Forestry" ideas. By default on lands being managed to grow timber, physical and regulatory restrictions create diverse habitats for multiple species across the landscape. Watercourse protection zones maintain all kinds of vegetative covers and habitat conditions. Regulatory restrictions are providing all kinds of late seral forest conditions. Retention and creation of woody debris is an ongoing process, and a continually changing vegetative cover provides habitats for a multitude of species. Fire and Mother Nature add to the mix by continuing to create and change habitats.

In the name of "New Forestry", landowners are being forced to do questionable things not supported by proven science and authorized regulations, and the way they are routinely forced to do these things is definitely not the result of compromise. Regulators are requiring healthy trees to be killed in an effort to create more snags. Tops are cut out of large healthy trees to kill them in an attempt to create more snags, dead materials, and nesting platforms. Unhealthy, diseased, and insect infested trees are required to be left which take up growing space and provide a source of infection for healthy trees. Road construction is forced to be done on steep, potentially unstable slopes; so, benign road use by watercourses will not occur. Woody debris is required to be left untouched which increases the potential for fire. In an attempt to create multi-canopied conditions and habitats for a special list of species, many unworkable "New Forestry" ideas are being forcefully applied. Unnecessary buffers are required which reduce income from the land and often results in a taking of value.

I can support justified light doses of "New Forestry". I can even support protecting the best and most unique habitats in preserves. However, the increasing lock-up of our public lands and unjustified regulatory restrictions on resource uses has gone way overboard and is more than a light dose.

In summarizing this chapter and what the pictures tell us, I provide the following food for thought.

"New Forestry" as a management tool is deficient in the following ways.

1. It ignores the real world and what really happens.

2. It creates unhealthy and low producing forest conditions in an attempt to service a special group of species at the expense of many other species.

3. It ignores the increased risk of loss from fire, disease, and insects.

4. It uses a lot of unsubstantiated and unsupported ideas to restrict use of natural resources and to unjustifiably take private property.

There is a prevalent thought in this country that we can continually reduce natural resource productivity and hoard our resources in preserves without having to face any consequences. I provide the following two stories for you to think about.

The first story involves a visitor from India. This visitor said we were wasteful when he saw all the beach driftwood that was left to lie on our beaches, and someone from this country said not having to use driftwood was a credit to how well we manage our resources. The fact we defaulted into having an abundant amount of resources which our population level does not require be utilized was not even considered by the person from this country. Sadly, too many in this country share this same naïve thinking.

The second story also involves India. There was a severe drought in India, and owners of elephant herds were running out of food to feed their elephants. India had this one of a kind special forest preserve which was very unique and protected by law. This uniqueness kept the protected preserve from being utilized for forage for a long time. The drought and lack of feed became critical. Rather than lose their elephants, the herders broke the law, entered the protected preserve, and cut limbs from trees to feed their elephants.

This story illustrates why only areas with very unique and special qualities should be set aside; so, there are powerful reasons to leave them untouched. The uniqueness of the India preserve saved it for a long time, and this preserve was only entered because there was no where else to go.

This story also shows how pressures to use resources can build, become powerful, and be unstoppable. While this country is not facing resource problems found in India, an awful lot of ongoing importation shows this country is not internally fulfilling resource needs.

Properly maximizing use of resources outside protected areas could help us maintain the luxury of leaving protected areas untouched. Unfortunately, proper maximization of available resources is not being allowed. Based on some pretty weak and indefensible reasons, we keep hoarding and restricting resources, and this is lowering the bar keeping us out of protected areas. In the extreme, hoarding and restricting resources can lead to what happened in

India, and the lowered bar may not be enough to stop the mob at boundaries to legitimately unique areas.

The reduced production and use of natural resources by such things as "New Forestry" need to be seriously reviewed and overhauled.

Need and greed are powerful forces that reach out and take what they want, and you never want to say never.

And away we go

**The blind but powerful
leading the sheep to the cliff**

BURN BABY BURN

Chapter Seventeen

As the west burns, the debate over how to manage our wildlands continues through broken hearing and politically driven legislative processes. There is no clear direction or end to all the B.S. that is flowing through these processes. Everyone fiddles with half truths and point and counter point presentations. It is no wonder confusion and friction exist regarding proper management of our Public Trust lands.

Fire problems and land management choices involve very complex issues, and there is a lack of discussion and understanding of the total picture. The involved decision process requires society to choose how and where to leave the land untouched, and how and where it should be managed. Because vegetative growth, fuel loading, and wildland management situations are constantly changing, management methods have to also keep changing.

An internet report(435) helps to show how complicated the fire issue is by having the chairman of the National Association of Forest Service Retirees say the following. "Too often, proven, professionally applied forest management practices are ignored, harming the very public forests we cared for during our careers. Perhaps the most persistent misconception is that forests should be undisturbed by humans.", and left to "…become overgrown and more susceptible to fire, insects and disease." "Another misconception is that our overgrown forests are simply the result of past fire suppression efforts." "…the history of our Western forests,…" shows they "…are overgrown because of a complex combination of factors,…" including "Substantial fluctuation in climate and reduction in forest harvests (and I would add interference with needed management activities)…" "Thinning…where sunlight can reach young trees and ground vegetation…helps create healthy forests." By only "…thinning our forests near communities…we are inviting catastrophic wildfire, insect infestation and disease, threatening public health and safety, devastating the ecosystem and its wildlife, and damaging our watersheds." "…fire treatments must be implemented across broad landscapes in order to modify fire behavior."

Amen!

HINDSIGHT

LOSS OF ACCESS AND FUNDING NEEDED TO MANAGE OUR PUBLIC TRUST LANDS

My direct contact with the forest and forest management decisions on private and public lands for over 38 years allows me to present some food for thought.

Management activities involving recreation, fire control, timber, and environmental studies require reliable, efficient access. Construction and maintenance of needed road access is currently haphazard and poorly handled. Public land road programs have gone from using low environmental impact minimum standards to using overbuilt, paved highways. Unjustifiable, costly elimination of road access is occurring for questionable reasons. Limited road maintenance and construction funds are not being properly distributed.

In the past, timber harvest sale programs provided benefits to local communities and created access for other uses. Timber harvest sales provided funding for rural schools and local community roads. Jobs and economic support was provided to rural communities. Funding was generated to support various public activities such as recreation.

Things have changed. The timber harvest sale program has been made into a dysfunctional and uneconomic process, and lost sale revenues to schools and roads has been replaced by taxpayer dollars. For all practical purposes, the opponents of timber sale programs have successfully killed the timber sale golden goose and taken away provided benefits.

A magazine article(436) outlines how "In 1998 the (U.S.) Forest Service took in $788 million while spending $2.3 billion to manage..." national forest "...assets" In the past, the national forests contributed money to the national treasury, and now the national forests with zero cost in the forests' assets have become cost plus forests having to be funded by the taxpayers.

This same article(436) goes on to say "By the Forest Service's own estimates, 60% of..." national forest "...lands nationwide are today in an unhealthy and fire-prone condition. They are going to get more unhealthy. The U.S. Forest Service announced a moratorium on road building on 43 million acres, which..." by not having needed access "...will further limit the ability to reduce excess wood loads."

If there is no change in how natural resources on public lands are managed, marketed, and sold, then the cost plus situation where the forest becomes a suction point for tax dollars will not change. Having a continual adverse and unnecessary drain on local economies and this country's treasury is not justified.

HOW DID IT HAPPEN??

What created cost plus forest, loss of access, stumbling, and bumbling? Public agency staffs have become bloated, and staffs are doing all kinds of questionable things. Regarding some management issues, inexperienced staffs are using improper accounting procedures, and inaccurate numbers are being used to make some management decisions. Political pressures and quota requirements have got staffs all shook-up and caused a loss of experienced professionals.

Natural resource sale programs have become dysfunctional. Too many inexperienced Johnny-come-lately pseudo scientists and untrained and inexperienced public employees are allowed to run the show. Experience has been replaced by politically correct thinking that routinely keeps factual site specific review, peer reviewed and proven ideas, and use of a little logic and common sense from being applied in determining what restrictions and costs are truly required and applicable to timber harvest activity.

One argument used to justify not having public timber sales is the charge that the government is subsidizing purchasers of timber sales by giving away timber or paying others more to harvest timber than is returned to the government. Support for this argument comes from faulty accounting procedures and inappropriate application of cost factors.

Many unsupported and unjustified costs and cost procedures are inappropriately applied to timber harvest activities. Such things as hand piling of slash that should not be piled so it can return to the soil, road beautification work, biological survey and wildlife work not related to timber harvest operations, inappropriate accounting procedures for road costs, road maintenance costs for recreational purposes, and inapplicable administrative and training costs are inappropriately applied to timber sale accounts.

It is interesting how Public Trust lands, with zero cost basis assigned to natural resources, routinely no longer produce an economically acceptable product to the market. When experienced and knowledgeable professionals apply historical knowledge and common sense to what is now happening, they find inappropriate and unjustified accounting and operational procedures being applied. Changes allowing use of proper standards and procedures would allow environmentally acceptable sales of resources to

290

again produce positive returns. With no base cost and existing road systems, there is no excuse for Public Trust lands not paying their way and adding to the public treasury. Windfall damaged timber left to rot along existing roads would be a good place to start.

The old saying "people are promoted to their highest level of incompetence" has never been more true than in many governmental agencies. In the effort to fulfill mandated personnel quotas, many people have been advanced beyond their knowledge and capabilities. With inexperienced, lower seniority, and less qualified people being promoted over them, experienced people have left public agencies to avoid dealing with coming problems and for not being treated fairly.

When folks laying out sales do not know what it takes to have an economically viable sale, is it any wonder a lot of sales do not return positive returns to the government. Rotten and small timber is routinely chosen for removal that has no market value. Sale volumes are kept small which makes it hard to cover costly harvesting requirements and makes timber removal a cost plus operation. Unnecessary and unsupported species protection restrictions prevent economically viable timber from being included in sale volumes.

The issue of inexperienced people running the show was discussed by many regarding deaths of firefighters on the Thirty Mile fire in the North Cascades. According to a recopied report(437), rare reprimand actions are suppose to be applied regarding this matter. This report states "Eleven U.S. Forest Service employees should be disciplined for their actions..." "...punishments range from losing their jobs...being placed on leave without pay, to a letter of reprimand in their personnel files." "...investigation after the fire concluded that fire bosses and managers broke safety rules of firefighting and disregarded numerous warning signs of danger." Whether inexperience was the main culprit or it was decided, right or wrong, someone, anyone had to take the blame may never be fully disclosed. It would be interesting to know how high up in the supervisory chain the reprimands went. In any case, it appears the supervisors that broke firefighting safety rules and disregarded numerous warning signs of danger were not adequately prepared to be doing what they were charged to do.

Then there is the story(438) about a forest technician patrolling to enforce a fire ban and letting a campfire she started get out of control. The story says 100,000 acres was scorched in the Pike National Forest and 22 homes were destroyed. While the technician could be sentenced up to 10 years in prison and fined up to $250,000 (in your dreams), someone up the ladder handling this untrained technician and other technicians needs to be checked out, because this someone has the potential to allow this to happen again.

Due to broken and long drawn out hearing and review processes, there have been delays in implementing proper management techniques and ideas in the field. An absence of proper peer review and loss of knowledge provided by experienced personnel, has allowed political, media, and feel-good pressures to force many unproven ideas to be applied often to the detriment of the environment and rural communities.

During hearing and regulatory development processes, there is a push to have one approach or silver bullet when dealing with fire issues. This push ignores how site specific conditions differ on different areas, and a variety of approaches are required to handle different and changing conditions. The need to focus on solutions that fit site specific conditions seems to get lost in the debates. A politically correct large tree forest with its snag and windfall problem needs much different treatment than a young forest with low canopy fuels. In the right places, pruning, thinning, and prescribed burns reduce the potential for uncontrollable fire.

Also, a major item needing more attention in the fire debates is inappropriate and unjustified elimination of access. The push to not create and maintain permanent watercourse crossings and to purposefully eliminate roads is going to spell trouble in the future.

NO MANAGEMENT OPTION

Supposedly to benefit some species and to fulfill societal demands, some areas are not actively managed, and the consequences of "no management" need to be understood. When an area covered by older vegetation is made a roadless area, fuel loading already exists and continues to build over time. Maybe frequent lightning strikes will occasionally occur to reduce fuel loads. Realistically, hot burns can not be avoided on such areas, and after these burns, pristine areas will no longer be pristine, resources will be gone, erosion will occur, and area uses will be limited to what is provided by uncontrolled vegetative re-growth.

Routinely unproven and misguided thinking supporting "no management" options is presented by many introduced as experts and knowledgeable professionals. Such thinking and support for no management ideas is illustrated in news article(439) where "...U.S. Geological Surveys Jemez Mountains Field Station at Los Alamos, N. M..." person says

"...epidemic of bark beetles is killing millions of trees...And an eight year drought is killing many of the trees the beetles don't get." This is "...really a natural ...self-thinning of forests...response..." "...it may in effect reset many ecosystems, wiping them out and forcing natural selection to start over from scratch." "Nature's version of forest thinning creates...millions of dead trees like standing cordwood awaiting a match."; however, "...once the needles drop off the conifers, researchers said they are less prone to the wind-driven tree-top fires that have become more prevalent and fed western firestorms in recent years." Person from "U.S. Geological Survey's Desert Laboratory in Tucson, Ariz. says "...this drought is punching hundred-thousand acre holes in ponderosa pine forests...and million-acre hole from bark beetles..." and "Letting nature take its course may be practical, if not inevitable." "...California ecologist for the U.S. Forest Service" says there is "...pressure to quickly replant the devastated area(s) with something drought- and fire-resistant to prevent erosion and mudslides, even if that means introducing exotic species like giant sequoia." "The best the scientists could offer is that managers should do what's best for whatever springs back, whether that is juniper and pinion forest, oak woodlands, or ponderosa pine forests."

If you buy into what this article says, you believe some things are too big for humans to handle, and it is best to let beetles haphazardly kill trees. Supposedly fires, which haphazardly wipe out all kinds of species and habitats, will not be too bad, and except on areas where man tries to do something, haphazard re-growth will allow everything to supposedly cycle back to whatever was there before. We should let brush fields form, and wait hundreds of years for Mother Nature to maybe reforest them. Everything will be honky dory if we just leave the beetles to do their thing and let Mother Nature run the show.

While this article does provide some truths and useful information, and describes the overwhelming task to correct a lot of the dying forest and fire problems that now exist, this article's overall "no management" message ignores the benefits of active management and is more than a little dangerous.

The article also falls short by not adequately explaining how we got into the current mess and how to properly handle the current situation. Could it be the enviro and protectionist movements at the end of the Nineteenth Century and partly portrayed in this article caused a pull back from active forest management on our public lands? Did this lack of active forest management cause many of the fire and dying forest problems we now see?

There are benefits to replanting and reducing erosion and mudslide potential, and having more giant sequoia trees; however, I think we can do better. Active management like thinnings, removal of diseased, dead, and dying trees, creating fuel breaks, and maintaining road access can do a lot more in reducing damage from fire, disease, and insects.

There are many, many examples of what can happen if active management is not pursued.

The Booth and Bear Buttes Oregon fire as described in a news article(440) "...merged into one 83,000 acre complex fire burning through beetle infested Ponderosa pine..." which indicates dead pine trees had been left untended and unharvested. In discussing what to do on the 500,000 acre Biscuit fire in Oregon, a newspaper article(441) has the Dean of the College of Forestry at Oregon State University saying "...without cutting dead trees and replanting, the half of the Biscuit area that burned intensely was doomed to grow back as brush and hardwoods that burn over and over." Another article(442) regarding this fire discusses what to do on the burned areas. This article describes how ideas from Canada, Australia, and Hawaii are being considered which conflict with input from a professor emeritus of forest ecology and silviculture at Oregon State University. The professor says "...trees grow back bigger and faster..." by planting trees and clearing brush.

Nonlocal input favors leaving dead materials in place and leaving burned areas to the whim of Mother Nature. This input conflicts with an experienced professor's input and other local input which says leaving things to Mother Nature will result in flammable forest brush fields and heavy fuel loads. Any benefits from leaving large downed logs and dead trees will be quickly lost when consumed by another wildfire.

Use logical and practical local input or use ideas from out of the area? I know what I would do.

A series of news articles(443)(444)(445) all make reference to the ongoing beetle-kill and bug problem being a major contributor to the large fires in southern California and throughout the west. California Licensed Foresters Update Newsletter(446) mentions "...spruce bark beetle infestation has killed an estimated 3,400,000 acres of trees in the state (Alaska) over the past decade, and officials...say they fear about 1,400,000 acres in Kenai National Wildlife Refuge... vulnerable to fire." Another news article(447) describes the Boulder fire in Wyoming as "...feeding off beetle killed spruce trees..." A news article(448) tells how "...stands of drought and beetle-killed trees ignited like matchsticks to create a wind driven firestorm near Lake

Arrowhead…in the San Bernardino Mountains…" in "…Last fall's fires east of Los Angeles and San Diego…"

My personal observations and information from many others shows large amounts of beetle damaged trees exist in the Lake Tahoe area, and this information coincides with a newspaper article(449) which indicates the Tahoe area is ripe for a major burn. This newspaper article says "The forest surrounding Lake Tahoe, in particular, is an enclosed tinderbox."

A person in a Letter to the Editor(450) provides an overview by saying "I had occasion to drive from Phoenix to Williams and the Grand Canyon…last spring…and observed…up to 5 percent of the visible timber stand recently dead…" With no timber removal activity in sight to accomplish "…fuel reduction without cost to the American taxpayer…", "…the good governor of Arizona wants the federal government to send her taxpayer dollars so she can do forest "sweeping and dusting" around residential areas."

These articles show there is an obvious lack of effort to remove dead, beetle killed trees, and if these beetle damaged trees are not removed and the land treated, a lot of bad fire is still on the way.

No matter how it is spun or who spins it, "no management" ideas with the resulting haphazard results and damage look like a real bummer to me.

IT JUST KEEPS
GOING AND GOING AND GOING AND GOING…

Despite what is said otherwise, once fire is ripping and roaring in roadless areas with heavy fuels, there is no way to assure control of fire. A series of news articles that covered the Canoe and King Range fires in Humboldt County in 2003 provide real world examples of what can happen under "No Management" option.

Starting with 9/5/2003 newspaper story(451) covering ongoing lightning fires and status of fire control efforts in northwestern California, lightning caused fire on the King Range wilderness area is estimated at 50 to 100 acres. The fire is burning tall brush. Due to a shortage of fire resources and personnel and fire being located where it is deemed unsafe to fly-in firefighters without adequate back-up, the CDF has decided to put no one on the fire. Other fires stretch from Garberville area to Orick.

News article dated 9/10/2003(452) says Honeydew fire also called the Kings Range fire is worrisome in steep, brushy terrain with no roads. Firefighters have been held back, because they could get trapped by the bad fire fighting conditions.

Fire crews had difficulty forging a trail into another fire in a roadless area in Humboldt Redwoods State Park. Firefighters will hike into this fire and be supplied by helicopter.

The park folks said that all fires burned slowly and gently, reducing the fuels on the forest floor, and this will help thin the forest understory and provide new growth that will feed deer and elk. The park folks make things sound nice and predictable, but as demonstrated over time by these fires, reality and history show other results are possible.

As described in other newspaper articles and verified by studying the situation, both fires are located in areas that are roadless with dangerous access for fire fighting purposes. Both areas are designated to be managed as natural preserves and to remain untouched by human hands. Obviously fighting fire by humans is considered okay.

A 9/20/2003 news article(458) basically says the Canoe fire is still going, and Honeydew fire in the Kings Range is now at 9,600 acres and 900 personnel are on the Kings Range fire which has to date cost $8,500,000 dollars to fight.

The 9/23/2003 news article(459) states the Canoe fire is "romping and stomping" and says fire has grown from 600 acres to 1,650 acres and has cost $11,200,000 to fight. Canoe fire has been contained inside the State Park.

Continuing, a 9/24/2003 news article(460) says Canoe fire is up to 2,000 acres and 1,700 people are fighting the fire. The Canoe fire is now heading for 100 homes and 400 structures and evacuations are being conducted. Firefighting official says there have been some extreme burn conditions.

Comments by the State Park official are interesting in light of the comments found in another news article(461) dated 8/28/2003 regarding fire in old-growth redwood. In this article, a State Park Ranger says fuels build up substantially over time and when ignited can generate particularly hot fires in old-growth redwood forests. Regarding the fire in the article, a CDF spokesperson said there was a potential for serious damage to the involved old-growth redwoods, and the fire was actually burning very aggressively.

My experiences with fire in the redwoods leads me to believe the 8/28/03 and 9/23/03 articles(461)(459) information versus the comments in the 9/10/03 article(452). I have seen and experienced how fuel loads can build to high levels in redwood forests, and redwood fires can burn very hot. I have seen severe fire in old-growth redwoods and the potential for damage to old-growth redwood trees is high.

9/30/2003 news article(469) says Kings Range charred 11,777 acres. This fire with the Canoe fires has involved 2,277 personnel, has cost $21,100,000, damaged two structures, and injured 59 personnel.

10/1/2003 news article(454) says Canoe fire has burned 10,056 acres and Kings Range fire has burned 11,861 acres. These fires have cost $23,800,000. A local television report says the main concern is for firefighters as fire is in snags which are unsafe to be around.

The color picture (see photo#15 in center of book) appearing with a 9/28/2003 article(466) should raise questions about burns in old-growth forests being low level, nondamaging fires. The picture shows heavy fuels bucked to allow for placement of a fire trail in an old-growth forest, and shows a high intensity fire that is routinely found in old-growth area burns.

Once fire fuels are consumed, slow, lower intensities fires may occur for awhile; however, based on history and site specific facts, it is wishful thinking to believe random lightning fires will provide enough natural fire to reduce fuel loading and eliminate hot burns in old-growth forests. Large trees are continually coming apart, dying, and falling which increases fire fuel loads. Old-growth fires will always burn hot, consume small and large materials, damage old-growth trees, and cook critters, soils, and vegetation. Without manipulating fire fuels, the cycle of hot burns will repeat itself over time over and over and over and over again in "no management" areas.

Let's see now. In their dream world, park folks said these fires burned slowly and gently, reducing the fuels on the forest floor. These fires helped thin the forest understory, and the new growth will feed deer and elk. Fire in old-growth redwood stands is good because it burns off ground fuels and brush, and the fire is not hot enough to hurt the old-growth redwoods "at all".

Words used by experienced firefighters to describe the two fires included hazardous, tall flames, blown up, romping and stomping, particularly hot, burning very aggressively, treacherous, firestorm, and fierce. Words used to describe firefighting conditions included unsafe flying conditions, trapped by bad conditions, safety was a concern, dangerous access, and fire hammering the lines.

These two simple, low intensity under burns that do more good than harm as described by the park folks put firefighters at risk, injured 59 of them, cost $32,800,000 to fight, caused evacuations, destroyed property values, destroyed a lot of species and species' habitat, burned up a lot of trees and other vegetation, and increased the potential for erosion and landslides.

Don't you just love that "no management" dream world?

The benefits of active management was demonstrated in another fire that did not get much attention. This fire occurred in the Mendocino National Forest under hotter and more severe fire conditions than the Canoe and Kings Range fires. A 10/3/2003 news article(471) says this fire covered 2,000 acres and more than 1,000 personnel including tanker and helicopter crews were used to fight the fire. The news article says the fire was hard to control "...because it is burning in very steep, rugged terrain in lots of timber, grass and old logging debris." Having timber cruised, appraised, and managed the area burned in the past, I have personal knowledge of the burned area and where the fire started in heavy old-growth timber that had been lightly or never logged.

I was told the only reason the fire was stopped, held to only 2,000 acres, and costs were kept down was due to an existing road system. The roads were used as fire lines and provided access for fire fighting equipment and personnel. Additional reasons for the fire being controllable can be attributed to reduction of undergrowth and control fires that reduced fire fuels on areas being managed for timber production. Some untreated logging debris was mentioned as a concern; however, the handling of this fire demonstrated how direct, active management such as constructing fire breaks, control burning, and maintaining access roads provides the means to control all types of fires.

These three actual fire situations show the ability to safely and efficiently control fire and reduce fire damage goes up or down depending on the amount of allowed management activity. If the "no management" option ever becomes the preferred choice for handling our forests, we are going to be in big trouble.

POOR MANAGEMENT, LACK OF MANAGEMENT, MISMANAGEMENT, NEW FORESTRY

Even with all the examples of hindsight demonstrating the folly of "no management" thinking, the environmentalists still fight efforts at direct and active management.

A 2003 article(472) outlines the damage and cost of fires, and goes on to show how the enviros still do not get it.

The article states "...fires in California this year have burned more than 700,000 acres, destroyed more than 2,500 homes, caused $2,000,000,000 in costs and damages, and killed 22 people." "Last year's wild fires in the West burned 7,000,000 acres, destroyed 800 homes, cost $1,500,000,000, and killed 23 firefighters."

Ignoring reality, enviro groups advocate natural and controlled fire as a good thing, and enviros say in the article "There is no forest management plan that does the job as efficiently or effectively as the great forces of nature." They additionally say "...let nature take its course. If that means big fires -as long as they are not near populated areas-so be it." If you look past the callus disregard for human losses, this rhetoric shows a lack of concern for species and species habitat losses and environmental damage caused by fire.

Without some active management, Mother Nature is not going to voluntarily stay away from populous areas. The Oakland fire storm is a good example that shows fire is not just a rural issue that can be blamed on humans for encroaching into wildland areas. Mother nature is very unpredictable and letting her do what she wants exploded all over southern California in 2003.

An editorial(473) discusses another instance of inaction that lead to a build-up of major fuel loads and damage from fire. The editorial describes how a wind storm "...ripped through Northern California, knocking out power and uprooting or shearing the tops off of millions of trees in the region's vast forests. Damage was especially severe on a 35,000 acre area of the Lower Trinity District." The involve 35,000 acre area included some nonroaded wilderness area and contained large, mature timber which some folks would call old-growth.

The editorial goes on to say "Agency experts envisioned a two-fold approach to reducing fuels: salvage logging followed by controlled burns. Logging would remove the larger materials - downed timber and standing trees with blown-out tops." "No healthy trees would be disturbed." Environmentalists used legal procedures to hold up full application of the proposed fuel load reduction work, and by the time the Megram fire came along, only "...900 acres of the 35,000 blowdown acres had received any fuel treatments..."

The Megram fire "...exploded and gobbled up thousands of acres only to slow when...it...finally feasted...through the heavy blowdown." This fire burned "...tens of thousands of contiguous acres of mature timber...", destroyed northern spotted owl habitat, and "...completely devastated...upper reaches of Horse Linto Creek." where an ongoing...fishery restoration success story." was in progress.

Executive director for involved environmental group, the Northcoast Environmental Center, showed little remorse or concern for the damage that occurred. He, "...says he wouldn't do anything differently if he could turn back the clock." An agency spokesperson shows a more responsible attitude by saying "where we treated, it fared well..."

A 2003 news article(474) illustrates the size of area in this country that is being left inaccessible and hard to manage for fire and other purposes. The article states "The U.S. Forest Service rule prohibits road-building for logging and other commercial purposes on 58,500,000 acres, nearly one-third of all national forest land...Most...in the west." The article mentions "The rule exempts roads needed for fire protection."

The exemption sounds like road construction for fire control purposes can occur; however, there are no guarantees such road work will ever get done. As provided by the Megram fire story, management activities are fought and hindered by the environmental community. Additionally, funding needed for building roads has been reduced and eliminated by not allowing use of natural resources and by political pressures to not fund such projects. The result is limited ability to access and safely control fire on 58,500,000 acres under custodial care of the U.S. Forest Service and many millions of other acres under the custodial care of other public agencies.

An example of how successful the roadless area thinking has become is illustrated by a news article(475) in which a National Park spokesperson proudly describes how roads in the Redwood National Park are being eliminated. While some roads need to be put to bed and restored, the program to restore roads in Redwood National Park has gone overboard.

Based on visual review and working adjacent to the park, my knowledge of Redwood National Park situation is pretty good. I know that stabilized roads with heavy layers of rocked surface, re-vegetated trees of good size, and stabilized watercourse crossings have been unnecessarily torn up. Naturally weathered, stabilize, and re-vegetate unstable areas not detrimentally contributing sediment to a watershed have been entered and disturbed.

The tearing up process used to eliminate roads has included digging into hillsides and road fill areas to move large quantities of soil around. The act of disturbing and piling soils obviously creates areas of freshly exposed soils and destabilizes things. In the short term, the work to eliminate stabilized roads and unstable areas probably causes more sedimentation and instability than existed before the work was done.

In the real world, short term accelerated sedimentation can be more detrimental than letting benign amounts dribble over time. Mother Nature naturally puts tons of sediment into watercourses every year; hence, we get spawning gravels and all kinds of beneficial habitats. Without sediments in watercourses, all kinds of unwanted things happen. As proven by studies and field observations, sudden flushes and heavy deposition of sediments cause major short term damage to watercourse habitats. No matter how much stabilization work is done (grass, straw, mulch) large soil movement involved in putting roads to bed can not avoid creating freshly exposed soils and accelerated erosion.

Why this road restoration work is being done is answered by the quote in the news article(475). "There's an absolute recognition across the service that this is what we want to do." The news article mentions $1,200,000 will be spent for one year's work. Since the Redwood National Park was created, 415 miles of road over decades have been restored (or destroyed depending on your point of view), and millions of dollars have been spent doing this work.

While some worthwhile, legitimate work has probably been done, has the expenditure of millions upon millions of taxpayer's dollars been well spent in the Redwood National Park? Considering the recent Canoe and Kings Range bad fires which demonstrated major fire control problems in roadless areas, hasn't the potential for damaging fires been increased on the Redwood National Park? Has the work in the park really stopped or reduced detrimental sedimentation and stability problems? Is all the restoration work really needed? Has work done by the National Park Service been peer reviewed by other than the Park Service; or, as indicated in the news article, have decisions to do the work all been internal Park Service decisions? Since the horse has already left the barn, it appears these questions involving governmental spending and resulting benefits will never be answered.

Tell me again how letting our natural resources and remote areas burn-up is a good thing and will keep populated areas from burning up.

I wonder how long it is going to take for the public to tell enviros to pound sand with the ideas stated below that were provided in a 2003 news article(472).

"There is no forest management plan that does the job as efficiently or effectively as the great forces of nature."

"...let nature take its course. If that means big fires-as long as they are not near populated areas-so be it."

It seems Mother Nature is telling the enviros they are all wet in their thinking, and if we don't actively corral her, she will do whatever she wants to do.

The firefighting business can be called a boom and bust business and not a stable source of community support. As areas are burned out, firefighting businesses are logically forced to move to unburned areas.

Of course, if the "no management" philosophy is allowed to prevail on a larger and larger scale, the fire fighting business could be made into a growth industry with a lot of boom. The "no management" option allows haphazard growth before and after fire to create flammable brush fields, and without manipulation of fuel loads, the potential for uncontrolled fires increases as dead materials and fuel loads accumulate. In a warped kind of way, some folks may even consider the increased employment and firefighting money a beneficial result of not actively managing our wildlands.

As further expressed in this cost of firefighting news article(487), some contractors even hope for bad fire years. A contractor is touching "...up his mobile kitchen..." and "...is cautiously hopeful the 2004 fire season will be good for business..." A kind of morbid comment follows which says "Everything looks great now because we've had five years of drought..."

It appears more fire fighting contractors are going to be needed, because many Forest Service employees say "That's not what I was hired to do and I'm not doing it..." I guess the Forest Service has turned into a bunch of specialists who do what they want.

In the final analysis, I hope everyone agrees the damage, loss, and misery from uncontrolled fire and an increased need for firefighting services is not a good thing. It is hard for me to believe a logically thinking person would say otherwise.

While fire can never be completely eliminated, how can anyone justify not managing our wildlands in an effort to reduce the risk of fire?

Why would anyone not support doing everything possible to avoid loss of property value, destruction of homes, firefighting costs, restoration costs, loss of species and species' habitat, landslide and erosion losses, damaged water supplies, and death?

To deflect attention away from their part and "no management's part in the fire damage that is occurring in the west, enviros have added a couple new thoughts to their spin.

Enviros are saying the results of timber harvesting are the culprit causing the fires. They play up the fact timber harvesting creates slashy fuel conditions, and re-growing a forest results in dense undergrowth that increases the potential for bad fire. They blame the backlog of untreated and dense forest conditions on bad timber harvesting practices.

They make it sound like growing a new forest is a bad thing.

They conveniently do not mention how current problems have been long in coming and are due to a lack of active management. They ignore how their lawsuits have stopped needed fire prevention work and have driven logging equipment out of the woods that used to help in fighting fire. They ignore how they have stopped removal of existing beetle killed trees that currently provide fire fuels. They ignore how they are fighting the thinning projects that could eliminate tight forest conditions. They ignore how their "no management" ideas have allowed Mother Nature to determine in her haphazard way what happens on our wildlands.

Despite all the historical information to the contrary, the enviros are doing what they can to keep "no management" thinking alive. They have taken the tact of saying protect the populated areas, and do not worry about natural damage in remote areas. If they can instill the idea, remote fires are natural and do no harm, they will not have to back-off in their push for more restrictions on resource use in remote areas.

This new approach is supported by a logical argument that homes and private property being used by people are more important than far off distant wildland resources. While the need to protect residential areas is a legitimate one, it is erroneous to think concentrating fire prevention efforts around populated areas will keep fire away from these areas. As proven over and over again and as stated in an internet report(489), "…fire treatments must be implemented across broad landscapes in order to modify fire behavior."

Sadly priorities are getting fuzzed-up, and a lot of people are buying into the new spin. Arguments promoting active management and road access to reduce fire damage seem to get less play, and politicians put compromises in place that reduce resources available for management and fire control in remote areas.

Changing priorities are demonstrated in a 2003 news article(490). This article discusses forest bills being considered by Congress, and says "The compromise also moves closer to the environmentalists desire to see the forest-thinning effort focus on protecting homes. It directs that half of the $760 million to be spent annually on fuel reduction go into clearing around communities."

Over a few years, I have observed the results of "no management" philosophy on a particular burn just west of Weaverville, California. It appears some of the burn was on private ownership, and the private area was quickly salvage logged and treated. Cal Trans appears to have done some erosion control work and planted some trees. A lot of burned timbered area appears to be Public Trust lands, and this area was left untreated. Photos number 16, 17, and 18 in the center of the book show how the untreated timbered area looks after a few years.

It is hard to understand how any good has come from the "no management" philosophy that has been applied to this burn. Waste and rotting trees are over the place, and the viewshed is not pretty and possibly getting worse. Bug infestation is evident, and this bug infestation appears to be spreading to live trees outside the burn area. Late in the game, some rotting, bug infested and dead trees were put in piles that remain in place. Due to bug and rot infestations, most if not all the piled wood is no longer good for anything. Would you want to use lumber full of bugs and rot in your home or back yard?

Some real world fire truths as I see them are as follows:

1. "No Management" leads to bigger and more uncontrollable fire. Building fuel loads, haphazard lightning, lack of access, and hazardous fire fighting conditions in "no management" areas will result in "BAD" fires and a lot of unnecessary damage.

2. Concentrating fire management efforts such as road access, fire trails, vegetative management and removal around residential and urban areas can be a recipe for disaster. As Canoe fire, Kings Range fire, and other fires stories demonstrate, fire is unpredictable and once started can overwhelm fire prevention efforts. As stated in internet report(435) "…fire treatments must be implemented across broad landscapes in order to modify fire behavior."

3. Letting Mother Nature haphazardly re-vegetate burned areas will result in brushfields and repeated burns. Active management can reduce fire potential and provides the means to reforest areas.

4. As demonstrated by Canoe fire, Kings Range fire, and other fires stories, random lightning does not provide a dependable and effective way to keep fuel loading at safe levels.

5. Big trees, even big redwoods do burn and die from fire.

6. Controlled prescriptive burning has its place, and should not be applied in all areas. Those wanting to dangerously apply prescribed burns in roadless, old-growth areas should be forced to stand on the firelines.

If you like nontimbered, mature brush covered areas that are unwalkable and of limited use by most species, the "no management" option is your cup of tea. To me, this kind of thinking is wasteful and selfish when you consider all the benefits that could come from the land.

One thing is for sure. Thousands of acres left inaccessible and unmanaged will lead to a lot of roaring unsafe fires, a lot of damage and cost, a lot of unproductive land, a loss of species and their habitats, a lot of waste, and harmed and dead humans.

WHERE OH WHERE HAVE OUR NATURAL RESOURCES GONE?

RESTORATION!   RESTORATION!
SET-ASIDE!   SET-ASIDE!
CONSERVATION EASEMENT!
CONSERVATION EASEMENT!
PARKS & WILDERNESS!   PARKS & WILDERNESS!

READY OR NOT
TAXPAYERS HERE WE COME

Chapter Eighteen

A slow lock-up of our natural resources and a drain on the taxpayer's checkbook is occurring in the name of environmental protection. All forms of governmental agencies and legislative bodies are having a field day spending taxpayers' money on land set-asides (parks, wilderness, historical monuments), on agreements limiting land and natural resource use (conservation easements, coastal use permits), and on a mixture of restoration activities. As discussed throughout this book, these activities are having an adverse affect on the availability of natural resources.

Public and governmental agencies have demonstrated an ability through use of regulatory powers and various forms of taxpayer funding to reduce and restrict full and proper use of natural resources.

Conservation easements are being put in place that restrict full and proper use of natural resources.

As natural resource availability is restricted, infrastructure producing natural resource products such as milling, food processing, and various manufacturing facilities is shut down.

As primary industries go away, service businesses such as Fred's grocery store and Mabel's Beauty Salon and tax revenues needed to fund public services such as schools and road maintenance fade away.

In the long term, tying up our resources is increasing this country's dependence on the rest of the world.

While curbing society's demand to lock-up lands looks unstoppable and there is no reason to stop beneficial restoration work, there is still a need to step back, take a good look at what is happening, and modify some things.

USING TAX DOLLARS TO CONVERT PRIVATE LANDS INTO PUBLIC TRUST LANDS AND A REDUCING ECONOMIC AND TAX REVENUE BASE

The following stories and Chapter Seven highlight why converting more and more private lands into Public Trust lands needs to be questioned.

Newspaper article (495) says "A robust real estate market helped push Humboldt County's property assessments over $7,000,000,000" which sounds good until the impacts from added service costs and higher residential land prices are considered. Tax revenue gains go to cover added service costs, and higher residential land values create pressures to sell lower valued open space lands into residential use. County costs are going up for "...routine repairs and maintenance..." which includes road repairs and maintenance in residential areas.

The article goes on to say "...county officials indicate the timber industry faced with downsizing and mill closures continues to ask for property reassessments." These reassessments are resulting in reduced tax revenues to the county as the article goes on to say "Pacific Lumber Co.'s annual property taxes paid to the county have dropped by an estimated $800,000 over the past year..." Converting private resource producing income lands to Public Trust lands reduces lands on property tax rolls, and this conversion is part of the reassessment process which is reducing the amount of taxes paid to the county.

Letter to Editor(496) gives more insight to how much one county can be affected by a reduction in tax rolls from reduced use of natural resources. "...ceased operations..." on "...timber-related properties..." reduced "...property tax value..." as follows: "...Pacific Lumber Co...$800,000 per year...Simpson properties in Fairhaven...$176,000 per year...Simpson Korbel property...$200,000 per year...Samoa Pacific... $300,000 per year." This adds up to a $1,476,000 reduction in taxes which is a pretty big hit for any county.

A 2001 Letter to the Editor(497) provides additional insight to the impacts of land set-asides to counties. "Humboldt County has 2.2 million acres (2.293 million acres per 2003 Summary Assessment report by California Fire and Resource Assessment Program)." Of this acreage "...Forest Service has 337,183 acres, National Park land 70,264 acres, Bureau of Land Management 62,537 acres, state parks 75,000...That totals 545,984 (I add 544,984) acres." without listing some "...Fish and Wildlife land and county parks..." and other public lands. This tells us "By simple math, over 25 percent of the acreage in the county..." and "...maybe as much as 33 percent if you count Fish and Wildlife land and county parks...is off the tax rolls." "...in-lieu payments...amount to "...$131,036.16...24 cents per acre..." Letter appears to be in opposition to "...proposed Lost Coast (local) Headlands properties (an assumed park set-aside project)..." When 24 cents per acre in-lieu tax rate is compared to "...$2.87 per acre...lowest tax rate of the proposed Lost Coast (local) Headlands properties (park project)...", it appears "The county is...losing $1,435,937.00 from this land." While the potential loss tax number feels high, there is no doubt the logic and significant adverse impact to rural areas from such set-asides expressed in the letter are correct.

As most people know, there are millions of acres off the tax rolls in National Parks, Bureau of Interior Lands, wilderness set-asides, newly created historical heritage areas, National Forests, and various other parks, but how many of us know about set aside, off the tax rolls lands managed for species use by the Fish and Wildlife Service(FWS). Internet report(419), shows there are 95,875,284.35 acres under control and management of the FWS.

Another 2004 article(498) further discusses how arrangements are sometimes made for taxpayer payments to rural areas "...from the federal government in lieu of taxes lost when lands were purchased for the public." This article says "The federal and state governments own about a third of the land in Humboldt County." and "Humboldt County (with 2.293 million total acres per 2003 Summary Assessment report by California Fire and Resource Assessment Program) will get $96,000...Del Norte County (with 649,000 acres per 2003 Summary Assessment report by California Fire and Resource Assessment Program and with about 75 % of its land in public ownership) will receive $87,512...from the federal government in lieu of taxes lost when lands were purchased for the public."

The provided information shows the large amount of public ownership in private ownership would be generating far more income and tax revenues than are being provided by in-lieu payments.

Additionally, note the reduced Humboldt in-lieu payments between the 2003 letter(497) with $131,036 in payments and the 2004 article(498) with $96,000 in payments. This shows the reducing resource use trend on Public Trust lands is also showing up as reduced in-lieu payments to rural communities.

On top of reducing in-lieu payments, governmental agencies have been known to completely reneg on paying promised in-lieu money. Already referenced 2004 article(498) and another 2004 article(499) regarding

Redwood National Park expansion say "In 2002, the Interior Department stopped paying Humboldt County for the taxes lost due to the 1977 expansion of the Redwood National Park, and the county's payments were cut by $630,000." One article says "Despite still owing $5 million...the...reason..." for stopping the Redwood national park payments was "...The 23 years the government gave itself to pay off the debt was up,..." In another article the Redwood Park is mentioned as still owing "...the county some $6,000,000 in payments associated with a 1979 Redwood National Park expansion." Both these articles demonstrate National Park Service's failure to fulfill promised economic help.

Don't you wish you could just not pay until the end of your loan agreements, and then say tough luck, time is up, ooly ooly oxin free.

A 2004 news article(500) demonstrates how many in the U.S. Forest Service still think not enough national forest land has been given wilderness protection. These folks say "...a great opportunity..." has been "...missed...to permanently protect large areas of the forest for future generations,..." and "...100,000 acres..." in "...Southern California's four national forests..." are proposed for "...wilderness protection..." "About one-third of the forests or roughly 1.1 million acres is designated as federally designated wilderness.", and routinely U.S. Forest Service proposed management plans designate more and more area to be given wilderness protection.

Even the Bush administration has not changed the push for more wilderness preserves. A news article(501) describes how a U.S. Forest Service management plan for the "...Biscuit fire...biggest wildfire in the nation in 2002...includes proposal from the Bush administration to add 64,000 acres to the Kalmiopsis Wilderness,..." This plan "...has become the focus of an intense debate over whether it is better to cut burned trees to help pay for and hasten reforestation,..."; or, do as the enviros want, and leave the area untreated, let burned timber go to waste, and let the land revert to unforested brushfields.

Another news article(258) says there is a plan "...to create 1,100-mile necklace of coastal marine reserves..." along California's coast line. This plan "...could put up to a fifth of state coastal waters off-limits to fishing..." which is going to hurt rural areas that get economic support from the fish resource. News article(503) says Fish and Game Department of California wants to "...to start a chain of protected marine areas along California's 1,100 mile coast." Another news article(504) says "The idea is provoking ...a struggle between some of the world's wealthiest and most powerful

309

environmental groups and California fishermen who fear they gradually will be booted off the ocean they prowl for recreation and profit." Note the media slant about "prowling" fishermen that "profit" from the ocean. Bad, bad fishermen.`

A news article(505) says a plan by national environmental groups to steer more of California's taxpayer money to Pacific Ocean research and protecting fishing grounds passed (State) Senate. "Senate voted to add ocean protection to the mission of California's $3.4 billion Proposition 50 bond,…" Wonder if this fits the intent of those who voted for Proposition 50? This article goes on to say "…recreational fishermen maintain that…corporate environmental groups…want to put larger swaths of the ocean near California's coastline off limits." and "…to create a new network of no-fishing marine reserves."

The "bad fishermen" article(502) goes on to say "Gov. Arnold Schwarzenegger has taken no position…" on "…The proposals sponsored by the New York based Natural Resources Defense Council and Washington DC based Oceans Conservancy…" The proposals recommend "…a $5.5 million project of Philadelphia-based Pew Charitable Trusts…" for "…both a Cabinet-level ocean council (supposedly titled the Ocean Protection Council) and placing more areas of the ocean off limits to human and commercial activity." That's what we need, another cabinet level governmental body.

The Philadelphia and east coast connection is interesting. Is California's new governor's connection to the east coast resulting in more meddling by east coast in left coast's business? Is the cancer in California growing; or, is California being used to spread the cancer?

This looks like the real deal, and to-be-affected fishermen and associated rural communities have got a real big reason to be worried. Oh well, the solution is probably simple in the minds of the politicians. They will probably have the taxpayers buy out the fishermen, pay to lock up the fish resource, and convince rural communities to slowly go down hill by chasing low paying jobs provided by a tourism based economy.

Two news articles(506)(508) provide another example of how political influences and some big players are involved in the game of spending taxpayer funding for set-aside projects. These articles outline a project to purchase some coastal lands and put in place a conservation easement involving the Hearst Castle ranch between Los Angeles and San Francisco in California.

The Hearst Castle ranch project involves buying 1.75 or 1.8 square miles of coastal land or 1,500 acres, and putting in place a conservation easement that strictly limits development of 128 square miles or 80,000 acres. Funding is to come from bond funds already approved by California voters and federal transportation money. Asking price is $80 million and $15 million in tax incentives or tax credits (which would probably make for some interesting reading) with California Transportation Commission having already authorized $23 million for the project as part of state transportation improvement program.

As with other conservancy groups who handle these types of deals, the taxpayers will make sure the American Land Conservancy who is brokering this deal comes out well-healed.

Assuming some private acres will be converted to public ownership and conservation easements will reduce resource use, land use changes will result in reduced property taxes for any involved open space lands.

It is interesting how use of transportation funds has showed up in other similar land purchases not directly connected to transportation issues. Are the transportation tax funds being applied as intended?

There is another little sidelight to the tie-up of rural lands and natural resources that is worth mentioning. As discussed in a news article(553), Native Americans are starting to buy up a lot of land and "...apply to the federal Bureau of Indian Affairs (BIA) to acquire the land and take into trust..." This means "If the BIA approves, the land would become part of the tribe's reservation and protected by sovereignty rights, the legal status of the tribe as a sovereign nation for many purposes. Among other benefits, sovereignty exempts tribes from many state and federal regulations." including many environmental and tax laws and regulations. In short, it appears private lands can be bought and given to another nation which can do things the rest of us can not do. I assume land given to another nation is also taken off the tax rolls, and local property tax revenues are reduced accordingly.

"...Santa Barbara County officials...rebuffed... attempts..." by landowner to develop a hotel and golf resort..." Locals say the land was to be turned into "...a massive housing and country club development." "...the land owner...former "Daniel Boone" and "Davy Crockett" television star Fess Parker..." and tribe "...struck a deal in which the tribe would buy 745 acres for $12 million, building a hotel, golf course and 155 homes for tribal members. Another 200 homes would be for general sale." "The land is zoned for agricultural use, and such a massive development would require changing the zoning..." The race card has been played by the tribe by saying "...they are angered by the community's opposition, saying it smacks of racism in a valley where the largest towns, Santa Ynez and Solvang, the self-proclaimed Danish capital of the nation (what nation?????), are predominately white. We're asking to do things that are within our rights. We don't make the laws. The federal government made the laws."

It is interesting how Native American environmental concerns involving developing and using the land seem to be colored by their desire to have the good life. It will be interesting to see which interests and laws, Native American rights and federal law versus enviros and "preserving" agricultural lands, win out in this situation. These Native American deals have the potential to involve thousands of acres in rural areas as Native Americans get more and more casino money and make more and more deals to acquire private lands.

While some folks are going out of their way to give this country's rights and lands to other nations and some feel current Native Americans have some kind of reparation coming, it is bothersome to see private lands being transferred to another nation that does not have to follow the same laws as the rest of us. We are all one country or not? I do not know all the current arrangements between this country and the Native Americans, but I do know some of them are questionably justified and are going to lead to some hard feelings. Since there is a lot I do not know about this subject, I better drop it, and move-on before I get in trouble. Maybe some casino money will be spread around to offset losses due to conversion of private lands to reservation lands, and this money will make the rest of us feel better.

Another type of hypocrisy involves enviros and protectionist minded folks preaching they want to preserve agricultural land. As illustrated by their actions, this is a hoot. These folks are one of the most active groups promoting restrictive regulations for agricultural activities. They push hard to lock-up lands and resources in conservation easements and Public Trust lands, and both of these actions limit income producing abilities of open space lands which forces these lands to be sold and developed. While not openly noticeable, these folks have probably done as much to take land out of agricultural production as anyone else.

Take a good look at the listings of set-aside and conservation projects provided in this chapter to get a small feel of the land and resources being tied-up.

NATIONAL HERITAGE AREAS

A little noticed program to restrict land uses and use of natural resources involves creation of National Heritage Areas (NHAs).

An 2004 internet report(511) says NHAs "Established in the 1980s as experiments in involving local communities in protecting local traditions, history and resources."

This sounds like a pretty simple and worthwhile program that will not be a very big deal. Well, read on and see how simple and unatrusive you think this program has become.

This internet report goes on to say a Government Accounting Office (GAO) report mentions how "The national Park Service (NPS) oversees the NHAs...", and "their financial reports are often not audited, results-oriented goals are not in place and management plans are not reviewed."

While there is questionable control over expenditures, "Funding...does not seem to be a problem. Between 1997 and 2002, heritage areas received $156 million from the federal government - $94 million through NPS and its programs and $61 million from other federal programs. Another $154 million came from state and local governments and private funds."

The GAO report "...found there is no systematic process for identifying potential sites." "...24 National Heritage Areas (NHAs) have been designated by Congress,...", and "A map in the GAO report shows the entire state of Tennessee has been designated with two areas identified as 'Tennessee Civil War and Blue Ridge'. One-fourth of Iowa is a heritage area known as 'Silos and Smokestacks'."

As stated in the GAO report, it is not clear how the heritage designation process works. A 2004 news article(512) describes how "...300,000 acres of public land..." in the "...Northern California Coastal Wild Heritage Wilderness Act..." are now being considered by Congress for wilderness designation under the heritage program. This action by Congress indicates heritage designations can be loosely applied to Public Trust lands and to private lands surrounded by Public Trust lands.

It sounds like this program is just getting started, and it will be another way for the Fourth Branch of Government to control land uses and restrict use of natural resources.

WHAT DO WE SACRIFICE FOR
SINGLE USE RESTRICTIONS AND SET-ASIDES

If you take time to look, society is routinely not an active partner in reviewing the full costs and benefits attributed to setting aside areas for single purpose uses. Little oversight is going into how public agencies and politicians are spending a lot of tax dollars for single use purposes.

By default, other species may benefit from designated single use areas, but can we afford the luxury of tying up a lot of land and resources for questionably limited purposes.

Two news articles(252)(253) covering the Grizzley Creek land sale provides one example of the high prices ($18,200,000) being paid to protect a single species. Even though there is some question about murrelets using the sale area and the sale area being acceptable murrelet habitat, the sale area is still designated to be mainly used as marbled murrelet, old-growth habitat. Murrelet protection requirements and physical land features will basically prevent other uses of the area.

A Letter to the Editor(515) discusses plover restoration work involving BLM (Bureau of Land Management), State Parks, U.S. Fish and Wildlife, and others. While actual direct cost per bird is hard to pin down, provided information does give a range of $19,000 to $100,000 per bird.

No matter the real cost per plover, I think it is safe to say lot of money is being spent on seemingly few birds with questionable justification for the expenditures.

How much can we afford to spend and lock-up for single purpose reasons?

Tax dollars and restrictions are being applied in many ways to create and maintain single purpose areas. Wilderness set-asides and single species habitat preserves are continually being put in place.

There are consequences for doing this. Additional pressure is put on available resources, and local economies are being hurt.

THEN THERE ARE SO FREELY GIVEN TAX DOLLARS

There is a whole bevy of organizations using taxpayer dollars to reduce use of our natural resources. They come in all shapes, sizes, and configurations. Many of these organizations are public agencies, and many are funded directly or indirectly by taxpayers. The appetite for taxpayer and donor dollars by these organizations seems unending.

There are hundreds of existing taxpayer supported funds available to those wanting to tie-up natural resources. Routinely legislators pass bills containing funding, voters approve proposition bond money, and many public agencies budget money. Those wanting to tie-up resources just have to fish around and find the right connections. Because approved funding is routinely not returned unspent, a lot of effort must go into finding ways to spend approved funding. The Fourth Branches of Government seem more than willing to give out money, and indicated cross-over spending, shows there may be a lack of effort to make sure all funds are spent as intended.

There is a continual push to use bond monies as mentioned in a 2004 newspaper article(516) for "...protecting waterways and the coastal environment." As the article says "...bond sales bring $4,100,000 to Humboldt County annually.", and it makes you wonder how money spent for land and timber purchases is available to the county as mentioned in the article. Could it be bond monies are not being spent as intended by the voters?

As previously mentioned in 2004 news article(504), "Environmentalists...successfully taped taxpayer money to buy thousands of acres of California coastline..." and "...are targeting the Pacific ocean..." Proposals are being made "...to steer bond money to environmentalists ocean wish lists..." Also, as previously mentioned in another 2004 news article(505), "(State) Senate voted to add ocean protection to the mission of California's $3.4 billion Proposition 50 bond,..." The first 2004 news article(504) covered how this "...idea is provoking a renewed struggle between some of the wealthiest and most powerful environmental groups and California fishermen." I wonder if the voters would have approved the bond funding if they knew it might be used to hurt fishermen and their associated rural community?

A news article(518) mentions how "Clearly, there are people who have decided to get into this business for the purpose of enriching themselves." The article goes on "...to say that state and federal agencies have done little to ensure compliance by...the tax exempt sector." While it sounds like it is simply up to the taxpayers and donors to say when enough is enough, this is not likely to happen soon.

Another news article(519) describes a lack of oversight in how tax money is spent. California state auditors found "The state handed out millions in taxpayer dollars to community groups and local agencies without providing adequate oversight of how the money was spent." What a revelation. I'd say someone is late to the party. A review of "...state Parks and Recreation Department...revealed questionable business practices, poor record keeping and scant follow-up..." "...$24.1 million in pork barrel allocations were secured by individual lawmakers...", and one "...Resource Center received $500,000 grant earmarked for a community center that was never built."

As discussed in first article(518) about grants, "...fast expanding tax-exempt sector...is growing enormously..." My review indicates no obvious saturation point has been reached regarding projects associated with environmental issues. If there are too many groups competing for the same dollars, maybe it is time for some taxpayer bounty going towards restoration, conservation easement, and set-aside programs to be directed towards more legitimate and worthwhile problems.

An internet report(520) brings to light a process that indicates "...agencies and/or Departments can just turn..." restoration funds and some publicly owned lands "...over to Indian Tribes to manage..." "The Department of Interior has listed 34 national parks in 15 states (including Redwood National Park in California, Voyageurs National Park in Minnesota and Olympic National Park in Washington), all 16 wildlife refuges in Alaska (including the controversial Arctic National Wildlife Refuge)..." and other areas "...where it will entertain offers from recognized tribes to take on some or all operations."

Concerns exist regarding turning funds and management control over to Native Americans that are sovereign nations not fully subject to this country's laws and regulations. How will these sovereign nations be held accountable for inappropriate actions according to this country's laws and regulations? Will "...Tribal hiring practices...known as 'order of preference' and 'tribal preference'..." where "...first choice for jobs goes to enrolled members of the local tribe, then first generation descendants of the local tribe, followed by enrolled members of other tribal reservations, and finally non-Indians." be strictly followed? Who will review and approve expenditures prior to use of allocated funds? When a tribe decides who is hired, what assurance is there that work will be properly and efficiently done by qualified and experienced professionals? Without use of outside competition, contractors, and bids, how can proper expenditure of funds be assured? Many questions need to be answered before Native Americans are given a monopoly over managing our Public Trust lands.

Two news articles(521)(522) tell how the U.S. Congress is considering giving 990 acres to an Indian tribe, and tribe says it will manage the land as it has been managed by the Bureau of Land management into perpetuity. It is not clear what is going on here. This could be part of previously discussed custodial deal; or, it could be an outright give away of our public lands to another sovereign nation, the Pechanga tribe. This deal needs to be watched.

CONSERVATION EASEMENTS

There is a legitimate reason for an interest in conservation easements. Due to increasing regulatory restrictions on economic uses of the land to produce natural resource products such as timber, food, and minerals, there is less and less economic support for maintenance of open space lands in private ownership. To hold onto their lands and pay some bills, many landowners are turning to use of conservation easements to release tied-up capital

While my experiences allow me to talk about conservation easements, I am not a lawyer; so, take what I say with a grain of salt.

I see conservation easements as an agreement between parties (the holder(s) of the easement and the ones giving rights away) that spells out what will and won't happen on a piece of land, who will be the judge in interpreting how the easement agreement is to be applied, and who pays who what.

Main things to keep in mind about conservation easements are:

- Be careful and understand what you are buying into before you enter into a conservation easement.

- A partnership is formed where all partners gain a say in what happens on involved property.

- Easement requirements routinely reduce what can be done on involved property.

- Reduced use means reduced sale value to a knowledgeable and willing buyer.

Conservation easements are more fully discussed in Chapter 14.

An example of a conservancy group handling the purchase of a property is illustrated in a news article(524). "…American Lands Conservancy…is brokering…" a deal to buy "…the Barnes Ranch to increase water stoppage and restore wetlands on Upper Klamath lake…for endangered suckers…" possibly involving "…$4.6 million…" You can be sure the conservancy will be well re-imbursed for their efforts.

Another simple example of how the conservation easement groups and public agency folks work together to tie up lands which I believe is detrimental to rural communities is shown in a news article(525). In this news article "…the newly acquired…" family owned "…Ranch…" and "…newest public jewel on California's North Coast…is a showcase of natural splendor and family stewardship." This glowing description indicates the family landowners over the years must have done a good job managing and running the ranch. The family was receiving all kinds of pressure regarding what to do with the ranch. Options included adding "…land to nearby Manchester State Park,…", sell "…on the open market,…"; or, as part of the family wanted "…keep on raising cattle and vegetables."

The article does not elaborate on how regulatory restrictions played a part in final decision, but from personal contact with the landowners in the past, I know the landowners were business men who had the same problems as many rural ranchers keeping ranches economically viable. I know ranch's dairy operations had to expend extra effort and cost in order to conform to increasing water quality regulations. What was going to be required by newly developed Environmental Protection Agency Total Maximum Daily Load requirements and accompanying state water quality permit requirements was not clear, and the ranch faced the need to spend substantial sums of money in order to conform to the new regulatory requirements. "…North Coast ecoregion director for the Nature Conservancy, says many ranching families face dilemmas similar to the…" owners of the ranch; where, "Estate taxes are steep…, and ranching is hard…", and "the only way they can pay taxes is to sell property."

"The…family came up with a compromise…to sell part of the ranch, 1,132 acres, to the Nature Conservancy which in turn donated it to the Bureau of Land Management." They retained rights to "…75 acres of old farm buildings…, raise cattle on 579 acres…", and "For 10 years,…graze some cattle on the…public lands under a lease with the Bureau of Land Management."

"…state Coastal Conservancy…pitched in $3.3 million for the purchase price…,…Another $1 million came from U.S. Fish and Wildlife Service, and $3.3 million was contributed by the state Wildlife Conservation Board."

This deal has given a positive slant by saying it "…brought new hope to a region that, despite its scenic riches, has an uneven tourist economy and a history of battling over logging and fisheries." "Some…hope the newly acquired nature preserve will…help put Point Arena on the eco-tourism map."

"California has plenty of voter approved funding for land acquisition, but it doesn't have money to pay for day to day upkeep of parks and preserves…"; so, "…state agencies won't be managing the…land, even though state taxpayers are funding most of the purchase." "…Bureau of Management has somewhat reluctantly agreed to oversee the…property."

This sure is a nice sounding arrangement where everyone wins. A closer review provides the following unspoken truths.

1. While the landowners will be allowed to live a good life which they have earned, the local area will lose land off the tax rolls when "…Nature Conservancy …in turn…" donates the land "…to the Bureau of Land Management.", and it becomes Public Trust land.

2. As indicated in the news article, the ranch activities and production of natural resource products will be reduced in the "…newly acquired nature preserve…", and this will reduce ranch's contribution to the local economy.

3. Being familiar with the involved area, I believe the remoteness and various other factors mentioned elsewhere in this book will make the idea that tourism will save the day an illusive dream.

4. While it is nice that the California taxpayers have "…plenty of voter approved funding for land acquisition,…", it is interesting how the California taxpayers are willing to pay a lot of money for a sizeable chunk of land, and then give the land away "…to the Bureau of Land Management…" and to the federal government.

While additional information might explain away some of my listed problems with the purchase and conversion to Public Trust ownership, there is no disputing the reduction in production of natural resource products, and the reduced contribution by the ranch to the local economy. If you look closely, you will see what is happening to this ranch is being repeated over and over all over this nation.

A purchase and re-sale scheme frequently utilized by trust and conservancy groups involves buying into lands that have been restricted by regulatory actions. After purchasing restricted lands and with the co-operation of the regulators, trusts and conservancy groups seem to be able to find ways to overcome environmental concerns and regulatory restrictions hindering use by previous owners. The trust and conservancy groups are able to develop and re-sell all or portions of purchased lands on the open market or to various public agencies. Some groups such as the California Coastal Conservancy have been able to build quite a war chest in this manner.

The scheme to purchase lands from landowners having trouble with regulatory restrictions and then to develop and re-sell all or portions of the purchased lands on the open market or to various public agencies is not exclusive to coastal properties. In the intermountain states, ranchers are facing similar hard to handle regulatory restrictions, and they are also being pushed towards conservation easements being offered by various trusts and conservancy groups.

The way trusts and conservancies buy up properties restricted by regulators and then work with regulators on ways to develop and re-sell portions of purchased properties smells a little fishy. Since police powers are involved and involved parties seem to have similar self-interests, the potential for conflict of interest and governmental abuse is high. I believe many folks are looking the other way to avoid seeing any conflict of interest connections, and I am sure a lot of folks are hoping no one looks too closely.

Like any good business person, the groups involved in the set-aside and conservation easement business do what is needed to build their cash and total assets. They work to keep good things such as potentially profitable lands and to get ride of the losers. With non-profit money having to be tied-up or spent as required by nonprofit tax requirements, the folks and lawyers that work for trusts and conservancies make sure they are treated well regarding salaries, workload requirements, and perks on and off the job. You might say, some of them live pretty high on the hog.

An internet article(526) says Nature Conservancy has assets of $3 billion, and internet report says this group has an annual income of $700 million.

A news article(527) lists California Coastal Conservancy, "…a state agency, that seeded…projects …with $168 million (I assume seeded means used donations and taxpayer money) and leveraged $133 million more (possibly through development and re-sale projects)."

These groups build some pretty big war chests that are used buying and tying-up more and more lands and their resources.

RESTORATION! OH MIGHTY RESTORATION!

Ready or not. Right or wrong. Taxpayer here we come.

Isn't it nice how politicians and public agencies use taxpayer funded restoration jobs and buyouts to keep the natives quiet? Just throw some taxpayer money at those creating a fuss, and while underlying problems still

320

remain to crop up again at a later date, everyone becomes good buddies for awhile.

Based on a lot of pseudo science, millions of dollars are spent correcting benign uncorrectable things, and often feeble and questionable restoration work is done that Mother Nature routinely dumps-on and tosses aside.

LOVE OF GOVERNMENTAL (REALLY TAXPAYER) DOLLARS

Rural communities welcome the idea of a restoration economy and using government dollars to stimulate their economies.

However, if the goal is to have stable economic supports, governmental dollars are not a good way to go. For many reasons, there is no guarantee government funding is forever and won't suddenly go away. Governmental dollars are routinely only a short term fix.

As provided in an article(533) many of those advocating restoration work say nice things like "…former adversaries are rallying around a pro-active restoration agenda for public lands and watersheds. People throughout the rural west are coming together in order to nurse our forests, rivers and economies back to health."

It is interesting how the crowd advocating restoration work reacts when it comes to applying factual information and doing actual productive restoration work contrary to their beliefs and self interests. When they see a threat to their self interests or access to governmental dollars, the togetherness, all for one cause tone disappears. The dialogue turns to one of reducing resource use, protectionism, and negativism about what humans and Mother Nature together can accomplish.

Restoration industry has definitely become a multi-million dollar industry as illustrated in two 2004 news articles(534)(535) which state "Taylorsville based nonprofit firm Forest Community Research "…finds…" "…watershed and natural resource restoration…work as a significant element of the County's (Humboldt and north coast) economy." "Publicly funded restoration has become big business …and labor groups (and others living off grants wanting some of the money) are hoping good paying jobs can result from it." "In 2002, funding from state and federal agencies for (Humboldt County) restoration work totaled more than $14 million, the Ford Foundation funded study found." One article mentions this compares to $42 million for dairy, $34 million for nursery and flower industry, $18.5 million for cattle and calves, and $6.3 for commercial fishing. Production of timber products was conveniently left out of the article. "It (publicly funded restoration) has brought in $65 million (to north coast) in state and federal money between 1995 and 2002,..." One article states "...another $150 million of funding will be needed just to complete work to improve salmon passage on roads..." "...The backlog is staggering (I believe based on some questionable thinking)..." and "...They won't be working themselves out of a job for quite awhile..."

A Letter to the Editor(536) illustrates the mindset of many getting in on the governmental restoration dollar free for-all who may be affected by California's budget deficit problems. "...a relatively "tiny" reinvestment has begun, a little money is being converted into healthy watersheds, when people are being employed in the woods again (not to utilize and produce natural resource products but to live on the governmental dole), when out-of-work loggers are retraining for restoration,..." Signed by a "...restoration worker..." "Editor's note: We agree that restoration funding is critical for our region and many local residents, and said so in a recent editorial."

It would be interesting to know how much restoration money really gets to the ones doing productive work versus ones playing at being supervisor, lead contractor, researcher, and paper shuffler.

An editorial(537) shows how restoration is being considered as a permanent fixture in rural areas and a way to provide "...opportunities on the North Coast, particularly for young people who haven't finished high school and don't have many skills to offer."

Restoration jobs are a good summer time or starter job, and they can provide some economic help, but there is a better way. Viable and doable use of natural resources could be promoted, and associated better jobs with a real future could be created. It is sad to see how jobs that produce natural resource products are overlooked and downplayed, and lower paying, really going nowhere, restoration jobs are promoted.

Keep in mind, attached to restoration and conservation programs are governmental bureaucracies that are part of the Fourth Branch of Government. Once funded and put in place, it is rare to see governmental programs go away. Routinely tax funded and established overhead supervisory staffs just get lost in the governmental maze and keep going and going and going...

Take a look at the many numbers presented in this chapter and throughout this book which represent a tiny portion of what is being spent. Ask yourself how "tiny" has the restoration investment become? Are all the uses of government dollars well thought out and justified, and are all the dollars being wisely spent?

There is a whole lot of studying going on, and many dollars are not paying for actual restoration work. By default some good occurs, but has much of the restoration effort become another wasteful governmental welfare program like the ones that hurt the Native Americans and other welfare communities?

Instead of using these dollars to quiet some outspoken folks and make life easier for some politicians, wouldn't it be better to utilize them developing something more permanent such as building a rural community economy based on the proper use of natural resources and proper production of natural resource products?

A STUMBLING RUN AT A FEW OF THE NUMBERS

A review of restoration, conservation easement, and set-aside projects and large amounts of allocated money shows how big the environmental protectionist movement has become. This review also shows how much the taxpayers are directly and indirectly supporting and subsidizing this privately and publicly run movement. A review over approximately two years from my little corner of the world provides a small sample of where tax and bond dollars are going. The results of this review follow.

The following short list shows the variety and financial power of conservancy and trust entities.

Mendocino Land trust - 1/29/04 Fort Bragg Advocate/Mendocino Beacon news article

North Coast regional Land Trust - 3/7/2004 Times Standard news article - open space goals

Natural Resources Defense Council based in New York and Oceans Conservancy based in Washington DC - 4/5/04 Times Standard news article - Involved in report recommending more areas off limits to human and commercial activity, and involved in Pacific coast issues

The Conservation Fund - 12/20/03 Empire News news article - nonprofit enviro group /protected more than 3.4 million acres nation-wide.

Wildlife Conservation Board - 1/04 University California Bulletin - state agency working on conservation easements and grants for land improvements and restoration efforts.

Peninsula Open Space Trust - 4/6/04 Times Standard news article - San Mateo County Coast.

California Coastal Conservancy - 3/21/04 Times Standard news article - state agency seeded with $168 million and leveraged $133 million more.

$6 billion David and Lucille Packard Foundation - 3/9/04 Times Standard news article - Utilized by environmentalists/has contributed in the past to marine programs.

Save the Redwoods League - 2004 Annual Report - $64,346,230 total assets - Annual report still displays inflammatory picture of old old-growth redwood clearcut that helped to promote establishment of the National Redwood Park. Today a young and well stocked redwood stand now covers the area in the picture.

Pew Charitable Trusts based in Philadelphia - 4/5/04 Times Standard news article - Involved in ocean protection

Oceans Conservancy based in Washington DC - 4/5/04 Times Standard news article.

National Trust for Historic Preservation - 5/26/04 Times Standard news article.

American Lands Conservancy - 1/29/04 Times Standard news article.

Nature Conservancy - Undated Washington Post news article - assets of $3 billion with $700 million annual income.

Sierra Nevada Conservancy (Being considered by California legislature) - 8/1/04 Press Democrat news article - To be given $4.15 million dollars.

Ojai Land Conservancy - 8/8/04 Times Standard News article - Received $500,000 fine by someone who removed 300 trees.

Environment Now - 11/16/03 internet flyer(539) provided by reputable association source shows Environment Now has - End of year book value of $35,173,987 and end of year fair market value of $34,720,695. This same information shows someone is making a pretty good living off this group: Exec. director listed as getting $120,000 compensation; other highest paid employee at $82,500; Five highest paid independent contractors: Grantwriter - $56,845, Consultant-Land Acquisition co-ordinator - $75,000, Environmental Consultant - $60,000, Coastal Restoration Program worker - $51,600, and Urban Renewal Program worker - $59,407. Four largest charitable activities during the tax year: Coastal Restoration - $240,039, Urban Renewal - 488,341, Forest Restoration - 204,393, and Fresh Water Conservation - $32,520. Supplemental Information for other groups: Coalition for Clean Air, National Resource Defense Council, Liberty Hill Foundation, Whale Rescue Team, California Coastkeeper, San Diego Baykeeper, Ventura Coastkeeper, Environmental Defense Center, Orange County Coastkeeper, Santa Monica Baykeeper, Marine Fish Conservation

Network, Morro Baykeeper, Wild Coast, John Muir Project, Bigger Picture, Environment Protection Info CTR, Trees Foundation, Black Mesa Trust, Adopt-A-Highway Maintenance Org., For the Sake of the Salmon, Heal the Bay, Friends of the San Gabriel River, Other Environmental Organizations for $932,522. To summarize this information which is indicated to be yearly information, it appears this organization with a book value of over $35,000,000 is annually paying two people $202,500, paying consultants $382,852, and putting $1,897,815 into projects and towards helping other environmental leaning groups. Can anyone deny that the environmental protection business, whether in the right or the wrong, is not big business?

A longer list of groups vying and using funds for restoration and set-aside purposes is not provided, because this list does enough to show there are a lot of groups involved in the restoration and land set-aside game. Due to a continual drive by politicians, enviros, and governmental bodies to create such groups, it is doubtful a complete list could ever be compiled.

Doesn't it scare you just a little to think of all the unaccountable groups with the power to mess around and change things?

For just a two or so year sample period, my review found the following "conservative" numbers to apply.

- Over $3.6 billion dollars to be spent for restoration and set-aside reasons. Many of the expenditures will not be adequately oversight reviewed, and a lot of taxpayer money will be used for some pretty questionable reasons. Think of how a lot of this money might be doing more good if it was used for other more worthwhile purposes.

- Over 4.9 million acres of land (plus another possible 3.2 million park acres in Maine) will be tie-up and have resource uses limited and eliminated. It takes around three states the size of Delaware to cover 4.9 million acres. Eight percent of California is equivalent to the combined total of 8.1 million acres. At the currently rapid set-aside rate, there is the potential for an area equivalent to the size of California (100,915,000 acres) to be set-aside with resources restricted every 10 to 20 years.

- County and local governments facing tough budget problems will be asked to absorb tax and economic losses from direct reduction of contributions from over 1.3 million acres.

Legislatures and others are having a field day grabbing areas and putting them into all kinds of set-asides without any thought to the consequences. Money is being spent and allocated without much thought to budget problems and possibly other more worthwhile needs. The flow of dollars to projects with an environmental tag seem to be without end.

At the current rate of lock-ups, private property will shortly be in the minority versus public ownership in this country. Despite recent Supreme Court ruling giving local government eminent domain power for governmental self interest reasons, I do not think our forefathers ever planned for the government to be able to administer and control more land than the people. Our way of life, especially in Rural America, is headed for some bad times if the government is allowed a monopoly control over this country's lands and resources.

The environmental industry is a bigga-deal, and this does not bode well for this country.

While some folks may argue my numbers are wrong until the cows come home, I do not believe there is much doubt that a lot of taxpayer money is being spent and a lot of acreage and natural resources are being placed off limits.

There seems to be little concern anything wrong is happening, and to the contrary, there are a lot of folks who think peachy keen things are happening. As long as dollars are spread around and some things get protected, the public seems to be happy. There is little push for accountability, and what's a few dollars being mis-used and into the pockets of a few good folks. There seems to be no end to governmental and donated dollars that are available for the asking; so, what's the big deal? Full speed ahead. Spend the money and lock up the resources as fast as we can.

IT ALL ADDS UP TO THE FOLLOWING

As long as nothing is said by taxpayers and as long as Atlas does not stop producing income that generates tax revenues, the process of tying-up and locking up land and resources will not stop. Governmental entities will keep buying up, preserving, setting aside land and resources and open space income producing lands with our tax money, and needed resources will increasingly come from worldwide sources.

Spending taxpayer money on properly done and scientifically justified restoration can lead to good things, but the restoration mission has been corrupted by those running the show. Without adequate oversight and scientific justification, a lot of unnecessary and damaging work is being done in the name of restoration.

The Grand Canyon situation is a good example of where good things have happened and meddling restoration folks just can't leave good things alone. A lot of effort and resources are being used to study and change a cooked up, cock-eyed, and very very very very questionable Grand Canyon and Colorado River problem. This effort and the involved resources could be better utilized in more worthwhile endeavors.

In a 2004 news article(333), the Grand Canyon is described as "...cool and calm. Trout leapt, splashing back into the river with a plop. Stands of salt cedar lined the banks, offering shade from the desert heat." Sounds okay and pretty nice, but in the world of the enviros and regulators, this is a bad scene. "The salt cedar and trout are invaders, part of a wave of alien fish and plants that have moved in and devoured or crowded out the native species. The sandy shorelines are washing away (probably including some pockets of quicksand). Once-buried Indian archeological sites are slipping into the river." "...four of the canyon's eight native fish species have disappeared, and the prospects for a fifth, the endangered humpback chub, are grim..." due to...the cold water..." By putting in the Glen Canyon Dam, humans have caused the river to change from a river that "...would fill with snowmelt and flood violently in the early summer, then dwindle to trickle in the winter..." and ran "...warm and muddy...in Powell's day..." Man has done an awful thing. Because of this bad thing man has done, "...sediment gets caught behind the dam in Lake Powell...", river flow has been "...smoothed out..." and river now "...runs cold and clear..." Such bad things have been done to the river that "The best we can do is keep slapping on as many Band-Aids as we can and hope the patient survives..." We need to keep spending time, effort, and dollars to "...measure the ever-faint pulse of the patient". The enviros want to go back to a warm and muddy river with extreme high and low changes in water flow.

Give me a break. Talk about your cock and bull stories.

As mentioned in the referenced article, "Over the years, nearly $200 million has been spent assessing what the dam has done (supposedly bad) to the Grand Canyon (What about all the good it has done?) and exploring what can be done to fix it." The rest of the world wished it had it so good to be able to spend this kind of money and effort on fixing such benign problems as naturally eroding archeological sites that were somehow better off when violent flooding occurred. There is something illogical about the way this archeological problem is being presented when a smoother, calmer flowing river causes more erosive activity than a river having fits of flooding. Only the enviros and regulators would waste thousands of dollars trying to hold Mother Nature in her tracks and keep natural processes from changing things. As discussed throughout this book, nothing remains static and unchanged in nature, and trying to hold back nature is an impossible task.

The dam is in to stay (at least I hope it is), and everyone should just relax. Instead of concentrating on the negative so much, sit back, enjoy the good things, and put the time and money being wasted on windmills to better use.

I know! Let's spend more time and resources on raising a lot of genetically superior acceptable fish, and build up fish populations? Refer to Chapter Four titled "PROTECTING THEM TO DEATH" for a discussion on how healthy hatchery fish, equal or superior to wild fish, are being killed mainly because humans raised them.

While we twiddle our thumbs, the producers are slowly being replaced by the takers. When the producers are gone and income is no longer generated, we won't have to worry about misspent dollars, because there will be no dollars to worry about.

IT'S ACCOUNTABILITY STUPID

Chapter Nineteen

This chapter provides a summary overview of many things discussed throughout this book regarding inappropriate actions by the Fourth Branch of Government and ways to approach these actions.

As a professional who has had to apply many, many legislated unclear and poorly worded laws and regulations in the field, I have seen how producers and users of natural resources are having to adhere to incorrectly interpreted and inappropriately applied laws and regulations.

The first part of this problem comes from unclear and inappropriate laws and regulations.

As discussed in Chapter Five there are many inherent weaknesses and faults in the processes used to develop laws and regulations.

Many laws and regulations are the result of compromise and are not based on facts and time tested, peer reviewed science. Especially in regards to environmental law where many sciences are in their infancy, unproven pseudo science is erroneously mixed with political and personal bias to create a lot of bad law.

Those making laws and regulations routinely lack the ability and technical expertise needed to make good laws, and after laws are put in place, there is little oversight to make sure laws work as intended. Since those making laws suffer little consequence from their actions, there is little incentive for them to correct their mistakes and make better laws.

A second part of the problem involves not being able to hold those interpreting and applying laws and regulations accountable for inappropriate actions.

This unaccountable regulatory group includes the many public and governmental agencies, the many appointed boards of control and review, and the layman courts that exist at all levels of government (state, federal, county, district, local). Combined this regulatory group makes a Fourth Branch of government that really runs things.

As a public participant and permitee reviewing why application of laws and regulations has become so distorted and adversarial, you find many permit requirements and regulatory actions are not based on authorized regulations and accepted professional standards. Due to ineffective ways to hold them accountable, regulators are routinely given a pass regarding unjustified and unprofessional actions. This lack of accountability gives the Fourth Branches of Government a free hand in interpreting and applying many unclear laws and regulations.

The following incident provided in a L.A. Times news story(432) regarding a potential candidate for Congress illustrates how many of our public officials are very naïve about what affects their constituents. This candidate from a major metropolitan area "…had just arrived at a Mendocino County sawmill…", and "…hoped to persuade loggers, truck drivers, and small-town merchants that…" the candidate "…could effectively represent them in Congress." "…pointing to a series of numbered signs on the lawn behind the…" sawmill offices the candidate said "Is that where you measure the logs?" "No…" said the mill owner "That's the employee driving range. The markers tell you how far you've hit your golf ball."

When elected representatives do not know the difference between a golf driving range showing yard markers many many yards apart and a log scaling yard that measures logs usually less than 42 feet in length, is it any wonder public officials are making unclear and hard to interpret laws. They and their staffs just do not know better, and unless it is to their benefit, a lot of them do not try to know better.

To illustrate how bad thing have become, one only needs to consider what a California Department of Fish and Game (DFG) representative, a member of the Fourth Branch of Government, said at a workshop on how to apply their regulations. He said "You will know what we (the regulators) want when you get your plan (permit) approved".

Chapter Two provides additional discussion about how the Fourth Branch of Government controls our lives and determines where this country is headed.

There is no indication our stumbling and bumbling regulatory processes as controlled by political correctness and easily swayed politicians are going to change; so, we have to find ways to overcome bad law problems outside rule making processes.

PERMIT REVIEW AND APPROVAL DELAYS

Regulatory authorities routinely ignore permit review and approval time-line requirements without any repercussions. Because their complaints are ignored and confrontation can result in additional costly delay, there has been an acceptance by permitees to tolerate the practice of missed regulatory deadlines.

A LISTING OF UNAUTHORIZED, UNJUSTIFIED, AND UNSUPPORTED ACTIONS

As a standard practice, permitees are routinely forced to provide more information for review than is required by basic environmental law such as the California Environmental Quality Act (CEQA). Basic environmental law requires disclosure and discussion of possible environmental impacts and mitigations developed to reduce disclosed impacts; however, permitees are routinely forced to provide inappropriate, unsubstantiated, speculated, and theorized impact information. Based on unnecessary and often inappropriate information, questionable permit requirements in excess of that required by basic environmental law are developed and put into permits.

A review of CEQA (California Environmental Quality Act) dated 1997, which is one of the most strict environmental laws in this country, shows "The Legislature further finds and declares that in the event specific economic, social, or other conditions make infeasible such project alternatives or such mitigation measures, individual projects may be approved in spite of one or more significant effects thereof." This shows CEQA requires disclosure, discussion, and mitigation to lessen impacts, but does not require "total" elimination of any impact especially when alternatives or mitigation measures are made infeasible, unrealistic, or damaging by economic, social, or other conditions. Interestingly, the regulators in California have shown little inclination to acknowledge and apply this section of CEQA.

Other CEQA sections say, "The decision as to whether a project may have one or more significant effects shall be based on substantial evidence in the record of the lead agency.", and "Substantial evidence shall include facts, reasonable assumptions predicated upon the facts, and expert opinion supported by the facts." Note the key word "facts". Regulators side-step these CEQA requirements, and they routinely do not provide clear written justification and factual basis in the record for their own requested mitigation requirements.

Theories and personal opinions, that have not undergone peer review or stood the test of proper and adequate scientific review, can be called pseudo science, and this pseudo science is routinely used to justify many inappropriate actions by the Fourth Branch of Government.

As discussed in earlier Chapter Four, an example of misguided pseudo science taking over regulatory processes occurred in the 1970s in California under a California Department of Fish and Game's (DFG) debris removal program. The DFG and California Department of Forestry (CDF) required all debris to be removed from watercourses, and not doing the work to the satisfaction of the DFG and CDF would result in violations, citations, and fines. This regulatory action was never properly peer reviewed and placed in authorized regulations.

This unauthorized debris removal happened because politicians and regulators bought into pseudo science provided by many in the Fourth Branches of Government. This pseudo science promoted removing all debris, because the idea was pushed that all debris had the potential to collect and restrict the migration of fish.

Because knowledgeable peer review did not occur and experienced professionals were ignored, politicians and regulators fell in love with the program. In an effort to help out-of-work fishermen, tax money was allocated for all kinds of stream cleaning programs.

With no effective way to stop the damage and make regulators accountable, this program went on for years damaging hundreds of miles of watercourses.

Another regulatory abuse story revolves around the northern spotted owl (NSO) timber shutdown in the western United States as more fully discussed in an earlier Chapter Three. This issue is still an ongoing festering unresolved sore, and a lot of information is coming out that indicates many regulators and biologists have acted inappropriately.

Natural Marine Fishery Service (NMFS) now understood to be the National Oceanic and Atmospheric Administration (NOAA) has also shown a willingness to utilize pseudo science as outlined in earlier Chapter Three. This agency has internally developed habitat guidelines without adequate time tested, peer review, and these guidelines are routinely applied as permit requirements without adequately considering site specific conditions. Inappropriately, the State of California routinely incorporates NMFS guidelines as requirements in state permits.

An example of not understanding the real world by NMFS is the constant push for no disturbance in watercourse protection areas and a conflicting desire for conifers to be established and grown in these areas. As discussed several places in this book, the approach to "no disturbance" will not result in wanted establishment and growth of conifers, because, in areas near watercourses, nonconifer vegetation usually captures and holds the site which inhibits the establishment and growth of conifers.

California Department of fish and Game (DFG) is constantly dreaming up unauthorized species protection requirements which are internally developed and inadequately peer reviewed.

An example of internally developed DFG guidelines that do not fit the real world involves a snag retention formula. Dead standing trees or snags are wanted for wildlife purposes, and this formula is suppose to determine how many green trees need to be left standing (locked-up, value taken) to eventually die and meet a theoretical dead tree goal.

The formula has been internally developed and has undergone questionable peer review. The formula is not found in state authorized regulations, and while DFG says there is a scientific study basis behind the formula, DFG has refused to answer questions and provide information that would support the formula.

Based on this formula, DFG requested 19 large green replacement trees per acre to be retained (never harvested) for snag recruitment purposes in one harvest plan. The site specific situation found some of the best, uncut stands in the timber harvest plan area did not even have 19 large green trees per acre. The DFG was requiring landowner to leave more threes than a lot of the land was producing. While the good lord might be able to make this happen, asking the landowner to do it was just a little over the top.

The snag formula is just one way DFG routinely requires questionable and unrealistic species protection requirements to be applied and routinely operates outside the authorization and intent of California's Forest Practice Act and CEQA.

Without being made accountable for their actions, governmental agencies are routinely allowed to restrict use of natural resources and to spend various budgeted and legislated funds in questionable ways.

Per an internet report(548) the U.S. Forest Service and Bureau of Land Management (BLM) are making plans "...to create a defacto...160,000 acre...Refugia ...mineral withdrawal and lockdown...closure..." area "...in the San Bernadino National Forest..." and on adjacent lands administered by the BLM in Southern California.

This action involves withdrawal from mineral entry "...a major portion of Pacific Southwest's high grade calcite limestone...that is used in plastic, paints, rubber, putty, drywall, and other construction materials as well as having chemical and pharmaceuticals uses. Cement is 79% limestone...,...is...used in water and air pollution control.", and "Each citizen uses 1,000 lbs per year..."

Federal Land Management Policy Act requires any withdrawal of more than 5,000 acres to be approved by Congress, and in this case, the Fourth Branch of Government is being allowed to set up a withdrawal without Congress' approval and without adequate review. Adjacent rural areas and

California are going through some tough times and money shortages, and per this internet report, this closure action will take $92,000,000 out of the economy.

Without adequate peer reviewed information and a more thorough proper survey for the species of concern, this planned mineral withdrawal is being done to protect "...the Arroyo toad and...limestone endemic plants..." called "...invader...weed...species that require open space, disturbed soils, and/or wildland fire for habitat expansion." As indicated for these species, disturbance creates habitats favored by many protected species, and not allowing disturbance is the same as protecting them to death. In their quest for power or something, regulators routinely ignore how disturbance helps many species.

An example of inadequate control of legislated funding is provided in internet report(468) which covers handling of Yosemite Park's flood restoration work in California.

"...Congress awarded a flood recovery package of $187,321,000...for reconstruction and emergency expenses..."; however, under the Clinton administration "...Park Service had in mind a different kind of restoration..." where "...ultimate goal..." was "...to remove virtually all human imprint." and "...turning...park...into a living museum,..." The park "...embarked on a three-year planning process on how best to restore park's "natural environment" - which would mean the way it was before white explorers and settlers entered the valley."

All the planning and inaction has resulted in delayed flood damage restoration work while "Local communities and businesses that depend on tourism were deeply impacted,..." The new plans for the park included having "...less asphalt (less places to park), fewer automobiles (commuting visitors into the park was to replace direct access by private vehicles), less development (remove and reduce existing available facilities), less congestion (less people allowed into he park)..." to provide an "...improved and enhanced visitor experience."

"Implementation of the...Plan, originally estimated to cost $343 million, will cost at least $442 million, and some critics predict it could go as high as $1 billion." The report does not make it clear where the appropriated flood restoration money has gone or how it has been used, and there is no mention of where the money needed for implementing the newly devised plan is to come from. "The...severely damaged...sewer infrastructure has not been properly repaired and is so poorly maintained, the California regional Water Quality Control Board voted to fine the Park Service for negligence because of ongoing sewage spills."

In 2003, the plan is still being implemented and money is still being spent on "...15 projects that comprise the first phase of implementation, and these include a redesign of trails and approaches to Yosemite Falls (not believe related to flood damage), building a new Indian culture center, removing a dam on the Merced River and buying new shuttle buses." "The tab for all 15 (projects) is reported as being from $105.2 million to $110 million..." which report indicates is not part of already listed funds.

In short, this report indicates Park Service is able to spend over $700 million to possibly around $1.3 billion without any oversight to assure the funding is spent as intended.

Come on taxpayers! When are you going to wake-up? I know I am awake for all the good it is doing.

Unjustified and unsupported actions are occurring due to poorly worded regulations that allow public agencies to apply mitigations without site specific and regulatory justification.

Section 14 CCR 1037.5 (f) put in place by California's Board of Forestry (BOF) provides an example of a poorly written regulation. Section 1037.5(f) wording found in 2003 Forest Practice Rule Handbook is as follows:

Mitigation and protective measures developed by members of the review team shall be consistent with 14 CCR 1037.3, 1037.5(b), 1037.5(h), and PRC 4582.6(b). Unless the RPF (California Registered Professional Forester) and review team member agree to mitigation measure(s), such mitigation and protective measures shall be explained and justified in writing based upon the evaluation of site-specific conditions at the appropriate scale

As stated in written correspondence, the CDF interprets this regulation to say "...if the RPF and review team member agree to a recommendation, the Forest Practice Rules do not require an explanation and justification."

CDF's handling of this type of situation sounds like a savings of time and paper, and as long as there is agreement, what's the problem?

A professional, real world review finds the modified regulations have actually reduced the level of accountability.

As being applied by the CDF, explanations and justifications for mitigations are not mandatory when initially presented.

Explanation and justification information may never be provided during the whole review and approval process unless formally requested by the RPF.

If RPF makes a formal request for this information, permit review and approval processes will be disrupted and delayed which may put permit preparation costs at risk, possibly increase permit restrictions and operational costs, and may adversely affect market and financial considerations. For these reasons, there is increased pressure to not make requests for this information.

Some public agency folks say explanations and justifications are routinely prepared and provided to support mitigations; so, there is no problem. To those who do provide explanation and justification for requested mitigations, I say more power to you and a "professionally well done pat on the back"; however, as the following information shows, adequate explanations and justifications are routinely not provided by everyone.

My review of 93 California harvest plan permits found 48 plans were passed on for approval with 105 examples of mitigation items lacking site specific or regulatory justification. When questioned about the lack of explanation and justification, CDF provided "beat around the bush" information and still did not provide site specific information to justify many mitigation requirements.

I personally know of one situation where a request for more explanation and justification was going to be made under rule 1037.5(f). The involved RPF was told the consequences of such a request would not be favorable to RPF's client. The implication was not one of professional co-operation by the public agencies but rather an abusive exercise of regulatory authority.

A close look will find many other problems with this poorly worded regulation.

This described justification problem is not limited to just the California timber harvest permit process. Many environmental permit processes have the problem of inadequate explanation and justification for proposed mitigation requirements, and routinely public agencies are not required to use site specific facts and authorized regulations to support proposed mitigation requirements.

HUMAN NATURE

Everyone dealing with regulators quickly learns regulators can take things personal when confronted, and bull-headedness, lack of open-mindedness, and unprofessional conduct can occur. Regulators can do many things to delay permit review and approval and to make permit requirements more costly. During later field inspections, regulators have the ability to be excessively strict in enforcing regulations, and it is possible for inappropriate application of regulations, issuance of unnecessary and unjustified violations, monetary fines, probation, and jail time to occur.

Since there are few sideboards that get their attention, regulators generally resist backing off until they see a "big" lack of support for their position.

Because exposed inappropriate actions by any member of the Fourth Branch of Government can rub off on all members, the regulators will do things to protect and defend fellow regulators. This protection is even more intensely applied at the department and local levels. While loyalty is generally a good thing, it has interfered with exposing inappropriate and wrongful actions.

LACK OF REGULATORY AND SUPERVISORY CONTROLS

A lack of reported reprimands and penalties indicates little is being done to penalize inappropriate behavior by public officials and public servants. While some might say this lack of reprimands and penalties indicates a good job is being done, the following listed examples of misconduct say otherwise. The provided examples of problem incidences show governmental supervisors need to do a better oversight job and need to do more when those under them act inappropriately.

Goddard Gulch story in following Chapter Twenty tells how California Fish and Game and State Water Quality accommodated a reporter disguised as a Fish and Game employee, and tells a story of destroyed trust among field professionals.

There are many kinds of regulators and many ways they can utilize their authority without being held accountable. A news article(470) provides a complicated story about how "...local water master..." was "...blamed...for opening...dam without... permission...leaving treacherous muddy banks..." causing two cows to struggle in mud with a pregnant cow ending up dead. A lawsuit "...discovered the (water) district was selling water to a hydroelectric plant and they found canceled checks showing district officials got paid by the power company." Local ranchers "pooled resources to form Hot Springs Valley Irrigation District...to store water...and to release water for irrigation, stock, and wildlife..." "Each fall for three years, large quantities of water mysteriously flowed down..." and "...swamped...pasture." It appears the district "...was making good on a settlement with Pacific Gas & Electric..." "...locals learned that checks totaling about $560,000 were paid to the district..." and "...paid three Hot Spring board members to work on dam improvements or release water from their dams." "...water belonging to all district members was being released...and all should be compensated, not a few individual ranchers." This situation indicates some water board members may have misused their public employee position to enrich themselves and some of their friends.

Another case of gotcha involving public officials is outlined in three news articles(482)(488)(494) which describe how "...State of California Department of Transportation (Caltrans) desires to transfer to the National Park Service...the Freshwater Spit." which is "...300 acres bordering the Pacific Ocean..." This spit "...has been a popular camping spot...for the recreational vehicle crowd, which spent a lot of money in Orick (the nearest rural town)." "...Caltrans...in-house appraisal determined...Spit's 300 acres...had nominal or insignificant value." "...under $100,000..." "Under state law,...transfers of more than $100,000 must be reviewed by the California Transportation Commission." and "...California Department of Transportation regulations...state that excess property valued at $100,000 or more be offered for sale." In addition "...enabling legislation...when park was created...specifically prohibits the park from purchasing land from the state of California, but it can accept donated land from the state..."

The creation of the Redwood National Park resulted in big economic downturn for the town of Orick, and there are bad feelings between park and many town's people and local fishermen. The park has restricted beach use to fishermen, and shutdown of spit camping area was another big blow to Orick. Already referenced news articles mention "The spit was leased to Redwood National Park beginning in 1990." and "The park halted camping at the spit in January. This camping ban...has devastated Orick's already anemic economy." A news article(507) further mentions "...park is a federal agency,..." not "...subject to coastal permits..., but California Coastal Commission staff say the park was supposed to filed paperwork with the state when it actually changed the spit to a day-use facility." "...federal consistency supervisor for the commission..." said "Without filing a federal consistency determination, the park could open itself to litigation."

Local opposition to the transfer found out what was going to happen and is making the two involved public agencies follow their own laws and be accountable to the taxpayers and the public. Referenced news articles tell how "A judge...ruling does express distrust of Caltrans..." and "...orders...Caltrans to bring the matter to the California Transportation Commission for a full public hearing."

This Caltrans and Redwood Park spit deal shows it is hard to hold the Fourth Branches of government accountable for doing inappropriate things. Redwood National Park did not follow proper procedures in closing down a camping area and caused damage to a local community's economy. Caltrans developed a low appraisal of the spit, and put in motion an inappropriate process that would make transfer to the park easier. It appears an attempt was made to make the transfer look like a donation which was not restricted by enabling legislation and would not require a lot of public scrutiny.

In the end, the involved Fourth Branches of Government will probably get what they want, and I doubt private enterprise will ever be able to productively use the spit area. Overcoming the desires of the three involved powerful public agencies, Caltrans, Redwood National Park, and California Coastal Commission, who have shown a desire to stop camping and limit use of the spit area, will probably be insurmountable. As discussed in already referenced news article(494), "...spit is inside park boundaries..."; however, "...the California Coastal Commission has influence over development at the spit..." and "...has more impact on its commercial value than the park's boundaries..."

I know of other situations where Caltrans has acquired private lands without obvious transportation connections, and at a later time, ownership has been transferred to other public agencies. During the situations I reference, Caltrans has closed historical public access without much if any public scrutiny, and it appears Caltrans controls land use until arrangements are made to transfer ownership through a kind of secretive process.

Complexity and confusion makes it hard to uncover governmental misconduct and to hold the governmental bodies accountable for inappropriate actions. The provided examples illustrate how hard it is for average folks to make sure public agencies such as the Federal Park Service and Caltrans are toeing the line. It takes a lot of time, effort, and resources.

Kudos to those making the effort to hold public agencies accountable.

THE SWEET LIFE ON THE GOVERNMENTAL DOLE

The Fourth Branch of Government has been able to cut a pretty sweet deal for a lot of governmental positions.

Out-of-line salaries are routinely paid for many governmental positions that are obtained through political connections and are not given based on merit. It is common for experience and knowledge to be overlooked in promoting and placing people at their highest level of incompetence.

Salaries should be adjusted downward for jobs of low responsibility which produce little, and public payroll jobs producing little should be eliminated.

So, you say what's new? Why bring up this problem in a discussion about accountability?

I bring up the subject of overpaying governmental employees and poor hiring practices, because the governmental payroll situation provides another example of unaccountable actions by the Fourth Branches of Government.

Politicians and governmental agencies can pretty well do as they want when hiring people and establishing payroll levels.

Many of the people who can not make it in private industry are hired by the government and inappropriately put into positions of authority. Because many of these people lack the experience and skills needed to do a proper job, they cause problems.

The old line "the public sector has to pay high salaries to get and keep qualified people" has been worn out and routinely can not be substantiated. Most private sector jobs do not come with a benefit, job security, and payroll package comparable to governmental packages for similar levels of responsibility and production. Job security provided by not having to be accountable is worth a lot.

Information from my friends and family in the firefighting and law enforcement fields and from other sources tells me those controlling governmental payrolls have got some messed up priorities. While some folks serving the public are not getting their due, a lack of oversight and public scrutiny is allowing taxpayers to inappropriately foot the bill for some fat cats.

A news article(489) provides an insight to how high level regulators receive excessive salaries, and there is little the taxpayers can do to control a run away public payroll situation. "...between fiscal years 1996 and 2003...San Francisco's...payroll costs grew from $1.3 billion to $2 billion...workers earning more than $100,000 annually almost tripled in the last three years ...city added thousands of employees...municipal workforce grew 14 percent...overtime spending grew substantially..." Other than regulators can do what they want, no other obvious reason is provided by the article for such large public payroll increases. "...city's population grew about 5 percent..." and "...resident satisfaction with city services didn't improve."

Across the Bay a news article(303) has Oakland's "...18 percent of the city's employees..." earning "...at least $100,000 between July 2003 and June 2004,..."

Another news article(513) has "Bart...general manager..." getting "...$309,000 in 2005..." How would you like to get public agency perks and benefits and still walk away with this kind of money?

A 2004 news article(514) illustrates high public employee payrolls are all over the country. "...County agricultural commissioner and scaler of weights and measures..." is retiring, and "...a search for his successor..." has been started. Currently the retiring commissioner is getting around $90,000 per year. The article indicates no seniority is required, and "The job pays just under $72,000 per year." for a new replacement.

While my contacts with the retiring commissioner indicated he did a good job, is an all around good guy, and his leaving will be a loss for the community, I have to question why this job is paying so much. While I do not know all the pressures associated with the job, I know they do not appear to be substantial. You get the opportunity to deal with some of the best people in the world and to live in a pretty darn good place.

Instead of using the job's pluses to bargain down the salary level, county officials seem to be avoiding their responsibilities to the taxpayers by offering an awful lot to get a new, untested employee.

BEWARE FALSE SCIENTISTS WHO CREATE AND DISTRIBUTE FALSE SCIENCE AND OUTRIGHT LIES

As illustrated by the increasing number of violent protests and violent actions, there are a lot of people willing to do bad things in the name of protecting the environment, and some civil servants and regulators in the professional scientific and regulatory communities have joined the bad conduct crowd.

While there have not been many in professional fields identified as creating outright false information or knowingly misapplying laws and regulations to further chosen environmental agendas, those in decision making positions with the authority to hurt others should never be given a pass for misrepresenting the facts in order to enhance their authority.

Throughout this book, examples of inappropriate governmental actions and examples of some outright misconduct situations are provided.

Following internet report(528) information outlines two misconduct actions involving purposely created false information by public employees and mentions the dangers and potential damage caused by such misconduct.

"...the highest bidder on a sale of Bald Mountain timber from the Eldorado National Forest in California ...was denied the award of the sale. The reason: Studies performed by Forest Service wildlife biologists claimed that harvesting would cause unacceptable damage to wildlife habitat." "...after a four year court battle...U.S. Court of Federal Claims found the evidence marshaled by the Forest Service lacked any rational basis in scientific fact and appeared biased by the "personal predilections (per a Webster Dictionary this means taking a stand without full consideration or knowledge) of governmental officials." This hoax had the potential to affect "...the management of millions of acres..." and "...served to illustrate the dangers of failing to ensure that environmental decisions are above suspicion of bias."

This internet report(528) also mentions a 2002 case where, "...two government scientists submitted samples of hair from the endangered Canada Lynx as part of a survey being conducted...were falsely labeled as coming from Washington state forests, when in fact they were laboratory samples..."

Another internet report(529) dated 2002 outlines three misconduct actions involving purposely created false information by public employees and again mentions the lynx false data situation. "...U.S. Fish and Wildlife Service are coming under fire for manufacturing evidence that Canadian and Grizzly Bears inhabited areas where they had not been previously thought to exist - which would justify restrictions on land use in order to protect the two endangered species..." and "...U.S. Forest Service (USFS) has been forced to admit it falsified the number of annual visitors to the nation's national forests." This report says "...USFS purposefully padded the (visitor) figure to advance an agenda...away from its (USFS) traditional multiple-use mandate toward extreme preservation..." by making it appear "...Americans were flocking to national forests in unprecedented numbers."

Regarding the false lynx data situation, an internet report(530) says "...the behavior of seven federal and state scientists wasn't criminal..." according "...to a report issued by the U.S. Department of Agriculture's inspector general.", and "The results of this investigation were discussed with an assistant United States Attorney, Western District of Washington, who declined criminal Prosecution." In an effort to try and smooth things over (try and bury what has happened), the report goes on to say "U.S. Forest Service Chief... hasn't decided on further action..." but "...has issued a code of ethics (Does this indicate they did not work under any ethical standards before this happened?) in an effort to move beyond the controversy." "Federal authorities have refused to release the identities of federal scientists involved, and Forest Service officials have deferred inquiries to...national headquarters." In short, why don't we just forget all this happened.

An internet report(531) goes further into the lynx false data situation and says "Interior Department (how they got involved is not clear)...adopted...Code of Scientific Conduct...that...states...employees will not hinder the scientific and information gathering activities of others nor engage in dishonesty, fraud, deceit, misrepresentation, or other scientific research or professional misconduct. Employees must report their activities honestly, thoroughly and without conflict of interest. And they must place quality and objectivity of scientific activities and information ahead of personal gain or allegiance to individuals or organizations. Under the new federal policy, misconduct is defined as fabricating, falsifying or plagiarizing research. Safeguards are also included for employees accused of misconduct in the future, including confidentiality."

These are some pretty nice and noble words. I wonder why they were not already in place and applicable? Maybe the public agencies don't want to advertise the misconduct restrictions that are already in place as mentioned in last internet report(531) which say "Federal employees are already prohibited in existing regulations from lying, cheating, or stealing while in the performance of their duties. There was and is, all the necessary civil service regulations necessary to punish any employees who falsify documents, reports or other products of their government employment duties,..."

This internet report(531) additionally says "Three of the federal scientists belong to the Wildlife Society, which reportedly found that the three did not violate its set of ethical standards, which say that scientists should avoid even the suspicion of dishonesty, fraud, deceit, misrepresentation or unprofessional demeanor." So much for the believability of the Wildlife Society's ethical standards.

As indicated by common sense and a practical application of civil service professional conduct standards, any rational person would conclude civil service standards of conduct have been broken and violated in the provided situations; however, no civil service reprimands were reported in the provided information.

This last internet report(531) goes on to say "...the lynx hair study falsification was never properly publicized and the perpetrators were never disciplined..." "The employees were orally reprimanded, but later received bonuses." Already referenced internet report(530) adds "...some of..." the "biologists got a pay raise after the fact,..."

Could the lynx false data situation be another situation where the regulators and other fellow scientists are just protecting their own? Sure looks like it.

Based on what happened in the lynx false data situation and other examples of misconduct by members of the Fourth branch of Government provided in this book, it looks like professional and ethical standards do not do much in making public employees accountable.

The earlier mentioned internet report(528) says these examples of misconduct illustrate "...the dangers ...of failing to ensure that environmental decisions are above suspicion of bias.", and the need "...to screen out expert testimony based on unsound science, and call for outside peer review."

This internet report(528) goes on to say "Much as we would like to believe that environmental decisions are simply based on science, far too often this is not the case. In fact, there have been an increasing number of cases over the past decade in which faulty science has been used to justify poor environmental decisions. So prevalent have such cases become that it increasingly appears to be too much to ask of government environmental scientists to put their personal values aside (and act responsibly and professionally) in the interest of producing the best, most reliable information. This leaves the courts to determine whether the science underlying environmental policy is sound; something they can do only if that science is subject to meaningful outside peer review and thoroughly scrutinized in the courtroom." In short, personal bias and inadequate peer review is allowing a lot of pseudo unproven scientific thinking to be utilized by public bodies in making environmental decisions, and the lack of accountability sideboards is forcing a lot of environmental decisions to be decided by the courts.

The already discussed case involving the highest bidder on a sale of Bald Mountain timber from the Eldorado National Forest in California provides one example of where the courts had to be used to correct misuse of governmental authority and use of unsupportable personal opinion.

Association of Consulting Foresters report(540) provides another example where court action was required to correct and inappropriate environmental decision. In this example "...Federal District Court rules that the FWS's (Fish and Wildlife Service's) critical habitat designation for the cactus ferruginous pygmy-owl was unlawful...", because "...designation was overly broad, lacked sound scientific research, provided little evidence to justify such stringent federal regulation,..." and "failed to fully evaluate economic impacts..." This unlawful designation was going to affect "...land development restrictions covering 730,000 acres of land in Arizona's Pima, Pinal, Maricopa and Cochise Counties..."

Apparently there are enough misconduct situations involving some government employees to force acknowledgment of an accountability problem once in a while. In a news article (541), "The head of the U.S. Bureau of Land Management says she's demanding more accountability of her field managers to try and rein in an agency that lacked discipline under the Clinton administration." "…under President Clinton… freelancing bureaucrats…pursued personal interests and agendas…" "Individual priorities were pursued…" and "…personal interpretation of how things should be done became an issue,…" While these are good assertive words, you have to keep in mind they are coming from a government employee that is talking to the "…Interstate Oil and Gas Compact Commission…" interested in "…drilling permits on federal land in the West…"; so, it is a wait and see if the words are followed by action.

And the list of accountability problems goes on.

LAYMAN COURTS ARE ADDING TO THE FRAY

A news article(543) which states "The highest court in the land has made it eminently clear that the EPA (Environmental Protection Agency) has ample authority to protect the public health and the environment from harmful effects…" and "The Clean Air Act allows state officials to make some (some is emphasized) decisions…within their borders, but…gives the EPA wide authority (wide is emphasized) to enforce…law passed by Congress…" The provided articles illustrate how the courts as a part of the Fourth Branch of Government have been given far reaching and massive controls over how this country is run. Layman judges, who do not understand the issues and are not qualified to make technical decisions affecting site specific field situations, are routinely allowed to made decisions that affect timber harvesting, fishing, and other uses of our natural resources. Numerous news articles and examples of the layman judge problem are provided in Chapter Twelve and throughout this book.

WHAT A CRY BABY!

At this point in the book, you may want to say horse pucky. You may think I have overstated things, and the Fourth Branches of Government can not get away with all the unprofessional things that have been stated.

If all the provided information and real world examples have not convinced you there is a legitimate problem that needs to be confronted, then you and I have to agree to disagree.

My experiences and the experiences of many, many others along with all the provided real world examples say there is a "Big" governmental accountability problem.

To me, the obvious solution to this problem is to develop and use effective ways to confront wrongful actions and make things right. Logically and morally, anyone not ethically and professionally applying the truth should be confronted and forced to do the right thing.

Grrrrrrrrr!

A LONG ROAD TO ACCOUNTABILITY
(The Goddard Gulch Story)

Chapter Twenty

This tale begins long ago in a place called Goddard Gulch and is a true tale. Except for my identity, other involved individuals have not been identified.

There was an ongoing battle between public agencies in the Fourth Branch of Government and many timber landowners regarding photos taken during timber harvest plan review. The photos themselves were not the problem. A lack of responsible handling of the photos was the problem. Public file information is available to anyone looking at the files, and a proper description of what the photos portrayed is routinely not provided by the public agencies. This lack of responsible handling of the photos was routinely resulting in misuse of photo and files information by many who were against timber harvesting.

A story adversarial to timber harvesting appeared in a major Los Angeles newspaper and in other papers having access to the story. Accompanying this story was a picture of Goddard Gulch timber harvest operations which were in my area of responsibility. Upon seeing the story and picture, I contacted the involved area forester and asked if he knew how and when the picture was taken; so, the files holding the picture could be identified. It was concluded the best opportunity for the picture to have been taken was on a preharvest inspection. The preharvest inspection participants were identified as someone from the Regional Water Quality (WQ) staff, a locally known Department of Fish and Game (DFG) Employee, area forester, and another person identified as a DFG summer employee who was along to learn about preharvest inspections.

Further investigation found the photo used in the story was one taken by WQ. As the photos taken by WQ were in a file open to the public, use of the photo was not restricted. No one could provide the means of how the photo got into the story.

Further review of the DFG personnel that were on the preharvest trip, provided the name of summer employee who was the only unknown person on the trip. A check with DFG personnel office found provided DFG summer employee name was not on DFG's payroll.

Both DFG and WQ said they would look into the matter and let me know what they found.

Silence was the result.

We contacted an association group for help. They provided the identity of reporter who wrote the story. To see if the area forester had seen this reporter before, a photo was provided for the area forester to review. Alas, the area forester could not be sure if he had seen the reporter before.

A deadend was reached, but the tale was not over.

In the not too distant future, I received a call from another area forester on a two-way radio. He had found four folks who identified themselves as DFG personnel taking pictures of Osprey nests in my area of responsibility, and I was asked how to handle the situation. I instructed the area forester to request all the DFG people provide written identification; so, we would know who they were, and to explain why they were taking the pictures. The area forester called me back, and to the best of my memory, he said "two DFG people had written identification, another had some kind of identification that was questionable, and the last person could not identify himself as working for DFG".

What to do? Let this matter slide and maybe have another Goddard Gulch or what? I instructed the area forester to request they give him their cameras, and after we had developed the pictures and saw what was on them, the cameras and pictures would be returned to them.

Later that afternoon, the area forester showed up and dropped rolls of exposed film on my desk. When I said this was not what I said to do and exposing the film was unnecessary, the area forester said the DFG people pulled the film out of the cameras when they heard my instructions on the radio. The DFG people said they had pictures they did not want us to see. Makes you wonder what was on the other pictures.

The excitement regarding this matter was over, almost!

Shortly after the exposed picture incident, I received a call from the Director of DFG in Sacramento. At first I just let him take me to the woodshed and listened to what he had to say. To him, I had acted in high-handed manner and been wrong in what I had done. After he had done his thing, I told him that up to recent times we had been nothing but co-operative with DFG personnel, but things such as the Goddard Gulch incident had changed how we were forced to handle unexplained activities by governmental agencies. When asked if he had heard of the Goddard Gulch incident, he replied "no". I explained what had happened regarding Goddard

Gulch, and the conversation ended with him saying I was still in the wrong, but he would check this Goddard Gulch thing out.

I figured, another end of the tale, but I was wrong.

One day while sitting at my desk this fella came in to see me with another fella. He introduced himself as the Director of DFG. He was in town at a meeting, and he wanted to personally come by to give me a letter of apology for what had happened at Goddard Gulch. The other fella with him was some kind of internal investigator, and he had investigated the incident. It had been discovered the DFG summer employee was really a reporter who had been misrepresented as a DFG employee. This reporter was the one who wrote the story that was in the Los Angeles paper. The DFG employee who knowingly mislead everyone on the preharvest trip was transferred out of the area, and I guess got some kind of reprimand.

Luck, lots of luck, and perseverance solved the mystery of where and how the Goddard Gulch pictures were obtained. Whatever damage the story had done could not be corrected and remained in place. This incident showed how you had to be on your toes and stand your ground when in the right when handling inappropriate Fourth Branch of Government actions.

With this lesson under the belt, the tale goes on.

WQ continued to want to take pictures on preharvest inspections. On another preharvest inspection, WQ said they wanted to take pictures. My request that WQ sign a written agreement stating they would properly describe, label, and identify photos in the open public files was rejected. I in-turn stated no photos could be taken. I was then told the photos were required; so, a WQ supervisor could better understand what the field situation was like. I suggested WQ not send people into the field to do field review if they were not qualified or experienced enough to make the field decisions required during such reviews. I stated we could delay the preharvest inspection until a WQ person qualified to make decisions in the field could attend the preharvest inspections. No photos were taken, but a later preharvest trip occurred which involved the attendance of eighteen public agency people and included supervisors from WQ and California Department of Forestry (CDF). I understand the lead CDF person on this last preharvest inspection visit asked the lead WQ person what he was going to do when the CDF approved the timber harvest permit, and the lead WQ person was said to say "Nothing".

The involved harvest plan was approved.

For awhile things settled down.

Then I got a call from WQ that they had flown over a harvest plan, and from the elevation required to be flown by a fixed wing aircraft, they thought they had seen a violation. WQ requested that they be allowed access to go take a picture of this violation. I requested some things which I believe included a request that WQ sign a written agreement to properly describe, label, and identify photos in the open public files. I can not remember exactly what was said; however, there was disagreement on exactly what WQ wanted to do. I eventually told WQ they would have to get a search warrant. WQ then set things in motion to do just that.

The court proceedings were pretty straight forward but interesting. Our attorney wrote up a judgment allowing for a picture of the identified potential violation location with requirements to have photos properly identified in the public files, and presented it to the judge. The judge wanted to know what was going on, and our attorney said we had no problem with WQ looking at a potential violation and properly handling any required photos. WQ's legal representative stated that was all WQ wanted to do, and their photos had never been misused.

All through the court discussions, our attorney had kept a copy of the Goddard Gulch story on his desk for all to see, and he kept handling, touching, and moving the copy of the story around on his desk in the courtroom. The WQ folks were breaking their necks to try and see what he was playing with. When WQ's legal representative said WQ photos had never been misused, our attorney said he had a copy of an incident to prove otherwise. WQ turned to their staff in the room and asked if the photo in the story being presented was taken by them, and the WQ person who took the photo was in the room and had to acknowledge that his photo was the one used in the story.

This last matter involving the Goddard Gulch incident was the icing on the cake. The judge signed the judgment just the way our attorney prepared it. WQ went out to the potential violation location, took a couple pictures, said there was no violation, and sent us copies of the pictures they took. I have no idea if the pictures ever ended up in a public file, and if so, if the photos were properly handled. I do know a lot of time and taxpayer money was spent for no useful public purpose, and I know there were benefits from acting professionally and holding the involved regulators accountable.

I FELT GOOD!

While luck and coincidence can play a lot in how things turn out, this tale shows gumption, doing the right thing, and complete follow-through can be rewarded. This tale should provide encouragement to those who have the will to push for accountability by the Fourth Branch of Government. Such accountability will not come easily or quickly. Persistence and developing a moral high ground position are needed. Even at that, you win some and you lose some, but you lose it all if you do nothing.

FACE-OFF

WHAT TO DO?

HOW DO WE STOP THE SKY FROM FALLING?

PUTTING ACCOUNTABILITY BACK INTO THE REGULATORY PROCESS

Chapter Twenty One

I thought it would be worthwhile to end this book on available ways to make the Fourth Branch of Government accountable.

Some approaches to the accountability problem are already in play, and while they seem to produce little positive results, they need to be discussed to help everyone understand what really has to be done.

Meeting with regulators is a nice professional thing to do, but without much incentive to make changes, regulators have shown little to no interest in acting on suggestions presented at such meetings. Regulators generally refuse to acknowledge problems exist, and to avoid complicating their jobs and their lives, they routinely do nothing. Regulators routinely consider political, uninformed public, and lawsuit pressures more important than correcting wrongs done to producers of natural resource products.

Associations and leaders representing the producers of natural resource products and rural communities are another potential means of getting something done; however, as discussed in Chapter Eleven, these folks are dropping the ball. While these folks do a little public relation work and have a lot of cocktail meetings, they routinely run at the sign of confrontation and continually play a losing compromise game.

While hearing and legislative processes are the basic means for change in this country, little governmental accountability regarding environmental issues is being achieved through these processes. As discussed in Chapter Five, the weaknesses of these processes routinely results in a lot of bad law and more harm than good for producers of natural resource products and rural communities. To participate in these processes requires a lot of time, money, and access to the right people to accomplish anything, and a lot of time, money, and access to the right people is not available to most advocates for accountability.

You would think the academic community would be helpful in getting regulations and governmental actions to be based on professional standards, time tested and proven science, and site specific facts. Instead, this group has shown a reluctance to get involved with accountability issues. While some academic folks routinely give input supporting more and often incorrect regulations, this group as a whole has been AWOL when regulatory thinking is technically and scientifically in error.

Opinion article(549) outlines how the academic community as a group could be more accountable and more involved. This article correctly points out the academic community's slant towards invented wrongs and failings, and this group does not spend enough time and effort in providing a well rounded, real world understanding of issues and the truth. This article focused on patriotic and political issues, but what the article said could readily be applied to environmental and rural community issues. Students are routinely taught past detrimental land practices are still occurring, and positive constructive things being done on the land are given inadequate play.

At this point, many may ask "What about all the many laws and regulations that are in place to counter governmental misconduct?" What about appeal and petition review processes?

Existing laws and regulations that are supposed to provide protection from regulatory abuses are routinely utilized; however, positive results have been spotty to nil. The first thing to keep in mind is that the Fourth Branches of Government are the ones interpreting and applying these laws and regulations, and when requested to apply the involved laws and regulations, they routinely concentrate on defending themselves and other public officials. Who do you think is looking out for who, and who is there to make them do the right thing?

It can not be said penalties and reprimands have never been given for inappropriate governmental actions. There are a few rare cases of regulators being taken to the woodshed; however, by being rare with routinely light punishment, such reprimand actions have provided little incentive for regulators to toe the line.

While obtaining compensation for damage from inappropriate governmental actions would provide a proper and effective way to get the attention of members of the Fourth Branch of Government, this approach has very limited application, because many public servants and public agencies are shielded from being sued and held liable for damages.

The second thing to keep in mind is appeal processes don't work, because proper focused, open minded, scientific and factual peer review of appeals and presented problems does not occur.

Without an open mind and all the facts being considered, there is little chance for the right thing to come out of existing review and appeal processes.

Obviously, we need to keep in mind there are many regulators who do not go out of their way to cause problems. Some regulators are top notch, dedicated professionals who know their business; however, they face the same real world problems faced by private industry professionals. While civil servant status gives them more protection, they are human and like to avoid problems for themselves and their families. When told to do something by higher levels of government, even the good ones will do things they know are wrong. While the good regulators should do more to eliminate unprofessional actions by their fellow regulators and to eliminate regulatory problems, there is little chance they will stand tall and do what is needed.

While those who are improperly trained and poorly supervised will make honest mistakes and deserve fair treatment, they are still professionals, and unprofessional and unauthorized conduct needs to be identified and corrected. Regulators no doubt are having problems interpreting and applying the many unclear and hard to interpret laws and regulations, but this difficulty does not provide an excuse for being overzealous and abusive. They should be able to see through the bull and act according to regulatory interpretations supported by site specific facts, peer reviewed science, logic, and common sense.

I have heard an example of true public assistance is being provided by some public servants in Texas. These folks are actually practicing the art of helping the public in working with the victims of Hurricane Katrina. Public employees actually escort people to other offices to make sure they are properly helped. Simple forms are being used, and public officials actually work directly with applicants in filling out forms. Questions by applicants are being answered, and public servants accompany applicants to new job, housing, and school locations. Personal attention is given and phone calls are answered by an actual voice. Stupid regulations are by-passed.

The rest of the country's Fourth branch of Government needs to take a lesson from Texas.

A little quiz illustrates how public employees are no longer trained to be public servants for "all".

Ask (public servants) the following questions:

1. What did they learn they should do in their job during their training?
2. What is the most important part of their job?
3. What do they feel is the most important thing about their job?

Expected truthful answers:

1. Do not let wrongs occur as interpreted by them.
2. Protect the public from wrongdoers and those that do not follow regulations.
3. Interpret and apply regulations and "get" those that do not follow regulations.
4. Protect the environment.
5. Protect themselves and be comfortable in what they do.
6. Interpret regulations in the strictest sense.

Some answers that should be provided, but will not be openly and easily provided:

1. Be a public servant to all.
2. Help guide producers in the private sector to get needed permits.
3. Speak up about and give advice on the rights and wrongs of regulations and regulatory interpretations.
4. Work with producers in the private sector to solve regulatory problems.
5. Be sure decisions, application of regulations, and regulatory interpretations are supported by the site specific facts, proper science, logic, and common sense.

I see the current public servant mindset getting in the way of helping permitees during permit review and approval and finding practical and factual ways to resolve regulatory conflicts. Factors contributing to this problem are as follows:

- Use of inexperienced personnel.

- Lack of supervisorial input and training.
- Routine misinterpretation and misapplication of rules and regulations.
- Abuse of authority and lack of effort to keep governmental restrictions within authorized regulatory limits.
- Inappropriately trying to avoid conflicts with sister agency, public, political, and layman court concerns at the expense of permitees.
- Lack of effective accountability processes. Appeal and petition processes are unworkable, complicated, costly, and not functionally reliable.
- General attitude enhanced by training and supervisorial direction that regulators are there to enforce regulations and restrictions and not to help find ways to reduce and avoid restrictions. Do it our way; or, no way!

At the start of my professional life, the things I now say did not apply to most regulators, but at the end of my professional life, I now have to say I sadly believe the things I say do apply to most regulators.

OH! HOW WE NEED TRAINING!
OFF LIKE A HERD OF TURTLES

Experienced field professionals will readily admit there is a need for continued training and education, and practical training is really needed in the Fourth Branches of Government where the school of hard knocks has not adequately weeded out the untrained and inexperienced.

There is a problem with most training sessions that seems to elude those running and setting up training and educational meetings. Many in academic institutions, associations, and regulators have missed going to the school of hard knocks and do not know how to practically apply real world information. There is too much "Throw it out there and see if it sticks" thinking.

While topics and presented information may follow a common theme, "experienced" field professionals routinely leave training and so-called workshop meetings trying to figure out how to apply an often disjointed jumble of ideas and information. A lot of information is heavy to theory, and information showing how to resolve real world and "You will know what we want when you get your permit approved" situations are a rarity at training meetings.

HOW ABOUT SOME CLOSURE AND PRACTICALITY

Training sessions routinely provide a flood of discussion about bad things, but it is like pulling eye-teeth for good things to be mentioned. Why can't training sessions include more closure by providing descriptions and examples of acceptable and beneficial levels of disturbance? There seems to be a pact to not present positive vibs.

Examples of how regulators and enviros want to see things can be diamonds in the rough that can be utilized in the real world of balancing second guessed interpretations of rules and Johnny-come-lately ideas.

The cry "we need more studies and just haven't had the time or money to study and learn" is routinely provided when specific information is requested. With the wealth of information now available, this cry has become a worn out weak excuse for not providing factual success stories.

Obviously, examples of good things are occurring and decisions are being made within the permit review and approval processes that could be shared. More real world information about current tools and knowledge, key variables needing to be considered, and pertinent regulatory interpretations could be provided. Examples of harvest operation mitigations that worked, stability projects that did the job, follow-up information on stream restoration activities, and examples of successful wildlife habitat mitigations could be discussed.

Instead of always talking about trade-offs and economic choices involved in a conflict between environmental protection and human needs, why can't some real world positive and pro-active ways humans can help the environment be presented? Available information showing proper operational activities can increase populations of fish, frog, salamander, mountain lion, spotted owl, and many other species seems to be held back. It is rare to have a speaker describe what levels of disturbance can be good in the short and long run.

Could it be too much practical, useful knowledge would disrupt the agendas of many regulators and pseudo scientists?

A TRAINING WE GO

Unproductive training sessions can be a waste of time and money for experienced professionals. The purpose of a training session is to train, and people should come to listen and learn.

Too often training sessions are mixed with continuing education, and for nonprofessional reasons many show up that like to hear themselves talk and give slanted speeches. While there can be some benefit to raising and noting unclear and confusing regulatory situations for future review, those running training meetings need to keep the audience on track and to avoid frivolous discussion.

While everyone is on their own in reviewing training session content and deciding where to spend their time and the uneducated public needs to be accommodated, coming to advertised training sessions and finding them set-up to handle the lowest level of regulatory and educational understanding can be a real bummer. Time is taken up discussing layman problems and irresolvable issues, and time is taken away from legitimate training issues.

Training sessions conducted at an experienced professional level provide better longer lasting benefits. Participants, especially members of the Fourth Branch of Government, get a better opportunity to learn how difficult it is to balance continually changing regulatory interpretations in the real world.

Single day field training sessions targeting specific subjects or topics can be very productive, and there needs to be more of them. Field training provides a look at the real world, and short focused sessions provide a more thorough review of topics and issues. I have found short informal field sessions to be a practical way for field professionals and regulators to closely interact in learning real world problems.

Knowing what makes your regulator happy can pay the cost of attending a training session. The trick is to get the regulators to tell what makes them happy. In the regulatory world of multiple interpretations, regulators have a lot of opportunity to avoid confrontation and to find justifiable resolutions to regulatory problems, and there is no excuse for regulators not being able to clearly state what they require to be done.

For those who are afraid of pseudo protectionist ideas that may spew forth if there are more training sessions and more give and take, I say you better wake up and smell the roses. The regulators have the power to make a lot of things happen, and it is better to know what is coming; so, you can prepare to confront the inappropriate stuff.

A practical and productive training program needs to include the following elements:

GET INTO THE FIELD
(Crowded rooms lacking visual aids and speakers lacking answers are the pits)

ALLOW PARTICIPANTS TO LEARN FROM EXPERIENCED FIELD PROFESSIONALS
AND DO NOT WASTE FIELD PROFESSIONALS' TIME

1. Training material and information needs to be provided from an experienced professional perspective.

2. Speakers need to be experienced and practicing professionals, and speakers need to have experience in dealing with current regulatory processes and issue(s) being discussed. Speakers who have never had to apply what they are discussing can not do an adequate job.

3. Issues being discussed that do not have a clearly written and understandable regulatory resolution should not be utilized, because while it is good to air ideas and problems, training sessions are not the proper forum for spending time trying to develop answers to complicated possibly unanswerable questions. Trying to cover too much information or too broad a subject creates less focus on specific problems and dilutes the usefulness of the information being presented.

4. Real world questions and examples need to be utilized and presented. Field examples are needed that clearly illustrate the results of applying provided information. What has been the result of applying certain mitigation measures? Effects over time need to be discussed. What are the lasting effects? How long does it take for recovery? What are the beneficial as well as the negative effects? What peer review and scientific proof is available to verify validity of presented ideas and information?

5. While keeping in mind too much variety can cause confusion, having a mix of speakers per listed agenda item can be beneficial. Try to balance speakers among "experienced" regulatory, private, and academic professionals. Unless strongly supported and justified, there is a need to not have the speakers collectively provide a one-sided viewpoint that conflicts with a large portion of the audience. While a little

confrontation and disagreement can be good, unjustified and unnecessary confrontation can be destructive.

6. Information on ways to effectively handle regulatory problems associated with discussed issues needs to be provided. Too often, a bunch of varied ideas and information is thrown to the audience, and no acceptable way to resolve regulatory conflicts is provided. A purely scientific training presentation providing little real world application can be a waste of time. Training programs need to be geared to provide resolutions and not to perpetuate questions and confusion.

7. Any training session moderator should maintain order and not let the discussions wonder off the issues being discussed. General discussion that is not to the point and goes in circles needs to be cut-off.

8. The simpler, least costly, and easier to attend training session the better. Avoid big, formal shows in distant cities with a lot of speakers lacking field experience. Meetings in locations where issues are being encountered allow for more participation and more factual input.

9. Unless other experienced speakers are not available, avoid using local or state in-breed speakers. This is a major problem in California where speakers with the same ideas and limitations are used over and over again, and this repeated use of the same speakers has resulted in application of inappropriate bias and incorrect information in the field. In California, new ideas, research, and information from other areas is routinely stifled and not fully utilized.

10. A "SMALL" screening, program committee made up of "experienced" field professionals acquainted with the issues to be discussed should be employed to screen and modify training materials.

11. Have a good mix of different academic people, public agency regulators, private professionals, and landowners at training sessions. Too often training sessions only consist of members of one group, and the lack of exposure to differing schools of thought and landowner concerns can result in biased and improper application of ideas and regulations.

POTENTIAL TRAINING AND MEETING ISSUES

1. Watercourse Protection Issues - These issues are all over the place, because of many unclear regulatory requirements.

    Unfortunately the regulatory community and many other professionals continue to hang onto the use of protection requirements that are tied to watercourse classification systems. Any watercourse classification system involves subjective and changing decisions about all kinds of changing factors (presence of water, seasonal changes, critter use, and on), and determining protection requirements based on an ever-changing watercourse classification results in improper protection requirements. To properly protect beneficial uses, requires identifying applicable beneficial uses, and then developing mitigation measures that properly protect these beneficial uses. The use of watercourse classification systems to determine watercourse protection measures has outlived its usefulness, does not properly protect beneficial uses, causes a lot of unnecessary and unjustified operational problems, and just plain causes a lot of aggravation and people problems that we would all be better off without.

    You would think after all this time someone would have come up with a working definition of a healthy watershed, watercourse, or instream condition. It seems those running the water protection show are purposefully avoiding the idea that a healthy watershed, watercourse, or instream condition can exist, and if they are not avoiding this type of thinking, why haven't they developed a range of acceptable conditions. The old and tired cry there are too many variables and we need more study is no longer justified. In all the information that has been collected on key variables such as water temperature, sedimentation sizes, canopy cover percentages, pool riffle ratios, large woody debris levels, and insect population counts there has to be a hint of what is good and what is bad. There is a need to identify good things; so, unnecessary restrictions on use of natural resources can be avoided in healthy watersheds. The way regulators and some others avoid the subject of healthy conditions leads you to believe there is no such thing or can never be such a thing as a healthy watershed, watercourse, or instream condition.

2. Species Habitat Needs – Species protection is all over the place and needs to be based on site specific factors. How authorized regulations are supposed to be used in developing protection guidelines needs to be better defined and understood.

3. Silviculture Management Issues - There is a need to understand how canned regulatory prescriptions do not fit the real world, and there is a need to understand how to modify regulations to fit the real world.

4. Rules and Regulations - As provided by any written regulations, there is a cornucopia of potential ideas and subjects needing to be discussed and understood.

5. Can't we just get along? The simple process of just listening to and applying other factual and practical viewpoints needs to be emphasized and taught more. Many training sessions focus on doing things one way, and this lack of open-mindedness routinely leads to unnecessary and unjustified confrontation.

My training and experience while working for governmental agencies left me with the impression governmental regulators are not encouraged to work with contractors and permitees in acknowledging viewpoints and resolving problems. Of course, a lot of private industry also pushes this inflexibility, but in nongovernmental sectors, there is more incentive to modify behavior and come up with alternate courses of action. It seems a lack of real world experience and confidence causes governmental personnel to be trained to say "do it our way; or, no way."

A VIEW OF WHAT IS REALLY HAPPENING AT MOST TRAINING SESSIONS, WORKSHOPS, SEMINARS, OR CONTINUING EDUCATION SESSIONS

A lot of time and money is spent attending. Everyone gets together and throws a bunch of ideas and information around. A lot of questions are asked and most go unanswered. Some interesting ideas are captured, but little of a real world and practical nature is accomplished. A lot of coffee is absorbed and there is a lot of good fellowship talk. Most everyone says the meeting was a good one, and someone always says there is a need to have more similar meetings. Everyone goes home.

A lot of time and money is spent attending. Everyone gets together and throws a bunch of ideas and information around. A lot of questions are asked and most go unanswered. Some interesting ideas are captured, but little of a real world and practical nature is accomplished. A lot of coffee is absorbed

362

and there is a lot of good fellowship talk. Most everyone says the meeting was a good one, and someone always says there is a need to have more similar meetings. Everyone goes home.

A lot of time and money is spent attending. Everyone gets together and throws a bunch of ideas and information around. A lot of questions are asked and most go unanswered. Some interesting ideas are captured, but little of a real world and practical nature is accomplished. A lot of coffee is absorbed and there is a lot of good fellowship talk. Most everyone says the meeting was a good one, and someone always says there is a need to have more similar meetings. Everyone goes home.

A lot of time and money is spent attending. Everyone gets together and throws a bunch of ideas and information around. A lot of questions are asked and most go unanswered. Some interesting ideas are captured, but little of a real world and practical nature is accomplished. A lot of coffee is absorbed and there is a lot of good fellowship talk. Most everyone says the meeting was a good one, and someone always says there is a need to have more similar meetings. Everyone goes home.

A lot of time and money is spent attending. Everyone gets together and throws a bunch of ideas and information around. A lot of questions are asked and most go unanswered. Some interesting ideas are captured, but little of a real world and practical nature is accomplished. A lot of coffee is absorbed and there is a lot of good fellowship talk. Most everyone says the meeting was a good one, and someone always says there is a need to have more similar meetings. Everyone goes home.

Away we go,
Not knowing where we go,
But knowing we must go,
Because someone said so.

FACTUAL FORCEFUL INPUT IS AWOL
LOSS OF COMMON SENSE

An obvious solution to regulatory problems is to professionally and logically approach and resolve our problems. To start this process requires there to be a recognition and acceptance that there is a problem, and the refusal to recognize the flood of poor regulations being put into play drives many experienced professionals nuts.

Regulatory decisions and regulations need to be based on peer reviewed and time tested science, site specific facts, logic, and common sense, the "truth", and this is routinely not being done. The result is creation of many unclear and unjustified regulations open to multiple interpretations that are hard to understand and hard to enforce.

Current, new supported ideas and information can not seem to filter through the bureaucratic maze, and decisions are often based on old and tired ideas or who wins the point and counterpoint and perception battle. We seem to have lost the ability to state the obvious in simple terms, and to solve problems by the old, tried, and true way of collecting site specific facts, using experienced field professionals, using the people who know the land, applying time tested and peer reviewed science, and applying some logic and common sense.

The mess just keeps getting worse for the producers of natural resources. As discussed in Chapter Eleven, rule making bodies do their own thing, and the hearing processes continue to let social and public concerns override physical truths. All the competing interests and opinions have been forced into "stakeholder" groups, which is a laugh since the only ones with money at the table are the producers of natural resources, and a lot of effort and resources are expended in playing point and counterpoint games. The result is a mess that is handed to the experienced field professionals to try and implement.

The current mixing of technical and social issues is causing confusion, and not providing correct and usable answers.

The process of environmental review and development of regulations needs to be broken into two processes. One process is needed to develop technical information and physical solutions to problems, and another separate process then needs to take this technical information into the public arena where social issues and general public concerns can shape final regulations. In this way, the physical basis and impacts of regulatory actions can more clearly be identified for all to see. If society and general public are willing to accept adverse consequences from decisions that do not heed physical truths, then there is not much that can be done in our democratic society. Hopefully having a clearer factual picture of what is coming will cause some common sense to prevail.

If not, se la vee said the old folks.

The cry that the sky will fall if all perceived environmental problems are not covered by some regulatory process is not supported by the facts. Mother Earth has taking a lot and still keeps ticking. In fact if you take a serious look around, you will see she has done some pretty miraculous healing, and disturbance has create some pretty beneficial things to happen. Jumping to the cry the sky is falling and being careful to a fault is resulting in a lot of bad law and damage to people and the environment.

Properly collected common sense "truth" will set you free. Many large, costly, and complicated research projects advocated by inexperienced pseudo experts do not need to be conducted to get a lot of the needed "truth". Just let experienced professionals back into the game. By utilizing logic and common sense and state of the art practices now in place, they can come up with all kind of efficient and low cost ways to get the "truth".

BLACK IS BLACK
WHITE IS WHITE

The idea that when making technical decisions all available information must be used and decisions have to be a gray compromise is wrong. Societal decisions may require compromise, but technical decisions should be based on smaller black and white (right or wrong) decisions based on peer reviewed and time tested science and factual information.

Technical review should include the use of experienced field professionals. Without their involvement, bogus information and improper action can not be properly identified and eliminated from the decision process.

Theorized and not scientifically proven ideas should not be part of a technical decision process. Mixing factual information with theorized and not scientifically proven information results in compromised information that distorts and makes factual information less relevant.

A lot of hearing input is routinely useless by frequently being incorrect and misleading.

In the dark ages, ridged control by those in power allowed many unproven ideas to be applied, and this caused bad things to happen. Especially if information would take away their power to control others, those in control would not let decisions be made based on factual information. As time moved on, factual information could not be held back, and the right and wrong, the black and white of what was happening forced everyone out of the unknown into the known.

Today we have not reverted back into the unknown and into another Dark Age, yet; however, our decision making processes are evolving into a mix of fact and fiction, caution and compromise, and who wins the political and perception point and counter point battle. This mix is not taking us to a good place.

HAZARDOUS WATERS AND THINGS THAT MAKE THE SWEAT POP

Before I move-on and start talking tough, I need to tell a story that applies to those that take on the Fourth Branch of Government and those in the enviro community.

This story is told in a news article(551) and an opinion article(552) which describes what happened to one person who became a member of a regulatory board and went out of her way to learn how regulatory processes affect permitees. This person "...decided to investigate...experiences with staff..." and "...outrageous conditions imposed..." by this staff on citizens of a city. This action resulted in Grand Jury accusations involving a questionable conflict of interest, and an action was filed by the county District Attorney. The opinion article author says she attended the Grand Jury meetings, and "...after reading the grand jury transcripts...", she said the testimony given was not what actually happened. The news article mentions "...the city attorney..." said before any involvement "...there was no conflict as long as the project was 12 months in the future.", and the opinion article said nothing was hidden. "...everything...was done with the council's and the staff's knowledge." The opinion article goes on to say "...a nightmare was endured..." by someone who "...stood up for a citizen's rights." Other news articles mentioned how a substantial amount of private funds had to be used to pay for a legal defense and how life had been turned upside down. In the end, a mistrial was declared, and the matter appears to have been dropped.

I tell this story; so, it is clear being a tough guy and doing the right thing may have adverse consequences. Being a naïve good citizen and participating on a public body exposes you to many types of potential conflicts which helps to explain why public bodies have trouble getting good qualified members. Right or wrong, your life can be turned upside down by being cited for violating some unexpected, little known, vague, and poorly applied law, and you could be forced to use up personal assets defending yourself.

Additionally, this story shows how you do not want to depend on governmental agencies such as staffs to do the right thing or to protect you.

As you read on, keep this story in mind and don't be naïve. Be very clear about what you are going to do, and be sure you understand the potential consequences. I know I have felt the sweat pop on a couple of occasions when I have gone out on a limb. Fortunately, the truth has helped me persevere.

PUTTING ACCOUNTABILITY BACK INTO REGULATORY PROCESSES

Needed change and regulatory relief is not being provided by existing compromise and get-a-long approaches; so, something else needs to be done.

A close professional review of accountability problems finds a simple and common theme behind accountability problems. Simply put, members of the Fourth Branches of Government are not always required to base their actions on authorized regulations, time tested and peer reviewed science, site specific conditions, logic, and common sense. If regulators and all involved professionals were forced to justify their actions based on these elements, a professional, factual basis would be provided for eliminating many inappropriate actions, and a factually correct, authorized level playing field would exist for all participants.

Being accountable under this simple, irrefutable, and logical standard would be a bitch for abusive regulators and those providing pseudo ideas.

Since there is little incentive for regulators to voluntarily change, forcing change seems to be in order.

A look at how our forefathers and enviros accomplished change finds confrontation leading the way. In the case of our forefathers, severe change required severe confrontation. In the case of the enviros, confrontation has not been as severe as in the Revolutionary War, but it has not been without its violence. Enviro confrontation, especially violent confrontation, has got the attention of the media, politicians, and general public. When confronted by the enviros, regulators and politicians have run scared, routinely giving-in to enviro demands.

Without the violent part, this information tells us some confrontation is needed to get the attention of the Fourth Branches of Government. Simply put, those acting inappropriately without authorization and justification need to be confronted.

I have learned respectful and professional confrontation utilizing the truth brings better results than a heavy handed approach utilizing a lot of mistruths.

While it is tough to confront regulators when a project or a lot of value is at stake, I have found the long run pay-off to usually be worth the cost and effort. I have played the game of compromise and avoided confrontation with some useful results; but, the longest lasting and most beneficial results have come from not backing-off professionally presented truthful positions.

Confrontation based on professionally presented truth does get good results.

For those with the gumption to confront inappropriate regulatory actions, there are some regulatory review processes that hold some promise.

THE GRAND JURY CAN BE A BIG HELP

The Grand Jury processes are a potential means of correcting governmental misconduct, but based on my experience with one Grand Jury situation, this process has its limitations.

I was on the way to being put in the pool for a County Grand Jury when I became aware of a muzzle problem and weakness in the process. Per an opinion article(328), "...secrecy and confidentiality requirements..." and "...constraints remain in effect forever!" Jurors "...cannot discuss what..." they hear "...as a juror..." or what they know "...about the proceedings of the previous jury." A juror discussing these matters violates jury oath, a penal code section, and "...is guilty of a misdemeanor." Questioning of court staff confirmed the opinion article to be correct.

I realized, if I got on the jury and issues covered by my expertise and of interest to me were brought-up, technically and legally I could never again discuss them at any time in the future or even in this book. While I am sure many jurors are getting away with not following the straight and narrow interpretation of the law, I did not want to put myself at risk of being a target for someone I may cross. Maybe I am just paranoid, but I decided it would be wise to drop my name from the potential list for the Grand Jury.

As on many public boards, commissions, and committees, I do see how these secrecy requirements reduce the quality and expertise of the jury pool, and this in turn reduces the quality and completeness of the review and determinations made by Grand Juries. Those active in public issues may not want to participate and be muzzled, and qualified professionals may not participate due to potential interference with business activities.

Since I have seen Grand Juries do a lot of good, I believe this process provides a lot of potential for handling governmental misconduct. I just wish the process could incorporate more experience and knowledge; so, it could do more.

368

OFFICE OF ADMINISTRATIVE LAW UNDERGROUND
REGULATION REVIEW PROCESS

In California, there is a review process conducted by the Office of Administrative Law (OAL) that reviews and makes a legal determination regarding underground type regulations. Regulations targeted for review are internally developed guidelines that are inappropriately applied as authorized regulations.

Some applicable regulatory wording is as follows:

Section 11340.5: No state agency shall issue, utilize, enforce...any guideline, criterion, bulletin,... which is regulation as defined in subdivision (g) of Section 11342 unless guideline...has been adopted as a regulation and filed with the Secretary of state pursuant to this chapter.

Section 11342 (g): Regulations means "every" rule, regulation, order, or standard of general application or the amendment, supplement, or revision of any rule... adopted by any state agency to implement...the law enforced or administered by it (it being the involved state agency)...

In the King's English these two regulatory sections mean:

No regulations can be applied by state agencies which are not legal regulations, and all legal regulations have to be reviewed by the OAL and filed with the Secretary of State.

Seems logical and straight forward, right? Check the many requirements being applied by governmental agencies, and I believe you will find many regulations fall short of being authorized regulations.

For some unclear reason landowner and other various associations of California have demonstrated a resistance to supporting utilization of this review process. Maybe there is a fear of losing control over political situations if anyone can request and start a review of inappropriate regulations.

Governor Arnold Schwarzenegger sparked some hope when he issued Executive Order S-2-03 requiring a California Performance Review (CPR). This order required all state agencies to work with OAL in doing a review of how they were internally applying state laws and regulations. Hope for regulatory relief soon faded when this review was assigned to only state agencies, and outside input was restricted. This review became the fox checking to see if the fence was good enough to keep it away from the chickens.

A good look at the California OAL review process finds it to be a professional and factual review process that could be utilized anywhere in this country. It provides a way for the average person to confront legitimately improper regulatory actions.

OMBUDSMAN AND PERMITEE'S BILL OF RIGHTS

Another process in place with the California Environmental Protection Agency (CAL/EPA) also holds some promise.

This process involves use of unbiased, peer review by a third party ombudsman.

Webster's Dictionary describes an ombudsman as an individual, government or otherwise, that investigates complaints by individuals regarding abuses or capricious acts by public officials, reports findings, and helps to achieve equitable settlements.

As I have never heard of anyone exercising the rights listed under the Cal/EPA Bill of Rights, the existence of this Bill of Rights may be more lip-service and window dressing than a practical way to protect permitee rights, but at least, it does provide a pattern for review already in place that can be utilized. Re-copied Cal/EPA Bill of Rights (November 2, 2000) is provided as follows:

BILL OF RIGHTS FOR ENVIRONMENTAL PERMIT APPLICANTS

The California Environmental Protection Agency (Cal/EPA) endorses the following precepts that form the basis of a permit applicant's "Bill of Rights"

1. Permit applicants have the right to assistance in understanding regulatory and permit requirements. All Cal/EPA programs maintain an Ombudsman to work directly with applicants. Permit Assistance Centers located throughout California have permit specialists from all State, regional, and local agencies to identify permit requirements and assist in permit processing.

2. Permit applicants have the right to know the projected fees for review of applications, how any costs will be determined and billed, and procedures for resolving any disputes over fee billings.

3. Permit applicants have the right of access to complete and clearly written guidance documents that explain the regulatory requirements. Agencies

must publish a list of all information required in a permit application and of criteria used to determine whether the submitted information is adequate.

4. Permit applicants have the right of timely completeness determinations for their applications. In general, agencies notify the applicant within 30 days of any deficiencies or determine that the application is complete. California Environmental Quality Act (CEQA) and public hearing requests may require additional information.

5. Permit applicants have the right to know exactly how their applications are deficient and what further information is needed to make their application complete. Pursuant to California Government Code Section 65944, after an application is accepted as complete, an agency may not request any new or additional information that was not specified in the original application.

6. Permit applicants have the right of a timely decision on their permit application. The agencies are required to establish time limits for permit review.

7. Permit applicants have the right to appeal permit review time limits by statute or administratively that have been violated without good cause. For state environmental agencies, appeals are made directly to the Cal/EPA Secretary or to a specific board. For local environmental agencies, appeals are generally made to the local governing board or under certain circumstances, to Cal/EPA. Through this appeal, applicants may obtain a set date for a decision on their permit and in some cases a refund of all application fees (ask boards and departments for details).

8. Permit applicants have the right to work with a single lead agency where multiple environmental approvals are needed. For multiple permits, all agency actions can be consolidated under lead agency. For site remediation, all applicable laws can be administered through a single lead agency.

9. Permit applicants have the right to know who will be reviewing their application and the time required to complete the full review process.

While this ombudsman process could do a lot in providing regulatory relief and resolving many regulatory conflicts, the Fourth Branch of Government seems to collectively resist any oversight ideas. Regulatory relief is routinely promised, but when something logical and simple comes along such as the Ombudsman idea, the Fourth Branch of Government stone-walls, runs, and hides from the idea. Public agencies routinely avoid bringing legitimate problem issues to the attention of their companion boards and commissions.

An attempt by a California Registered Professional Forester (RPF) to put CAL/EPA Bill of Rights and Ombudsman process into California's forest practice regulatory process provides an example of how the Fourth Branch of Government resists such oversight. This RPF petitioned the California Board of Forestry (BOF) to implement a "Timber Harvest Plan Submitters Bill of Rights" on 6/18/2001. The BOF acknowledged the idea, thanked the RPF for the idea and his time, and then stone-walled on doing anything. Although justification for not endorsing the timber harvest plan submitter's Bill of Rights as similarly done by Cal/EPA has not been provided, the petitioned Bill of Rights is not in place as of 7/18/2005. It appears the petitioned Bill of Rights (re-copied below) is dead as far as the BOF is concerned.

DRAFT

BILL OF RIGHTS FOR TIMBER HARVEST PLAN SUBMITTERS

The California Board of Forestry endorses the following percepts that form the basis of a timber harvest plan submitter's "Bill of Rights". This "Bill of Rights" is based on the "Bill of Rights for Environmental Permit Applicants" published by the California Environmental Protection Agency.

1. Timber harvest plan submitters have the right to assistance in understanding regulatory and permit requirements. The Board of Forestry will maintain an Ombudsman to work with timber harvest plan submitters at each location where the Director of the Department of Forestry and Fire Protection accepts timber harvest plans for filing and/or review.

2. The term "timber harvest plan", includes all forms prescribed by the Board of Forestry to be submitted to the Department of Forestry and Fire Protection for review, including but not limited to: timber harvest plans, modified timber harvest plans, non-industrial timber management plans,

the exemption for Christmas tree, dead, dying, or diseased, fuelwood or split products, the exemption for removal of fire hazard trees within 150 feet of a residence, the notice of emergency timber operations, the exemption for substantially damaged timberlands unmerchantable as sawlog, the exemption for public agency, private and public utility right of way, timberland conversion permit, and the exemption for less than 3 acre conversion.

3. Timber harvest plan submitters have the right of access to complete and clearly written guidance documents that explain the regulatory requirements. The Department of Forestry and Fire Protection must publish a list of all information required in a timber harvest plan, using the rules of the Board of Forestry, and of the criteria used to determine whether submitted information is adequate.

4. Timber harvest plan submitters have the right of timely completeness determinations. Pursuant to Public Resources Code Section 4582.7 and Title 14, California Code of Regulations, Sections 1031 to 1052.3, the Director of the Department of Forestry and Fire Protection shall have 10 days to determine is a timber harvest plan is accurate, complete and in proper order.

5. Timber harvest plan submitters must know what "accurate, complete and in proper order" means.

6. Timber harvest plan submitters have the right to know exactly how their plans are deficient and what further information is needed to make their harvest plans complete. Pursuant to Public Resources Code Section 4582.75 and California Government Section 65994, after a timber harvest plan is accepted as complete, the Department of Forestry and Fire Protection and/or the agencies that participate in the review team process outlined in Title 14, California Code of Regulations, Sections 1037.1 to 1037.5, may not request any new or additional information that was not specified prior to filing of an accepted timber harvest plan.

7. Timber harvest plan submitters have the right of timely decision on their timber harvest plan. The Director of the Department of Forestry and Fire Protection must uphold the time period for review and a decision pursuant to Title 14, California Code of Regulations, Sections 1031 to 1052.3.

8. In the event that a timber harvest plan is returned to the submitter without a determination that it is accurate, complete and in proper order, the Director of the Department of Forestry and Fire Protection shall provide the Ombudsman and the submitter with the information needed to make the plan complete. The Ombudsman shall work with the plan submitter and/or the Department, if requested, to clarify the regulatory requirements. The Ombudsman shall provide the Board with reports about issues related to filing and processing of timber harvest plans.

9. Timber harvest plan submitters have the right to work with a single lead agency. Pursuant to the Z'Berg-Nejedly Forest Practice Act of 1973, Public resources Code Sections 4511 to 4628, the certification of the timber harvesting program pursuant to Public Resources Code Section 21080.5, and the rules adopted by the Board of Forestry in Title 14, California Code of Regulations, Sections 895 to 1115.4, the lead agency is the Department of Forestry and Fire Protection.

10. Timber harvest plan submitters have the right to know who will be reviewing their timber harvest plans and the time required to complete the full review process.

While all the pretty verbiage would probably be ignored and be of little use, the creation of an impartial Ombudsman who could review and report on problems could do a lot to make regulators more accountable. Examples of where an ombudsman and Permitee Bill of Rights review process could be applied are as follows:

1. In this example, the California Department of Forestry refused to approve a timber harvest plan permit unless a Civil Engineer Geologist (CEG) field review and report wanted by an inexperienced Water Quality (WQ) representative was completed. This requirement for permit approval was requested despite having Registered Professional Forester (RPF) who prepared the plan, California Department of Forestry (CDF) RPF and field representative for the CDF, and Department of Mines and Geology (DMG) field representative saying CEG input was not needed. Although three experienced professionals did not support the need for using a CEG and the involved WQ representative was not qualified to make the involved determination that a CEG was needed, CDF refused to

proceed with permit review until they had the requested CEG report. Doing the CEG report took time and delayed plan review and approval. Permitee had to absorb the extra cost for additionally required RPF time and for hiring a CEG. When CEG review and report was done, it did not change permit requirements from those determined needed before WQ requested use of a CEG. Additionally, the WQ did not review CEG information prior to plan approval, and WQ refused to participate in a field inspection of the work WQ had required be provided by a CEG. This abusive use of regulatory authority resulted in a waste of time and money for everyone including the involved public agencies and accomplished nothing but some hard feelings.

2. The California Department of Fish and Game (DFG) and California Department of Forestry's (CDF) 70s damaging debris removal program could have been brought under review. If permitees had access to someone to stand up to this questionable regulatory action at the beginning of its enforcement, a lot of watercourse and species damage would have been avoided. What happened under DFG's watch shows a blind trust in public agencies knowing what is best can lead to bad things, and unbiased third party review is routinely needed.

3. Many regulators are inappropriately pushing to eliminate road access and to ding around on healed slide areas. This is causing many unjustified and damaging permit requirements to be put in place, and again, unbiased review is needed.

4. A misguided effort to not allow disturbance in areas adjacent to watercourses needs to be site specifically peer reviewed. While improperly applied disturbance next to watercourses can cause sedimentation and damage to watercourses, no disturbance means little to no mineral soil which favors the establishment of conifer trees, less sunlight needed for better tree growth, and more competition from nonconifer vegetation which restricts conifer tree growth. The overall result of not allowing disturbance in areas adjacent to watercourses is reduced conifer tree growth in areas adjacent to watercourses, an unnecessary and unjustified taking of timber value, a reduction in production of large woody debris and related beneficial uses, and a reduction in the cover and food production for species using the areas adjacent to and in watercourses.

There is one common theme that runs through these provided examples. Routinely permit requirements are not authorized by rules and regulations, are not based on intended interpretations of legislated rules and regulations, and are not justified by site specific facts and time tested, peer reviewed science. Unbiased third party review would bring a lot of this inappropriate activity out into the open where it could be professionally and properly handled.

If a permitee can not get a straight, truthful answer from the Fourth Branch of Government to a legitimate regulatory question, where are permitees and others to go to get the truth?

MONITORING
SUCH AS COULD BE DONE IN AN OMBUDSMAN PROCESS COULD BE USED TO IDENTIFY PERMIT REVIEW AND APPROVAL ACCOUNTABILITY PROBLEMS

A big plus for using an ombudsman review process is the feedback that could be generated and used to correct unintended application of rules and regulations.

A more consistent, unchanging, logical interpretation of rules and regulations would occur. Mitigation recommendations not justified by site specific conditions and not backed by authorized regulations would be weeded out of the review and approval processes. Inappropriate layman court decisions and sister agency requests would be more thoroughly scrutinized. A better effort at meeting regulatory deadlines would occur.

An actual case, involving a timber harvest plan permit being abusively handled during review, helps to illustrate the problem with ever-changing instructions and inappropriate deviation from authorized regulatory procedures. In this example, the CDF had appropriately instructed personnel that public agency reports and recommendations not received within required permit review deadlines and in time for adequate review by the RPF, plan submitter, and the CDF were not to be considered. Within a two week period after giving out these instructions, a public agency report required to be provided prior to a second review was handed to a RPF at the door to the second review meeting. The shortness of time to review the report made it impossible for the CDF, RPF, and permitee to adequately review and address the report. In this example, the CDF ignored a sister agency's unprofessional conduct and ignored their own instructions and other authorized regulations by forcibly requiring second review period be extended until the delinquent public agency report could be provided and reviewed through routine channels. The RPF and permitee were given no voice in the matter, and while the late report slowly wound through routine channels, harvest plan permit review and approval was inappropriately delayed for a substantial amount of time at permitee's expense.

A monitoring process would allow for review and identification of regulatory application problems which could then be reported in a timely manner to any involved board or commission. Such a watchdog monitoring process would improve communication between the boards and commissions and their partner public agencies.

Any monitoring program should incorporate the following:

A. Assign an open-minded representative of any involved board or commission to actively participate in the monitoring process. Easily done reviews of available permit reports and unannounced attendance at review meetings by this board or commission representative would do wonders to putting accountability into the process being monitored.

B. A monitoring process should review how well the process handles the following:

   a. Site specific justification of requested mitigation measures.
   b. Authorized regulatory basis for requested mitigation measures.
   c. Improper use of internally developed guideline type material as authorized regulations.

The information provided by a well run, unbiased monitoring program would be invaluable to any rule making process.

TIME TO GET REAL

ACCOUNTABILITY CAN BE MADE A BITCH FOR ABUSIVE REGULATORS AND FOR THOSE CREATING OR PROVIDING FALSE SCIENCE AND LIES

To this point, ways to get regulatory accountability have involved a lot of give and take with the Fourth Branch of Government doing most of the taking, and compromise and get-a-long approaches have not provided much regulatory relief.

377

So, is there something else that can be done?

While many do not want to acknowledge it, the enviros accomplished change with confrontation. Some confrontation has been properly done and some has been violent and in poor taste with the media eating up the violent stuff.

I visualize improving on what the enviros have done by using professional confrontation and the truth. I do not see violent confrontation as a useful tool.

While compromise has produced limited results, longer lasting and more productive results have been obtained from professional, truthful confrontation. On an individual level, I have seen how this type of confrontation has held the line and reduced unjustified governmental actions.

Needed change is not going to come without some hardship. Some hurdles may seem insurmountable, but permitees and professionals have to get off the sidelines and put more effort into confronting inappropriate actions. For the short term, permit delays, increased expenditures, added mitigation costs, and increased regulatory pressures and requirements may be unavoidable. Forcing regulators to defend themselves against the truth using currently available appeals, petition, and personnel review processes will not happen without some cost.

THE FORMULA

Based on a lot of thought and actual practice, a "formula" outlining what is needed to effectively confront the Fourth Branches of Government has been developed. Simply put the "formula" is as follows.

1. Pick a winner. Too often indefensible positions are taken. If you do not have a winner do not start the fight.

In the case of environmental issues, landowners and producers of natural resource products have to meet higher standards than their opponents. Having a morally right, high ground position is mandatory to having a winner.

2. Keep your message short, to the point, and simple to understand. Pro-resource presented arguments and information are often too complicated and hard to follow. Your message needs to be logical, interesting, and easy to understand; so, it will be easily absorbed and accepted.

Be sure to show regulators you understand what you are doing. Make it clear not answering legitimate questions violates applicable laws and be prepared to mention the laws being violated. Explain how not answering questions can provide the basis for a lawsuit.

3. Be professional, factual, friendly, and smart in your presentations. The words professional and smart are emphasized. Be firm, maybe a little confrontational to get everyone's attention, but never get personal.

Ask yourself, whose information will be taken more seriously? Those who forcefully and professionally make good clear points in a cool reasonable manner; or, those who come across as loud, obnoxious, babbling, hot heads?

When your opposition is factually wrong, do what you can to put them on the defensive with the power of the question. Bring out their lack of professionalism and destroy their credibility whenever the opportunity presents itself. Do not be afraid of good clean confrontation.

Do not be side-tracked by general nonfactual answers to legitimate questions. Do not let comments like "A violation of California Environmental Quality Act, Endangered Species Act, Environmental Protection Agency regulations...etc...etc...will occur if what you want is done" scare you off. Make your opposition provide in writing specific regulatory wording and site specific information to support their position.

4. Frame your position and suggested solutions in such a way they are supported by factual information that can not be rebutted or ignored by decisions makers.

Do not make it easy for decision makers to settle on a compromise position that does not solve involved problems.

Do not help your opposition.

Do not give your opposition the opportunity to attack your credibility.

Pro-resource use information is often multi-sided and nonconfrontational to a fault, and proponents of natural resource use often provide compromise positions and unnecessary information that is turned against them.

Support information should include the following:

a. A write-up describing the factual site specific situation(s) that supports your position.

b. A listing of applicable authorized regulations.

c. When information is utilized that is not part of the provided site specific and authorized regulatory information, a write-up describing why this information is relevant needs to be provided. Make sure this information is time tested and peer reviewed.

It is only proper that professionals on both sides of the fence act as professionals. If any involved professionals do not voluntary support their position in the above listed manner, force them to do it. The credibility of anyone and any information not peer reviewed and adequately justified needs to be called into question.

5. Do not let time slide by and do not back-off until all avenues of recourse have been exhausted. Routinely participants allow regulatory processes to overwhelm and outlast commitment and truth.

If you are getting nowhere in a timely manner, and I emphasize timely, do not let them stall you. Force answers from those contacted. Time and delay are your enemy. Time dulls memories, people change, ideas get muddled and confused, and examples of problems get stale. Don't let your issue be shuffled around and lost in committee.
Be a pest.
Do not be afraid to move-on to other courses of action such as going over the heads of those handling your issue. Get audiences with supervisors, higher boards, governors, and up. Use all available resources such as associations and politicians. If you have a justifiable and legitimate position, which you better have to even get started, do not hold back. Delay helps your opposition and hurts you.
If you reach a deadend, you reach a deadend. This possible reality better be part of your original decision process in deciding to confront those you are confronting.

6. Learn and study your options and map out a game plan including use of all your options. Hopefully this book can be help in this effort, but do

not settle for only using other people ideas. Keep an open mind, and work at creating your own ideas and options.

Work within more accessible and less complicated review processes available to you before committing to higher level and more costly courses of action.

This can mean starting with lower, field level folks. It is best to start at the very bottom, and give the bottom folks a chance to correct problems. As you work up the chain of command, keep the lower levels including field people advised of what you are doing. To maintain credibility and a strong position, do not advance to higher levels of the bureaucratic heap until you have built a strong base at lower levels.

Utilizing all hearing and review processes available to you may result in some bureaucratic road blocks, but this will be time well spent. This will allow you to learn how the game is played, learn the players, and pick-up information needed to modify, better organize, re-fine, and strengthen your position. As you learn more about involved processes and what needs to be presented, you might take some short cuts, but keep in mind, short cuts can result in missed information and a weaker position.

If there is no resolution by the end of bureaucratic administrative processes, you can look to other ways to continue the fight. Media or politicians may be a distant option. The court system may be a way to go if qualified and open minded lawyer(s) not afraid of new law can be found.

At this point or even earlier, it may be worthwhile to contact a legal foundation which is set-up to protect private property rights. The Pacific legal Foundation working the west coast and the Intermountain Legal Foundation working the intermountain states have done a lot of good and had some winners. These foundations are experienced in private property issues and may handle some or all legal costs, but be advised these foundations are made up of lawyers and as such are only looking for clearcut, winning cases. Like most lawyers, these foundations will shy away from new law and new science.

You might consider getting help in preparing your information and game plan.

If you can find practical legal counsel and other professionals, you might get them involved. As there are many professionals that will not think out of the box and will not work with you and your ideas, I emphasize the word "practical". Most lawyers and other professionals tend to present confusing and long winded presentations, and you need to be able to control them; so, your clear, simple, short, and supportable message is not lost in a bunch of babble.

Having such professionals add to your presentations can be a powerful tool in getting the attention of members of the Fourth branch of Government.

7. The final and maybe most important ingredients are commitment, resources, and backing. Without these things, you may be wasting your time and money.

Strategy and commitment need to be clearly defined. Are you going for a compromise or are you going until you win or lose the brass ring? Can you afford the loss if you get stopped short of a win?

If real world business and financial realities may get in the way, you might want to save yourself the misery of trying to change things and maybe having a bull's-eye placed on yourself. Even in playing the compromise game, you have to be careful of the bridges you may burn.

Simply put the "formula" is as follows:

- Pick a winner and don't fight losers.
- Develop a clear, understandable message that can not be ignored
- Present your message in a professional, unyielding way. Do not get personal.
- Provide a message supported by the truth and make your opposition do the same.
- Do not back off. Be a pest.
- Do not give-up until all your options have been exhausted.
- Be sure commitment, resources, and backing are in place. A little gumption wouldn't hurt.

Sounds tough doesn't it? Well, it is tough to be a winner using currently available review processes. If you do not want a win bad enough to do what is required by the "formula", maybe you better not start.

My stumbling application of the "formula" has shown me it will work, and the results have been well worth the effort.

The "formula" has been a big help during permit review and approval processes and application of regulations in the field. Applying "formula" ideas to two petition processes almost got effective regulatory change in place. One petition only failed because group backing was not forthcoming; however, this effort did open discussion and some eyes about regulatory accountability that had been avoided for years. Another petition was on the way to working until California budget mess shut-down the involved Office of Administrative Law.

I personally know of another situation where a landowner was unjustly denied needed work permits for years inside the Coastal Commission Permit Zone, and his use of the "formula" provided positive results. This landowner documented harassment and inappropriate actions by regulators, and by being persistent in using available review processes, the guilty regulators were identified and reprimanded. I seem to remember one regulator lost a month's salary and was suspended for a time from work. Other involved regulators also received suspensions and probation review periods.

Presenting information in the manner outlined by the "formula" makes it hard for those in power such as personnel review boards to avoid reprimanding those acting inappropriately. Unauthorized, unjustified, and unsupported Fourth Branch of Government actions and inappropriate use of pseudo thinking are brought out into the open. Regulators are forced to be professionally accountable often making them defend the indefensible. The provided information will allow better decisions to be made involving verbal and written reprimands, probation, and loss of payroll.

In addition to providing for direct change, the "formula" provides a way to build a factual base which has been badly missing in the debate over natural resource use issues. Introducing a strong proven factual basis can do wonders in overcoming enviro spin.

FACE OFF

CONFRONTATION COMES IN MANY FORMS

PROFESSIONAL HONESTY, TRUTHFUL FACTS, AND BACKBONE MAKE A WINNING COMBINATION

Some obvious things seem to not be so obvious. In the world of regulations, there is a winning approach that gets lost in everyday hassles. Simply put, this approach involves development of a respectful relationship between regulators and permitees. Development of this relationship often takes a backseat to everyday problems and the need to just get the job done; yet, such a relationship can yield many dividends.

In the good old days, respectful relationships with regulators came easy. I can remember when there was more give and take, and we all worked towards a common good. There was no need for frequent confrontation, and over time as regulators grew to know me and I grew to know them, we simply found ways to get along.

Now the push for more regulation and more restrictions has forced us all to develop different goals and to fight harder to hang onto what freedoms we do have. Today there is a more adversarial regulatory climate, and you have to work harder at developing respectful relationships with regulators.

One day I was preparing to go out on a field inspection with a regulator, and I was feeling apprehensive and did not want to go into the field with the regulator. It dawned on me I was apprehensive, because I was not going out with someone who would be working with me to resolve problems to the benefit of all involved parties and the environment. I was going out with someone that was going to go out of their way to cause me and my client trouble. In the past, I kind of looked forward to going out with regulators, work with them, hear their opinions, and share stories and information. The main goal of past regulators was not to find wrongs and to give tickets. They, like you, were going out with the idea to find the best ways to resolve any problem situations to the benefit of all. Maybe I am the one in the wrong by feeling this way, but this is how I see things have changed. There is a stronger mood among regulators to look for wrongs and to give tickets than to work at ways to resolve things. It appears enviro and supervisory pressures to find things that are wrong has won the day, and when in the field with regulators, good feelings have been replaced by having to be on guard all the time. As the old army song goes "MA, I just want to go home" and not have to be fearful all the time.

Over the years, I believe I developed good, professional relationships with some regulators, and it has taken constant, conscious effort to keep these relationships in place.

As I look back, I see some basic things that I had to do in developing a respectful relationship.

1. When I was confronted with inappropriate or unjustified behavior and I had a winning and supportable position, I would not back down. The regulators eventually learned this. Even when the regulators thought they had a winning hand, I rarely lost such encounters, because as I emphasize, I did not confront regulators unless I had what was needed to win. Eventually the regulators learned that I did not confront them unless I was serious with a legitimate position that they would have trouble rebutting.

I would work to present my position and facts in a clearly understandable manner, and I approached the regulators as one professional to another professional. I would provide an authorized regulatory and factual basis for my position, and I usually put my supporting information in writing. Letters can be a very useful tool and provide a way to put your position in the record in case it is needed at a later time to verify what happened. Because my position was defended by the facts, the regulators would more often than not back-off or at least attempt to find a compromise position.

2. I avoided arguing losing and indefensible issues, and sometimes I had to let discretion be the better part of valor. If I could not convince involved regulators they were wrong, if the regulators had the upper hand which is often the way things are now, if I did not have the backing and support of my client to do what was needed to win, or if it was in my clients' and maybe my best interest, I just capitulated. I believe the professional and respectful relationships I did build and the strong support I developed for my positions, allowed me to stand my ground more times than I had to back down.

3. With the participation of my contractors and clients, I had a standard practice of reporting any potentially legitimate violation to regulators, and we took our medicine. Reporting violations was not a simple matter due to the ever-changing unclear and questionable regulatory requirements regarding what should be called a violation and what should not be called a violation; however, I made sure potentially legitimate violations especially when environmental damage was in question were reported. This approach promoted an open working relationship with regulators, and ways were found to resolve potential problem situations without environmental damage and excessive punishment.

4. As a professional courtesy, I did not blind-side the regulators by going to their supervisors without their knowledge. I would explain my position to them and give them the opportunity to back-off. If the regulator refused to back-off, I would first request they contact their supervisor about the involved matter. If the regulator refused to contact their supervisor, then with their knowledge I would contact their supervisor. I

would continue to move up the chain of command in this manner until I got satisfaction.

5. I tried real hard to never let the situation get personal. There were some situations where this was not easy. If things started to get personal, I backed away and let the regulator's supervisor get involved. This approach allowed me to stay on the moral high ground and to not provide ammunition that could be used against me at a later time. Referring to possible supervisor involvement was a good way to cool things down and get things back onto the right track.

A lot of this simply comes down to treating others as you would have them treat you, and not being stupid and doing stupid things.

Examples of how this approach worked can be illustrated by the actions of past regulators that worked with me.

During work on a United State Forest Service timber sale contract (which is a rarity now days), I came in contact with a tough sale administrator that everyone was afraid of. He believed it was his job to religiously apply the wording in the contract as he had been trained to do. After he requested some things be done that I said were not required by the contract, he and I established a relationship that revolved around constant review of the wording in the contract. After a week or so of this and my winning many of my points, he said to me "you are the first contractor that has ever showed he understands and has read the contract".

Due to this exchange of information and not backing down, this inspector learned to trust us, and despite sometimes stretching contract interpretations, he worked with us in developing operational ideas that benefited both us and the government.

Eventually we saw very little of him on the contract area. While I heard other contractors say how they fought him and did not want to get him as your sale administer, we welcomed him as a good professional.

If I had backed down at the start, I do not believe this beneficial relationship would have ever developed.

A new California Department of Forestry (CDF) Forest Practice Inspector came to town one day that everyone said to avoid. During my first contacts with this inspector, I opened discussions about the multiple often incorrect interpretations of the rules, and we exchanged thoughts on the problem. I learned where he was coming from and found he heavily believed in regulatory wording. I and my co-workers acquainted him with some conflicts we were having with some regulations and took him into the field to review problem situations. Eventually, preharvest inspections started going faster with less unjustified mitigations and restrictions, and the inspector did not visit our operations as much as other operations. A feeling of trust and understanding was developed that benefited both of us. This inspector would even go out of his way to help us resolve field and regulatory problems when other inspectors would run away.

Along came stream alternation permits handled by the California Department of Fish and Game (DFG), and one DFG warden was assigned to cover operations on hundreds of thousands of acres. This inspector was the toughest of the toughest. Things started out a little ragged, but as he saw we were trying to do the right thing, and would do as he said, he started to trust us more. Eventually, he learned the lay of our ground and would give us permission to start operations before full review had been done. This freed him up to work on the tougher crossing situations and to spend more time going after the folks giving him trouble.

There was one incident involving a brushy watercourse protection zone where a tractor operator wondered into the zone. Except for some brush being knocked down, nothing was hurt, and having less brush would maybe allow for a tree to get started in the zone. We told the CDF inspector about what had happened and he came out and took a look. If you keep in mind this occurred in the days when humor was possible in the regulatory community, you will better appreciate what the CDF inspector wrote in his report. In the report he wrote "A tractor operator with dirty sunglasses looking into the sun wondered into the watercourse protection with no environmental damage having occurred". I suspect today this violation would be blown up into a major problem, and current regulatory interpretations might be used to apply monetary fines and jail time.

These examples show the benefits of standing tall when you are in the right. A professional respect is developed, and there is less friction and adversity with professionally acting regulators. This in turn can lead to less unjustified restrictions and costs and a better environmental and operational product.

I do not believe the same high level of professional respectful relationship can be developed if you back off when you are right. Backing off shows a weakness that many regulators feed on, and they just keep coming for more. I know I and others, including many regulators and enviros, have more respect for those, that do not back off when they support their positions with the facts.

Some may say I am wrong, but I feel this approach has resulted in the regulators, even the ones who do not like my positions, respecting me. I have remained in contact with a lot of the regulators over the years, and I think I can consider some of them my friends.

I am sure there are those who say it can not be this simple to get along. Some will advocate an adverse relationship with regulators is unavoidable, and some will say being confrontation all the time with regulators is required to stay in business. I say they are wrong.

While there have been a few, and I emphasize a few, regulators I came in contact with that refused to come around and be good professionals, these folks were definitely a minority. These few bad regulators seemed to be hard headed or simply unable to grasp the truth. A couple were simply school yard bullies who liked to lord their regulatory power over others.

When you run into one of these bad apples, you can capitulate to what they want and suffer the consequences; or, you can ignore them as much as possible which drives them up a wall. When you do have to deal with a regulatory bad apple, provide a logical and legitimate basis for what you need to do and stick to a straight and narrow application of authorized regulations. Tell them what you are going to do, hide nothing, present them with your interpretations of the rules, and stick the truth in their face. Do not let problems with them become personal which can lead to giving them something they can use against you.

Being professional and being in the right is not always going to be easy.

If you have not hidden anything and not cut any corners, you have no reason to back off. Even if they get you into a tight spot, I have found the consequences are routinely not bad. To the contrary, if you have acted professionally and done the right things, you routinely come out looking like the good guy. As a bonus, the bad apples have a tendency to be overzealous and make mistakes which supervisors and personnel review boards may not be able to overlook.

The very, very, very, low reprimand rate for civil servants indicates two things. Governmental folks rarely do anything wrong which is disputed by the information provided in this book; or, it is very tough to get a civil servant reprimanded. Real world information indicates public employee reprimand processes do not function properly and public agencies protect their own.

If you feel you want to go after a bad regulator through existing reprimand processes, you want to be very smart in what you do. You better be sure you can prove your case and the regulator can not side-step your efforts. The consequences of going after a regulator and losing are not good.

There are some who will say I am exaggerating the importance of getting along with the regulators. While it may not be right, regulators have the hammer, and you can find ways to keep them from hitting you or you can fight them and continually get hit over the head.

You can equate backing-off by producers and users of natural resource products to a contact sport or to the Viet Nam war. The other side is out to go full go, and there are no plans by them to back-off. The consequences of going easy and going for a compromise have been proven to result in getting the bad end of the deal. When I played football, every time I let up a little, I got the worst of the hit. I never saw North Viet Nam or the Viet Cong seriously back-off, and being politically correct or accepting a compromise in that war got a lot of guys unnecessarily hurt and killed. I hope I heard wrong, but the other day a supposedly good source said as in Viet Nam our leaders were letting political correctness get in the way of fighting the Irag war in an all-out way and our people were inappropriately being put in harms way. I support what we are doing in Iraq, but as with the Fourth branches of Government and Viet Nam, I see too many of our leaders not using their heads in doing all they can to do the right thing and to not unnecessarily put our people in harms way. War is war and backing off just a little can get a lot of people hurt. I see backing off as a way to eventually lose it all as demonstrated by what can happen on a football field and what did happen in Viet Nam.

I have learned the lesson that strength is rewarded when it is backed by the truth and is correctly and appropriately applied.

I have also learned every situation in life involves different consequences and facts. There is no silver bullet or one way to resolve all problem situations, and each problem situation requires a different approach in resolving it. Regulatory problem situations are no different.

Hut! Hut! Hike!

WELL?
YOU IN OR OUT?

If there was more commitment to confronting the regulators, better accountability could be achieved.

All that is needed to resolve many inappropriate governmental actions is to require all participants to play on the same ball field by the same rules. Without sacrificing any environmental protections, just make all participants, especially the regulators, act professional by justifying their actions with site specific facts, authorized regulations, and time tested peer reviewed information. Confronting and reprimanding those who do otherwise would do a lot to force everyone to work harder at doing the right thing. Throwing in a little logic and common sense can be a bonus.

A news article(547) written by a north coast of California legislator is titled "Faith is no replacement for accountability" The legislator states in the article "War funding should not be a faith based initiative. It requires tough questions and honest answers..." It is too bad he and his legislative colleagues do not practice what he is saying regarding the handling of many environmental and rural community problems that are mentioned in this book.

The chicken that never pecks back (stands up for itself when it is in the right) is the chicken that is pecked to death. Sadly the commitment and involvement needed to hold the line against the regulators is lacking and the chicken called Rural America is being pecked to death.

If the real world is not holding you back and you want to do some good, then join with me and a few others in confronting inappropriate actions by the Fourth Branch of Government. Think what could be done if groups instead of individuals did things like those outlined in the "formula" and the "Face Off" information.

If you are in,
Good Luck

In closing this chapter and this book, it is worth mentioning the Fourth Branch of Government routinely and falsely promises more accountability and regulatory relief. Proof is in the pudding, and so far, the licking has been pretty poor.

Since public agencies are full of people that want to keep their positions of power and influence, there is little incentive for public agencies to acknowledge there are accountability problems and to make needed changes. As illustrated earlier in this chapter by the California Department of Forestry bolding stating in writing they will not be requiring explanations and justifications, public agencies have shown a disregard for ethical and professional standards.

As illustrated by California Board of Forestry's ignoring and stonewalling potential reform and ways to improve regulatory processes, there seems to be no way to break through the resistance against peer review and oversight of public agencies.

The regulators and the enviro community have voiced objection to requiring regulatory actions to be based on authorized regulations, time tested and peer reviewed science, site specific facts, logic, and common sense.

So, here we are. The Fourth Branches of Government have not shown a desire to police themselves, and regulators and enviros have objected to using a simple, professional standard of conduct.

All this has given the old slogan "Question Authority" a much broader meaning.

Professional and truthful confrontation can be used to knock the regulators off their mountain and to get their attention. Once they are no longer King-of-the-Hill, they will be more willing to do their share in making things work.

I suggest all professionals do what I do. Base decisions on time tested and peer reviewed information, site specific facts (truth), logic, and common sense, and support others who do the same. You won't make some fair-weather friends and you won't please everyone, but you will sleep good at night.

Meanwhile back in the real world, examples of how the three branches of government in conjunction with the Fourth Branch of Government and enviros are hurting rural area working folks have been provided throughout this book. Bad laws, pseudo science, slanted media coverage, increased costs, increasing imports, inability to get permits, unjustified permit requirements, land lock-ups, permit restrictions causing reduction in operating season, increasing regulation, continual confusion in permit review and approval processes, and on and on and on, continue to reduce use of natural resources and to create disincentives to maintaining privately owned open space lands in private ownership.

As natural resource use is reduced, economic supports will disappear, rural communities will fade away, and this country will become more dependent on the rest of the world for needed resources.

As represented by the Hamil Iraq hostage story, Rural America's way of life has the ability to produce some exceptional and hard working people. These people have provided this country with many good values and many of the things that have allowed us to remain free and independent of many worldwide problems. In a news article(261), Hamil, a farmer, who was been forced to find other work shows his true grit by going to a foreign land under tough and dangerous circumstances to keep his family and rural way of life going. His hard working, patriotic, and practical upbringing is illustrated by his saying "...he would consider returning to the job in Iraq but worries about how it would affect his children. We got to get that country back on its feet,...". "...the rebuilding mission that nearly cost him his life must continue." As we lose the rural way of life, we lose the chance for the rural way of life to produce more clear thinking, practical, honest, patriotic, hardworking, family people like Hamil.

For many reasons, Rural America may be coming to an end as we know it. Because of all the good that comes from Rural America, you would think we would do more to find logical and practical ways to keep it going.

Will we simply shrug our shoulders, turn our backs, and say

"Rest in Peace Rural America"

"You have done well."

OR

FIGHT BACK?

REFERENCE INFORMATION

Reference
Number   Source of Information

Reference Number	Source of Information
1	1/17/04 - Times-Standard – Associated Press
2	1/29/05 - Times-Standard – Scrippe (Western Service-McClatchy)
3	3/22/04 – News article believed to be Times-Standard article
4	6/9/05 – Eureka FM 107.3 radio spot (6:50 AM)
5	1/17/05 - Times-Standard – Associated Press
6	2/1/04 - Times-Standard – James Tressler
7	8/8/04 - Times-Standard
8	2/8/04 - Times-Standard
9	8/6/03 - Times-Standard
10	2/5/04 - Times-Standard
11	3/16/04 - Times-Standard
12	1/31/04 - Times-Standard
13	9/5/04 - Times-Standard – James Tressler
14	9/18/03 - Times-Standard
15	9/18/03 - Times-Standard
16	8/17/03 - Times-Standard
17	5/4/05 - Times-Standard
18	9/17/03 - Times-Standard – Associated Press
19	6/18/04 - Times-Standard
20	6/17/04 - Times-Standard
21	6/30/04 - Times-Standard – Associated Press
22	8/7/04 - Times-Standard – Associated Press
23	9/11/03 - Times-Standard – Associated Press
24	3/23/04 - Times-Standard – Andrew Bird
25	4/23/04 - Times-Standard – Letter to Editor by Dorothy Santry
26	5/28/04 - Times-Standard – Associated Press
27	5/27/04 - Times-Standard
28	3/12/04 - Times-Standard
29	11/29/03 – Internet article - Foresters Group by Ken
30	5/4/04 - Times-Standard
31	5/20/05 - Times-Standard – Associated Press
32	6/22/04 - Times-Standard – Associated Press
33	5/26/04 - Times-Standard – Associated Press
34	6/23/04 - Times-Standard – Associated Press
35	3/22/04 - Times-Standard – Letter to Editor by Hollis McCoy
36	7/9/04 - Times-Standard
37	4/10/04 - Times-Standard – Letter to Editor by Liz Patrick

38	6/30/04 - Times-Standard
39	6/30/04 - Times-Standard – Associated Press
40	2/11/04 - Times-Standard
41	5/11/04 - Times-Standard – John Driscoll
42	8/27/05 - Times-Standard – Associated Press
43	4/14/04 - Times-Standard – Associated Press
44	1/29/04 - Times-Standard – Don Terbush
45	7/12/04 - Times-Standard – John Driscoll
46	6/13/04 - Times-Standard
47	9/5/04 - Times-Standard
48	6/8/04 - Times-Standard – Associated Press
49	7/22/02 – Internet article - Foresters Group
	(Washington Times by Audrey Hudson)
50	7/30/04 - Times-Standard – Andrew Bird
51	1/28/04 - Times-Standard
52	4/05 – University of California "Oaks'n'fols Newsletter
53	3/8/04 - Times-Standard – Associated Press
54	8/31/04 - Times-Standard
55	2/25/04 - Times-Standard
56	2/10/04 - Times-Standard – Andrew Bird
57	4/22/04 - Times-Standard – Meghan Vogel
58	1/28/04 - Times-Standard
59	6/10/04 - Times-Standard – Associated Press
60	9/12/04 - Times-Standard
61	12/5/04 - Times-Standard – Andrew Bird
62	10/18/04 - Times-Standard
63	7/8/04 – News article believed to be Times-Standard article
64	3/4/04 – Internet article - Foresters Group by Fred Grau
65	4/5/04 – Internet article - Foresters Group by Jim Beers
66	7/9/04 - Times-Standard – Associated Press
67	7/12/04 - Times-Standard – Associated Press
68	7/25/04 - Times-Standard
69	12/21/03 - Times-Standard – Associated Press
70	4/11/04 - Times-Standard – James Tressler
71	7/33/01 – Internet Action Bulletin – CARA Vote
	(Association Committee – Nick Kent)
72	5/10/03 – Internet article - Foresters Group from Saffell
73	8/7/03 – Internet article - Foresters Group
	(Mixed report from Fred Grau and James Gorman with reference to New York Times)
74	6/16/05 - Times-Standard
75	6/16/01 – Bill Gaines and David Vogel Testimony associated with California Waterfowl Association before House of Representatives Committee on Resources

76   9/15/03 – Internet article – Michael Crichton

77   6/2005 – SAF (Society of American Foresters) Newsletter by Steve
           Wilent

78   3/15/02 – Internet Comments from a Bill Dennison to a Silvia Milligan to
           undisclosed recipients that accompanied a copy of a
           Washington Times article.

79   4/02 – Internet article - Foresters Group from Ken and Jim Rathburn with
           reference to Environmental Climate News

80   5/14/04 – Willits News – Letter to Editor by Mike A'Dair

81   2/4/04 - Times-Standard – John Driscoll

82   8/1/04 - Times-Standard – Associated Press – Scott Sonner

83   8/18/05 - Times-Standard – Sara Watson Arthurs

84   9/13/04 – News article believed to be Times Standard article

85   7/25/04 - Times-Standard – Associated Press

86   5/11/04 - Times-Standard – Associated Press

87   9/25/04 - Times-Standard – Associated Press

88   11/16/04 - Times-Standard

89   4/20/05 - Times-Standard

90   4/22/05 – Internet report – U.S. Forest Service
           (Press Release – sei@sei.org)

91   8/8/03 - Times-Standard – Associated Press

92   8/15/03 - Times-Standard – Associated Press

93   3/31/04 - Times-Standard

94   12/3/99 – National Oceanic and Atmospheric Administration letter to
           California Board of Forestry signed by Rodney McInnis.

95   10/7/00 - Times-Standard – John Driscoll

96   5/29/01 – California Licensed Foresters Association Update Newsletter

97   2/12/01 – California Licensed Foresters Association
           Update Newsletter referencing Santa Rosa Press Democrat
           article

98   2/5,6, and7/02 – Minutes of California Board of Forestry

99   8/1/01 – Internet report from Ron Stuntzner of Stuntzner Engineering and
           Forestry.

100   6/28/93 – Ruling by Ninth District Court of Appeals regarding
           Dalbert/Dow Pharmacelticals Inc.

101   10/2/03 – Santa Rosa Press Democrat

102   5/9/04 - Times-Standard – John Driscoll

103   1/13/04 - Times-Standard – Associated Press

104   4/28/04 - Times-Standard – Associated Press

105   7/7/03 – Internet article - Foresters Group from Ken by Gary Youngblood

106   1/2/04 – Tree Farmer magazine by Jeffrey Jackson

107   9/30/03 – NCASI association report

108   5/20/01 – San Francisco Chronicle – George Ahmaogak

109   7/26/05 - Times-Standard – John Driscoll

110	12/03 – Yankee Magazine. com
111	4/9/04 - Times-Standard – John Driscoll
112	10/23/03 – Idaho Statesman – Jack Sullivan
113	6/8/05 – AG ALERT Newsletter – Weekly newspaper for California Agriculture
114	3/27/04 - Times-Standard – Associated Press
115	5/31/05 - Times-Standard – Mike Morrow
116	7/26/04 - Times-Standard – John Driscoll
117	2/16/03 – Internet article - Foresters Group – from Ken and Jim Beers (Biological Team article)
118	2/17/03 – Internet article - Foresters Group – from Ken and Jim Beers (Biological Team article)
119	11/30/03 – San Francisco Chronicle – Mike Chambers
120	3/5/04 - Times-Standard – Shaun Walker
121	6/3/04 - Times-Standard – John Driscoll
122	4/7/04 - Times-Standard – Associated Press
123	2/17/04 - Times-Standard – Associated Press
124	5/17/04 - Times-Standard – Associated Press
125	4/18/04 - Times-Standard
126	3/12/04 - Times-Standard – Associated Press
127	3/22/04 - Times-Standard – John Driscoll
128	4/26/04 - Times-Standard
129	5/8/04 - Times-Standard
130	undated – Sacramento Bee staff writer report
131	6-7/99 – Flyer on "Why We Have No Salmon" (A Video) about elimination of the Oregon Fish Hatchery Runs. By Ron Yechout
132	10/5/01 – AFRC News Report
133	5/28/04 - Times-Standard – Associated Press
134	5/28/04 - Times-Standard
135	8/11/04 - Times-Standard – Associated Press
136	5/17/04 - Times-Standard – Associated Press
137	8/16/97 - Times-Standard – Letter to Editor by Dave Bitts, Secretary Humboldt Fisherman's Marketing Association, Eureka.
138	8/18/95 - Times-Standard – David Anderson
139	7/10/04 - Times-Standard – Associated Press
140	7/14/04 - Times-Standard – Associated Press
141	10/20/03 – Oregonian – Howard Morgan
142	3/21/04 - Times-Standard – Associated Press
143	9/23/01 - Times-Standard – Editorial
144	2/13/04 – Santa Rosa Press Democrat – Associated Press
145	11/28/03 – San Francisco Chronicle – Glen Martin
146	7/5/04 - Times-Standard – Associated Press
147	9/10/03 – Internet – Jim Beers

148	9/25/03 - Times-Standard – John Driscoll
149	7/31/01 – Internet by O Sowens referencing letter to Ryan DeVries from Michigan Department of Environmental Quality.
150	7/26/04 - Times-Standard – John Driscoll
151	7/24/04 - Times-Standard – Associated Press
152	4/4/04 - Times-Standard – Associated Press
153	1/10/04 - Times-Standard – Associated Press
154	11/13/04 - Times-Standard
155	1/19/04 - Times-Standard
156	3/10/04 - Times-Standard
157	6/30/05 - Times-Standard – Associated Press
158	5/2/04 - Times-Standard – Associated Press
159	5/18/04 - Times-Standard – Associated Press
160	6/5/04 - Times-Standard
161	6/5/04 - Times-Standard – Chris Durant
162	6/7/04 - Times-Standard
163	6/9/04 - Times-Standard – John Driscoll
164	1/22/05 - Times-Standard
165	6/18/04 - Times-Standard
166	6/28/04 - Times-Standard – Associated Press
167	7/10/04 - Times-Standard
168	9/27/03 - Times-Standard
169	9/30/03 - Times-Standard
170	7/27/04 - Times-Standard – John Driscoll
171	8/20/05 - Times-Standard – Associated Press
172	11/19/04 - Times-Standard – Associated Press
173	6/28/05 - Times-Standard – Associated Press
174	3/9/05 - Times-Standard – Associated Press
175	12/9/04 – Times Standard – Letter to Editor by Scott Sinclair
176	11/9/03 – San Francisco Chronicle – Associated Press
177	8/26/03 - Times-Standard
178	9/26/03 – Santa Rosa Press Democrat – Carol Benfell
179	11/15/03 – San Francisco Chronicle – Amy Stewart
180	11/14/03 – San Francisco Chronicle – Steve Ruben Stein
181	3/5/04 - Times-Standard – John Driscoll
182	7/4/04 - Times-Standard
183	7/12/04 – Radio spot message
184	1/3/03 - Times-Standard
185	1/13/03 - Times-Standard
186	5/10/04 - Times-Standard – Associated Press
187	10/23/03 – Los Angeles – David Kelly – in Idaho Statesman
188	12/9/03 - Times-Standard
189	12/15/03 - Times-Standard

190	2/15/04 – Santa Rosa Press Democrat – Associated Press –Carol Benfell
191	7/13/04 - Times-Standard
192	12/1/03 – Los Angeles Times – Julie Cary
193	7/25/04 - Times-Standard – Associated Press
194	11/28/03 – Marin Independent Journal – Associated Press - Brian Melley
195	11/1/04 - Times-Standard
196	11/16/04 - Times-Standard – Chris Durant
197	12/7/04 - Times-Standard – Letter to Editor by Summer LaSalle
198	3/7/05 - Times-Standard – Associated Press
199	3/11/05 - Times-Standard – Associated Press
200	4/4/05 - Times-Standard – Associated Press
201	4/17/05 - Times-Standard – Associated Press
202	6/7/05 - Times-Standard – Associated Press
203	8/21/05 - Times-Standard – Associated Press
204	7/29/04 - Times-Standard
205	11/28/03 - Times-Standard – Associated Press
206	6/5/04 - Times-Standard – Associated Press
207	9/26/03 - Times-Standard – John Driscoll
208	2/4/04 - Times-Standard – Associated Press
209	2/21/04 - Times-Standard – Associated Press
210	8/24/05 - Times-Standard – Associated Press
211	5/5/04 - Times-Standard – James Tressler
212	5/17/04 - Times-Standard
213	5/25/04 - Times-Standard – Andrew Bird
214	6/24/04 - Times-Standard
215	6/19/04 – National Geographic radio spot message
216	7/15/04 - Times-Standard
217	11/6/03 – San Francisco Chronicle – Edward Epstein
218	11/26/03 – San Francisco Chronicle – Henry K. Lee
219	5/4/04 - Times-Standard – Letter to Editor by David Ravetti
220	6/2/04 – Internet article - Foresters Group – Jim Beers
221	6/9/04 – Times-Standard – Associated Press
222	6/22/04 - Times-Standard – Opinion article by William Safire
223	4/20/04 - Times-Standard – John Driscoll
224	6/1/05 - Times-Standard – Sara Watson Arthurs
225	9/27/03 - Times-Standard – John Driscoll
226	9/3/03 - Times-Standard – John Driscoll
227	10/10/03 - Times-Standard – Associated Press
228	3/2/04 – California Licensed Foresters Association Action Alert
229	10/2/03 – Fort Bragg Advocate News – staff
230	1/23/04 – Times-Standard – Associated Press
231	11/30/03 – Santa Rosa Press Democrat – Carol Benfell
232	12/12/03 – Times-Standard – Associated Press

233   2/9/04 – Times-Standard – Associated Press
234   9/2/04 – Times-Standard – Associated Press
235   8/29/03 - Times-Standard – John Driscoll
236   3/18/04 - Times-Standard – Meghan Vogel
237   3/18/04 – Times-Standard – Associated Press
238   11/21/03 – San Francisco Chronicle – John Heilprin
239   8/18/05 – Times-Standard – Associated Press
240   Undated – Associated Press
241   3/19/04 – Times-Standard – Associated Press
242   5/14/04 – Times-Standard – Associated Press
243   4/18/04 – Times-Standard – Andrew Bird
244   2/9/04 - Times-Standard – John Driscoll
245   4/23/04 – Times-Standard – Associated Press
246   2003 – Buckeye Association Newsletter by Tom Herman
247   2/9/04 – Times-Standard – Associated Press
248   3/14/01 – Ninth District Court of Appeals Ruling – Arizona Cattle
         Growers Association and Jeff Menges / Bureau of Land
         Management and U.S. Fish and Wildlife Southwest Center for
         Biological Diversity.
249   3/21/04 – Times-Standard – Associated Press
250   6/24/05 – Times-Standard – Associated Press
251   1/15/04 – Times-Standard – Editorial
252   9/27/03 - Times-Standard – John Driscoll
253   10/2/03 - Times-Standard – John Driscoll
254   1/13/03 - Times-Standard – John Driscoll
255   1/9/04 - Times-Standard – Editorial
256   7/30/05 - Times-Standard
257   1/10/04 – Times-Standard – Associated Press
258   1/14/04 – Times-Standard – Associated Press
259   1/13/04 - Times-Standard – John Driscoll
260   2/8/04 - Times-Standard – Opinion article by Uri Driscoll
261   5/9/04 – Times-Standard – Associated Press
262   2/9/04 – Times-Standard – Associated Press
263   4/9/04 - Times-Standard – Letter to Editor by Don Amador
264   3/10/04 - Times-Standard – Dobrowolski
265   4/23/04 - Times-Standard – Letter to Editor by Judy Walker
266   2/11/04 - Times-Standard
267   1/8/04 - Times-Standard – Meghan Vogel
268   11/22/04 – Times-Standard – Associated Press
269   4/30/05 – Times-Standard – Associated Press
270   5/26/05 – Two radio spot messages – Neil Bork on 790 AM
         Eureka, California, and Shawn Hannity on 980 AM
         Eureka, California

271	5/26/05 – Radio spot message – Neil Bork on 790 AM Eureka, California
272	1/4/04 - Times-Standard – James Tressler
273	1/15/04 - Times-Standard
274	11/24/04 – AG ALERT newsletter article by Robyn Rominger
275	11/24/04 – AG ALERT newsletter article by Robyn Rominger
276	4/4/04 - Times-Standard – AP investigation
277	4/30/05 – Times-Standard – Associated Press
278	1/14/04 - Times-Standard – James Tressler
279	4/18/04 - Times-Standard – Letter to Editor by Patrick Tobin
280	9/10/03 - Times-Standard – Marcele Allen
281	10/1/03 – Times-Standard – Associated Press
282	1/28/04 – Times-Standard – Associated Press
283	3/2/04 – Times-Standard – Associated Press
284	4/27/04 – News article believed to be Times-Standard article
285	6/2/04 – Times-Standard – Associated Press
286	10/11/03 – Santa Rosa Press Democrat – Allan Heavens
287	2/16/02 – Internet article - Foresters Group – Ken – Referenced New York Times article by Ted Albracht.
288	3/12/03 - Times-Standard
289	2/8/04 – Times-Standard – Associated Press
290	8/18/03 – Times-Standard – Associated Press
291	9/7/04 – Times-Standard – Associated Press
292	1/9/04 – Times-Standard – Associated Press
293	5/6/04 – Times-Standard – Associated Press
294	7/25/03 – Times-Standard – Associated Press
295	2/4/04 – Times-Standard – Associated Press
296	2/16/04 – Times-Standard – Associated Press
297	2/16/04 – Times-Standard – John Driscoll
298	11/18/03 – Times-Standard – Associated Press
299	1/17/04 – Times-Standard
300	4/21/04 – Times-Standard – B.J. Bassett
301	3/26/04 - Times-Standard – James Tressler
302	9/2/05 – Times-Standard
303	12/9/04 – Times-Standard – Associated Press
304	8/13/03 - Times-Standard – Two articles by Tressler and Driscoll
305	8/17/03 - Times-Standard – John Driscoll
306	8/29/03 - Times-Standard – John Driscoll
307	10/13/03 - Times-Standard – Opinion article by Diane Beck
308	12/5/03 - Times-Standard – John Driscoll
309	12/18/03 - Times-Standard – Meghan Vogel
310	1/8/04 - Times-Standard – Andrew Bird
311	1/9/04 - Times-Standard – John Driscoll
312	1/21/04 - Times-Standard – John Driscoll

313   4/29/05 – Internet report – Foresters Group – Harry Wiant with reference to Pacific Legal Foundation

314   1/21/04 - Times-Standard – Letter to Editor by Marsha Mello

315   1/25/04 - Times-Standard – John Driscoll

316   2/27/04 - Times-Standard – John Driscoll

317   10/6/04 - Times-Standard

318   2/24/04 - Times-Standard – Opinion article by William Safire

319   5/5/04 – Radio spot message

320   Spring 2001 – Society of American Foresters (SAF) Newsletter article by Clare Nunnemaker

321   1/16/04 - Times-Standard

322   1/20/04 - Times-Standard

323   2/24/04 – Internet – Foresters Group – From H. Wiant – Referenced as Notes from Alleghenny Society of American Foresters (SAF) Winter Meet

324   8/2/05 – Times-Standard – Associated Press

325   9/9/05 - Times-Standard

326   5/25/05 – Times-Standard – Associated Press

327   7/24/05 - Times-Standard

328   6/15/05 - Times-Standard – Opinion article by Marilyn Benemann

329   4/21/04 - Times-Standard – Letter to Editor by unknown writer

330   7/9/03 – Internet article - Foresters Group – Jim Beers

331   11/1/00 – NCASI Newsletter

332   5/7/03 – Internet article - Foresters Group – Ken – References Pulp and Pulpworkers Resource Council and Potlatch Corp.

333   6/9/04 - Times-Standard – Associated Press

334   3/30/04 – Internet article - Foresters Group – Jim Beers

335   4/12/04 – Times-Standard – Associated Press

336   4/30/04 – Times-Standard – Associated Press

337   5/21/04 – Times-Standard – Associated Press

338   5/21/04 – Times-Standard – Associated Press

339   9/1/04 – Times-Standard – Associated Press
            No # 1/27/03 – Time Magazine by Terry McCarthy (fully referenced in body of book)

340   3/23/04 – Times-Standard

341   9/1/03 – Times-Standard – Associated Press

342   9/22/03 – Times-Standard – Sara Watson Arthurs

343   3/30/04 – Times-Standard – Associated Press

344   4/13/04 – Times-Standard – Associated Press

345   5/1/04 – Times-Standard – Associated Press

346   12/1/04 – Times-Standard – John Driscoll

347   4/18/04 – Times-Standard

348   4/26/04 - Times-Standard – Opinion article by Ted Trichilo

349   2/17/03 – Times-Standard – James Tressler

350   5/6/04 – Times-Standard
351   6/22/04 – Times-Standard – James Tressler
352   1/16/04 – Times-Standard
353   4/27/04 – Times-Standard
354   4/27/03 – Times-Standard – Associated Press
355   3/8/04 – Times-Standard – Paul McHugh
356   8/18/05 – Times-Standard – Associated Press
357   5/29/04 – Times-Standard – Editorial
358   3/15/04 – California Licensed Foresters Association Newsletter Update
359   4/1/04 – Internet Action Request from George Hollister with reference to
           California Farm Bureau
360   5/10/04 – Times-Standard – Associated Press
361   3/27/04 – Times-Standard – Associated Press
362   10/6/03 – Fort Bragg Advocate News – Tony Reed
363   2/9/03 - Times-Standard – Opinion article by Martyn B. Hopper
364   1/6/04 – Santa Rosa Press Democrat – Katy Hellenmeyer
365   2/4/04 - Times-Standard
366   11/27/04 – Times-Standard – Associated Press
367   3/28/04 – Times-Standard – Sarah Watson Arthurs
368   1/9/04 – Internet Action Request from George Hollister with reference to
           Mendocino California Farm Bureau
369   5/29/04 – Times-Standard – Associated Press
370   4/27/03 – Times-Standard – James Faulk
371   6/18/03 – AG Alert Newsletter article by Rubyn Rominger
372   3/18/04 – Times-Standard – Associated Press
373   7/16/04 – Times-Standard – Associated Press
374   6/23/04 – Times-Standard – Associated Press
375   6/9/04 – Times-Standard – Associated Press
376   3/7/04 – Times-Standard – John Driscoll
377   10/8/03 – Times-Standard – John Driscoll
378   10/9/03 – Times-Standard – Editorial
379   1/04 – Forest Landowners Newsletter – Dan Weldon
380   9/18/03 – California Licensed Foresters Association Newsletter Update
           referencing Sacramento Bee Editorial
381   8/24/03 – Times-Standard – Editorial
382   8/29/03 - Times-Standard – Letter to Editor by Barry Gossi
383   9/5/03 - Times-Standard – Ed Cox
384   Spring 2001 – Society of American Foresters (SAF) Newsletter
           referencing comments by Greenpeace fella
385   Winter 2004 – Center for Watershed Studies "Watershed Review"
           Update on watersheds – University of Washington – Carol Volk
386   4/14/04 - Times-Standard
387   11/15/03 – San Francisco Chronicle
388   4/29/04 - Times-Standard – Opinion article by Dorothy Iversen

389	5/29/04 - Times-Standard – Associated Press
390	3/23/04 - Times-Standard
391	3/6/04 - Times-Standard
392	3/23/04 - Times-Standard
393	3/24/04 - Times-Standard – Andrew Bird
394	4/22/04 – North Coast Journal
395	4/5/04 - Times-Standard – Associated Press
396	5/6/04 - Times-Standard – Letter to Editor by Ward Mengel
397	11/29/04 - Times-Standard – Associated Press
398	4/20/04 - Times-Standard
399	4/21/04 - Times-Standard
400	1/29/04 - Times-Standard
401	2/20/04 - Times-Standard
402	3/13/04 - Times-Standard
403	3/14/04 - Times-Standard
404	3/13/04 - Times-Standard – Associated Press
405	3/10/04 - Times-Standard
406	1/21/04 - Times-Standard
407	3/21/04 - Times-Standard – Associated Press
408	4/1/04 - Times-Standard – Meghan Vogel
409	5/7/04 - Times-Standard – Meghan Vogel
410	5/28/04 - Times-Standard – Associated Press
411	5/2/04 - Times-Standard – Associated Press
412	5/1/04 - Times-Standard – Sara Watson Arthurs
413	6/18/04 - Times-Standard – Associated Press
414	6/25/04 - Times-Standard – Associated Press
415	2/6/04 - Times-Standard – Associated Press
416	7/4/04 - Times-Standard – Associated Press
417	8/31/04 - Times-Standard
418	9/1/04 - Times-Standard – Associated Press
419	7/5/04 – Internet article - Foresters Group – Jim Beers
420	5/2/04 - Times-Standard – Associated Press
421	5/6/04 - Times-Standard – Associated Press
422	8/21/04 - Times-Standard – Associated Press
423	6/18/04 - Times-Standard
424	8/1/02 – Internet – John Stossel – 20/20 ABC News – reference 8/2/02 date
425	9/29/03 - Times-Standard – Associated Press
426	9/29/03 - Times-Standard – Associated Press
427	10/20/03 – The Columbian – Blaine Harden
428	11/3/03 – San Francisco Examiner – Ron Harris
429	11/20/03 – San Francisco Examiner
430	1/19/04 - Times-Standard – Associated Press

431	8/29/02 – Internet article - Foresters Group – Paul Johnson – References CNS News, Marc Marano, and 8/29/02 date
432	10/8/96 – Los Angeles Times – Frank Clifford
433	6/6/03 – Internet article - Foresters Group – Jim Beers
434	8/16/05 – Radio spot message – 1480 AM Eureka, California – Tom Hartman
435	6/5/03 – Internet article - Foresters Group – Ken – Article from Washington Times by Douglas Leisz from NAFSR Report "Forest Health and Fire Overview and Evaluation"
436	9/18/00 – Forbes Magazine by Robert H. Nelson
437	6/1/02 – Internet article - Foresters Group – References Associated Press
438	6/16/02 – Internet article - Foresters Group – References Jennifer Hamilton Associated Press writer.
439	6/1/04 - Times-Standard – Associated Press
440	9/8/03 - Times-Standard – Associated Press
441	1/13/04 - Times-Standard – Associated Press
442	6/27/04 - Times-Standard – Associated Press
443	10/25/03 – San Francisco Chronicle – Peter Filmrite, Ryan Kim, Stacy Finz, Chuck Squatriglia
444	10/31/03 – Two San Francisco Chronicle articles – One by Robert Salladay, Zachary Colie and one by Ryan Kim, Chuck Squatriglia, Joe Garofoli
445	11/1/03 – Two San Francisco Chronicle articles – One by Robert Salladay, Zachary Colie and one by Peter Filmrite, Ryan Kim, Stacy Finz, Chuck Squatriglia
446	3/15/04 – California Licensed Foresters Association Newsletter Update
447	8/23/04 – Random news article
448	1/22/04 - Times-Standard – Associated Press
449	11/2/03 – Two San Francisco Chronicle articles – Tom Stienstra
450	3/30/04 - Times-Standard – Letter to Editor by William German
451	9/5/03 - Times-Standard – John Driscoll
452	9/10/03 - Times-Standard – John Driscoll
453	9/11/03 - Times-Standard – Shaun Walker
454	10/1/03 - Times-Standard
455	9/14/03 - Times-Standard
456	9/18/03 - Times-Standard – John Driscoll
457	9/19/03 - Times-Standard – John Driscoll
458	9/20/03 - Times-Standard – John Driscoll
459	9/23/03 - Times-Standard – John Driscoll
460	9/24/03 - Times-Standard – John Driscoll
461	8/28/03 - Times-Standard – John Driscoll
462	9/26/03 - Times-Standard – John Driscoll
463	9/26/03 – Santa Rosa Press democrat – Mike Genella

464	9/27/03 - Times-Standard – Chris Durant
465	9/27/03 – Santa Rosa Press democrat – Mike Genella
466	9/28/03 – Santa Rosa Press democrat – Mike Genella
467	9/29/03 – Radio spot message – FM 105.5 Eureka, California
468	5/12/03 – Internet article - Foresters Group – Ken – References World Net Daily and Sarah Foster
469	9/30/03 - Times-Standard – Chris Durant
470	4/11/04 - Times-Standard – Associated Press
471	10/3/03 - Times-Standard – Associated Press
472	11/20/03 – Internet article - Foresters Group – Ken – By Duane D. Freese
473	2/6/00 – SACBEE BEE Editorials – William Wade Keye
474	11/15/03 – San Francisco Chronicle – Bob Egelke
475	8/26/03 - Times-Standard – Dan Murphy
476	7/7/04 - Times-Standard – Associated Press
477	7/7/04 - Times-Standard – Associated Press
478	8/19/04 - Times-Standard – Associated Press
479	6/25/05 - Times-Standard – Associated Press
480	6/27/05 - Times-Standard – Associated Press
481	7/1/05 - Times-Standard – Associated Press
482	4/25/04 - Times-Standard – Andrew Bird
483	8/4/04 - Times-Standard – Associated Press
484	12/6/04 – Santa Rosa Press democrat – Robert Jablun
485	12/29/03 - Times-Standard – Associated Press
486	12/1/03 – Los Angeles Times – Janet Wilson
487	3/1/03 - Times-Standard – Associated Press
488	5/25/04 - Times-Standard – Andrew Bird
489	3/29/04 - Times-Standard
490	10/2003 – U.S. Forest Service Pamphlet – Picked up in Boise, Idaho Hospital
491	8/21/04 - Times-Standard – Associated Press
492	1/17/04 - Times-Standard – John Driscoll
493	10/25/03 – San Francisco Chronicle – Associated Press
494	6/3/04 - Times-Standard – Andrew Bird
495	1/4/04 – Times Standard – James Tressler
496	11/27/04 - Times-Standard – Letter to Editor by Aldo Bongio
497	3/31/01 - Times-Standard – Letter to Editor by Margot Casanova Wells
498	6/18/04 - Times-Standard – John Driscoll
499	1/4/04 – Times Standard – James Tressler
500	5/8/04 - Times-Standard – Associated Press
501	1/25/04 - Times-Standard
502	4/5/04 - Times-Standard – Associated Press
503	1/25/04 - Times-Standard
504	4/2/04 - Times-Standard

505	5/26/04 - Times-Standard – Associated Press
506	2/4/04 - Times-Standard – Associated Press
507	1/31/04 - Times-Standard – John Driscoll
508	6/5/04 - Times-Standard – Associated Press
509	7/19/04 - Times-Standard – Associated Press
510	7/26/04 - Times-Standard – Associated Press
511	4/5/04 – Internet article - Foresters Group – Jim Beers
512	7/3/04 - Times-Standard – John Driscoll
513	6/27/05 - Times-Standard
514	6/10/04 - Times-Standard – James Tressler
515	4/20/04 - Times-Standard – Letter to Editor by Aaron Libow
516	1/5/04 – Times Standard – James Tressler
517	6/12/04 – Times Standard – Sara Watson Arthurs
518	6/21/04 - Times-Standard – Associated Press
519	9/13/04 - Times-Standard – Associated Press
520	6/10/03 – Internet article - Foresters Group – Jim Beers – References Public Employees for Environmental Responsibility 6/9/03 Report
521	9/22/04 – Times-Standard – Associated Press
522	9/23/04 - Times-Standard – Associated Press
523	2/3/04 - Times-Standard – Opinion article by Felice Pace
524	1/29/04 - Times-Standard – Associated Press
525	7/25/04 - Times-Standard – Stuart Leavenworth
526	9/2/03 - Internet article - Foresters Group – Ken – American Land Rights Association referenced
527	3/21/04 - Times-Standard – Associated Press
528	5/7/03 – Internet article - Foresters Group – Ken – References Gary Stevens National Resource Law Group of D.C. Law Firm Saltman and Stevens
529	3/5/02 – Internet article - Foresters Group – Ken – References Daily Policy Digest 3/1/02 report from a James Taylor article.
530	5/7/02 – Internet article - Foresters Group – Ken – References 5/4/02 Columbian article and Erik Robinson a Columbian staff writer.
531	6/2/03 – Internet article - Foresters Group – Ken – References 6/2/03 Washington Times article and Audrey Hudson
532	7/29/04 - Times-Standard
533	2/6/04 - Times-Standard – Opinion article by Chris Larson
534	3/17/04 - Times-Standard – John Driscoll
535	4/5/04 - Times-Standard – John Driscoll
536	1/20/04 - Times-Standard – Letter to Editor by David Simpson
537	3/25/04 - Times-Standard – Editorial
538	1/9/05 - Times-Standard – John Driscoll
539	11/6/03 – Information provided through contact with California Licensed Foresters Association and provided internet information

540	10/25/01 – Internet - Association of Consulting Foresters (ACF) weekly update report
541	10/23/04 - Times-Standard – Associated Press – Scott Sonner
542	11/17,19,20/03 – Summarized Talking Points from California Department of Fish and Game Hearings on Coho
543	1/22/04 - Times-Standard
544	8/6/04 - Times-Standard – Jeff Pearce
545	6/18/03 – Internet article - Foresters Group – References Dale E. Anderson President Pennsylvania Forest Industry Association
546	Undated – News article by Larry Modell – Petaluma, California – References Lafferty Ranch, Sonoma Mountain.
547	9/18/03 - Times-Standard
548	7/9/03 – Internet article - Foresters Group – Ken – References American Land Rights Association
549	9/23/03 - Times-Standard – Opinion article by Thomas Hannah
550	9/93 – Pacific Fishery Management Council – 2000 SW First Avenue, Suite 420, Portland, Oregon 97201-5344 – Historical Ocean Salmon Fishery Data for Washington, Oregon, and California
551	6/25/05 - Times-Standard – Kimberly Wear
552	9/11/05 - Times-Standard – Opinion article by Sue Long
553	6/7/04 - Times-Standard – Associated Press

Note: As should be obvious, my local newspaper is the Times-Standard of Eureka, California. Since it may seem I am picking on this newspaper at times, I want to let it be known I no longer apply the "SubStandard" label to this newspaper as so many do. In my reading of many newspapers in my travels, I have found the Times-Standard to be better than most papers. While this may indicate other overall general problems with newspapers and I routinely disagree with content and see problems, I found this newspaper has a lot going for it.

Note: As shown in the reference information, Jim Beers has provided a lot of useful information and has shown a working knowledge of the issues presented in this book. Per his internet information, Jim Beers is available for consulting or to speak. Contact him at: JimBeers7@earthink.net

Note: During the final phases of publishing my book, I was told about a book written by Michael Crichton titled State of Fear. I bought this book and pleasantly found it touches on many issues I raise in my book. This touch is done differently and in a very informative and entertaining way that is beyond my abilities. I found this book to be a "must read" book.